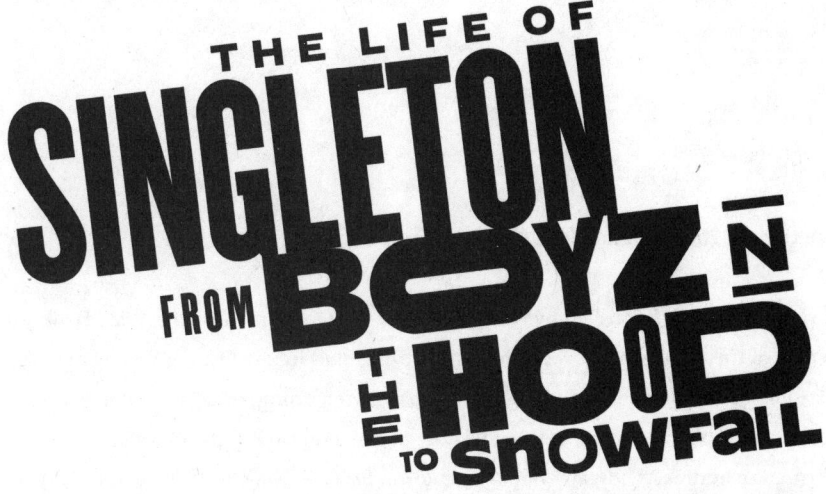

THE LIFE OF SINGLETON
FROM BOYZ N THE HOOD TO SNOWFALL

THOMAS GOLIANOPOULOS

ANDSCAPE
LOS ANGELES   NEW YORK

First Edition, July 2025
10 9 8 7 6 5 4 3 2 1
FAC-004510-25135
Printed in the United States of America
This book is set in Baskerville MT Pro, Knockout, and Decimal
Designed by Amy C. King
Library of Congress Control Number: 2024952511
ISBN 978-1-368-09594-5

The authorized representative in the EU for product safety and compliance is
Disney Trading B.V., Asterweg 15S, 1031 HL, Amsterdam, The Netherlands
email: DCP.DL-EU.bookscontact@disney.com

Reinforced binding
www.AndscapeBooks.com

SUSTAINABLE FORESTRY INITIATIVE

Certified Sourcing

www.forests.org
SFI-01681

Logo Applies to Text Stock Only

*For Karen, Emery, and Giannis*

On September 27, 1984, seventeen-year-old Robbie Stringer, nicknamed Monster, was shot in the chest in an alley near 101st and Vermont in South Central Los Angeles by the same Rollin' 90s Neighborhood Crips he'd been in a shoot-out with about a year earlier.

Somehow, Monster made it back home alive. He cried for his mom, and when he saw her, he lifted his shirt to reveal the wound. Paramedics were called, but he was dead before they arrived.

News traveled fast. Monster was a 107th Street Hoover Crip. Members of the gang loaded into a 1984 gold Cutlass to find who had killed him.

Sixteen-year-old John Singleton never called him Monster. He knew him as Robbie. And as soon as word got to him at home, Singleton left the house to find the rest of the Hoovers.

It didn't take long. They were sitting in an alley. Waiting. Not hiding.

Singleton, painfully thin with thick-lensed glasses, approached the driver. He carried the gun he'd stolen from his father. Kevin Orange, known as Big Twin, turned toward him.

"Go home, John," he said. "Now."

"Robbie got shot?" Singleton asked.

Big Twin hesitated, then he decided Singleton needed to know.

"Robbie's dead."

Though just a year apart, Singleton viewed Robbie like a big brother. He had status in the streets that made him seem older than his birth certificate claimed. Robbie built his reputation by breaking into people's homes. Around 1982, he started selling cocaine. He was the neighborhood bully to some kids—and a protector to others. Like Singleton.

Singleton, his fists balled and teeth clenched and fighting tears, tried opening the door.

"Let me in."

Orange shook his head. "This is not what *you* do," he said. "This is what *we* do." And he rode off in search of Robbie's killers.

John Singleton never forgot that moment. What would have happened if they'd let him in? Would he have used his father's .357 Magnum? Would he have been shot? Why wouldn't they let him go with them? And what did it all mean?

Singleton still talked about it nearly a decade later. "Remember Robbie Stringer?" he'd ask his best friends, Michael "Fatbacc" Winters and Jimmy Ray.

Robbie's death came on the heels of the summer of 1984. Crack had exploded. "Jam on It" by Newcleus was pumping out of every boom box. Carl Lewis and Mary Lou Retton won gold at the Summer Olympics and Lionel Richie sang "All Night Long" during the closing ceremonies of the global get-together that made the people of South Central feel uninvited in their own city.

Singleton spent that summer at the movies. Over three months he saw *Breakin'*, *Sixteen Candles*, *Firestarter*, *Indiana Jones and the Temple of Doom*, *Star Trek III: The Search for Spock*, *Beat Street*, *Ghostbusters*, *Gremlins*, *Top Secret!*, *The Karate Kid*, *Bachelor Party*, and *Conan the Destroyer*. He saw *The Last Starfighter* three times. *The NeverEnding Story*. *Revenge of the Nerds*. *Red Dawn*, *Dreamscape*. He saw *Purple Rain* at least three times, not counting the film's premiere at Mann's Chinese Theatre, which he attended as a fan and where he touched Morgan Fairchild's hand as she approached the red carpet, a moment he endlessly bragged about.

And it was that summer his friend was murdered.

That year, 1,438 people were killed in Los Angeles County. On the news, it would be just another gangbanger shot dead. But Singleton knew that Robbie did what he did in the street, but he also had a story and a soul. He had friends and a mom and a girlfriend who watched him die.

Orange had a very good reason to leave John behind that night: Danny Singleton, John's father.

"Yo, Kevin, let me talk to you," Danny might say in passing.

No matter what Orange might be getting into, he stopped for him.

"Do you know any Black-owned stores over on Vermont—not just Black people working there. Black folks that own them?"

Orange could only shrug.

"Think about that," Danny would say. "Spend some of that energy opening your own business or buying some of this land."

They were thinking about Danny when they turned John away.

Danny never gangbanged but had their respect; Stanley "Tookie" Williams, a cofounder of the Crips, was a friend. For many in the neighborhood, Danny was the first person they heard talk about knowledge of self. Whenever he noticed someone gravitating toward trouble, he encouraged them to do better. Some of his philosophies came from his mother, Ethel, a follower of the Nation of Islam.

Born in Fresno, Danny was the sixth of Leon and Ethel Singleton's children. His parents were both born in Mississippi and met there before heading out West for work and to start a family. Leon toiled as a farm laborer in the South. Once he arrived in Fresno, he got a job as a storekeeper. He then moved the family to Los Angeles, when Danny was three. From a young age, Danny oozed self-confidence. He grew to be six feet, three inches and 220 pounds of muscle. With his short Afro and dark skin tone, he resembled Richard Roundtree. As a teenager, he often took the bus to the Japanese movie theater downtown to watch Akira Kurosawa films. Toshiro Mifune, who starred in sixteen of the director's films, was his favorite actor. Danny was a hard-nosed guy. But not as hard-nosed as John Singleton's mother, Sheila.

Sheila Ward-Johnson was the third and youngest daughter of John and Audrey Morgan. The Morgans lived in Pennsylvania, where John worked as a chauffeur at a Retail Auto Sales. He married Audrey Myers in Seattle in 1946. A descendant of farmers from South Carolina, Audrey grew up in Philadelphia. Henry, her father, worked as a laborer in the Philadelphia Navy Yard. In 1939, he made $1,175. Audrey was a boisterous lady; Singleton credits her with teaching him how to tell dirty jokes. She was the storyteller in the family. Audrey taught Sheila how to be tough and fight for what she wanted.

Now in Los Angeles, Sheila became pregnant by Danny in the spring of 1967. They planned to raise their son together. But Danny said he was deployed to Vietnam three days before John was born on January 6, 1968, at the John Wesley County Hospital. Although this is difficult to confirm, Danny said that he put an engagement ring on Sheila's finger. He told *Wright Enterprises Community Spotlight*, a publicist-generated newsletter, that he received a "Dear John" letter from Sheila during his yearlong tour of duty.

For the bulk of his childhood, and his entire life, really, Singleton's parents were at odds—a "fractured" family, as he put it in a later interview. When an interlocutor mistakenly referred to Danny as Sheila's husband, she tersely corrected him. "He wasn't my husband," she said during a panel discussion in 2022. "I made certain that people knew he was not my husband. I was very lucky not to have executed a marriage after the engagement. Very lucky."

Once back in Los Angeles, Danny enrolled at Cal State LA, where he also played football. In January 1976, he got a job at Thrifty's Drug Store in South Central off Vermont and Manchester. He ascended to a management position and ran a chain of stores. From there, he earned his real estate license and became a mortgage broker. But still, money was an issue throughout Singleton's childhood.

"My father said that he couldn't afford to pay child support," Singleton said, "but he could pay moral support."

Danny loved his son and had high expectations for him. When he'd see him, he'd teach him how to be independent and navigate the world. Danny parented through proverbs and adages that he dispensed at random.

Over dinner, he'd say, "John, are you a leader or a follower?"

"I'm a leader!"

"Everyone says that," Danny would say. "Until it's time to make decisions. Remember what you said."

John would nod, silent.

Another favorite was whenever John struggled with anything, from assembling a toy to doing homework, Danny could look over, show John a simpler way.

"I always tell you, John. Work smarter—"

"Not harder," John would add.

"That's right."

At times, Danny didn't treat his son as if he were a child. John would absorb his long monologues about life, death, and the origins of the universe, which Danny often delivered while lifting weights. They'd go fishing down at Palos Verdes. Danny would pack a loaf of bread, a can of tuna, mayonnaise, and relish, and make sandwiches while casting a line. Rarely, if ever, did they catch anything, but that wasn't the point. They'd talk about what kind of man John would become and whatever was on their minds.

"What do you know about sex?" Danny asked him once.

"A little."

"Oh, yeah," Danny said, smiling. He picked up a big slimy snail off a rock. "John, what's this look like to you?"

"I don't know."

"Heh—one day you'll get it."

For parts of John's childhood, Danny lived with his mother, Ethel, and other family members in La Puente, a small Latino community twenty minutes outside LA in the San Gabriel Valley. Once he entered the real estate game, he'd sometimes stay in fixer-uppers he worked on. Then he'd sell them and move into the next project. Danny didn't settle down in his place of residence—or in his personal life. He bounced from one relationship to another and juggled multiple women simultaneously; they loved his build, his good looks, his confidence. He fathered at least seven children after John was born: Rashabar, Marshay, Latoya, Danny Jr., Dannielle, and Tanesa, whom John was closest with. Samira Singleton, born in April 1998, is the youngest.

"I looked up to my father like most people look up to Superman," John said. "My daddy walked around like he was the only father on the block who had a Magnum by his bed. He's bad and had all the chicks, [quick to] knock a nigga out. He was that dude."

As a child, Singleton primarily lived with Sheila in the Darby-Dixon neighborhood of Inglewood, a part of town known as the Bottoms, a six-block area just south of the Hollywood Park racetrack and casino that consisted of two-story apartment houses and duplex homes. Located at the bottom of a sloped terrain, the community became a stronghold of the Crenshaw Mafia Gangster Bloods after the group was founded in the 1970s.

They lived at 3406 Lawrence Street in a one-bedroom apartment that became a two-bedroom after Sheila converted the dining room into Singleton's bedroom. When Singleton was a toddler, Sheila enrolled at Cal State Dominguez Hills in Carson, California, about a twenty-five-minute drive from LA, where she studied medical technology. Later on, she earned a master's in health care management. Sheila also studied accounting at Cal State University, Los Angeles, and in 1995 received a master's in business management.

With his mother busy with school, Singleton was a latchkey kid. He spent a lot of time alone, and the library became his babysitter. While in elementary school, he read *The Autobiography of Malcolm X* and Anne Moody's memoir *Coming of Age in Mississippi*. He learned about history that school ignored: the Civil Rights Movement, the Nation of Islam, Black pride, Pan-Africanism.

When he heard that Malcolm X had copied the entire dictionary, he set out to duplicate the feat; he only got through the letter *A*.

Sheila loved the theater and wanted to expose Singleton to a wide array of culture. She'd visit museums with him when there was enough time to do so with all her studies. Sometimes, they'd drive around in her Volkswagen and mock pedestrians while waiting for the light to turn green, making up dialogue in an improv exercise of sorts.

Sheila also took him to the movies often. In the summer of 1975, when Singleton was seven, they saw *Cooley High*, a coming-of-age story about Black teen-agers from the North Side of Chicago. At the end of the film, after the tragic hero Cochise was murdered, he heard his mother sniffling.

"Why are you crying, Mama?" he blurted out. "It's make-believe."

"Because it's such a good movie. It feels real, John. It feels so real."

Up to that point, Singleton had experienced movies as sheer entertainment. From his apartment on Lawrence Street, he could look out the back window and watch whatever played at the Century Drive-In a block over. The Century showed mostly kung fu movies, slasher films, and blaxploitation flicks. He later joked that "seeing Pam Grier's titties" in *Coffy* and *Foxy Brown* inspired him to make movies.

But in the dark, watching *Cooley High*, he grasped how movies connected with their audience—the emotions they stirred; the feelings they created. Once he started making movies, *Cooley High* stayed nestled in the back of his mind. He wanted to generate *that* reaction from people.

Movies were one thing Sheila and Danny agreed on. When Danny had John, he'd take him to see martial arts films and Godzilla movies at the same Japanese theaters he'd frequented as a teenager. One afternoon, during the summer of 1977, Danny took John to see *Star Wars*. They stood in line for over an hour outside Mann's Chinese Theatre before taking their seats.

Like millions of other kids, Singleton stared at the screen in awe from the moment he read the words "A long time ago in a galaxy far, far away. . . ." He'd seen the commercials but had no idea about the world he'd soon enter. He tried making sense of the opening crawl: Why are the rebels at war with the Galactic Empire? How do you destroy an entire planet? Who's Princess Leia?

As soon as it was over, he wanted to go back again and again, and over the next three years he'd see *Star Wars* around a dozen times in the theater. Each time he loved something different about it. On his first viewing, the special effects drew him in. *Jason and the Argonauts* and *Godzilla* looked primitive compared to the Death Star's explosion.

Later on, he became obsessed with the characters: Luke Skywalker's heroism; Han Solo's detached cool; Princess Leia's beauty and bravery; Darth Vader, the perfect villain; all the weird creatures and robots.

He quoted the film at any opportunity:

To his friends in the school cafeteria: *"You'll never find a more wretched hive of scum and villainy."*

To himself acting in the mirror: *"Who's the more foolish, the fool or the fool who follows him?"*

To his neighborhood friend: *"I find your lack of faith disturbing."*

Finally, he started paying attention to the technical aspects of the film: the dichotomy between the desert light on Tatooine and the darkness of outer space; the cool camera work like the low-angle shot when the stormtroopers chase Han, Leia, and Chewbacca through the Death Star; how director George Lucas transitioned from scene to scene. Later on, he'd learn they were called wipe transitions.

When he went to the library now, he'd read film reviews from old newspapers on microfiche. At recess he'd draw flip-books, little animated shorts, with friends.

One night, in January 1978, Singleton was up late, way past his bedtime, watching television, when he came across *Tomorrow with Tom Snyder*, a talk show airing after *The Tonight Show*. Snyder's guest that evening was Steven Spielberg, promoting his new film *Close Encounters of the Third Kind*. Singleton loved the sci-fi epic but didn't know much about the man who wrote and directed it. For the next hour, he listened to Spielberg discuss his inspiration for the story, his upbringing, and the filmmaking process.

Afterward, Singleton said to himself, "I want to do what that guy does."

★★★★★

One summer night, when Singleton was around eleven or twelve years old, he was in the street with friends waiting for the sun to go down. It was a few days after the Fourth of July. He had saved a couple of M-80 firecrackers from the holidays. The plan: Blow up a chunk of the sidewalk once it got dark.

"John, it's time to come inside," Sheila called.

"Not yet, Mom," he said.

"Now," she said, raising her voice.

"All my friends are still out."

"I don't care. Now."

"Look, it's still light outside," he said. "Why do I have to go in the house?"

Sheila marched toward him. She raised her arm, opened her palm, and swatted at his face. Singleton put up his arms just in time to block the slap, but hit his mom's arm in the process.

Knowing he couldn't win this battle, he apologized and followed her back to their apartment, sulking.

"Dad would let me stay out," he mumbled under his breath.

"Oh, really?" she said. "Well, I think it's time you go live with your father."

As Singleton told it, that's how he came to live with his father. He soon moved into his grandmother Ethel's house on 101st and Vermont, where Danny stayed in a back room. He made fast friends. One Saturday morning, while skateboarding out front, his dad's neighbor, a teenager named Kevin Orange, approached him. A few steps behind him stood a boy about Singleton's age, Michael Winters. He too carried a skateboard.

"John, this is my godbrother Mike. Maybe you can teach him how to ride," Orange said. "Mike, that's Danny's son John. You might want to play with him. He can actually ride a skateboard."

"Do you ride, man?" John asked.

"Not really," Winters said. "I just get on my knees and push."

Singleton laughed.

"At least I'm allowed to cross the street," Winters snapped back.

Nicknamed "Fatbacc," he would become one of Singleton's closest friends. Along with another boy, Jimmy Ray, the trio would go on adventures across the city, riding the bus to different neighborhoods, going to parks, the mall, pro wrestling shows at the Olympic Auditorium, and the movie theater. As they got a little older, they ran a three-man operation on the RTD bus for pocket change.

"Okay, okay, listen, everybody, we have a very special guest on the bus this afternoon," Singleton would say. "Please welcome Michael Jackson! Hit it!" Fatbacc would insert a cassette of *Thriller* into a boom box, press play, and Jimmy Ray would emerge in full Michael Jackson cosplay to perform a routine.

"Give it up for Michael," Singleton would say afterward, collecting money from passengers.

Another favorite activity was playing cat-and-mouse games with the police helicopters hovering over the neighborhood. Singleton would run out in the street, zigging and zagging, daring them to trap him in their spotlight. Why? "It was really beautiful," he said. "When they'd point the spotlights at the ground, the light would come through that tree in hundreds of tiny little shafts, dappling through the leaves."

Founded in 1956, the LAPD's Air Support Division is the largest local airborne law-enforcement unit in the United States. Police copters were first deployed to monitor traffic. But around the time of the Watts uprising in 1965 they evolved into the LAPD's eyes in the sky. In the years afterward, the helicopters became a continuous presence in South Central.

The constant thick whooshing blades—that *thwup, thwup, thwup* sound. The blinding spotlight. South Central residents learned how to sleep through their sights and sounds. Their fleet grew from three in 1965 to fifteen less than a decade later. Thank the city's aerospace industry for spurring the growth. The LAPD began utilizing them as a patrol vehicle of sorts—at least two were airborne at all times. Researchers found that they reduced crime in the areas they patrolled. But other studies debunked those results, finding the copters' presence to be nothing more than performative security and a dumb use of resources that accomplished little but terrorized a population.

"I've heard copters all my life," Singleton once said. "It's an incredible kind of psychological violence. It makes you think not in terms of the future, because who knows if you'll be around. So you say, 'Not next year. Not next week. I'm going to get mine now.'"

Since this was Los Angeles in the late 1970s and early 1980s, Singleton and his friends had to be careful about where they trod, who they talked to, and how they navigated certain situations.

Gang culture in Los Angeles exploded in the aftermath of the Black Panther Party's collapse. This was in large part due to the FBI's Counterintelligence Program, better known as COINTELPRO, a series of clandestine and sometimes illegal schemes carried out between 1956 and 1971 designed to discredit, disrupt, and destroy organizations that the bureau considered threats. Initially, gangs filled the void left by the Panthers in serving the community and protecting Black Angelinos from the LAPD; the name Crips is sometimes said to be a backronym for Community Revolution in Progress. As the economic conditions in Los Angeles worsened and the drug trade became more lucrative, their focus shifted.

Singleton was affiliated due to where he grew up. He was never a gangbanger. He just knew a lot of them. Kevin Orange and Robbie Stringer were Crips. Later on, Fatbacc joined as well. But he had friends on the other side. The Bottoms was Bloods territory. Singleton's older cousin Avance "Smokey" Smith was a Blood.

"John was fascinated by gang life," Smokey says today, "but nobody would let him participate in it." Not Smokey. Not Big Twin. Definitely not Danny nor Sheila. "Sheila never did like me, because she always thought I was a bad influence for John."

Singleton lived the gang life through their eyes and stories.

He had his own stories too. His slight stature and dorky glasses made him a target for bullies. But he could scrap. Danny taught him well. In the end, he probably won just as many fights as he lost.

By the time he got to Monroe Junior High School, he carried a box cutter in his pocket for protection. He kept it hidden but always had the metal Afro pick his dad gave him. One day, his shop teacher caught him using it in class.

"Singleton, are you halfway intelligent enough to understand the rules?" he said. "Those metal picks are banned."

He walked toward Singleton's desk. "Give it to me," he demanded.

Singleton sighed heavily and avoided eye contact.

"Give it to me," he said, outstretching his hand.

Slowly, Singleton yielded the comb, and slumped in his chair.

The teacher placed the comb on his workbench and sawed it in half. Singleton's eyes started to well up. Then the teacher cut it in half again. And again.

Singleton bit his lip, choked back tears, got out of his chair, and walked to the classroom door. He turned around. "Fuck you, motherfucker," he said. Then he walked out.

Soon after, he transferred to Portola Junior High in the San Fernando Valley. He'd stand at the bus stop on Ninety-Second and Hoover a little after six a.m. for the long ride into the Valley. Immediately, he noticed how well funded the school appeared to be compared to the schools he had attended. They had a computer lab and an after-school program where he learned how to code. For a moment there, he thought of pursuing tech and becoming an engineer, but the thought of all the math classes he'd have to take intimidated him.

It was his first time at a school that wasn't primarily Black and Latino; a recent influx of Israeli and Japanese immigrants had joined the predominantly white student body.

"John had white friends, Hispanic friends, Black friends. John got on with everyone," says his friend Carl Austin. "John was a fucking chameleon. He blended in everywhere he went. It was fascinating to watch."

Later, Singleton would say that Austin was the popular guy who got all the girls and played sports. Today, Austin corrects his friend.

"We all followed John. He was the leader. He would never say it—but he was."

Singleton met Austin on his first day at Portola. He noticed him reading a Batman comic and struck up a conversation with him on the bus about Frank Miller's *Daredevil*.

"We got pretty tight there and back in the neighborhood as well," Austin says. "No one was into the things we were into. We were into movies. We were into comic books. We were into computers."

Together, they indulged their geekdom. Fantasy Castle, a comic-book store near the school, was their heaven on earth, ground zero for all things related to film—posters, scripts, the novelizations of new movies. They'd hoard their allowance money and then splurge.

"What did you get?" Austin asked.

"Oliver Stone's *Conan the Barbarian* script," Singleton said. "Not gonna read it until we see the movie, though. I don't care that John Milius's version is different. You?"

"A novelization of *Poltergeist*."

"Should've told me. I woulda let you borrow it."

"Is it good?"

"Dunno. I didn't finish it. Don't want to spoil the ending."

"I'm gonna read the whole thing."

"Go ahead, but don't tell me a damn thing about what happens at the end," Singleton said. He put his arm on Austin's shoulder and looked him in his eyes. "If you say anything, I will hurt you."

Soon, they talked about writing their own movies and started reading books like Syd Field's *Screenplay*. Toward the end of the school year, for the first time, they ditched to go to the theater.

Singleton masterminded the plan. On the morning of May 28, 1982, Singleton and Austin got off the bus and walked into the school building. Instead of going to their classrooms, they hid in the bathroom stalls.

"John, I—I don't know," Austin said.

Singleton could hear his short breaths from the next stall.

"Don't chicken out now."

"Whi-which exit are we using," Austin said, suddenly forgetful and stuttering.

"Just follow me."

A few minutes later, the school bell rang. Singleton and Austin climbed out of the stalls, walked the empty halls, snuck out through the back door, hopped a fence, and ran to the bus stop. Their destination: The Cinerama Dome in Hollywood. Why? *Rocky III* opened that morning.

When they arrived at the theater, Singleton furrowed his brow and emitted a loud groan. The line stretched around the block. He approached a group of college kids near the front.

"This guy is a wrecking machine," he said, quoting Burgess Meredith from the film's trailer using the same distinct voice as the actor.

"Within fifteen minutes we're part of their group," Austin says. "He did stuff like that all the time. I have no idea how he got to be that charming at the age of fourteen."

Singleton had little choice but to excel at making fast friends. Every fall, he was the new kid at school. He moved around often as a teen, much more than he divulged in interviews once he became famous. Life wasn't predictable or comfortable. He never truly felt settled. After Portola, he attended Bassett High School in La Puente. Then he did a year at Morningside High School in Inglewood. After Robbie Stringer's murder, Ethel urged John to live with family in Rialto, about an hour east of Los Angeles; Danny was nearby in San Bernardino. In October of that year, Singleton enrolled in Eisenhower High School in Rialto. Then, after moving in with Sheila, he spent his senior year at Blair High in Pasadena.

Film became the one constant during his nomadic formative years. At Eisenhower, he reviewed movies for his school newspapers. Initially it was more of a hustle, a scheme to see movies like *Sixteen Candles*, *Mask*, and *The Breakfast Club* weeks early and for free. But the more he watched, the more he learned, and the more he believed he could do it.

In 1985, the summer between his junior and senior years, he took a cinematography course at Pasadena City College. For the first time, he had access to film equipment. He'd rent out Super 8 cameras and shoot films around Pasadena with Austin, such as a music video for Phil Collins's "In the Air Tonight"; *Miami Vice* was an obsession at this point. He used Austin and his new Pasadena friends as actors, including a blond girl who lived a few blocks from him that he had a crush on. By the time senior year started in the fall, he'd made four or five films.

He read *Skywalking: The Life and Films of George Lucas*, Dale Pollock's definitive biography of the *Star Wars* creator, which tracked Lucas's life from the hot rod scene of Modesto, California, to USC film school to Hollywood. *That's it. I've got to go to USC*, he remembered thinking.

Like most kids from South Central, Singleton knew USC was right there. But he always felt like it didn't belong. Then he read about how the film school had recently opened new buildings: the George Lucas Instructional Building, the

Marcia Lucas Post-Production Facility, and the Johnny Carson and Harold Lloyd Sound Stages.

One afternoon in the fall of 1985, Sheila decided to check out a master's program at the school. "Mind if I tag along?" John asked. Shortly after walking onto campus, he wandered off. Singleton joined a horde of students, and followed them in through the front door into the George Lucas Instructional Building. Every classroom was full. Not a single Black face. He roamed the halls and stopped a student.

"What's your major?" he asked.

"Production."

"So, you're going to be a producer."

"No, I'm going to be a cinematographer."

"So, you work on camera shots and with the camera operators?"

"That's right. Are you interested?"

"No," he said. "Any fool can figure out where to point the camera. I have a story to tell."

He moved on, leaving the student dumbfounded. He bombarded others with more questions, and then he found a professor.

"I'm John Singleton. I'm seventeen years old and I'm from South Central. I want to go to film school."

The professor took in the young man's intense gaze and stole a glance at the book Singleton carried, Stephen King's short story collection, *Skeleton Crew*. He pointed down the hall.

Singleton knocked on the door. An older man opened it. "I want to go to school here," Singleton said.

The man shook his hand. "Okay, what do you want to do?"

"I want to write and direct stories about real people and the things we go through."

"That's refreshing," the older man said. "Most people who walk in these doors want to be the next Spielberg or Lucas. They want to get rich and get the sports car and the blond. How are your grades?"

Singleton shrank in his chair. "C-plus? B-minus, maybe?"

"Let's try to improve that."

He told Singleton all about the school: how to apply and how to take advantage of its resources without being enrolled. "Aim for the filmic writing program," he said. "It's new but it's what you're looking for. To get where you want to go you have to learn how to write scripts. You'll find time to shoot stuff on the side."

He handed Singleton his card. Singleton looked at it and realized he'd been talking to Russ McGregor, the interim dean of the film school.

From that moment, Singleton plotted his course to USC. He improved his grades at Blair, ultimately graduating with a B average and scoring a 900 on the SAT (out of 1600). Whenever he could, he made his way back to campus during his senior year. He volunteered on student films, doing mostly production assistant work. But his favorite thing to do on campus was watch films in the cinema stacks at Doheny Memorial Library.

When he told his parents about his decision, he received a mixed response. "What about real estate?" Danny said. "A lot of money out there and you can get started right after graduation in June." Sheila, meanwhile, had spent the last seventeen years telling Singleton he could do anything he set his mind to. She wasn't going to discourage him no matter how difficult the road ahead seemed.

In the spring of 1986, he got the news: He had been admitted to the filmic writing program at USC Film School and would be part of the class of 1990.

In July he returned to campus for freshman orientation. He already knew his way around the buildings, what he planned to do. When asked to introduce himself, he smiled and said, "My name is John Singleton. I'm a local from the community and I'm here to study film."

"He had this shit-eating grin on his face the whole time, like he knew something that we didn't," says Pat O'Hara, a football player from Santa Monica in Singleton's orientation group. "Out of that group of twenty people, the only person I remember was John."

Earlier that year, Tracey Willard, a friend of Sheila's, told Singleton to apply to her job's film program. He gave her one of his short films It was about a Black man who was so in love with a white girl that he killed himself over her. Willard worked at the NAACP. It didn't go over so well.

She still wanted to see Singleton get a leg up in film.

"I need to introduce you to my friend Spike Lee," said Willard. "You remind me of him."

"What does he do?"

"He's a writer and a director."

Just a few weeks later, Singleton sat alone in a Santa Monica movie theater, in the middle seat of the middle row, waiting to watch Akira Kurosawa's *Ran* for the third time, when he saw a trailer for a black-and-white film called *She's Gotta Have It*. A twenty-nine-year-old NYU film student from Brooklyn named Spike Lee had directed it.

One week later, Singleton was in line at the same theater for *She's Gotta Have It*. Lee was standing outside the theater, handing out promotional buttons.

Singleton walked up.

"Do you know Tracey Willard from Spelman?"

"Yeah, I know Tracey," said Lee, a Morehouse graduate.

"My name is John Singleton. She said I should meet you."

"Cool, John. Welcome. Let me know what you think."

They dapped up and John went inside.

Once in the theater, Singleton couldn't believe what was on the screen.

"It was the first movie for me where I felt Black people were fully well-rounded people," Singleton said. "They weren't archetypes. They weren't just good or bad, they were three-dimensional. They didn't play that color shit where the bad guys were dark-skinned. It was really just Black. I came out the theater and I was galvanized."

Afterward, a crowd formed around Lee trying to compliment him in his moment of triumph. He locked eyes with Singleton—he couldn't miss him in that bright yellow shirt—and made his way toward him.

"What did you think?" Lee asked.

"I loved it. By the way, I'm going to USC film school in two weeks. Watch out for me. I'm coming."

In September 1986, eighteen-year-old John Singleton arrived at USC with the goal of adding to the school's rich history of producing top-tier writing and directing talent. Soon, he'd take his place next to George Lucas, John Carpenter, John Milius, and Ron Howard. He was USC's next great filmmaker, in his mind at least.

Since its founding in 1929, the same year as the first Academy Awards ceremony, the USC School of Cinematic Arts maintained its status as the world's most prestigious film school. And at the time of Singleton's attendance in the 1980s, it was awash in donor money. Ray Stark bestowed $1 million toward a new graduate program. Lucas, the school's most famous alum, had underwritten $4.7 million of the recently opened $14 million postproduction building. As its biggest moneymaker after the football team, the film school felt detached from the rest of the university—and with good reason.

During an era known for greed, excess, and superficiality, USC, a private school in a state with a robust public university system, embodied some of the decade's more vulgar traits. Tuition soared around this time. Beginning in 1985, a year prior to Singleton enrolling, it escalated approximately 9 percent each of the next four years. For the 1988–89 academic year, attending USC cost $11,302, up from $5,310 in 1980. The acceptance rate hovered around 70 percent. A recruitment poster from the 1980s featured a well-endowed blonde in a sports car, as though the school were promoting itself as a home for America's frat bros and their future trophy wives. To some, USC stood for the University of Spoiled Children.

Singleton assumed film school would be different. But even there a hierarchy existed.

Production, where future producers, directors, and below-the-line crew members learned their craft, was the most prestigious major at the School of Cinematic

Arts. Production majors chased a golden ticket: At the end of the semester, five students were selected to direct a thirty-minute sixteen-millimeter color film, which
would then be screened for a theater full of agents, managers, producers, and
studio executives.

Critical studies, the more white-collar and academic discipline, landed next.
While production majors aspired to be the next Spielberg, the most likely end-
game for a critical studies student was writing for a literary magazine or landing
a tenured position at some overpriced institution like, say, USC.

Where did that leave the filmic writing program?

"The filmic writing program was the ugly stepchild of the film department,"
says Paul Lucey, a USC film school professor from 1980 to 1993.

Margaret Mehring, an activist and documentarian, founded the program in
1982. She was a polarizing figure on campus in that she was a woman in a position of power. According to interviews with faculty and students, for one reason
or another, Mehring was never embraced by the faculty as one of their own. She
hadn't worked as a technician. She didn't have enough credits to her name. She
hadn't fought in the war. She insisted on using the term *filmic writing* over *screenwriting*. *Too pedestrian*, she thought. Her teaching methods? Similarly hippie-dippie
and eccentric.

"Find the most beautiful thing in the world and then tell us about it" went one
of her classroom assignments.

USC featured a murderers' row of instructors during Singleton's time,
including recent Oscar winner William Kelley, and Syd Field, the best-selling
author of *Screenplay: The Foundations of Screenwriting*, which popularized the three-
act structure model and introduced the term "inciting incident" into the lexicon.

Abraham Polonsky, the blacklisted Oscar-nominated screenwriter of 1947's
*Body and Soul*, was his favorite writing professor. Polonsky could be grouchy. "All
the people you're studying didn't go to film school," he'd say. "They figured it
out by studying literature and having a point of view." But he had a soft spot for
Singleton.

In time, Singleton was tasked with picking up Polonsky from his Beverly Hills
home and driving him to campus.

"John, once you're done with this place, get ready for a life with few triumphs
and a lot of potholes."

"What do you mean?"

"You will not believe what writers must endure," Polonsky said. "Actors who change dialogue to suit their persona and not the scene. Directors who turn a good screenplay into a bad movie."

"Do you really think I'm going to make it?"

"If you keep writing about reality. What do I always say?"

"Write what you know."

"Write what you know," Polonsky said. "What else did I say in class the other day?"

"At the rate all of you are going, this is the only guy who's ever going to get a job making movies."

"I meant it."

Initially, film school lived up to his expectations. On the first day his Cinema 190 class met, Singleton sat in the front row of the 365-seat Norris Theatre pinned to his chair, eyes wider than dinner plates, watching *Singin' in the Rain*. Afterward, Professor Drew Casper opened the floor to students. Singleton's hand shot straight up. When called on, he underscored how Gene Kelly's dance numbers were shot. He ended his monologue with a reference to *Papillon*, the 1973 prison drama starring Steve McQueen and Dustin Hoffman.

Now among his people, he indulged in his love of film. People who didn't flinch at subtitles. People who avoided *The Maltese Falcon* on PBS to see it for the first time on the big screen. People who devoured everything from experimental black-and-white student films to blockbusters like *Star Wars*. They weren't film snobs. These were all cinephiles.

Toward the end of his first semester, Singleton began to view them suspiciously. From the start, the lack of Black students both in the filmic writing program and the film school in general bothered him. The slights accumulated. Became harder to ignore. The dearth of Black films in the syllabus. Professors quick to dismiss his point of view. His peers telling him he'd never get a movie made.

"Why are you even here?" one white student asked him.

"I took out twenty-five thousand dollars in loans to be here. Why the fuck do you think I'm here? Why are you here?"

He viewed them as trust fund babies unwilling to get their fingernails dirty. No drive. No point of view. No heart. No soul. "USC was a cultural wasteland," Singleton told *Rolling Stone* in 1991. "Everybody wanted to get rich, but nobody wanted to work to get there."

Singleton put in the work. He referred to himself as a "filmic soldier," a warrior on the front lines spreading the gospel of cinema, learning the craft in order to leave his mark on the world.

"Going to film school wasn't about partying. It wasn't about drinking," he said. "It was nothing but studying film and living life the best I could."

He felt an internal pressure to succeed. He remembered, as a kid, hearing older folks discuss their ambitions—this plan, that plan, a new path, some grand scheme that, more often than not, didn't pan out. He didn't want to end up like that. He couldn't fail.

Singleton utilized all the resources USC film school offered. He attended every screening and extra seminar. Helped out on student projects. Met with professors during office hours. Read biographies of great filmmakers and then binged their work. He studied Academy Award–winning screenwriters like Paddy Chayefsky (*Network*, *The Hospital*). "What makes this work?" he'd ask after reading a great script. Then he'd list all the reasons in his journal. He was clocking his ten thousand hours. He was Kobe shooting in the gym.

Singleton took on the manner of a future first-round draft pick; college was a pit stop for him on his way to the pros. On campus, he cut a striking figure—the short, thin Black kid with Coke-bottle glasses dashing from class to class, usually with a stack of papers under one arm. He adopted a steely persona—harder than hard—similar to that of a no-nonsense reality show contestant who declares early on "I'm not here to make friends" and actually means it. In reality, it was a defense mechanism constructed to withstand slings and arrows, both real and perceived.

In response, the white students in class didn't invite him to film school parties. They talked about him behind his back.

*"It's so obvious he doesn't give a shit about anyone."*

*"I'm not like John. I actually care about what you're working on."*

*"He thinks we don't like him because he's Black. We don't like him because he's a dick."*

Though he didn't exude warmth and friendliness, Singleton didn't struggle to make new friends outside of film school. During the first week of the semester, he struck up a conversation with a politically minded and socially conscious student from Seattle outside of her dorm room in Fluor Tower.

"Hi, my name is John Singleton. I'm running for student senate and I need your vote."

"What's your platform?"

"Huh?"

"What are you trying to do if elected?"

"Ummm, make student housing more affordable. Do I have your vote?"

"I don't know."

"Okay, I'll see you around."

They became instant friends.

"That moment defined our relationship for the next thirty years," says Adrianne Shropshire. "John being totally self-assured and me being totally skeptical and side-eyeing him. The thing I never asked him was if he was saying that to all the women. Was it a pickup line? Because John never ran for student senate."

A few days before the semester started, Singleton befriended a six-foot-three kid from Harlem named Yon Styles. A graduate of the prestigious Bronx High School of Science, Styles applied to USC on a whim after determining late senior year that he wanted to attend college near the beach. Styles rocked fatigues and shell-toe Adidas. In high school, he lettered in tennis, basketball, and going out, earning the nickname the Recreational Director. He didn't look, or act, like a teenager. He was a regular at downtown Manhattan nightclubs.

On campus, Styles attracted like-minded freshmen—Black kids from the East Coast echoing him in both spirit and swag. Students from Connecticut, New York, New Jersey, Miami, Chicago, Detroit, and Maryland by way of Africa entered his orbit. Prep school kids. A diplomat's son. Former valedictorians. And a film student from South Central.

Kenneth Baines, a Harlem native nicknamed Busy for his active social life, christened the crew Black Pack.

Singleton became fascinated with his new friends. Despite all he'd seen as a kid in South Central, he grew up sheltered compared to this collection of East Coast cosmopolitans. He hadn't been on a plane or to the Palladium. Though not a virgin, he was much less experienced than his new friends.

"When John was interested in a girl, he'd want to date that girl," Baines says. "I would tell him all the time that he was going too easy on them and getting in his feelings a little too much."

Black Pack upended the caste system at USC, the one placing freshmen at the bottom of the social pecking order.

Styles's dorm in the Century apartments turned into their clubhouse after they scared off all his suitemates. They nicknamed it Black Pack Headquarters, or BPHQ for short. On weekends, Styles threw parties that attracted football players, cheerleaders, and cool kids from all cliques, crews, and backgrounds. Black Pack wasn't a gang or a fraternity—though it shared certain traits with them, like dressing uniformly and adopting a one-for-all-and-all-for-one philosophy.

One night, Black Pack showed up almost ten deep to the Topping Student Center in black trench coats and backward baseball caps. Heads turned upon their arrival. "Oh, they're here," someone murmured. Trouble started a few minutes later once Moose, an African student whose father was a diplomat, flirted with someone's girlfriend.

"You need to back the fuck off."

"Or what?" Moose taunted.

"Or else me and my boys are gonna fuck you up."

"Your boys? Oh, you have boys?"

Black Pack then stepped in. During the ensuing melee, there's a possibility that Singleton threw a kid down the stairs and broke his arm.

"People look at John and see this thin dude, flattop, glasses, a straight nerd. But his appearance belies his character," Malcolm Norrington says. "John was street. He always had my back."

Norrington, who attended Cal State Northridge, first met Singleton at an Omega Psi Phi information session. Some friends were startled at the idea of Singleton rushing. *John? Rushing? He's not a joiner. He won't make it through pledging.* But frats offered something he yearned for: the camaraderie of his fellow Black man.

In the spring of 1987, Singleton pledged the Beta Omega Chapter of Kappa Alpha Psi Fraternity. He wasn't a prototypical Kappa. They were pretty boys with a reputation as smooth, debonair types, which he was not. Still, Singleton stepped on campus with his fellow pledges in crimson and cream, twirling the frat's signature accessory: a miniature red-and-white striped cane.

The traditions went back decades. To the time of Jim Crow. To the time of an ascendent Ku Klux Klan.

Founded in 1911 on the campus of Indiana University, Kappa Alpha Psi was "born in an environment satured with racism" according to its website. Bloomington was a KKK hotbed in a state full of KKK hotbeds. The founders persevered; a USC chapter opened in 1947. The ties of brotherhood bonded them all, down to Singleton's pledge class.

He found the Kappas also offered friendship, fun parties, and postcollegiate networking opportunities. It came at a price. Pledging a Black fraternity in the 1980s meant an ass-kicking, and Singleton was not spared. They'd roll up a magazine and grind it into his ear. Friends remember seeing him marked up. At one point, he sported a black eye. One night during the spring semester, he banged on Adrianne's door.

"Let me in. It's John."

He barreled into her dorm room and slammed the door shut.

"What's going on? It's late."

"I need to hide here for an hour."

"Why?"

"I just need a place to hide."

"Why are you doing this stupid shit, getting humiliated on campus?"

"It'll be worth it in the end. It's just a few more weeks."

Singleton would then stumble back to Fluor Tower where he worked as the overnight front desk clerk three times a week from midnight to seven a.m. One night he fell asleep at his post with both his elbows on the table and his head in his palms.

"Eh-hem," said Beverly Watson, the customer service manager at Fluor Tower.

Singleton jolted awake. He looked at the clock.

"Oh, I just fell asleep," he said, rubbing his freshly shaved head.

"You haven't been sleeping all night?"

"No way. What time is it now?"

"It's quarter to seven, John."

"I'm so sorry. Won't happen again."

"Go home. Get rest. It's the graveyard shift. It happens. But don't let it happen again."

Watson sympathized with Singleton. She assumed he had cancer, due to his bald head. *Oh, he's going to school and he's sick,* she thought. *He's trying so hard.* She gave him a second chance and a third chance and a fourth chance.

A few weeks later, Watson marched into Fluor Tower only to find the front desk unmanned. Across the lobby, Singleton had passed out on a couch in front of the television. She shook him awake. By this point, Watson knew the truth. Singleton hadn't undergone chemo. He was pledging a frat.

"John, I'm sorry, but I have to get rid of you," she told him.

"Okay. I get it," he said. "I'll see you around."

"He didn't care," Watson says. "Working at Fluor Tower was the least of his worries. He had so much other stuff going on."

★★★★★

During the summer between his freshman and sophomore year, Singleton got his first showbiz job. He worked as a production assistant/security guard on *Pee-wee's Playhouse*, the hit Saturday morning show starring Paul Reubens as his childlike alter ego Pee-wee Herman.

Every morning, Singleton would cheerfully walk into Hollywood Center Studios, the former home of Desilu Productions and Francis Ford Coppola's Zoetrope. He'd sit on a metal folding chair outside the soundstage door with the flashing red light. He couldn't stop smiling over being on a studio lot.

"Good morning, John," Reubens would say on his way in.

"Good morning, Mr. Reubens."

"I have a question for you, John."

"Yeah?"

"When it's all said and done, what's one single word you want used to describe you?"

*"Incredible."*

Reubens would bow to Singleton and make his way inside.

"He was such a sweet kid," Reubens said, shortly before his death in 2023. "I had him check credentials. We weren't worried about someone coming in and doing something dastardly. I didn't want a kid to walk in and see me smoking on the set."

On his first day on set, Singleton ambled near the catering table.

"Hey, do you want some coffee?"

"Nah, I'm cool," Singleton said.

He looked up. "Oh wow, you're Larry Fishburne."

"You can call me Fish."

"Hey, I'm John Singleton. I'm a student at USC film school. I'm going to make movies."

"How old are you, John?"

"I'm nineteen. One day, I'm gonna write a really good role for you. Then I'm going to direct you in it."

"How old are you again?"

"Nineteen."

"Go on, brother!"

Later that day, he recounted the entire experience to a friend in the dorms.

Singleton loved meeting celebrities. Even more, he loved telling stories about meeting celebrities.

"It's Larry Fishburne! Do you know how many movies he's made with Coppola? Four! *Apocalypse Now. Rumble Fish. The Cotton Club. Gardens of Stone.*"

Singleton learned Fishburne had spent the spring in Atlanta shooting Spike Lee's next film *School Daze.* For the rest of the summer, whenever he got the chance, he peppered him with questions about the director.

Once school started, Singleton moved into a four-bedroom ranch-style house about a mile from campus that came to be known as BPHQ2. Singleton and three other names appeared on the lease. But on most nights the second iteration of Black Pack Headquarters passed for a flophouse.

"It was a sty," says Bobby Thomas. "It was Black *Animal House*—a lot of drinking, a lot of blunts, a lot of girls, and a lot of craziness."

Parties sprang up every night of the week. Sometimes they'd get so live and sweaty police would break them up. Young MC once DJed a Black Pack party; George Clinton stumbled in once or twice to smoke weed with the crew.

Singleton's bedroom was located in the back of the house, past the smoldering ashtrays and empty forty-ounce bottles piled up in the living room. Once inside, he'd blast Public Enemy on his stereo. "Miuzi Weighs a Ton." Papers would be scattered across the floor. Notes. Ideas. Old homework assignments. He set up a tiny projector to watch black-and-white movies.

Every so often, he'd emerge. He'd check the fridge just in case someone brought home food. Then he'd hang in the living room, scribbling in his notebook. One afternoon, he sat down while Yon was telling a story.

"You have to understand. We went to high school together. I knew her from Science. Before college, her mom asked me to look after her. I had to do something."

"Wait? What? What happened?" Singleton asked.

"One of my friends from New York, the one with the white roommate. Last night they got invited to a house. Someone at the party called her a 'Black bitch.'"

"Oh shit. What happened next?"

"She tells me and I go ballistic. I grab a baseball bat and tell Big Rob. We head down there. She gets me in the house and shows me who said it. I took him outside. Made him apologize."

"Then what did you say?" Singleton said, leaning forward, hands on his knees.

"If I ever have to come back again, I'm going to bust your head open with this baseball bat."

As always, Singleton took notes.

Singleton's time at BPHQ2 would be short-lived. One morning, in the fall of 1987, a sharp knock woke up the house. Bobby Thomas stumbled into the living room.

Singleton's mom, Sheila, pushed her way inside and looked around. The trash, the food, the laundry, the smell.

"Oh no," she said.

A few weeks earlier, she called to check in on Singleton following the Whittier earthquake. It was sometime around eight a.m.

"Do you live here?" she asked Bobby.

"Um, kinda."

"When you see John, you tell him to call his mother."

"Yes, ma'am."

One week later, Singleton moved out.

Throughout his sophomore year, he balanced classwork with a series of odd jobs. He drove a car for SuperShuttle, ferrying passengers to and from LAX. On the weekends, he conducted exit poll audience surveys for *Entertainment Tonight*. He got paid twenty-five dollars per movie, but the fringe benefits—free movies— made it worth it for him. Singleton also gave tours at the California African American Museum at Exposition Park.

In the spring of 1988, he became one of the founding members of the African American Film Association (now the African American Cinema Society). David L. Watts, a critical studies major from Cerritos nicknamed Money Train, founded the group to highlight the contributions of Black filmmakers. He appointed Singleton as his vice president. One of their first endeavors was curating a Sidney Poitier film festival.

Declaring any new Black organization at USC was deemed a political act. AAFA faced pushback.

"Why Sidney Poitier?" a white student asked an AAFA member.

"He's the first Black person to win the Academy Award for Best Actor."

"I find that offensive," the white student said. The student was a member of Young Americans for Freedom, a conservative youth activist group with a substantial footprint on campus.

"It's not offensive when there's a retrospective on Jimmy Stewart!" the AAFA member said.

In April 1988, Singleton and Watts attended a campus screening of *Colors*. Norris Theatre buzzed with energy. Directed by Dennis Hopper, *Colors* was one of Hollywood's first movies about LA gang culture. Singleton looked forward to seeing his neighborhood depicted on the big screen. The lights went down. But Singleton could barely hide his disgust. He squirmed in his seat and rubbed his forehead. *Colors*, which centered on two white LAPD officers played by Robert Duvall and Sean Penn, offered a beat cop's perspective of life in South Central. Afterward, the film's writers and producers took questions from the audience.

*"What was the toughest part of the shoot?"*

*"How was it working with Sean Penn?"*

*"Did Madonna ever show up to set?"*

Then Singleton stood up.

"This movie is bullshit!" he squawked. "How dare you make a movie about my neighborhood that glorifies the police."

Boos engulfed the theater. "Sit down!" someone cried.

"No, I take a personal affront to the film. That's not how it goes down in South Central. Nothing about this movie is true."

"Well, Ice-T wrote the music," said one of the producers.

"Well, Ice-T didn't write the fucking script," Singleton rebutted.

He also may or may not have called the filmmakers on stage a bunch of "white motherfuckers."

It was around this time Singleton started to find his voice as a writer. Sheila had gotten him a ticket to see *Fences*, the August Wilson play that swept the Tony Awards in 1987, and it sparked a light. Wilson's characters spoke with a specific rhythm and soul; Singleton could feel the brown liquor in their voice. He soon started work on a script about sisters reuniting for their mother's funeral. He titled it *Twilight Time*.

He didn't get behind the camera until Cinema 290. For the class, he was responsible for writing and directing three-minute Super 8 shorts. One of them was *Pickin' Boogers*, named after the Biz Markie song. In the film, a commuter accidentally glued his finger to his nose while flirting with a girl at a bus stop. Another film, *Baby*, was about a woman hallucinating about the child she had lost.

Like most student filmmakers, he relied on friends to be his cast and crew. That changed one afternoon at the Crenshaw Plaza mall.

"Hey, man, you played Dr. Feelgood!" Singleton said.

Cylk Cozart stopped and looked around. A former college basketball player turned actor, he had just appeared in Spike Lee's *School Daze* as Gamma Phi Gamma Big Brother Dr. Feelgood. When he saw Singleton wearing a baseball hat, glasses, and varsity jacket, he did a double take. "He looked like Spike, dressed like Spike, and talked like Spike," Cozart says.

"I'm John Singleton. I'm a student at USC film school. I'm going to be a director."

"What do you mean going to be? You're either a director or you're not."

"I am a director." Singleton dug around his backpack. "Hey, I wrote this script for class. Would you mind reading it? It's a love story."

"Sure. But where are you coming from, man? Why'd you write it?"

"Man, I was in love," Singleton said. *Faith, Don't Leave Me Now* told the story of a girl who leaves her boyfriend for someone rich and famous.

"That's all I needed to know," Cozart says. "He had the enthusiasm. Now I knew he had depth—that it meant something to him. So I said I'd help him out. Besides, I thought it could be good for my demo reel. I was just relieved he didn't ask me to finance it."

By the end of his sophomore year, Singleton's talent started to get noticed.

"John has really blossomed as a writer, a filmmaker, and a person," Margaret Mehring wrote in her progress evaluation. "It is possible that he will receive the Nicholson Scholarship next year. I hope so. He is very much alive, eager, and so full of hope and promise. He has charted his course and stuck to it. He recognized the need to learn screenwriting in order to do what he wants to do in production and has done so. I think that John will make some history, not just for Black films but for films per se. I am so happy for him."

A few months later, Mehring's prediction turned prescient when Singleton's script for *Twilight Time* won the Jack Nicholson Award, the most prestigious screenwriting award at USC. Singleton banked eight thousand dollars toward his tuition. More importantly, it announced his arrival onto the scene.

★★★★★

Singleton almost didn't make it to graduation. In the summer of 1988, he learned that Spike Lee would be shooting his next feature film in New York from mid-July through September. Immediately, he mailed his résumé to Lee's company, 40 Acres and a Mule, hoping to land a production assistant gig. He told friends he planned to drop out of USC. He even found housing in Brooklyn for the duration of the shoot. But when he never heard back, he resumed his course.

Singleton stepped back from AAFA that summer just as preparation for the Sidney Poitier film festival went into overdrive. "He ghosted us," says Watts, who soon fired Singleton as VP.

From there, he joined another student organization. At the start of his junior year, Singleton became cochairman of the Black Student Union. Following his election, members awaited his first act with bated breath. As a freshman, Singleton led a sit-in that took over an administration building to protest USC's continued investment in the apartheid state of South Africa. There was no shortage of issues he could tackle: police brutality; racial profiling on campus; the lack of diversity in the student body.

"We should put on a Spike Lee film festival," he proposed.

"John, this isn't AAFA," the cochairman said. "Besides, Spike's made two films. That's not much of a festival."

Singleton moved on to a familiar issue. He refocused on USC's divestment from South Africa.

By this point, Capitol Hill had already acted. In the fall of 1986, Congress overrode Ronald Reagan's veto and passed the Comprehensive Anti-Apartheid Act, imposing sanctions on South Africa and prohibiting the US government from investing in or trading with the rogue nation. USC then announced a phased-out divestment plan starting in 1988. As BSU cochairman, Singleton kept pressure on the USC Board of Trustees. He organized rallies that coincided with board meetings and courted media coverage. "If USC wants to clean up its image," he told reporters, "it better clean up its act."

Black students at USC banded together. On Wednesday afternoons, around eighty Trojans would gather for lunch in front of Tommy Trojan, an area dubbed Ethnic Square or N—National Park. There was an intense sort of bonding that happened as a result of being segregated on a very wealthy, very white campus.

"USC was a big white island in a big Black neighborhood," Singleton said.

Located in the heart of South Central, the school seemed to take an antagonistic stance toward the community. Fences covered the perimeter in sections. According to interviews conducted for this book, White students referred to Black residents as "locals" in the most derogatory way. *Should we call campus security? There sure are a lot of locals around.*

Once, Singleton observed campus security detain two Black kids, who couldn't have been older than ten, cutting across campus on bicycles.

"Why are you bothering them?" he asked.

"It's a closed campus. They need to go around."

"They're already halfway across! You're gonna make them double back and walk around? This is their neighborhood!"

As BSU cochair, he was an ambassador to local schools and chaperoned campus tours. He tried recruiting high school seniors to USC despite knowing how difficult it was being Black at the school. The prejudice he faced ranged from simple microaggressions (a white girl clutching her purse in the presence of a Black man; the underrepresentation of Black films in studies) to more overt acts of racism. Black students were regularly met with affirmative-action taunts. It wasn't out of the ordinary for a Black man to be asked *What sport do you play?*

Then there was the constant harassment from authorities. Show-us-your-papers stops from USC's campus security. They'd often detain Black students, both male and female, and ask for identification. Being stopped on campus because you "fit a description" shouldn't be part of the college experience. But it was reality for Singleton and his friends.

Campus security followed the lead of the Los Angeles Police Department.

Accusations of police brutality and racism soared following the appointment of LAPD chief Daryl Gates in 1978. Considered the father of SWAT, Gates promoted an aggressive, almost paramilitary approach to policing. In the 1980s, police often conducted violent sweeps in South Los Angeles, going house to house with battering rams and bulldozers, hunting for suspected drug dealers and gang members. These raids, dubbed Operation Hammer, resulted in razed buildings and scores of Black people arrested on petty crimes. Gates ignored community leaders. He showed disdain for its residents. When asked to explain the disproportionate number of Black people dying from police choke holds, Gates theorized that "their arteries do not open as fast as they do in normal people." (Gates's mentor, former police chief William H. Parker, once compared Black people to "monkeys in a zoo.")

The rank and file carried out his directives. Stop and frisk became the norm. Patrol cars followed groups of Black men for no reason. Police officers refused to differentiate between a Black economics major and a Black kid in a gang.

"Everyone was painted with the same brush," Kenneth Baines says. "It was very typical to be thrown against a car and told to put your hands up. We were Black kids approaching an isolated place of privilege. If you're approaching USC, the castle on the hill, you're a potential threat."

Other threats resided off campus. One night, Baines and a few members of Black Pack were walking near USC when a car slowly pulled up next to them. Baines wore a blue Knicks jersey with orange-and-white trim. The backseat driver's-side window rolled down. A handgun appeared. Pointing at him.

"What set you claim?"

"What are you talking about?"

"What set you claim?"

"What's going on?"

"What's up with all that blue, homie?"

"I'm just a student. I'm going to—"

The driver lowered his window. He turned and faced the gunman in the back seat.

"Hey, bro, hey, man, leave them dudes alone," he said. "They just some mark-ass busters. Them just students, man. They ain't about this life." The car then drove off.

Clashes with fellow Black men. Harassment from racist cops. Violence that could erupt anytime, anywhere. Living in a constant state of outrage and anxiety. These themes went hand in hand with being a Black man at USC in the late 1980s. Soon, they'd find a home in John Singleton's films.

# CHAPTER THREE

**O**ne afternoon during the summer of 1989, Singleton spotted a cute girl eating lunch all alone in a sandwich shop on the USC campus, and drifted toward her table.

"Sister, you don't have to sit by yourself—if you don't want to" was his opening line.

Vestria Barlow, a four-foot-eleven-inch-tall Black girl from South Central visiting her former ballet instructor on campus, put down her lunch, picked up a napkin, and dotted the area around her mouth with it. She looked Singleton up and down. Barlow preferred eating alone but found him intriguing. "Just the fact that he called me 'Sister' showed he had a sense of consciousness," she says.

Barlow pushed an open chair toward Singleton, inviting him to share her table. They spent hours walking together on campus that afternoon, sharing their hopes and dreams as college kids do: Barlow discussed her prep school background and her current studies in design school; Singleton, as expected, talked about an idea he had for a script, one about his neighborhood and his friends growing up. At the end of that first date, she gave him a ride home. Before they departed, Barlow scribbled her parents' phone number on a piece of paper.

"Brother, I'm going back to Atlanta soon," she said. "You can call my parents if you want. But I think the next time I see you, it's going to be on television."

Singleton walked away, thinking about the girl he'd just met and the script he'd been obsessing over.

Over the next year or so, Singleton would write his magnum opus, sign with a big-time agent, get a movie deal, and meet the people who'd change his life, some of whom he'd remain close to for the next thirty years. And the inciting incident to all this—to use a Syd Field term—was a July 1989 screening of *Do the Right Thing*.

The opening credits reeled him in. John Singleton fell in love with *Do the Right*

*Thing* from the moment Rosie Perez, all hips, lips, and *oomph*, powered onto the screen backed by Public Enemy's "Fight the Power."

Spike Lee kept the plot to his third feature film simple: Racial tensions burst on the hottest day of summer in Bed-Stuy, Brooklyn. *Do the Right Thing* pulsed with urgency; an argument can be made that it helped elect New York City's first Black mayor that fall. Singleton thought it was the best thing he'd ever seen—so good that it inspired him to create his own masterwork.

"*Do the Right Thing* made me write *Boyz N the Hood*," Singleton would say.

Singleton and Lee had crossed paths a few times since their first meeting. These encounters followed a pattern. Singleton would find out Lee was in Los Angeles for a book signing or screening and show up to it. Then they'd have a quick, meaningful exchange.

"Spike, people at SC tell me I'll never get a movie made because I'm Black," Singleton once revealed to him.

"Do not allow closed-minded people to change who you are and what you do," Lee responded.

Singleton's heart raced when he spotted Lee afterward chatting with audience members. "Go say hi to him," a friend suggested.

"Nah, man," Singleton snapped back. "I don't want to say nothing to him."

Singleton looked at Lee with equal parts envy and awe. He craved to make something as dope as *Do the Right Thing*. He knew he was on the right path—the Nicholson Award for *Twilight Time* was proof positive of that. But it wasn't happening fast enough for his liking. Outside the theater, he fumed, "I'm outta here."

He marched down Hollywood Boulevard with renewed determination, brushing past anyone in his path. "I got to do my shit," he muttered to himself. "I'm making my fucking movie. I'm gonna tear this motherfucker up—watch."

Once he settled down, he analyzed *Do the Right Thing*. Why did it work? What could he learn from it? Right away he noticed how Spike had claimed Brooklyn as his cinematic turf and filled the screen with characters native to it: the sweet old rummy who likes his Miller High Life and calls himself Da Mayor; Radio Raheem, built like a tank, flattop fade, rocking four-finger rings, African medallions, and a boom box; the white gentrifier in the Larry Bird jersey; the Korean grocery store owner and so forth and so forth. *I need to do something for Los Angeles*, he thought. *I have to come from LA so hard, so people really know that it has its own type of flavor.*

That's when it hit him. "Write what you know, John," Professor Polonsky told him during their rides to campus.

And what did twenty-one-year-old John Daniel Singleton know? He knew how to survive in South Central Los Angeles.

He researched the script. During the summer of 1989, he rolled down to the corner of Century and Vermont and linked with old friends like Fatbacc to talk about their childhood—postadolescent therapy sessions that took place on barstools, park benches, or stoops.

"Hey, man, I've been having these dreams," he confided during one of those visits.

"What kind of dreams?" Fatbacc replied.

"Dreams about things we've seen—things from when we were kids, things from our teenage years," Singleton said.

Both knew where the conversation was heading.

"Remember Robbie Stringer?"

Later on in life, Singleton referred to these visions as "PTSD moments," the result of witnessing the neighborhood change from the proliferation of cheap cocaine. "It was like the Wild, Wild West," he said, recalling the violence that exploded in South Central during the early 1980s. "We were all intimately around people who were experiencing it."

People like Robbie Stringer.

When Singleton applied to USC, he included a one-paragraph pitch for a screenplay about three friends navigating life in South Central called *Summer of '84*. But now, more than ever, he realized its potential. Immediately, he workshopped the story using his own narrative as its foundation. He'd explore themes like the importance of male role models while using vignettes from his own upbringing (or some borrowed from his friends) to dot the script with life and color.

"Remember that time my pops shot at that guy trying to rob our house?" he'd ask with eyes wider than the bullet holes Danny Singleton's Magnum left in the wall that night. "That's gonna be in the movie."

The wheels started turning. "Remember the barbecue in Big Twin's backyard?" he asked. He could picture it now. The domino tiles slapping down on picnic tables. The smell of grilled meat piled high in aluminum trays. Egyptian Lover on the stereo. He would take an anecdote from here, an incident from there, a joke he once heard, and then Frankenstein characters and scenes out of them.

It would be a teen movie like *Risky Business, Cooley High*, and *American Graffiti*. High school sweethearts would bicker about whether or not to do it. The jock stressed about the SATs. Bullies threatened the main characters. Except this teen movie would take place in John Singleton's world. The specter of AIDS weighed on their mind. The jock was a teenage dad. The bullies were Bloods. Though no one rapped in the film, it would be a hip-hop film made by a hip-hop filmmaker for the hip-hop generation.

When he sat down to write, Eazy-E's *Eazy-Duz-It* and N.W.A.'s *Straight Outta Compton* played on repeat. Sometimes, while listening to the albums, he'd close his eyes and zone out to Dr. Dre's production for inspiration. He'd visualize the lyrics as a series of scenes or short films.

"What they were doing in music was giving voice to everything I had seen growing up," he said. "I thought, 'If I can get a little bit of that life on film, then I'll have something that will affect people.'" He settled on a title: *Boyz N the Hood*, after the Eazy-E song of the same name.

One morning in September 1989, Singleton walked into Professor Viki King's classroom, sat at his desk, put his feet up, and opened an issue of *Daily Variety*. One by one, students pitched ideas for their senior thesis, an original screenplay that would make up the bulk of their grade for the semester.

"Next up is John Singleton."

He stood up and scanned the class full of white faces.

"My script is called *Boyz N the Hood*. It's about South Central LA, where you hear automatic gunfire and helicopters in the distance. It's about three boys growing up. It's my magnum opus. This is the movie I was born to make. One day I'm going to direct it." A few students snickered at the last part.

Later, while classmates talked behind his back, Singleton sat on the fire escape with Morgan Ward, a filmic writing student from Indio, California, a small, rural town in the Coachella Valley. "See, one brother is a star football player," Singleton explained. "He's like the next Marcus Allen. The other brother just got out of jail. They're brothers but they're half brothers. They have different dads—"

"John, I don't get the title."

"What do you mean? It's an Eazy-E song."

"Who?"

"Never mind."

"What does *Boyz N the Hood* mean, anyway? Does it have anything to do with Robin Hood?"

Singleton laughed. "Oh my God, you're so fucking stupid."

He started writing that fall in the basement computer lab in Waite Phillips Hall. For the next three weeks or so, he'd write all night into the morning before stumbling into class if lucky. He skipped meals. A small patch of hair fell out from the stress.

"Many times, when I was working on this," he said, "I'd sit there and tears would come to my eyes because I was purging all this stuff that was inside of me."

Writing was not a sedentary activity for him. "I'm writing the best fucking screenplay of my life," he'd holler, clapping his hands to urge himself on. He stood up and acted out scenes, reciting different characters' dialogue.

"Hey, can you keep it down?" an exasperated voice pleaded. "I'm writing a disserta—"

"Shut the fuck up! Don't you know I'm writing a fucking classic movie right here?" Singleton barked back. "Mind your own damn business."

Then he would return to his desktop and continue writing as if nothing had happened.

Singleton went into salesman mode as soon as he submitted the script to his professor. He knew he had a winner and wanted to share bits and pieces of it with friends on campus.

". . . She downs the forty and then hands the empty bottle back to Doughboy. He goes, get this, check it, it's so good."

He was holding court under Tommy Trojan, squinting from the fall sunlight reflecting off the bronze statue, doing his best to get to the punch line. "Doughboy goes, check it, 'You better take yo' ass to the store with that.'"

Technically, he hadn't finished the assignment. He still had to find an actor and stage a scene from his script. And for that, he turned to a recent USC graduate named Baldwin C. Sykes.

Singleton became familiar with the Compton native following his appearance in Evening of Soul, an annual showcase for Black student performers held each February in Bovard Auditorium. They'd seen each other on campus until Sykes, a theater major, graduated in the spring of 1989. A few months later, they reconnected after Singleton saw him featured on *The Oprah Winfrey Show* in a segment on young actors titled "Making It in Hollywood."

He called Sykes. "Can you come to campus and read a scene for class?" Singleton asked.

"Sure, what's it called?"

"*Boyz N the Hood.*"

"Cool title," Sykes said.

"John had won a Nicholson Award. He was already a big cheese," Sykes later said. "I thought he would eventually become something—in about ten years or so."

When Sykes arrived on campus, Singleton shoved a script at his chest. "We have about fifteen minutes," he said. "Flip to the end. Last scene. You'll be reading Doughboy."

Sykes read the scene. Immediately he thought of neighborhood legends who had suffered Doughboy's fate. "Damn, this is about us," Sykes said, exhaling. "I'm gonna get you this A. We're gonna give them this heat. Let's go."

His eyes welled up early on in the scene. "They either don't know, don't show, and don't care what be going on in the hood. They had all that foreign shit instead . . . They didn't show nothing about my brother."

"When I was done," Sykes says, "there wasn't a dry eye in the audience."

Except for one set of eyes. Singleton bristled afterward. "You were supposed to cry!"

"I'm a gangster," Sykes said without missing a beat. "I'm too hard to cry."

Singleton nodded his approval. "When I come up, you're gonna come up."

Singleton received an A on his senior thesis and collected another Nicholson Award, making him a back-to-back winner and the school's first two-time honoree. He began to get an idea of just how far the script could take him.

★★★★★

Despite Sykes's powerful performance, he never had a shot at the role. Singleton wrote Doughboy for the N.W.A. rapper Ice Cube. An Inglewood native born O'Shea Jackson, Cube had no acting experience, but Singleton believed his sneer and swagger embodied the role based in part on Fatbacc. He planned to cast the entire group in the film with Dr. Dre as Monster, MC Ren as Dooky, and Eazy-E as Little Chris. But Cube went solo in December 1989, citing a contract dispute with N.W.A. manager Jerry Heller. By that point, Singleton *kinda, sorta* knew Ice Cube.

He met the rapper in early 1989 at his internship. During the spring semester of his junior year, Singleton was a director's intern on *The Arsenio Hall Show*. He had little interaction with the host. Sometimes he shadowed the director during filming. For the most part, he copied scripts and ran errands around Stage 29 on the Paramount lot. "This is BS," he'd moan to friends. "I didn't take this internship to get coffee." He took the internship for the networking opportunities it presented—and eventually his gambit paid off.

One day while backstage he heard a voice that left him frozen. It sounded familiar but he couldn't pinpoint who it belonged to. He stopped and listened. Still nothing. The voice got louder and angrier as an argument got out of hand, and that's when it clicked. Singleton picked up the pace as if drawn to the voice. When he ducked his head around a corner and spied the rapper, his suspicions were confirmed.

"Don't you know who this is?" Singleton yelled, breaking up the dispute. "That's Ice Cube! He's with N.W.A."

Singleton took Cube aside. "Listen, my name is John Singleton. I go to USC film school. I got an idea for a film. I want you to know that I'm gonna make it and I want you to star in it. I want you to act in my movie."

Cube didn't know how to respond. For all he could tell, John spoke another language. A film? Acting? Not part of his agenda. Cube aimed to be the best rapper in the world, not some actor.

"You're gonna star in my movie, Cube," Singleton said. "It's gonna be so good."

"Cool," said Cube, walking away.

A few months later they ran into each other again at Louis Farrakhan's Save the Black Family rally on the UCLA campus.

"Remember me?" Singleton asked Cube. "I'm gonna make that movie with you, watch."

"Yeah. Cool," Cube said dismissively.

In February 1990, Singleton and some friends arrived at the Palace in Hollywood for a Public Enemy concert. Walking into the venue that evening, he felt a tinge of electricity. Public Enemy's new single "Welcome to the Terrordome" had just dropped. *Fear of a Black Planet*, their new album, was scheduled to come out in April. Sensing an industry crowd, Singleton scanned the floor, looking to make connections.

While Singleton worked the room, his friend Bill Straus started to feel a bit self-conscious. As one of the few white guys in the club, he felt he was "cramping John's style."

"John, I'm going to bounce," he shouted into Singleton's ear sometime during Public Enemy's two-hour set.

Singleton glided toward the stage, weaving his way through the crowd, determined to get a better look at his favorite rap group. As he got closer, he noticed someone in a hooded parka standing near DJ Terminator X's turntables. It was Ice Cube.

"Ohhhhhhhh shit!!!!" Singleton shrieked.

The union between Public Enemy and Cube blew minds. East meets West. Socially conscious rap and gangster rap. Soon it would be revealed that Cube had linked with the group following his bitter divorce from N.W.A. and had collaborated with them in New York. Singleton wasn't thinking about music.

"I have to talk to Cube," he said. "I need him in my movie."

After the show, Cube held court in a parking lot near the Palace. "Yo, man," someone asked, "why'd you do it? Why'd you leave?"

"Jerry Heller," Cube said without blinking.

"Still a fool for leaving."

Singleton approached the scrum. "Hey, they need him more than he needs them," he said. "You know he wrote all of Eazy's shit?"

"Exactly," Cube said. He turned to get a better look at his unknown advocate.

"Remember me?" Singleton asked.

"Yeah, I remember you," Cube said.

They ended up kicking it until past midnight, at which point Singleton realized he needed a ride home. "Hey, can you drive me back to campus?" he asked.

Cube glared at him. Normally, he would have declined. But something about Singleton's energy and passion appealed to him. "Fine," Cube said. "I'm going to see my girl anyway, and she lives around there."

They hopped in Cube's Suzuki Sidekick, a two-seater with a tinted hardtop, and drove down the Harbor Freeway. Cube popped a cassette into the stereo.

"These beats are going to be on my solo album," he said. "It's going to be called *AmeriKKKa's Most Wanted*." The instrumental for what would become "Once Upon a Time in the Projects" filtered through the stereo.

"Hey, man, remember that script I told you about?" Singleton said, nodding along to the funky Betty Davis sample. "I wrote it. I got it done. And we're gonna do it."

"I'm with it," Cube said stepping on the gas. "If it actually happens."

I n the fall of 1989, Singleton went to work for the same studio executive he'd cursed out eighteen months earlier. He started an internship at Fried Films, a small production company that had a first-look deal with Columbia Pictures. Two or three times a week, he'd take the bus to Burbank, where Columbia and Warner Bros. shared a lot known as the Burbank Studios.

Fried Films didn't have much in development. When Singleton wasn't making copies or running errands, he buried his head in a book or would skim the trades.

Karen Teicher, a recent graduate of USC and Fried's development executive, supervised him. On some afternoons, she'd ask for his opinion on recently submitted scripts. "Another wack-ass screenplay, huh?" he'd ask.

A few hours later he would return to her office, toss the script on her desk, and hand her his typed-up coverage: a one-paragraph summary of the script and his notes on it. "Another wack-ass screenplay."

"John, do you really think you can do better?" Teicher asked.

He glared at her from behind his glasses. "I won the Nicholson last year."

"Let me read it, then!"

He eventually gave her the script. *Oh my God, he's a real writer*, she thought after reading *Twilight Time*.

"John, this is good," she said.

"Wait until you read *Boyz N the Hood*," he responded.

"What's *Boyz N the Hood*?"

Singleton dug into his backpack. "This is *Boyz N the Hood*," he said, handing over his script.

About two hours later, Teicher called Singleton back to her office. She closed the door. "I read it. I loved it," she said. "Now the question is what do you want to do with it?"

"I want to direct it," Singleton responded.

"I know a few agents," she said. "I know a guy at William Morris. I know a couple of people at CAA. Why don't you let me take your scripts around town and see what comes of it? But first let me show it to Rob."

Singleton sighed.

Rob Fried was one of the new breed of film executives that studios turned to in the 1980s. An Ivy League grad with an MBA, he had no relevant film experience when Columbia Pictures hired him in 1983. His job was to bring a Wall Street–like analytics-based rationality to the green-lighting process; he crunched numbers to determine the rate of return for specific actors and genres. A legal thriller starring a former Oscar nominee, say, might make this much at the box office. A Chuck Norris martial arts movie might make that much. This was a risk. That was a safe bet. Fried was an early version of a *Moneyball* executive, a data-driven manager guided by a spreadsheet and not his gut.

"Aspiring Moguls Take MBA's to Hollywood," blared a *New York Times* trend piece from 1986 that centered on Fried and this new ilk of D-suite guys. After leaving Columbia, he became director of business development at 20th Century Fox and then VP of production at Orion Pictures, where he oversaw *Hoosiers, Bull Durham*, and a certain gang movie that John Singleton despised.

"I was deeply involved with *Colors* as a young executive," says Fried, who upon taking over the project collaborated on a draft with the screenwriter Michael Schiffer and the film's director Dennis Hopper. "This was a bunch of white guys writing and developing a story about gang life in LA."

Fried returned to Columbia in 1988 as executive VP of production but quickly lost a power struggle with his boss. Like many former execs, he then pivoted to production and formed Fried Films.

Singleton didn't care for him much, with all the screaming Fried did around the office. There was also the matter of his taste or lack thereof. Fried hung a theater-sized poster of *Colors* behind his desk. When summoned to his office, Singleton lingered in the doorway, eyes cast down, refusing to enter. Fried thought it was a quirk, unaware that Singleton was the USC student who, eighteen months earlier, may or may not have called him a "white motherfucker" at a campus screening of the film.

When asked nearly thirty-five years later about the incident, Fried says, "I remember that happening. That's amazing. I didn't know John was the student. I just remember it was a kid—and I ended up hiring that kid."

That kid had also written a brilliant screenplay. "It was so lean and real,"

Fried says. "When I read John's script for *Boyz N the Hood*, it occurred to me. 'Holy shit, this is more authentic than *Colors*.'"

Fried considered *Boyz N the Hood* saleable but didn't think Columbia, or any studio for that matter, would hire the college senior to direct it, yet Teicher submitted it there. She also passed it on to an agent at William Morris and to her friend Bradford W. Smith, a young agent at Creative Artists Agency.

A Midwestern native new to the business, Smith had a nose for good material. He graduated from Yale with an MFA in Drama Theater Administration/Producing. As associate managing director of the Yale Repertory Theatre, he worked on two August Wilson productions: the national tour for *Joe Turner's Come and Gone* and the Broadway opening of *Fences*. After reading *Twilight Time* and *Boyz N the Hood* over a single weekend, he set up a meeting with Singleton for early that next week.

Singleton arrived at the new CAA building in Beverly Hills on time. He took a deep breath and absorbed the sight before him: a postmodern sixty-five-thousand-square-foot property designed by the same architect who did the Louvre. A year earlier, when he'd made the rounds with *Twilight Time*, he'd walked away with nothing but an extra layer of thick skin.

Smith cut to the chase. "I read your material and I think you have that flavor that reminds me very much of August Wilson," he said. "I'd like to sign you. Let's see what we can do together."

"Oh, that's good to hear," Singleton said, acting as nonchalant as possible. A fistful of quarters jangled in his pocket as he raced out onto Wilshire Boulevard in search of a pay phone. "Karen! CAA wants to sign me," he shouted over the sounds of traffic.

"He was so excited," Teicher says. "He was completely disarmed. More than anything, I think he was relieved."

He had reason to be excited. "When John signed in 1990, we were king of the hill, top dog. We ran the city," says former CAA senior agent Mike Marcus. "I don't think anybody has seen the likes of that kind of power in one place since."

Singleton canceled his meeting with William Morris.

Known for packaging its A-list roster of stars and directors together, CAA was the most dominant agency in town. They had so much muscle that they created a whole new genre of film: the CAA movie.

On *Rain Man*, the agency bundled Tom Cruise and Dustin Hoffman with Barry Levinson directing. *Wall Street* paired Michael Douglas with director Oliver

Stone. Steven Spielberg directed *Hook* with Robin Williams starring as an adult Peter Pan and Hoffman as the titular villain, and on and on and on. Costner, De Niro, Pacino, Oprah, Scorsese, Coppola, Kubrick, and other first-ballot Hall of Famers were all clients at the time. CAA chairman and cofounder Mike Ovitz frequently topped magazine lists as the Most Powerful Person in Hollywood.

Singleton knew what this meant for his career. But in the moment he focused on something else entirely: the bragging rights. "White boys couldn't tell me nothing," he said.

★★★★★

CAA shopped Singleton as a writer in early 1990, introducing him to actors and producers in hopes he could land some work. His first such meeting was with Jasmine Guy, the star of *A Different World*. They met at a coffee shop in LA to discuss a Dorothy Dandridge movie she hoped to get off the ground. During these meets with Tom Cruise or a pre–*Thelma & Louise* Brad Pitt, he'd often steer the conversation back to his little script about three friends named Tre, Doughboy, and Ricky.

At times he didn't wait for his agency to set up meetings. One afternoon, bored at his internship, Singleton wandered Burbank Studios when he came upon a sign reading GRIO ENTERTAINMENT GROUP. As an avid reader of the trades, he knew this to be Quincy Jones's motion picture and television operation. "Can I talk to Q?" he asked, only to be led into the offices of Doug McHenry, a Harvard Law graduate, who, along with his producing partner George Jackson, ran Grio.

"Did you like *Do the Right Thing*?" Singleton asked.

"Of course," McHenry answered.

"I wrote this script," Singleton said, "that will do for South Central what *Do the Right Thing* did for Brooklyn."

The next day Singleton returned with *Boyz N the Hood*.

McHenry and Jackson both loved it but couldn't pursue it. They'd started their own production company, Elephant Walk Entertainment, and were negotiating with Grio over which projects they could take with them. "John wanted to get his picture done immediately—like he wanted it done yesterday," McHenry says. "We just didn't have time to devote to it because we were trying to convince Warner Bros. to do *New Jack City*."

When McHenry broke the news, all Singleton said was "This shit is going to happen with or without you."

Brad Smith continued sending the script out to production companies, where it gained some traction. John Hughes read it. Brian Grazer and Imagine were interested. Jonathan Demme, who was also developing Taylor Branch's *Parting the Waters*, the Pulitzer Prize–winning book about Dr. Martin Luther King Jr., considered optioning it for Orion Pictures.

"Jonathan was in love his whole life with Black culture," says Demme's producing partner Ed Saxon. When he read *Boyz N the Hood*, "it felt like, 'Here's a voice! This is the real deal!' Here was this incredibly vivid piece of writing that felt like neorealist cinema from Italy after the war—like this is what's really happening."

Word started to get around about the hotshot kid from USC with the buzzy script.

Around this time, *Boyz N the Hood* found its way into the lap of Russell Simmons. One of the first rap moguls, Simmons, a rude, crude, and shrewd loudmouth from Queens, made a name for himself managing the biggest stars in hip-hop, including his brother's group Run-D.M.C. He then cofounded hip-hop's most iconic label, Def Jam Recordings. From the start he dreamed of building an empire beyond music. He dipped his toe in the movie industry producing the Run-D.M.C. vehicles *Krush Groove* and *Tougher Than Leather*.

Now he wanted to become a real Hollywood player.

He had recently launched a new venture with Stan Lathan, the director of *Beat Street*, and they were already talking with HBO. Simmons had also been negotiating a production deal with Columbia Pictures. He wanted *Boyz N the Hood*—even though he couldn't be bothered to read the thing.

Singleton arrived for his breakfast meeting with Simmons and Lathan at Le Mondrian hotel in West Hollywood armed with a plan. He wouldn't let the fast-talking New Yorker push him around. He nudged past tourists grazing in the lobby and made his way toward the restaurant where Lathan and Simmons waited.

In a few hours, Simmons would be on a private jet returning to New York. "Pitch it to me."

Lathan, wary of Simmons's approach, intervened. "Russell, you got to read this—"

"No, no, no, I want him to pitch me," Simmons told his partner. He turned his attention back to Singleton. "You're supposed to pitch me the story."

Singleton had contempt for pompous New Yorkers like Simmons. It wasn't difficult for him to return fire. "I don't need to pitch you shit," Singleton said. "This isn't *Krush Groove*. This isn't about New York. This is about growing up where you hear helicopters every night over your house and automatic gunfire in the distance. It's about LA. You don't know about that shit."

Simmons got what he wanted: for Singleton to pitch him.

"You've seen *Jaws*," he said. "What happens before the shark eats someone in *Jaws*? You hear the music, right? '*DUNDUNDUNDUNDUNDUNDUNDUN.*' In my movie, before someone gets shot in a drive-by you hear the 808 beats coming out of the booming system."

Simmons now understood—sort of. "LL got a song called 'The Boomin' System.' It'll be out in a couple of weeks," he said, referring to the next single from LL Cool J's upcoming album *Mama Said Knock You Out*.

Simmons read the script later that day during his flight on MGM Grand Air. "The script was so fucking good," Simmons remembers, "that I was almost crying." While still in the air he called his connection at the studio, Jon Peters, who just so happened to be the new Sony cochairman, and told him that he wanted to produce this intern's movie called *Boyz N the Hood*.

While all this was happening, a young Columbia executive had gotten her hands on the script. She didn't have much pull. But she believed in *Boyz N the Hood* and was almost as determined as Singleton to turn it into a film.

★★★★★

Stephanie Allain studied prelaw at USC before dropping out at nineteen and moving to Hawai'i to pursue a career in ballet. After returning to California, she bounced around for a while. She changed schools. Switched majors. Nothing stuck.

Out of necessity, she became less interested in her own creative pursuits and got practical. She learned of a job called a story analyst where she would read scripts and then write summaries for agents or film executives—crib notes for important people who didn't have time to read but wanted to speak semi-intelligently in meetings. She'd recently given birth. "It was something I could do with a baby," she says.

At first, she did it for free. Then she got paid twenty-five dollars per script. Soon, her rate doubled. After a while, Allain got the form down and it became innate: a log line, a paragraph synopsis, followed by notes and critiques. A position opened up at CAA, and she called the hiring manager once a week until securing the job. She wasn't at the agency long; Allain soon left CAA for 20th Century Fox, where she met her mentor Amy Pascal. A VP of production, Pascal handpicked Allain to be her personal reader. She also showed her the ropes: how to talk to writers and directors, how to get a movie off the ground.

When Pascal left for Columbia, Allain followed her out the door, heading to Warner Bros. But she lost her job during the 1988 writers' strike, at which point Pascal hired her at Columbia. About a year later, she received a promotion. Allain then began fielding candidates to fill her old job, and that's when she met John Singleton.

Following Allain's departure, the Columbia story department went from predominantly white to completely white. She made it known that her replacement would be a Black person. Karen Teicher, whose office was also on the Burbank lot, recommended Singleton when she heard of the opening.

The job interview quickly went off the rails as the conversation turned from the story analyst position to Singleton's scripts. "So, I read *Twilight Time*," Allain said, "and I thought it was promising."

"Promising?"

"There's a lot to like," she said. "What impressed me was that all the female characters were nuanced and believable. But structurally—structurally it's off. It doesn't have a strong three-act structure. It's more like a slice of life. It feels more like a play."

"He looked at me like I was crazy," Allain recalls now.

"Okay, what else are you working on?" she asked.

"*Boyz N the Hood*," Singleton said, his eyes lighting up. "It's about South Central LA, where you hear automatic gunfire and helicopters in the distance. . . ." He launched into the same pitch he had given countless times to friends, classmates, and professors, except now he delivered it to someone with clout, even if just a little. ". . . This is the movie I was born to make. One day I'm going to direct it."

As a native Angelino, the premise intrigued Allain. More importantly, she bought into John Singleton. "He was scarily, crazily, absolutely and completely confident," she says. "It wasn't even braggadocio. It was like it had already happened for him and he was here from the future telling me about it."

"I'd love to read *Boyz N the Hood*," she said.

"Jonathan Demme is reading it," he said. "Actually, it's out with John Hughes's company. Look, if they don't buy it, I'll let you read it."

After the interview, she called Brad Smith, who confirmed Singleton's story.

Yes, Hughes Entertainment had the script. That further piqued her interest. Now here's where it gets murky. Allain claims that Smith sent her the script about two weeks later—the official coverage sheet from Columbia credits Smith with the submission.

But Singleton has said that Teicher sent it to Allain, which Teicher also confirmed. Either way, Allain had it, and as soon as she did, she closed the door to her office and read it cover to cover. By the end, she was in tears. Afterward, Allain says she was "overtaken with a singular goal to get that movie made. It was just really clear for me that's what I was supposed to do."

★★★★★

At the time, Columbia Pictures was the most dysfunctional studio in town. Sony had acquired the fading Torch Lady in a giant overpay—$3.4 billion plus $1.6 billion in debt—and were looking to make a splash. So they turned to Peter Guber and Jon Peters, the producing team whose most recent film, *Batman*, had scored the biggest opening of all time. In September 1989, Sony hired them as cochairmen of the newly created Sony Pictures Entertainment. As part of the deal, the Japanese electronics giant bought Guber and Peters's production company, GPEC, for $200 million (another staggering overpay) and created a one-time bonus pool of $50 million; the fringe benefits reportedly totaled between $150 and $200 million. There were a few more red flags involved: Guber and Peters had no experience running a studio and both were still under contract at Warner Bros. A flurry of lawsuits followed. In the end, Sony settled for a reported $800 million. The ROI wasn't great.

As producers, Guber and Peters had a strong hitmaking track record. But their reputation was that of expert marketers and promoters. They weren't hands-on filmmakers. Guber got his start at Columbia, where he was one of the first studio executives to recognize how modern technology, including the VCR, would upend the industry. At thirty-one, he was named VP of worldwide production. Upon leaving in 1975, he produced big hits like *The Deep* and the Oscar winner *Midnight Express* and made a killing in the record industry. In *Hit & Run*, Nancy Griffin and Kim Masters's bestseller about Guber and Peters's reign at Sony, they describe Guber as "brilliant, manipulative, seductive, and virtually without close friends."

Peters, a seventh-grade dropout and former hairdresser, broke into the business as Barbra Streisand's wigmaker turned boyfriend. They were the Brangelina of the 1970s, with the gossip pages portraying Peters as a Svengali-like character after he produced Streisand's 1974 album *ButterFly* and her blockbuster remake of *A Star is Born*. He had a knack for big-picture ideas—and volatile outbursts. Peters had a rough upbringing, and the scars never really healed. Once, he pulled a gun on a repairman. In the office, he could be a sweetheart one minute before morphing into the Tasmanian Devil.

Guber and Peters became producing partners in the early 1980s. Together they notched hits that ranged from highbrow (*The Color Purple, Gorillas in the Mist*) to lowbrow (*Flashdance*) to somewhere in between (*The Witches of Eastwick*). Their plan at Sony? Spend, spend, spend, and take big swings in the mold of *Batman*—blockbuster films that generated sequels and Happy Meal tie-ins. Guber and Peters targeted Warner Bros. executive Mark Canton to run Columbia, but when Canton couldn't wiggle out of his contract, they settled for Frank Price.

A former writer and a veteran executive, Price returned to the position he held from 1978 to 1983. During his first tenure at Columbia, he green-lit *Kramer vs. Kramer, Tootsie, Gandhi, The Karate Kid*, and *Ghostbusters*. He then went on to lead Universal. Though credited with huge hits like *Back to the Future*, the infamous bomb *Howard the Duck* marred his time at the studio, and predictably, sealed his downfall.

Price didn't have much to work with when he started at Columbia in early 1990. "We were in a dead period," says Michael Nathanson, president of production at the time. Coca-Cola and the management team in New York had slowed down production prior to selling the studio to Sony. "We had no development money," Nathanson says. "We had no production money."

Columbia's slate was barren aside from a ghastly *Lord of the Flies* adaptation, a cheap cash-in on the Lambada fad called *The Forbidden Dance*, and *Texasville*, a sequel to *The Last Picture Show*. The studio sat out the 1990 summer movie season, releasing just one film (the Julia Roberts thriller *Flatliners*) between Easter and Labor Day. There was tremendous pressure at Columbia to hit the ground running, and Guber and Peters were ready to splurge; they had just won a bidding war for *Radio Flyer*, a spec script from a young screenwriter named David M. Evans. By the spring of 1990, Columbia hungered for product, making it the perfect time for Stephanie Allain to pitch *Boyz N the Hood*.

Allain had waited out the drought. She knew that *Boyz N the Hood* likely would die a quick death if she submitted it while the studio was in its long period of stasis. Instead, she hoarded the script for around two months until it was time to strike.

In the meantime, she built support for the project. Allain approached each executive in the building. She tailored her pitch depending on her audience. One of her first stops was the third-floor office of her boss's boss's boss, Jon Peters, where she pushed the script's up-from-the-streets Horatio Alger–type aspects on him.

Peters, a self-described "street fighter," was sold on it. As Allain walked out, he hollered, "You tell Frank that I'll pay for the movie myself if he doesn't want to do it." Whether he would do that or not, his energy as cochairman boosted her efforts.

On June 1, 1990, Allain submitted the script to the story department for coverage, a formality prior to putting it on the executives' weekend read schedule. Crotchety lifers in secure union gigs filled the story department at that time. Allain lucked out. The story editor assigned *Boyz N the Hood* to Jeff Stockwell, one of the fresh faces Columbia had recently hired. An aspiring screenwriter, Stockwell was a white guy from suburban Massachusetts. *Boyz* was out of his milieu. But it pulled him into its world. "I'd been teaching for several years, so my head was very much in that adolescent space," he says.

Stockwell awarded the script a grade of "good to excellent" for its characterization and dialogue. "In the hands of a director committed to its message, [it could] be a powerful black film, capitalizing intelligently on rap and crossing over into some commercial success," Stockwell wrote. "There's a good chance that a film based on this will reach out past urban black audiences (who will undoubtedly welcome its freshness). And it would not, finally, be expensive to produce. . . . Recommendation: maybe."

Allain arrived early to the office on Monday morning ready to notch the first big win of her career. The week prior she had circled the wagons. She figured that she'd drummed up enough backing to get the film green-lit. In her mind, Stockwell's positive coverage was the October surprise needed to tilt undecideds to her favor. Then the meeting started.

"The writing is undeniable, but I don't know," said one executive. "This John Singleton is an unknown entity."

"It's an urban tale about Los Angeles," said another. "On paper, that doesn't sound commercial."

It snowballed from there. Colleagues who had pledged their support were now shooting arrows at the project.

With each negative comment, Allain clutched the conference room table tighter and tighter. Her thoughts raced. Her breath shortened. Suddenly, she blurted out, "Look, if we all agree that the writing is undeniable—" She halted before completing the thought. The room then turned to Frank Price.

"This movie is very clear. It's all there," said the Columbia chairman. "I hadn't been moved in that particular way since I had seen [the 1948 Vittorio De Sica film] *The Bicycle Thief.* That's why I think we should make *Boyz N the Hood.* If I can identify with an Italian family that doesn't speak English, why can't a white American identify with this family in the inner city of LA? I think quite a few people will. Let's do it. Let's bring him in."

Columbia prepared to offer Singleton six figures for the script, but there was one problem: He insisted on directing, despite being woefully unqualified to handle a feature. Up to then, he had directed a few silent eight-millimeter student films and two rap music videos (one for the Bay Area rapper Morocco Moe, and "Steppin' into the House" for the frat-rap group the '06 Style).

"John, this isn't the kind of reel you'd show to get a job," Allain told him after watching "Steppin' into the House." "We're not going to tell anyone about it. We're going to bury these."

Singleton winced, but deep down he knew Allain was right; the '06 Style hired an editor to finish the clip after Singleton showed them his first cut.

But how difficult could directing be, anyway? "Other guys were doing it and they weren't as smart as me," he said. "What did they know that I didn't?"

Still, he prepared to walk away from the deal if Columbia didn't agree to his terms, and considered his other options for the fall. Having graduated a few weeks back, he needed a job. He thought of applying for an entry-level studio gig or working as a PA while scrounging for independent financing for *Boyz.* He could also double down on debt and pursue his MFA following acceptance to USC's graduate program. Teaching elementary school remained another option, though he was self-aware enough to know he'd be miserable doing it. "I would be some crazy cat teaching, talking about all the screenplays I have at home," he said.

Singleton had added another member to his team while negotiating with Columbia. Around this time, his aunt Karen introduced him to Michael Frisby, an attorney who shared office space with her boss.

"I met John," Frisby says. "He was very intelligent, very committed, very determined. I thought, 'Wow, this is an impressive young man.'"

Singleton's interest in him surprised Frisby. "Not only was I a young attorney. But I am a Black attorney," he says. "Back then, a lot of Black artists, entertainers, singers, preferred to have non-Black representation. They wanted a white or

Jewish attorney. I've had two instances where artists told me that they didn't think a Black attorney or manager could get them to where they wanted to go. John was opposed to that. He was a supporter of Black folk, Black causes, Black issues, the whole bit."

Singleton carried a my-way-or-the-highway attitude into the meeting with Price, Nathanson, and Allain. In many ways, he was overmatched. However, he held all the leverage.

Columbia needed product and wanted to get into business with him—the kid rocking jeans, sneakers, and a Public Enemy T-shirt to the most consequential meeting of his life.

"We read the script. We love it. We want to make this movie," Nathanson said to Singleton. "But we hear that you want to direct it."

"No, I *am* going to direct it," Singleton responded. "I'm not gonna let some fool from Idaho or Encino direct a movie about my neighborhood. Either I direct it or I step."

Nathanson pushed back. "What makes you think you can do it?"

"This is the movie that me and my friends talked about when we rode the bus back home from some wack movie," Singleton said. "This is the movie that we talked about when kicking it on the porch. This is the movie we wanted to see. This is the movie I was born to make."

"What if we told you we wanted to give you a hundred and fifty thousand dollars for the script?"

"Then we have to end this meeting, because I'm directing this movie. If you're not going to make this movie, someone else will."

"It was shocking," Nathanson would say years later. "But he had to shock us to get the job."

Singleton touted the film's commercial prospects. "Look, it's like *Easy Rider,*" he said, comparing *Boyz N the Hood* to the hip 1969 counterculture road film that earned $60 million at the box office against a $400,000 budget. "It's going to tap into something that's happening in the world that has yet to be expressed on film. Besides, it's not going to cost a lot of money."

Ever budget conscious, Price now piped in. "But you have a helicopter in multiple scenes," he said. "That costs money."

"I don't need a real helicopter," Singleton said. "At night, we can just use xenon lighting, then we add the sound in postproduction. Sound design was one of my favorite classes, even though I didn't get an A."

Price liked Singleton's answer. "Well, he thinks practically," he said to himself. More than that, he loved his confidence. Later on, Price would say, "The last time I met someone that young with so much self-assurance was Steven Spielberg."

Singleton learned later that afternoon that he had talked his way into his dream job. He would direct *Boyz N the Hood*.

"When do we start shooting?" he asked Price.

"Fall."

"When do we start preproduction?"

"Immediately."

Singleton faced a long road ahead—and he was scared to death.

**F**rank Price's first order of business after green-lighting *Boyz N the Hood* was making sure Russell Simmons had nothing to do with it. Even budgeted at $5.7 million, the film carried risk for Price. As Guber and Peters's fallback option, each and every move he made as chairman would be heavily scrutinized. Now he had just handed a directing job to a twenty-two-year-old screenwriter. Price had been in this situation before with a first-time director like Singleton and knew how to handle it: Keep the cost down and hire a strong, experienced producer to ensure production runs smoothly and on time.

Russell Simmons was not that kind of producer. Despite his notable connections—he kept in touch with Peters throughout the process—Simmons lost his grip on *Boyz N the Hood*.

"What they did to me was almost criminal," Simmons says today. "To think that Frank Price would take it out of my hands—a film that was about the Black community—and give it to a white [producer]. Can you imagine that? And to bully me like that? I'm a civil rights guy. I'm a fighter. I've always been involved in the public discussion on justice and equality. But there was nothing I could do."

The studio still hadn't found a producer. Jackson and McHenry were deep into postproduction on *New Jack City*. Rob Fried wasn't a candidate either despite his assertion that he had a submission claim on the film. As per his first-look deal with Columbia, if he brought a project to the studio—as Fried claimed to have done with *Boyz N the Hood*—Fried should be attached as a producer. But his presence on the film was a nonstarter. At one point, Michael Nathanson announced, "If Rob Fried is the producer, it's not getting done here."

In the end, Columbia paid Fried a settlement to go away.

Price then set his sights on Steve Nicolaides, a frequent Rob Reiner collaborator (*Stand by Me, The Princess Bride, When Harry Met Sally*) and the best friend of Allain's then husband. In his mind, Nicolaides's background in physical production made him a perfect partner for a budding auteur such as Singleton and a young executive like Allain, recently promoted to a VP post to supervise development of the film. "Steve was also good at catering to and understanding the needs of a sensitive director," Price said. "He had done it with Rob. He wouldn't try to crush the new guy."

Nicolaides had just completed work on Reiner's Stephen King adaptation *Misery*, an aptly titled production, he says. Once it wrapped, he intended to spend the summer of 1990 in Cambridge, Massachusetts, with his preteen son. At first he stuck to the plan, even turning down Billy Crystal's request to work on *City Slickers*. Then Stephanie Allain called.

Immediately, she started pitching. "Oh my God, I just read the greatest script I've ever read in my life," she said. "You have to read this within the next two days."

"I don't want to work this summer, Stephanie," Nicolaides said. "I want to spend it with Aaron. Tomorrow we're visiting the Basketball Hall of Fame in Springfield."

"No, no, no, you must read this. It's the best thing you've ever read."

"The best, huh?"

"The best. This script—"

"Okay, okay, FedEx it to me."

Two days later it arrived. "You know how there are times in your life when a new taste or a new girlfriend or some literature changes your life," Nicolaides says. "That's what happened to me with *Boyz N the Hood*."

Nicolaides grew up in the business. His father was an accountant for the production company that produced *The Beverly Hillbillies*, *Green Acres*, and *The Addams Family*. At eleven years old, Nicolaides answered Mister Ed's fan mail. He then worked as an errand boy on the lot. Early on, he learned that behind the glamour and glitz, showbiz truly was a blue-collar gig. There were long hours. No one went home until the job was done.

In the late 1960s, Nicolaides studied English literature and history at UC Santa Barbara. He wanted to write fiction but lacked the confidence to do so. Instead, he gravitated toward the protest movement against the Vietnam War. A self-proclaimed "long-haired hippie," he dodged the draft for two years until receiving a medical exemption. He then dropped out of school and returned to the entertainment industry.

He started out as a secretary and PA before ascending to production coordinator and ultimately to production manager, where he was tasked with overseeing the day-to-day operation of a film—budgets, shooting schedules, managing the below-the-line crew, and ensuring it ran smoothly and on time.

Reading *Boyz N the Hood* took Nicolaides back to the feeling he had when protesting the war. When he turned to the last page of the script, he started thinking this movie could make a difference in the world. He called Allain. Within a week he returned to California.

Nicolaides met John at Sheila's house in Pasadena.

"Why me?" he asked Singleton.

"Because you worked on my favorite movie of all time," Singleton said.

Nicolaides took a sip of homemade lemonade. "Oh yeah? Which one?"

*"Stand by Me."*

As Nicolaides described his vision for the film, Singleton's smile widened. "A few summers ago, we were in a production office right next to Dennis Hopper's movie *Colors*," he told Singleton. "Anyway, I would wander into the art department and look at all the pretty murals. It felt like it was 'Hollywood Goes to the Ghetto.' I can't stand those kinds of movies."

Singleton laughed. He'd laugh with his entire body. His shoulders hunched up. His face would crinkle. It was a hissing, gurgling laugh that made him sound like Muttley, the Hanna-Barbera cartoon dog from *Wacky Races*.

Nicolaides could see Singleton's movie in his head. "I don't want to do 'Hollywood Goes to the Ghetto,'" he said. "I want to shoot it real. I don't want to move anything around. I don't want to paint beautiful murals on walls. You know, don't even hire a production designer. In fact, the art director should be more like a location manager. It should feel like a documentary."

Singleton shook hands with his producer and moved on to casting.

"Someone wants to put you in a movie."

Ice Cube had forgotten about *Boyz N the Hood* when his manager mentioned that a script had recently arrived for him.

Cube had become one of the most powerful voices in hip-hop since he'd last seen Singleton back in February. His debut album *AmeriKKKa's Most Wanted* went gold within two weeks of its May release and received a perfect five-mic rating in *The Source* magazine. He'd been crisscrossing the country promoting the album since then. A film? Acting? He still didn't have time for that.

"Remember me?" Singleton said when Cube walked into his first audition. "I told you I was making a movie!"

Cube shrugged and started reciting his lines. But he clearly wasn't ready.

"Man, did you read the script?" Singleton asked.

"Nah, I didn't read it."

"Come on, you know this guy. Nobody else can play this part but you," Singleton said. "I'm gonna give you one more shot, man. Take my script home tonight. Read that shit. Come back tomorrow."

Cube tucked the pages under his arm and slowly exited. A cool draft passed through the room.

As soon as Cube left, Nicolaides turned and said, "I have a bad feeling we're gonna get a phone call tomorrow and he's gonna say, 'Fuck this.'" Singleton nodded in agreement.

Cube called the next morning asking for a second chance. "This is about how we grew up" he realized upon finally reading the script. "John's making a movie about our neighborhood."

Later that afternoon, he made the most of his opportunity. He nailed it, and Singleton had his Doughboy.

He had already cast his Furious Styles, the father of Tre Styles, the film's teenage striver whose story mirrored Singleton's own and was named after his USC friend Yon Styles. "That was a no-brainer for me," Fishburne said. "I got the script. I read the script. I was in tears when I was turning the last three pages of the script."

Singleton had a clear vision of what he wanted for the rest of the ensemble. He wanted new faces. And he found them on the first official day of casting at the offices of casting director Jaki Brown, whom Nicolaides would hail as "the unsung hero of *Boyz N the Hood*."

One morning, actors read for Tre Styles. Morris Chestnut, a tall, dark, and handsome finance major from Cal State Northridge working as a bank teller between auditions, was first up. Chestnut's résumé consisted of an episode of *Freddy's Nightmares*, the syndicated *A Nightmare on Elm Street* spin-off series, but Singleton liked him. Just not as Tre. "Let's keep him in mind for Ricky," he said as Chestnut departed.

Cuba Gooding Jr. was third in the room that day.

As the son of Shirley Gooding, of the 1960s girl group the Sweethearts, and Cuba Gooding Sr., the lead singer of The Main Ingredient ("Everybody Plays the

Fool"), he was a born performer. At the closing ceremony of the 1984 Summer Olympics, Gooding Jr. performed with the break-dancing ensemble onstage at the LA Coliseum, backing up Lionel Richie as he sang "All Night Long" to ninety-three thousand spectators and more than ninety-seven million Americans watching on the tube at home. From there he got into acting and scored small roles in *Hill Street Blues*, *Amen*, and *MacGyver*, and a walk-on in Eddie Murphy's *Coming to America*.

Gooding Jr. instantly captured Singleton's attention. Initially, it had nothing to do with his acting. The yellow button-down shirt with black sleeves and a black dot on the chest. The black Z. Cavaricci pants he'd snagged from an earlier fashion shoot. The black dress shoes so shiny and plastic they squeaked like a dog's chew toy. He looked like Tre, a good kid with a retail gig at the Fox Hills Mall. Immediately, Singleton had him read with Fishburne, who was sitting in.

"He's going to be Tre, and the chocolate one," Singleton said, referring to Chestnut, "is going to be Ricky."

"John, I have a full waiting room," Brown said. "You have to see more actors."

"That's who I want," he said.

"Well, we got Ricky and Tre," Nicolaides said. "Do you want to go get some lunch?"

Singleton got his way throughout casting. Though the studio had doubts about Gooding Jr. and put him through an arduous screen-testing process, Singleton won out in the end. He cast Tre's mom Reva (Angela Bassett) and Brenda Baker (Tyra Ferrell), the rough-around-the-edges mother to Doughboy and Ricky, based on Fishburne recommendations. Regina King, a former Trojan, starring as good girl Brenda Jenkins on the sitcom *227*, ended up as Shalika after reading three lines for Brown. "I just wanted to see if you could be ghetto," Brown told her.

Nia Long, who had just one film credit to her name, beat out over thirty actresses, including Stacey Dash, for the role of Tre's girlfriend, Brandi. "It wasn't your typical audition," she said. "John asked me about my life. He wanted to know about my relationship with my father. He wanted to know about my mother. He wanted to know which street I grew up on." Born in Brooklyn, Long lived in Iowa City, Iowa, for a spell before moving to Los Angeles at the age of seven. "I grew up in the hood on Slauson and Western, which was ten to twelve blocks from where John grew up," she said. "There was an instant connection."

It went on like that as Singleton filled out the cast through a combination of happenstance and nepotism.

He cast *Sanford & Son*'s Whitman Mayo after running into him at Marla

Gibbs's acting school, which shared the same building as Singleton's production office on Forty-Third and Degnan Boulevard. Singleton discovered Dedrick D. Gobert, a member of a Volkswagen car club, while looking for cars to feature in the film.

"He used to suck on a pacifier because he was trying to quit smoking," Jaki Brown said of Gobert, who'd never acted before but would go on to play Dooky. "John thought it was such a cool thing that he ultimately used it in the film." Singleton found his Little Chris after Redge Green, another nonprofessional actor, rolled into his office in a wheelchair and shared his life story. He hired friends for small yet vital parts. Malcolm Norrington and Lloyd Avery II were cast as the antagonists Knucklehead #1 and Knucklehead #2.

When it came time to cast Doughboy's friend Monster, Singleton saw it as an opportunity to pull a prank.

He called Baldwin C. Sykes. "Hey, man, I forgot to tell you that I got an A on my senior thesis," Singleton said. "What are you doing now?"

"I got an agent," Sykes answered. "Just did my first commercial."

"You should read for this project I'm involved with."

"What's it about?"

"Gangs and shit."

"Cool."

Singleton greeted Sykes outside the audition. "Go in there and knock it out," he said before disappearing.

"I thought John was a PA," Sykes says.

Inside, Brown told him he'd be reading for the role of Monster. As he scrolled the sides he did a double take.

Afterward, Singleton, now wearing a production jacket, greeted him. "Congrats, man," he said. "You got the part." Singleton laughed.

Sykes gawked at him.

"This is *Boyz N the Hood*. This is my film. I'm the director."

Singleton took a particular interest in casting Tre's fantasy fling, Tisha. As described in the script, Tisha was "fine, body was boomin' like right out of *Jet* centerfold or something." On that afternoon, young actresses and wannabes dressed in short shorts, miniskirts, and a lot of spandex and heels filled the casting office. A *Soul Train* dancer named Leonette Scott strutted into the room. Singleton gasped at her curves and cleavage spilling out of her tube top.

"That's her," he said as soon as Scott finished her audition.

"John, she can't act," Nicolaides said.

"I don't care. That's her," Singleton said. "It's not about acting ability. We just want a hot girl."

★★★★★

Life had changed rapidly for Singleton since he signed on to direct *Boyz N the Hood*. While it thrilled him in so many ways, it left him uneasy. "When you get into the entertainment industry, a lot of people just lose their mind," he said. "I wanted to try to hold on to who I was as much as possible."

He now lived with his girlfriend, Melissa Maxwell, in an apartment near La Brea and Wilshire. They'd met at USC and got closer as interns at *The Arsenio Hall Show* in early 1989—though not as close as he would've liked. From the start, friends mocked him for doting on her despite her perceived indifference. Maxwell, however, believed in him from the outset. "Melissa was the person who gave me the 411 on John," Sykes says. "One day after class we saw John sprinting across campus and she said, 'Do you see that guy over there? He's going to do big things. He's next level.'"

Maxwell was one of the few students at USC who matched him in ambition. She too had designs to write and direct films. In turn, she became one of his trusted collaborators. Maxwell filled the role of production manager on "Steppin' into the House." She also offered constructive feedback on his scripts. More than that, he loved the feeling of walking into a room with her on his arm. The stares. The double takes. The whispers. "How the hell did he pull her?"

And yet throughout the summer of 1990, he felt an impending sense of doom. It had all happened so suddenly for him. A year earlier, he was an extra on the Sam Raimi action movie *Darkman*. Now, he was prepping to direct his own film. In quiet moments with friends he expressed doubts.

"I talked so much shit like, 'I'm going to be better than Spike.' Then it was like, 'Damn, I really got to do this.'"

By then, the national press had caught wind of his story. In the August 7, 1990, issue of the *Village Voice*, the New York–based alt-weekly's star writer Nelson George mentioned Singleton in his column about Compton. "Singleton, who is touted by some as 'LA's Spike Lee,' expects to be shooting this script in September," George wrote. "There's always a chance that the heat on him may cool—Hollywood is profoundly fickle. But to me it looks like he's got the young and understanding to challenge Compton's knucklehead rappers on their own turf—to illuminate not just the town's sicknesses, but its soul."

*LA's Spike Lee.*

Singleton was being compared to his heroes before he even shot a frame of film on *Boyz N the Hood*. He still had to learn how to direct. In the end, he rewatched his favorite films over and over again, sometimes for more than twelve hours a day, jotting down notes the whole time. Then he discovered the Columbia screening room, where he studied the greats on the big screen. *Taxi Driver. Seven Samurai. Jaws. Drugstore Cowboy. The French Connection. Raging Bull*, and youth movies such as *Stand by Me, The 400 Blows, Los Olvidados*, and *Pixote*. He watched movies the way a hip-hop producer listened to old records, searching for a groove or a break he could filter through his sampler and turn into something different and completely his own.

From Scorsese he learned how to "show characters in relationship with their environment." Kurosawa's films taught him the power of nonverbal communication. He analyzed the baptism scene in *The Godfather* for *Boyz N the Hood*'s climax. He didn't want to come across as a rookie. So he examined Orson Welles's *Citizen Kane*, perhaps the greatest directorial debut ever, and discovered that successful first-time directors didn't move the camera just for the sake of it. They moved the camera to serve the story.

Singleton also enrolled in acting classes at the Crossroads Academy. Adopting a fake persona as a UPS driver, he went undercover to gain a better understanding of the craft. He hoped to learn the language of actors and how to communicate with them. How to elicit a performance. How to be a guiding force in a comforting manner. One night over the summer, Singleton hosted Fishburne in his apartment.

"Fish, tell me everything Francis taught you as an actor," he requested of Fishburne, a veteran of four Francis Ford Coppola films.

Fishburne laughed. "Where do I begin?"

"What does Francis do with his actors?" Singleton asked. "What's his rehearsal process like?"

Fishburne shared Coppola's secrets, which were starting to become common among other directors at the time: They'd read the script over and over together before moving on to improvisation exercises that had nothing to do with the script but helped the actors flesh out their characters. "Then we'd eat a lot of pasta and drink wine," Fishburne said.

Singleton didn't become a director on his own.

He benefited from a sturdy support system, a crew that later became known as the Singleton Family. A collection of veterans and rookies, friends and strangers, Black people and white people (though mostly Black people), the founding members of the Singleton Family met on *Boyz N the Hood.* They'd stick together in some form for the next thirty years.

Nicolaides helped Singleton put the family together. When assembling the crew, he hired veterans for key roles, such as the first assistant director Don Wilkerson, the director of photography Charles Mills, and stunt coordinator Bob Minor, the first Black member of the Stuntmen's Association of Motion Pictures. But he also included some familiar faces. "The director's job is to answer a thousand questions a day," Nicolaides said. "You're trying to surround him with friends and confidants and people who give him security and confidence to make decisions."

He hired Maxwell, his girlfriend, to be his personal assistant and hooked up friends—and friends of friends—with jobs sight unseen. Singleton hired Bobby Thomas from Black Pack as a grip. A nineteen-year-old film student from Detroit named Joe Doughrity came on board without an interview to be the director's PA (a role described as a personal assistant to the director's personal assistant).

They had already crossed paths at Golden Apple Comics on Melrose and outside the Nuart Theatre on Santa Monica Boulevard, where they shared a quick convo about samurai flicks. "We would be the only two Black guys for Akira Kurosawa films," Doughrity said, "and would give each other the head nod that brothers do."

Doughrity knew all about Singleton even if he couldn't put a face to the name. While working as a temp at an ad agency, Doughrity read Nelson George's "Native Son" column in the *Village Voice* and decided he wanted to work with John Singleton, that kid from LA about to direct a film called *Boyz N the Hood.* He was in luck. Doughrity's coworker was a USC alum. The next day he came in with Sheila Ward's address, which he found in the USC student directory. So, Doughrity wrote a letter asking for a job.

Soon he was called in for an interview. When he arrived at the production office, Public Enemy's "Brothers Gonna Work It Out (Remix)" was blasting on repeat. Singleton then appeared. He lowered the music, smiled, and walked toward Doughrity.

"He slaps my hand, hugs me, and says, 'You're hired,'" says Doughrity, who dropped out of film school to work on the film.

Bruce Bellamy, the younger brother of Singleton's friend Brian Bellamy, would be the art director. Singleton had worked with the script supervisor Dawn Gilliam on "Steppin' into the House." Four days before shooting started, Bill Straus snared a production assistant gig after suddenly losing his job in New York City. He drove cross-country to make it just in time for the first day. "John really came through for me in such a profound way when I was at my nadir," he says.

Spike Lee had used majority Black crews since his first feature, *She's Gotta Have It*, and, in the process, changed the complexion of film sets along the East Coast. He negotiated with the guilds to get his crew members inducted into unions, which meant better pay, better hours, greater access to better shows. Steadier work. Overtime and meal penalties. Benefits and a pension.

Singleton wanted to work similar magic in California. But with a dearth of unionized Black professionals, Nicolaides prepped the film nonunion at first. Less than a month before shooting started, Nicolaides approached Sony's head of physical production Gary Martin about making a change, even though it would add another six-figure sum to the budget. With Martin's approval, Nicolaides pitched the International Alliance of Theatrical Stage Employees. "Look, you and I both know that you're not coming down to South Central to see which union members are working on a nonunion show," he reasoned. "Why don't you let me [reapprove] everyone who's on my payroll now into the union?"

The union bosses acquiesced. As many as thirty members of the *Boyz N the Hood* crew, including Bobby Thomas, earned IATSE union cards. Predictably, it inspired an outpouring of loyalty toward Singleton, which persisted long after the movie wrapped. "The crew would have jumped off a cliff for him," Thomas says.

The veteran hands also rallied around him. For them, it was a revelation to work amongst an all-Black crew, in a Black neighborhood, for a Black filmmaker telling a Black story.

Singleton grew close to Wilkerson, a taskmaster who dissected his shot list each morning before pushing him to make the day anyway.

"He was a great father figure to John," Nicolaides says. From his work on *Boyz N the Hood*, Wilkerson gained a reputation as a guru to rookie directors. He would steer the directorial debuts of Anthony Drazan (*Zebrahead*, 1992), Eric Meza (*House Party 3*, 1994), Martin Lawrence (*A Thin Line between Love and Hate*, 1996), Ice Cube (*The Players Club*, 1998), and Rick Famuyiwa (*The Wood*, 1999). Later on, Wilkerson lived with Singleton for a few months when he went through a divorce.

Nicolaides selected Charles Mills, a veteran director of photography working mostly in episodic television, to shoot the film. Though not flashy, he remained committed to the roughness of *Boyz N the Hood* and pledged to shoot with a lot of handhelds.

When Singleton landed the deal to direct *Boyz N the Hood*, friends assumed he'd hire Brian Bellamy as his cinematographer. Bellamy was a film student from Detroit pushing thirty when they met at USC. Despite being an undergrad, Bellamy already knew the nuts and bolts of the industry. In between classes, he worked full-time as a cameraman on music videos and on movies such as *I'm Gonna Git You Sucka* and *House Party*. Friends describe him as Singleton's "film mentor." He assisted Singleton on his student films, shot "Steppin' into the House" for him, and was the one guy in Black Pack who could go toe-to-toe with him about movies.

Singleton and Bellamy worked well together but couldn't have been more different. Bellamy was a smooth talker and, according to some, a world-class functioning pothead, whereas Singleton rarely drank and didn't smoke. But both had similar aspirations and gravitated toward similar material, which is partly why the relationship deteriorated.

While Singleton wrote *Boyz N the Hood*, Bellamy worked on a script about his formative years in Detroit. Characters shared motivation, philosophy, and themes such as the importance of Black male role models. From the start, Bellamy believed that Singleton stole his idea. He didn't work on *Boyz N the Hood* or on any of Singleton's subsequent films. "Brian did not hide that he felt like John had fucked him over," Doughrity says.

★★★★★

By the time the cast gathered for rehearsals, Singleton felt more confident. Ice Cube had found his footing with help from an acting coach and his castmates.

"I remember how nervous Ice Cube was," Gooding Jr. said. "Watching the process of him putting his character together and talking about his insecurities and the emotions about the character—that was him getting comfortable with himself for the movie."

Gooding Jr. remained on edge, albeit for different reasons. When he showed up on the first day of rehearsals, he learned he still hadn't booked the job. "Steve Nicolaides pulled me aside and said, 'I hate to do this to you. But the studio still isn't sure about you. We have to do another screen test,'" Gooding Jr. said. "I couldn't believe it. John couldn't believe it either. They put me in another room, put another camera on me, and made me read another scene. This is the first fucking day of rehearsal. I go home and get a call. 'Congratulations, you're in the movie. Your call time is ten o'clock.'"

Throughout the callbacks and screen tests, Singleton had one note for Gooding Jr.: Stop smiling so much. But the actor unearthed the right emotional beats for his performance once officially cast. With the character now embedded in him, he read with Nia Long—the scene where Tre arrives at Brandi's door after a Black cop shoves a gun in his face.

"I'm sick of this shit," he whimpered in character, growing more and more agitated. "I'm so tired of this shit."

Gooding thought of his own encounters with the LAPD. He started shadow-boxing. Lefts and rights. Hooks and uppercuts. Combinations. "Fuck this shit," he growled, swinging wildly. Tears flowed. "Fuck you, motherfuckers." He didn't stop throwing haymakers until he punched a hole through a wall. Later on, once he'd calmed down, he signed his name next to it.

Fishburne said to Singleton, "I really wish I was that connected to my own emotional stuff when I was his age."

When the read-through finished, Singleton raced toward Nicolaides and leapt onto his back. Then he leaned in and whispered, "I'm going to win a fucking Academy Award for this script."

# CHAPTER SIX

**F**og rolled off the Pacific and covered the streets of Inglewood as dawn broke on Monday, October 1, 1990, the first day of filming on *Boyz N the Hood*. Singleton arrived to the set about ninety minutes prior to the seven a.m. call time. As he waited for the production to show, he ambled through his old neighborhood, the Bottoms, down blocks named after former Inglewood mayors, like Lawrence, Darby, and Dixon. He took it all in, thinking about the moment. "Everything I'd wanted since I was nine years old," he said.

Even with temperatures in the sixties, Singleton began to shiver. He sat alone on the curb for a few minutes to regain his composure. "You can do this. You can do this," he repeated over and over. Soon, the fog started to break, the trucks and trailers rolled in, the cast and crew arrived, and it was time to get to work, whether he was ready or not.

Singleton prepared the first shot of his career: a basic tracking shot of ten-year-old Tre and three classmates walking down the street. Beforehand, he gathered the four child actors, all of whom were as nervous as he was. "Just chill," he assured. "I got this." Then he huddled with Mills and called it out. "Kids, you're gonna walk from right to left," he exclaimed. "We're gonna lay down thirty-five feet of track and track them. I want some trash over here. I want the stray dogs over there." It sounded like something a director would say.

"I didn't know what the hell I was doing," he'd later admit. "But I had seen enough films where I had seen tracking shots. That's what the dolly was for, right?"

As the day progressed, more and more people spilled from their homes into the streets. Hollywood productions didn't come around here often. Hollywood productions headed by a twenty-two-year-old Black kid from the neighborhood were a Halley's Comet–like event. "John-John, what are you doing out here?" an older woman called out.

"I'm directing a movie," he answered. She turned toward her building and yelled, "Flip, come down, John-John is directing a movie!"

"Okay, okay, I need everyone to be quiet," he said. Singleton returned to directing the scene where Tre walks past a craps game—an homage to Travis Bickle ambling through Times Square in *Taxi Driver*. Moments later after he said, "Cut!" the crowd exploded. "Great, I love it!" Singleton cried. "Let's move on!"

A bit of reality set in at the end of the first day after film popped out of a B camera in the darkroom. The film couldn't be salvaged. Would it be an omen for the production?

Singleton's naïveté was apparent early on. "I love it. Let's move on," he'd announce after calling "Cut," not realizing he could shoot multiple takes. At one point, Nicolaides took him aside. "You know, John, sometimes the light changes in the middle of a shot. Sometimes there's a beat or a line that doesn't hit perfectly. We have time. Don't think this is a race."

The studio waited for Singleton to lose control of the picture.

Before filming started, he learned he was essentially on probation. If the dailies were subpar, he'd likely be replaced. Guber and Peters had demonstrated a quick trigger finger. A few months earlier, they'd fired David M. Evans, the twenty-seven-year-old writer/director of *Radio Flyer*, three weeks into production of the film. Like Singleton, Evans was an unknown when Sony purchased his script for $700,000 and gave him an additional $300,000 to direct. But his vision became corrupted through Peters's micromanaging and the dailies were incoherent. Sony halted production (costing the studio $5 million), then hired the husband-and-wife directing-and-producing team Richard Donner and Lauren Shuler Donner, ringing up an additional $6 million in costs. Filming on *Radio Flyer* restarted on October 3, 1990, two days after *Boyz N the Hood* started shooting.

Unlike *Radio Flyer*, a high-profile acquisition, there wasn't much glare on *Boyz N the Hood*. Singleton flew under the radar both with the studio and the industry. Columbia aspired to make glossy popcorn films like *Bram Stoker's Dracula* and star vehicles like *The Prince of Tides*. A $5.7 million Black film like *Boyz N the Hood* wasn't a priority. South Central was about a mile from Sony's offices but could have been across the Pacific and it wouldn't have been much different. Singleton was left alone—for the most part.

Aside from Allain, Columbia executives didn't visit the set until Doughboy's welcome-home barbecue. Singleton modeled the scene after Connie and Carlo's wedding, which opens *The Godfather*. It's where the main characters first interact.

Character traits are formed. Relationships are established. Storylines are set in motion.

The scene fills the audience in on what's transpired during the seven-year jump in time: Doughboy's been in and out of jail; Tre is having problems with his girlfriend, Brandi, and he's still best friends with Ricky—who, oh, by the way, has a son now.

Pretty girls danced. Music pumped during setups. Extras hung out in the director's chair. Actors swigged apple juice from forty-ounce bottles of St. Ides and Olde English while playing real games of dominoes and spades. Production quickly fell behind schedule. "I think for the first time John got a little lost," Nicolaides says. "Those are the kind of scenes that are very challenging for any director. But certainly for a first-timer."

Sony's head of physical production Gary Martin ended the party. Singleton had to move on.

For filmmakers, a set visit from Martin equaled a call to the principal's office. Yet Singleton never feared for his job. "My attitude was, 'Who the hell are they going to get to come down here and shoot this movie? They ain't firing me,'" he said. He was never in real danger of losing it anyway.

Before wrapping the barbecue scene, Singleton talked it over with Mills. Until that point he had a habit of referencing his idols while calling out shots. "This is just like what Spielberg would do," he'd say. "This is like that Truffaut shot from *The 400 Blows*."

For this shot, he wanted Mills's camera to follow the action through the backyard. "I need the Steadicam working its way across the barbecue, following the kid around, showing the dancing, the dominoes," he said. "This is going to be like a Scorsese shot."

"No," Mills corrected him. "This is a John Singleton shot."

Singleton, quiet for once, nodded. Singleton benefited from Nicolaides's decision to shoot the film in sequence. With time, his fake confidence turned into conviction. He worked hard. Every night, he'd stay up late reviewing his shot list for the next day. *How many shots is it going to take to do this scene? How many pages can we film?* He'd write it out on a piece of paper, type it up, and distribute it to the crew in the morning. He was a fast learner and became more decisive on set. He could massage and inspire an actor to get the performance he needed. "This is your porch," he'd tell Cube.

One day, Cube was telling war stories from his time in N.W.A. "This dude Jerry Heller was a straight-up crook," he said to a group of extras who'd gathered around him. "I wasn't seeing any of the dough." Singleton overheard the rant. Suddenly, he had an idea.

"Hey, man, do you have any N.W.A. or Eazy-E gear?"

"I should. Why?"

"You'll see," Singleton answered. "Just bring it in tomorrow. Don't forget."

Cube arrived the next morning clutching a stack of T-shirts. They were filming a scene where Doughboy and his crew beat up a smoker for snatching Dooky's chain. Singleton held up a black shirt with *We Want Eazy* written on it. "Hey, man, what do you think about putting this on the crackhead?"

Cube laughed. "Yeah, let's do it. I don't give a fuck," he said. "John, you're crazy."

All of this was a prologue to the film's emotional climax: the death of Ricky Baker.

Gooding Jr. sat in makeup that morning brooding, trying to tap into the hurt and anguish he'd need for his performance. He then retired to his trailer, where he further worked himself up, preparing to witness his best friend's murder. As soon as he walked onto the location, he felt a rush of emotion.

At the other end of the alley, Singleton dissected the scene with Lloyd Avery II, the actor portraying Ricky's killer. Singleton reviewed meticulous details with Avery: how to grip the sawed-off shotgun as he emerged from the Jolly Rancher–red Hyundai, what to do with his eyes, his nostrils, his expression.

Avery wasn't a professional actor. A middle-class kid from a good home, he had gone to trade school and dabbled in music. Later on, he got involved with gangs. But he was eager to make his friend proud. After conferring with Singleton, Avery walked toward Gooding Jr.

"What's up, Cuba?" he asked. "What do you think about this—"

"Don't fucking talk to me right now!"

Avery, a real live wire, then lunged at Cuba. "Do you know who you're talking to?" he shouted. "What the fuck is wrong with you?" A PA separated them.

Chestnut missed the entire argument; he was busy listening to the stunt coordinator Bob Minor explain to him how to avoid getting his head blown off. "As soon as you see the Hyundai, you're going to turn and run," Minor instructed. "Just make sure to keep your head up and you'll be fine."

"Wait. What?" Chestnut said, startled. "What happens if I look down?"

"These are squibs," Minor said, pointing to the little capsules set to pop and turn Chestnut's white Henley into a blood-soaked mess. "They are mini explosives. Just don't look down. You'll be fine."

"Don't look down. I'll be fine," Chestnut said.

They shot the drive-by quickly with sparse coverage. Singleton's greatest concern was that his actors adhere to the storyboards and hit their cues afterward to pull off the most impressive shot of the film. As Tre holds Ricky in his arms, Doughboy's Chevy Impala arrives. Doughboy, Monster, and Dooky exit the car. Doughboy cradles his brother's head. In the background, Dooky rests his head on the hood while Monster teeters, shell-shocked. At that moment, Little Chris rolls in and steers left. Cube then looks up and utters, "Let's take him home."

"It's a long take," says director Craig Brewer. "Look at the positioning of everybody. The guy in the wheelchair coming up in the foreground. Ice Cube lifting his head. There's real apex-of-triangle focus by way of staging within the frame happening. Amongst us directors, that's when we applaud. 'Ooh, look at that.' You're not just cutting to tell us how to feel, you're staging for us to feel. That's when things feel like David Lean."

The action moved to the Baker house.

As written in the script, Mrs. Baker tries to remain calm upon seeing Ricky's body and dials 9-1-1. It didn't work in rehearsals. But Singleton was open to suggestions.

"Forget about the phone," Tyra Ferrell said. "I feel like it's crucial for me to show love to my son. What do you think?"

"Keep going," Singleton said. "Take the reins."

She choreographed the scene on the fly. "This is what's going to happen," Ferrell said. "You bring him in. I come in. I see him. I will not believe it. I want him to get up. I turn to Darrin and I melt in his arms because he's the only one I have left. But then I realize that he must have played some role in it, so I go off in a rage on him. Then I need Tre to do what he needs to do to get me off him and get out of the scene."

"I like it," Singleton said. "Let's go with it."

Ice Cube had one request before rehearsing the new scene: Don't touch his hat.

"I thought, 'Is he out of his mind?' We're acting in this scene and he is concerned about his hat," Ferrell said. "You don't tell an actor, 'Don't knock off my hat.' For me to get a real good reaction out of him, the hat is going to be the first thing to go."

Ferrell avoided the hat during rehearsals. But it was the first thing to go when cameras started to roll.

"It surprised the shit out of Cube. It surprised the shit out of everybody," Nicolaides says. "Tyra was a mad woman that day. She made the scene."

★★★★★

Shooting in South Central, the threat of violence remained present. The cast and crew never felt danger until what became known as the Crenshaw Incident.

From the start, Singleton lied to Nicolaides about the situation on the ground in Los Angeles. Yes, he said, the Bloods and Crips were still active. But no, Red vs. Blue was no longer a thing. "I didn't want the studio to start being all whatever about whatever," Singleton explained. "I wanted to make sure the film had authenticity. I didn't want to get into the whole political thing like, 'Maybe you shouldn't have red and blue.'"

"It was a bit of an oops," Nicolaides says. "I took John at his word. I didn't really go *bingo-bingo* at the Chicago Bulls cap and it didn't click in my brain about the red Hyundai either until the Crenshaw Incident."

Singleton had re-created Sunday nights on Crenshaw Boulevard, Los Angeles's long-running cruising spot, when it went down. Scores of extras lined the block near sparkling rides posted up curbside.

That night, members of Ice Cube's crew Da Lench Mob stomped out an extra who had "gotten out of line," Singleton said. Having witnessed the beatdown, Nicolaides alerted the two off-duty LAPD officers on hand. The extra fled the scene—but only after threatening to return with a gun.

Fears of a real drive-by shooting spread. Immediately, the crew erected a makeshift barricade around Crenshaw using camera trucks, prop trucks, and trailers. That night, there were no more fights. No one shot up the set.

The next day a member of the film crew, Wolfgang Bodison, received a phone call from Cle Shaheed Sloan, an Athens Park Blood known as Bone.

"The producer and I need to have dinner tonight," Bone said.

Later that night, Nicolaides, Bodison, and Fred Williams, a former gang-banger and a friend of the production, met Bone and an associate at the Boulevard Café.

"Look, I'm a businessman, I don't give a fuck about your little movie, but I can't control everybody," Bone said in a flat, even voice. "You need to know that the word is out that *Boyz N the Hood* is dissing the Bloods."

"We didn't mean to diss anybody," Nicolaides said. "There's no mention of Bloods and Crips in the movie. Besides, I was told that colors doesn't mean anything anymore."

Bone shook his head. "I know you're planning to shoot a scene where Ice Cube blows away three Bloods at the hamburger stand on Martin Luther King Boulevard. You would be stupid to do that. Some fourteen-year-old kid wanting to earn his stripes is going to ride over there and bust a cap in Ice Cube."

The next morning Nicolaides told Singleton, "We're not shooting at that burger stand on Martin Luther King."

"Why not?" Singleton asked.

"Bone said the streets think we're dissing the Bloods."

"But we're not dissing the Bloods."

"John, they're driving a red Hyundai," Nicolaides said.

"Fuck that and fuck him," Singleton said. "I'm doing what the fuck I want."

In the end, Singleton would be overruled by Nicolaides, Ice Cube, and the Fruit of Islam guards providing security. "John, listen to Steve, man," Cube advised. "It's me or you who's gonna get shot."

"My attitude was that we're not going to let them tell us what to do," Singleton said. "Then you're letting them have more power. You're giving them power."

He relented and changed the location to the Eat-a-Burger in the Crenshaw mall; on the night before Thanksgiving, he filmed it without incident.

A few days later, the cast and crew celebrated at the wrap party in Leimert Park. Singleton then retreated to his new home for the next ten weeks: the editing room.

Т he idea was that by hosting the screening at the studio instead of a multiplex, they'd have quiet and control.

So, on a chilly afternoon early in the spring of 1991, Columbia bussed an all-Black crowd from South Central onto the Sony lot and then made them wait in the cold for over an hour.

Finally, staffers ushered them into a screening room, where they were delayed once more.

The result was one angry focus group.

Inside the theater, Joseph Farrell, who revolutionized the test-screening process as chairman and CEO of the National Research Group, greeted the audience. "Good evening. Welcome to the first screening of Columbia Pictures' *Boyz N the Hood*. There are a few things I'd like to explain before we start the show," he said. "This is not a finished movie. Some of the sound is not perfect. The music is incomplete. When you see a white leader with squiggly lines, that indicates 'dissolve to.' When you see a—"

"Shut the fuck up and play the movie," thundered a voice from the crowd.

The lights dimmed. Singleton took a deep breath.

From the moment he got his deal he imagined how *Boyz N the Hood* would play with its intended audience. He loved the movie before he filmed it. Now, even in its rough form, he loved it more than ever. How would the people feel about it? He'd find out soon enough—once Farrell shut the fuck up and played the movie.

Postproduction had been nearly as intense as the shoot.

Since filming had concluded in late November, he faced a hard deadline. Singleton had ten weeks to submit his director's cut to the studio. He edited his film with Bruce Cannon in the same house where Cannon had helped cut *Body Heat* and *The Big Chill* as an assistant.

Cannon, a Beverly Hills native, secured the editing job after another editor passed and recommended him for it. His résumé wasn't notable aside from work as a second assistant editor on *E.T.: The Extra Terrestrial*, a gig Cannon says "had nothing to do with being an editor." But Singleton loved *The Making of Bikini School 3*, an unreleased mockumentary short directed by Bobcat Goldthwait, aka Zed from the Police Academy franchise, that Cannon edited. "Somehow John saw it," Cannon says. "It was silly and nuts, but he loved it."

They connected immediately. For the next ten weeks, they'd spend ten hours together daily, trading obscure film references, talking politics, eating Japanese food, cracking jokes, and exchanging countless high fives and fist bumps.

Yet early on there were challenges.

One morning Singleton called Cannon, sounding like he was still in the grips of sleep. "Hey, man, I'm not able to make it for nine," he said. "I'm going to be a little late."

"John, it's already nine o'clock. What happened?"

"I was up all night watching films."

"Where are you?"

"I'll be there soon. I'm turning on La Brea," Singleton said from bed.

From then on when Singleton called in late, which happened habitually, he'd say, "I'll be there soon. I'm turning on La Brea."

Inside the editing room, he was a writer to the core—protective of his words and his characters. "John liked to give his characters a lot of room and space," Cannon says, which resulted in scenes running long.

Eventually, Singleton learned to acquiesce, becoming more agreeable to cuts. "The tightening process, when we took some air out of the film, was when we saw it come together," Cannon says.

They promptly finished their first cut, giving the sound team an early start.

The film's composer, Stanley Clarke, got his hands on some footage about six or seven weeks into the editing process.

Singleton met the bass virtuoso just as Clarke was breaking into film composing with 1989's *Tap*, following a nearly two-decade run with the jazz fusion group Return to Forever. How they met in February 1989 should come as no surprise: Singleton rushed him backstage at a taping of *The Arsenio Hall Show*.

"You're gonna do my movie one day" was how Singleton introduced himself.

"I thought this guy was kinda crazy," Clarke says. About two years later, he got a call to meet a director named John Singleton. When Clarke arrived at

Singleton's Leimert Park office, the director was sitting on a sofa, Game Boy in hand. "Remember me?" he asked.

Singleton could hear the music in his head, both the score and the source music—the contemporary hip-hop and R&B that would play in the film. After screening a rough cut for Clarke, he declared, "I want the music to make the movie timeless." For Singleton, timeless meant traditional film scoring in the vein of his favorite composers such as Bernard Herrmann (*Cape Fear*).

Clarke agreed. "A lot of movies about the so-called hood are just Isaac Hayes knockoffs and wah-wah pedals," he said. "Please, John, no wah-wahs."

"I got one even better for you: I don't want to hear a guitar in the entire fucking score," Singleton countered. "Look, man, I really respect you. I want you to write what you feel."

"That was very, very refreshing to hear," Clarke says. "It gave me a sense of freedom."

Clarke sat with the footage. Even in its rough state, the film felt honest and true, which guided his compositions. "The score is what brought the film together," Cannon says.

"The Stanley Clarke–penned instrumental theme, titled 'Black on Black Crime,' became the music soul and spirit of the film," writes the journalist Stereo Williams. "With its foreboding melody and evocative combination of bass prowess and impending doom, it ripples throughout *Boyz N the Hood* and serves as both warning and rallying cry."

Everyone at the studio seemed to love the film when Singleton screened the temp mix sometime in January. There were a few notes. They wanted him to cut the scene where the police harass Furious and young Tre. "Why do you have to be so hard on the police?" they asked. Price also pushed for a stronger resolution between Furious and Tre at the end. Singleton won both battles. "We know Tre made the right decision and Tre knows he made the right decision," Singleton reasoned. "The father doesn't necessarily have to know."

Audiences reacted similarly. *Boyz N the Hood* received high grades from the South Central focus group. Sitting in on the screening, Price was transfixed by the crowd participation. People cheered at shots of the local corner store and laughed at jokes the older white executives didn't get. They warned Ricky when the red Hyundai surfaced and then openly wept as he died in Tre's arms.

Shortly after the test screening, Singleton got the news.

"We're taking *Boyz N the Hood* to the Cannes Film Festival. It's opening there."

★★★★★

Once Madonna was spotted jogging along the French Riviera in a *Boyz N the Hood* promo T-shirt, Singleton knew he'd hit it big.

"When I got to Cannes, nobody knew who the hell I was," he said. "But by the end of the week, everybody did."

As a student of film history, Singleton understood what a Cannes debut meant for his film: a splashy premiere, lots of press, and a friendly audience; despite what they claim, the French love American films. But he also recognized what it meant for him. Beginning in Cannes, Columbia placed Singleton front and center in the film's promotional and marketing campaigns. He'd be recognized as the industry's hot new auteur. The press—both the traditional film corps and the paparazzi—would be breathing down his neck.

Cannes has a rich history born out of anti-fascism. In 1938, the French, British, and American press stormed out of the Vienna Film Festival after Benito Mussolini and Adolf Hitler overruled the festival jury to award the top prizes to a pair of Italian and German propaganda films. A year later, the resort town of Cannes was selected to host a new festival beyond a dictator's reach. Then, on September 1, 1939, on the festival's inauguration day, Hitler invaded Poland. Cannes was postponed until 1946.

After the war, it was a showcase for the French New Wave. But over time Cannes became synonymous with glamorous red carpets and bold acquisition deals. Unlike most film festivals, there wasn't a vigorous submissions process. Cannes was political. All Frank Price had to do was pick up the phone.

The entire *Boyz* team flew in on the same plane: Nicolaides and Allain with their spouses, Cube and his soon-to-be-wife Kimberly, and Singleton with Melissa Maxwell.

Within minutes of arriving at Nice Côte d'Azur Airport, he detected the sights and sounds that characterized the next week. The stampede of paparazzi funneling toward their next target. The clamoring in French and broken English. The blinding flash fires emitting from cameras. Were they here for him? Was it for Ice Cube? Then, while on the escalator, he spotted Forest Whitaker, a Best Actor winner at Cannes a few years earlier, standing near the baggage claim, fending off the horde.

Singleton and Cube climbed into a cab for the thirty-minute drive from Nice to Cannes.

As they turned toward the Riviera, Singleton and Cube shouted in unison at their driver. "Yo, yo, stop the car." They exited and gaped at a graffiti-marked billboard perched against the cloudless sky. "That's for us," Singleton said.

Later that night, Singleton met up with Spike Lee, here in support of *Jungle Fever*, the thirty-four-year-old's fourth film in as many years.

At dinner, Lee recounted the highs and lows from his visits to Cannes. In 1986 he was the new sensation when *She's Gotta Have It* netted Lee the Prix de la jeunesse (Award of the Youth). Three years later, he arrived with even higher expectations. Based on pre-festival chatter, *Do the Right Thing* was the heavy favorite to win the festival's top prize, the Palme d'Or. Its premiere brought down the house. But it got shut out at the closing ceremony.

The more they talked, the more they realized what they had in common. The films they loved. The directors they admired. They were film school evangelists. They both found it troubling when the nineteen-year-old filmmaker Matty Rich proudly announced that he *hadn't* studied his craft.

A native of the Red Hook projects, Rich caused a stir when his semiautobiographical debut film *Straight Out of Brooklyn* won a Special Jury Prize at Sundance in January. In interviews, he bragged about dropping out of New York University film school after a month.

"I've never read a film book! I don't go to the movies! I don't know how to use a camera! I'm from the streets!" Lee once said, mocking Rich.

The rift between Rich and Lee boiled over at a photo shoot for a magazine article highlighting Black directors. "They got into it to the point where we had to separate them," recalls *House Party* director Reginald Hudlin.

Over dinner, Singleton and Spike made a pact. If they ever had a problem with each other, they wouldn't take it to the press. They'd hash it out in private. Man-to-man.

Lee's story about the jury's sucker punch stuck with Singleton. He walked on the famous Croisette boardwalk oblivious to the palm trees that should've reminded him of home. His mind wandered back to something Cube said on the plane ride over. "They're about to shit on our movie, John."

*Boyz N the Hood* premiered on May 13, 1991, at the Grand Palais. When the lights came back on, the crowd vaulted from their seats applauding like partisans at a political convention. Singleton could see Quincy Jones on his feet. Eddie Murphy standing. Spike Lee. Roger Ebert, now the most influential film critic in the country following Pauline Kael's recent retirement, wiping away tears.

The standing ovation continued for nearly twenty minutes.

A second screening failed to meet the public's demand for *Boyz N the Hood*, as roughly three hundred people were turned away.

"The movie is blowing up," he reported back to his friends stateside. "It just seems like it's getting bigger and bigger."

At times, when it got to be too much, he'd hide behind his camcorder; Singleton told reporters he was shooting a documentary about his first time at Cannes.

Shortly before leaving Cannes, Nicolaides spotted a swarm of paparazzi slowly moving forward like infantry soldiers approaching the front line. Shooting. Shooting. Shooting. He stepped off the sidewalk and into the street to make room for the photographers and get a better look at their prey.

"Jean Singleton," Nicolaides cried out in an overblown French accent.

Singleton peered from inside the scrum, met eyes with his producer, smiled, and continued on his way.

★★★★★

The Coen brothers' *Barton Fink* won the Palme d'Or, but *Boyz N the Hood*, which was screened outside of competition, was the breakout hit of the 1991 Cannes Film Festival. Singleton was its breakout star.

"Another annual tradition at Cannes is the discovery of an unsung new talent, and this year that talent was twenty-three-year-old American filmmaker John Singleton," said Gene Siskel, the *Chicago Tribune* film critic and cohost of the syndicated *Siskel & Ebert*. "If there was one thing the French, British, and American critics agreed on, it was that *Boyz N the Hood* was the most exciting film in this year's Cannes Film Festival."

The *Hollywood Reporter* called *Boyz N the Hood* "a booming, heart slam of a film" with "knockdown terrific" performances. David Ansen of *Newsweek* said it's "the work of a truly gifted filmmaker."

"I cried tears of sadness and joy during the final moments of hip-hop's first true cinematic epic, John Singleton's *Boyz N the Hood*," wrote Scott Poulson-Bryant in *Spin* magazine.

In the *New York Times*, critic Janet Maslin anointed Singleton a younger, West Coast version of Spike Lee—echoing Nelson George's prescient words in the *Village Voice* from a year earlier. "*Boyz N the Hood*, John Singleton's terrifically confident first feature, places Mr. Singleton on a footing with Spike Lee as a chronicler of the frustration faced by young black men growing up in urban settings. But Mr. Singleton, who wrote and directed this film set in South Central Los Angeles, has a distinctly Californian point of view. Unlike Mr. Lee's New York stories, which give their neighborhoods the finiteness and theatricality of stage sets, Mr. Singleton examines a more sprawling form of claustrophobia and a more adolescent angst."

Siskel compared Singleton to another of the director's heroes. "There's one good scene after another in *Boyz N the Hood*, a film that reminded me a lot of Martin Scorsese's early picture *Mean Streets* with its insights into the self-destructive life of an Italian American ghetto," the critic noted in his thumbs-up—"way up!"— review. "This director John Singleton has a seemingly effortless style that is based more on the content of his characters than any particularly flashy camera moves. It's a heartbreaking film as these lives take a natural, inevitable course and I think a major new director has arrived."

Roger Ebert deemed *Boyz N the Hood* "one of the best American films of recent years" in his four-star review in the *Chicago Sun-Times*. He applauded Singleton's talent both as a director ("His camera is so confident and he wins such natural performances from his actors") and a screenwriter ("Singleton's screenplay was built well; we feel we know the characters and their motivations, and so we can understand what happens and why"). He ended his review stating, "*Boyz N the Hood* has maturity and emotional depth: There are no cheap shots, nothing is thrown in for effect, realism is placed ahead of easy dramatic payoffs, and the audience grows deeply involved. By the end of *Boyz N the Hood*, I realized I had seen not simply a brilliant directorial debut, but an American film of enormous importance."

Now it was up to Columbia to make it a hit.

The job of selling the film to the public fell to Columbia Pictures' new head of marketing, a middle-aged white woman from New York named Paula Silver.

Silver had made a name for herself with her work on the *Gandhi* and *Ghostbusters* campaigns. Later on, she devised the rollout for the surprise hit *Mr. Holland's Opus* and was a strategist on the $368 million–grossing indie *My Big Fat Greek Wedding*.

On *Boyz N the Hood* she was tasked with performing a tricky balancing act: Build good word of mouth amongst the film's base in the Black community while attracting the white audiences needed for the film to become a crossover hit.

Shortly after Silver was hired in April 1991, Singleton watched *Boyz N the*

*Hood* with her. "John walks in bold with a little attitude because I was a white girl," Silver says.

"What did you think?" he asked her afterward.

"For the first time, I thought about what it was like to be Black in America."

"Well, you still don't know how to market the picture," he said.

"Why not?"

"Because you're white."

"Look, I know I'm not a California girl," she said. "I'm learning everything here for the first time. I can admit that. But I'm willing to say I don't know."

Singleton demanded a Black marketing team.

"We can hire a Black team," Silver said. "We can do that. But I have to tell you: This is about problem-solving. It's not magic. Let's talk about what we want to do here."

A few days later Singleton and Nicolaides were on the dubbing stage putting the finishing touches on the film's sound when Silver pulled them aside. "I have the tagline for the movie," Silver announced.

Singleton held his breath.

Taglines are the pithy slogans that appear on a poster to help market the film. Silver was around when some of the most memorable ones were created: "Who you gonna call?" and "In space no one can hear you scream." What would she think up for *Boyz N the Hood*? "Ready?" she asked. "'Are you brave enough to see this movie?'"

"Absolutely not," Nicolaides said.

Singleton had wanted "Increase the Peace" as a tagline, but the studio found it preachy and didactic. Eventually, they settled on "Once upon a time in South Central. It ain't no fairy tale," which everyone hated.

Columbia then hired UniWorld, a Black-owned firm specializing in marketing to Black consumers, to complement the efforts of Silver and her team. One of their first strategies was to screen the film for an assorted group made up of social workers, politicians, psychiatrists, police officers, and community leaders. By early July, more than three thousand people had seen the film.

The screenings weren't just intended to build buzz before its July 12 release date. According to the *Los Angeles Times*, their objective "was to identify and show the movie to LA's Black opinion leaders, who would get the word out to youthful and older audiences that *Boyz N the Hood* is, as the studio wants to emphasize, a 'coming of age movie' that does not endorse gang violence."

The message contradicted the studio's own ad campaign.

From the start, Columbia marketed *Boyz N the Hood* as an action flick, and not a coming-of-age drama. Nearly every violent act in the film is packed into the final twenty seconds of its trailer. Early television ads took a similar approach. "Five minutes away from your nice, safe neighborhood, there's a war going on," a menacing voiceover intoned at the start of one thirty-second spot.

Some Columbia executives were uneasy with the campaign, one that largely omitted the film's heart and message in favor of pushing gangs and guns. Predictably, they lost control of the narrative. "It's called *Boyz N the Hood*. A vivid movie about life in South Central LA is about to hit theaters nationwide, and police are fearing the worst. Will it touch off a wave of gang violence? Stick around" was the local news tease on KCAL9.

In March, violence erupted in and around theaters showing *New Jack City*, George Jackson and Doug McHenry's box office winner starring Wesley Snipes as Nino Brown, the fly Harlem drug lord based on 1970s kingpin Nicky Barnes.

A melee outside Mann Village Theater in upscale Westwood. Fifteen arrests in Vegas. A gunshot victim in Chicago. Three injured cops following a brawl in a Sayreville, New Jersey, movie theater lobby. In Brooklyn, an argument inside the theater led to gunfire exchanged outside the theater, killing a nineteen-year-old.

A media narrative emerged: The violence on-screen inspired the violence in real life. And who was to blame for this cinematic PR nightmare? The film and the filmmakers.

Singleton fancied having it both ways. He hoped audiences would get his message, which was *Increase the Peace*. But he also wanted to put butts in seats. "I did what I had to do to get people to see my movie," he said. "I wanted to make a really violent trailer because I wanted the people going to see *Terminator 2* to come see this movie and then find out that the film is much more than that."

He knew audiences might misinterpret his film's message of nonviolence.

Shortly after returning from Cannes, Singleton attended a friend's graduation party at Jim Brown's house. Every year, the retired football legend and longtime activist opened up his four-level mansion in the hills to a graduating college student, based, in part, on a letter-writing competition. For some time now, Brown had worked behind the scenes toward a gang truce. On this night, he had Bloods and Crips working side by side as security.

One of the Bloods stationed at the front door recognized Singleton and accused him of making Bloods look bad in the film.

"There's no good guys and bad guys," Singleton said, growing agitated. "Let me tell you what the movie is about. It's not about Bloods and Crips or who's right or wrong. It's not a gang movie. It's about a Black man raising his son."

"Fuck you."

"Fuck you. Just watch the movie."

"Fuck you."

"Watch the fucking movie."

Industry tracking pointed to an eight-figure opening, about double its production budget.

By seven p.m. on opening night Singleton was riding around Los Angeles in a rented limousine with some friends and some girls, dropping in on local theaters, gauging reactions to the film. The limo's first stop: the Baldwin Hills theater Singleton frequented as a kid. He had seen *Super Fly*, *Shaft*, and *Enter the Dragon* here.

Wearing his South Central Cinema baseball hat, he stood in the lobby, shaking hands like a politician at a campaign stop.

A couple approached him. "The movie was so good," the young woman said. "He really liked it too."

She pointed to her boyfriend. Eyes still watery, he looked up at the ceiling. "He might not be saying much now, but he did not shut up during the movie," she said. "He kept saying, 'That's my story. That's my story.'"

"That was the biggest compliment I ever received for that movie," Singleton said years later. "This was an OG, a gangster dude, you could tell he did time. His girl did all the talking for him. He couldn't express what he was feeling."

Later on, the limousine pulled up to the Cineplex Odeon in Universal City. He noticed people heading into the nine p.m. showing had something in common: They were all wearing red. On his walk back to the limo, he saw two teens draped head-to-toe in blue.

He scrambled back into the lobby to warn security. "Hey, hey, please don't let those two cats in the theater," he pleaded.

"If they have tickets, we can't stop them from going in," an usher said.

"Are you crazy?" he shouted. "These two guys are blue down, Cripped out and everything."

Later that night, he learned five people were shot in and around the eighteen-screen multiplex.

Pascal called Allain with news of the shooting that night. Columbia executives were on a corporate retreat in Santa Barbara and accurate information was tough to come by in real time. In all, two people were dead and around thirty were injured following violence in the vicinity of theaters showing *Boyz N the Hood*.

Shots were fired in a Minneapolis theater. Michael Booth, a twenty-three-year-old security guard, was killed in his car at a midnight showing at a drive-in in the Chicago suburb of Riverdale. Four people were shot in Upland, a city in San Bernardino. In Sacramento, a nineteen-year-old woman was shot six times when two men opened fire at police breaking up a fight outside a movie theater. There were also shootings in the Northern California city of Pinole and in Chino.

At around five a.m. Columbia executives decided to call a news conference for later that morning at the Four Seasons hotel in Beverly Hills. Singleton and Mark Gill, Columbia's senior vice president of publicity, would make a statement and then take questions from the media. Neither Guber nor Price attended the hastily called event. Studio executives with decades in the game expected Singleton to do damage control—an unfair amount of responsibility to heap on a twenty-three-year-old.

A few hours earlier Singleton had been dancing at a college party in Westwood. Now he was handling crisis PR for a billion-dollar multinational corporation.

Singleton approached the podium smoldering with resentment. Try as he might, he couldn't help but think about what went wrong and who to blame. The LAPD for putting the city on the brink. The media for pushing a narrative that became a self-fulfilling prophecy. The perpetrators of the violence. The people who missed the message of his film. The theaters for not taking better security measures. At the Black-owned Baldwin Hills Theater, management installed metal detectors, spaced out showings to avoid overcrowding the lobby, addressed the audience before each showing, and banned hats, gang colors, and babies. Why didn't more theaters do the same?

He kept his frustration in check while calmly addressing the media. Immediately, he expressed sympathy for the victims and asked for the violence to end. His voice wavered a bit. But he went on the offensive, blaming a society that "breeds illiteracy and economic deprivation."

"Do you take any responsibility for the violence?" a reporter asked.

"I didn't create the conditions which make people shoot each other," he said. "These acts were indicative of the degeneration of American society, not a reflection of my film, which is about family, love, and friendship."

"What would you say if you could speak directly to the people who caused the violence?"

"There's a certain segment of the population that wants you to do what you're doing to each other. But we don't have time for that," he said, sounding like Furious Styles (or Danny Singleton—same difference). "I won't turn my back on my brothers. I hope they don't turn their back on me."

Eight theaters, including the Cineplex Odeon in Universal City and Mann's Chinese Theatre, removed the film from their screens. But it didn't hurt business.

*Boyz N the Hood* opened at $10 million in third place behind *Terminator 2: Judgment Day* and *101 Dalmatians*. Playing in just 829 theaters, it averaged $12,091 per screen, the highest of any movie that weekend. In the end, *Boyz N the Hood* grossed $57 million and was Columbia's most profitable movie of 1991. Singleton now had a career. His life would soon open up in different ways as he gained access to money, women, and fame.

He also acquired something less tangible but as important.

Earlier in the night, before the violence ruined his moment, Singleton sat in the limousine with Yon Styles talking about the couple at the Baldwin Hills Theater. "That was really humbling," Singleton said. "These are people I grew up with. Nobody really cares about them. They're just fodder for most people in society."

"That's why you need to keep doing what you're doing," Styles said. "We all have opinions. But you have a voice now."

# CHAPTER EIGHT

**S**ingleton was the hottest new filmmaker in town and would be treated as such during the whirlwind summer of 1991 and beyond.

Later in life, when asked what he remembered most about the time around *Boyz N the Hood*, Singleton said, "Just being scared as hell. I kept up a front like, 'Okay, I'm not impressed.' But I was realizing all of my dreams.

"Life was changing so rapidly. I wanted to try to hold on to who I was as much as possible."

He confided in friends about his challenges—the test of character, the struggle to remain grounded, the fight to preserve a connection to his past self. But it was difficult. How could it not be?

For years, Singleton's underdog archetype motivated him in all aspects of life. Now an overnight sensation, he touched a new level of fame few directors reach. He became a rock star.

A Gen X icon.

A South Central legend.

A genius.

A young genius.

A young Black genius.

Suddenly, everyone wanted a piece of John Daniel Singleton. *The Oprah Winfrey Show. Good Morning America. The Tonight Show.* Alex Haley interviewed him for an episode of *Dialogue with Black Filmmakers*. He met with the Congressional Black Caucus in Washington, DC. The Bush administration reached out about a potential White House dinner.

Life turned into a movie montage. Parties at Eddie Murphy's mansion. Courtside with Spike Lee at the Great Western Forum for Game Five of the NBA Finals to watch Michael Jordan bag his first NBA championship. A few days after *Boyz n the Hood* opened, Ice Cube paused his show at the Apollo Theater in Harlem to introduce him.

"How many of y'all seen *Boyz N the Hood*?" Cube screamed. "I want to bring out the man who wrote and directed the film."

Singleton climbed onstage and looked out into a sea of New Yorkers cheering wildly for him. He laughed in disbelief. *They're clapping for me. A filmmaker from LA. I'm not even a rapper!* He chucked a few promo tees into the crowd. Then he turned and pumped his fist in the air before departing to more applause.

Celebrities stopped him in the street to sing his praises. "On the way to this interview, he ran into Living Colour guitarist Vernon Reid, who began raving about *Boyz*, compared Singleton to Orson Welles and offered—practically begged—to contribute music to the writer-director's next project," *Rolling Stone* reporter Alan Light wrote in his profile of him.

His heroes now sought him out. One night, Singleton and his friend, the comedian Joe Torry, went to the Comedy Store, the hottest comedy club on the Sunset Strip. During his senior year at USC, Singleton would go to the Store or the Regency West in Leimert Park where Torry did improv, and that's where they met.

Now, standing in the main room of the Comedy Store, Singleton locked eyes with the older man walking toward him. "You're John Singleton," the man said.

"Who wants to know?"

"My name is David Brooks. I'm an associate of Richard Pryor's," he said. "Mr. Richard Pryor would like to meet you."

Singleton gasped. He gripped Torry's shoulder. Seeing Pryor in the flesh transported him back to childhood. His mother's house. Rummaging through her record collection. Delicately placing the record on the phonograph so not to smudge the vinyl. Lowering the volume. Leaning into the speakers to hear Richard. Praying he didn't get caught.

Slowly, Singleton walked across the club.

Though the multiple sclerosis had taken hold, Pryor still possessed an aura about him. On this night, Al Pacino sat at the comedian's table. Yet as Singleton approached them, he barely blinked an eye at Michael Corleone.

Pryor drew Singleton in close. "You're the young man that made that movie," he whispered.

"Yes, sir."

Pryor embraced him as tightly as his muscles allowed him to.

Singleton hugged him back just as hard. Then he buried his head on Pryor's shoulder and sobbed.

While roaming the Sony lot in Culver City with friends, he mustered the courage to visit Stage Twenty-Seven, where Steven Spielberg was shooting his Peter Pan update *Hook*. Singleton walked past the *Jolly Roger*, the giant pirate ship constructed for the film, and scanned the set. Finally, he spotted Spielberg speaking on a cell phone.

"Go talk to him," his friends said.

"Nah, man, it might look like he's on break but he's working," Singleton said. "I can't."

Spielberg hung up the phone.

Singleton fidgeted, wrung his hands, and then adjusted his baseball cap. "Fuck it, I'm going to talk to him," he said, and marched toward the director. On the way, he bypassed Robin Williams, who Singleton later said in an interview seemed to turn and walk in the other direction when he noticed a handful of Black kids coming his way.

"South Central Cinema," Spielberg said, pointing at Singleton's hat. "Is that USC?"

"Yeah, I went to USC," he said. "Hi, my name is John Singleton."

Spielberg stuck out his hand.

Singleton wisely decided not to tell Spielberg a story about watching *Raiders of the Lost Ark* in the movie theater as a thirteen-year-old. "I was at Mann's Chinese Theatre," Singleton said years later in an interview. "I'm watching it, and I had to go to the bathroom. But I didn't want to leave, you know what I mean? So I took this cup—this lemonade cup—and I pissed in the cup. But when I reached down to piss in the cup, it was the first time I noticed I had pubic hair. While I was watching *Raiders of the Lost Ark* I realized I had my first pubic hair! I became a man watching *Raiders of the Lost Ark*!"

They had lunch a few weeks later. "Ricky's death was devastating. I felt like a fly on the wall in that room," Spielberg said. "That's my favorite scene in the picture. The way you captured that pain and confusion and hurt and disappointment . . .

"Make sure your stuff looks as rough as possible for as long as possible," Spielberg added before leaving.

Coppola had similar advice for Singleton when he received him on the set of *Bram Stoker's Dracula*. "Write as many films as you can, keep them personal, and make films that you're passionate about," the *Godfather* director said.

Almost everyone in the business was intrigued by him and welcomed him with open arms. They loved his enthusiasm, his boyishness, his candor. He spoke no differently around Coppola than he did around Fatbacc—with little filter and boundless curiosity.

In meetings everyone nodded along to his ideas and catered to his whims even when he sounded naïve or bratty. No longer did he scream and shout about his own brilliance. Others did it for him.

While he still dressed in Spike Lee cosplay—the glasses, the Malcolm X medallions, the baseball jerseys, the self-promoting hats and varsity jackets—the industry eyed him as the anti-Spike. Based in New York, Lee shunned Tinseltown events and refused to join the Directors Guild. He was an outsider. Singleton, Los Angeles born and raised, graduated from the studio feeder system known as USC Film School and arranged for Sidney Poitier and Barbra Streisand to sponsor his Directors Guild application.

Creatively, his work was revolutionary, but his aims and intentions were not. Blowing up the studio system didn't appeal to him. He loved the studio system. For now, at least. Although he still idolized Lee, he termed Spielberg his "idol of idols" and hoped to emulate his career as a commercial filmmaker.

Columbia felt a great deal of pride to be in business with him. The studio bought ads in the trades touting their relationship and the three-picture deal they had signed him to. They showed appreciation in other ways too. One afternoon, the top honchos at the studio called him into a meeting. There, they handed him a check for a million dollars.

Singleton smirked and said, "I thought there'd be a car outside. I wanted a car."

"It was so funny," Allain says. "It didn't mean anything to him, because he wanted that old-fashioned Hollywood thing where they handed him car keys."

Singleton remembered it differently. "It was these three white men—course they all were white—and they handed me a check for, like, a large amount of money, okay? Large. And they were all waiting in there to see how I would react to it, like this nigger's gonna come in here and he's gonna jump up and down and say *I'm gonna buy me a Mercedes*! Another studio executive, a Black woman, said everybody had a bet on what kind of car I was going to buy. So, you know what I did? I didn't buy a car. They handed me a check and I said, 'When's the next one coming?'"

While his career was hitting peaks he could not have imagined, his relationship with Maxwell was coming to its end.

The split saddened colleagues from the film, though some saw it coming. "They had this stormy on-again, off-again relationship," Stephanie Allain says. "But I thought John and Melissa were made for each other."

Singleton still spoke of producing Maxwell's script about an interracial group of women in Los Angeles. Nothing came of it. In a *Los Angeles Times* article about up-and-coming women filmmakers, Maxwell said that she was raising funds for a short film. She also intended to pitch a television series for kids that tackled "contemporary urban issues." Eventually, she codirected a 1993 film about the LA riots, *The Fire This Time*. Press material referred to her as "John Singleton's creative associate from start to finish on *Boyz N the Hood*."

Following their breakup, Singleton's wandering eye could wander with freedom. There were more women than he could handle, though he tried his best to accommodate all of them, including the prime-time TV star and the singer in that one R&B group.

He always wanted to be a player but hadn't been capable of it until now.

"When I was in college, I was a bookworm," he said. "I would've been happy dating the fat girl." Then, post–*Boyz N the Hood*, "I had different choices of girls. I was happy for the attention."

For once in his life, women chased him.

The same questions popped into his head upon meeting someone new: *Does she want me for me? Does she want money? Does she want a role? Does she want a baby?*

Still, he embraced his new, uninhibited social life. Tall. Short. Light-skinned. Dark-skinned. Long hair. Natural hair. Skinny. Thick. He loved them all and wanted to please them all.

"A friend of mine who became intimate with him would say that he worked harder than any man she had ever been with," says Leslie Segar, a dancer and media personality from New York nicknamed Big Lez. "We think that pretty men or popular men are lazy. She was like, 'Oh no, he put in some work.' I guess his reputation was important to him in that sense."

He still had a chip on his shoulder. His insecurity about certain things—his height, his thinning hair, his slight build, especially when compared to his dad—made him self-aware enough to know his high batting average with the ladies wasn't on account of his looks. He never had a proper glow-up. No one suddenly considered him cute or hot. He didn't think he was handsome.

He was the same John, except he wasn't. He was now *Boyz N the Hood* director John Singleton.

Even friendships changed. Though once on the periphery of his crew, Singleton emerged as its nucleus. A whole clique—better yet, an entourage—formed after *Boyz N the Hood*. For his old friends, being in his inner circle now meant access to parties and celebrities and the women who didn't interest him or whom he didn't have time for. Usually the latter. While he didn't pick up bills left and right, he took care of his people. He secured jobs for them. Posted bail once or twice. They crashed with him during hard times. He became the rich friend with the big house and famous friends.

He now lived in a 4,900-square-foot six-bedroom perched at the end of a cul-de-sac in Baldwin Hills, an affluent neighborhood nicknamed the Black Beverly Hills.

The house, which he purchased for around $700,000, reflected aspects of both the old and new Singleton. When the sun came up in the morning, he woke up on Spider-Man sheets. Stacks of comic books piled up against a wall. A cat named Whiteboy lurked. Bottles of Evian lined the shelves of his otherwise empty refrigerator.

He splurged on three personal computers, thousands of dollars in laser discs, and all the equipment needed, like top-of-the-line speakers. He upgraded from a tatty silver Peugeot to a Pathfinder. Once he got rich, his wardrobe changed too. Armani glasses. Fresh Nike sneakers. Suede jackets. In time, he grew out a goatee and rocked a beret.

Like most twenty-three-year-old men, he was a work in progress.

Singleton shaped his persona in public and through the press. In interviews, he pushed certain narratives while shrouding parts of his past, such as his itinerant teen years. He sidestepped some questions about the autobiographical elements of *Boyz N the Hood*. When asked about USC, he never mentioned his fraternity. He didn't discuss his love for pop idols Wham!

"Back in the '80s, John took my little sister on a date to the Wham! concert at the Forum," his childhood friend Carl Austin says. "My sister took a photo of him at the concert. He had on this big *Choose Life* T-shirt. After *Boyz N the Hood* came out, I joked with him about sending that photo to the tabloids. John was like, 'I will fuck you up.'"

He quickly established a brand as the outspoken, street-smart whiz kid, although *brand* wasn't a term used back then. People listened when he spoke and he had a lot to say about film, race, politics, relationships, and even fashion. Gianni Versace "has a good sense of pattern," he told the *New York Times*. If anything he became a purer, more distilled version of himself.

And that version—the John Singleton the public met in magazines and on television—was cool.

But everyone who knew John knew one thing about him: John wasn't cool. He made cool films, but he wasn't cool.

"There was John Singleton and then there was John," Adrianne Shropshire says. "Both of those personalities existed at the same time. There was this sort of externally facing John Singleton doing all the publicity and hanging out in clubs and going out with his boys and all these different women. That was John Singleton. Then there was John, who'd read his comic books and watch Kurosawa films. Both of those characters existed simultaneously."

★★★★★

The world couldn't wait to see what he'd do next. People close to him suggested slowing down but he wanted to get a film into production as soon as possible, as did Columbia. "My biggest fear was to be a flash in the pan," Singleton said. "All I wanted to do at that time was be a guy with a career, a veteran."

But first he took a detour into MTV land.

Late one night in the fall of 1991, Michael Jackson called Singleton's house.

"Is this John?" asked a familiar voice.

"Yeah," he said, wiping his eyes. "Who's this?"

"Michael."

"Michael who?"

"Michael Jackson. Yeah, um, I want you to direct my next video."

"Let's sit down," Singleton said, getting out of bed. "Let's talk about—"

Before he could finish, the line went dead. The next morning Singleton called his agent, Bradford Smith, about the bizarre phone call. He soon set up a meeting at the Bel-Air mansion of Jackson's manager Sandy Gallin.

Singleton grew up listening to Jackson's 45s and eating Jackson 5 cereal. As a fan, he followed him through the eras: from the hit-making Motown child star to the post-disco smash *Off the Wall* to the Reagan-era global icon of *Thriller* and *Bad*. Working with him would allow Singleton to invade pop culture in a wholly unique way for a movie director.

Starting with 1982's "Thriller," Jackson elevated music videos to the point where his were no longer referred to as music videos. His latest short film, "Black or White," ran eleven minutes and was budgeted at $8.5 million, or $2.5 million more than *Boyz N the Hood*. The clip combined innovative photorealistic face-morphing special effects and an all-star cast featuring Macaulay Culkin, Academy Award–nominated actress Tess Harper, and George Wendt, the actor better known as Norm from *Cheers*. A young model named Tyra Banks appeared during the closing face-morphing sequence.

Singleton walked into the meeting with his chest out and head high. He always knew he would meet Michael Jackson. Unlike his encounters with Pryor and Spielberg, he didn't get starstruck around the King of Pop.

Jackson asked for Singleton's opinion of his new album *Dangerous*.

"I like the tracks that are getting played on Black radio," he said.

"What about 'Black or White'?" Jackson asked.

"Eh."

"You didn't like it?"

"You always do this," Singleton said.

"Do what?"

"Come with the weakest song off the album as the first single and still win with it," he said. "You did it with *Thriller*. You did it with *Bad*. Now you're doing it again with 'Black or White.'"

"What did you think of the video?"

"It was all right, but I could do better."

Jackson and his label Epic Records, a Sony subsidiary, selected "Remember the Time" as the album's next single. A breezy blast of New Jack Swing, the Teddy Riley–produced record was Singleton's favorite song on *Dangerous*.

"What are your plans for the video?" Jackson asked him.

"I want to put you with a whole bunch of Black people," Singleton said. "If you want to hire me, it's going to be all Black."

They kicked around ideas until sketching out a basic concept. Ancient Egypt. A beautiful queen. A jealous pharoah. Jackson as the queen's charismatic, magical suitor. A chase scene. A dance sequence. Elaborate special effects. Celebrity cameos. A spectacle. In other words, a standard Michael Jackson video aside from the added political subtext that Singleton insisted on: depicting the ancient Egyptians as Black.

Jackson hesitated, but Singleton won him over.

They cast Eddie Murphy as Ramses and the supermodel Iman as Nefertiti.

"Find something for Magic," Jackson said, insisting Singleton procure a role for Magic Johnson, who had recently retired from the Los Angeles Lakers after publicly disclosing his HIV diagnosis. Johnson appeared as a palace guard in the video. Singleton also cast his friends Malcolm Norrington and Jimmy Ray (p/k/a Roman Artiste) as sentries.

One thing remained unclear to Singleton. "What did you think of *Boyz N the Hood*?" he asked Jackson.

"I don't like violent movies."

"Wait. You never saw my movie? Why'd you call me, then?"

"What phone call?"

"You called me at, like, three in the morning."

"I never called you," Jackson said, laughing.

(Singleton soon learned that his friend Lloyd Avery II, aka the Blood who shot Ricky, had prank-called him impersonating Michael Jackson.)

Shot over two weeks on Soundstage Twelve on the Universal lot, the $3.9 million short film dwarfed *Boyz N the Hood* in terms of scale and star power. Singleton's first time on a soundstage involved working with camels, elephants, eagles, jugglers, fire-eaters, twenty-five dancers choreographed by Singleton's friend—the twenty-year-old wunderkind Fatima Robinson—multiple cranes, multiple cameras, and any technical toy he wanted.

David Bowie stood to the side on days his wife, Iman, filmed. Elizabeth Taylor visited the set. Sometimes Michael showed up late. Sometimes he wouldn't show up. Sometimes he'd leave early. At one point he fell and bloodied his face, halting production for a few days. Once he returned, he lit a stink bomb on the soundstage. On the day Jackson ate lunch with Singleton and the crew, he spent most of the meal rhapsodizing over his current obsession: *Innerspace*, a four-year-old sci-fi film starring Dennis Quaid and Meg Ryan.

Though beloved by its fans, the nine-minute "Remember the Time" video arrived during a turning point in Jackson's career. He faced blowback for the "Black or White" video—the crotch-grabbing; the weird aggression (destroying a car with a crowbar). *Entertainment Weekly* put him on the cover with the headline: "Michael Jackson's Video Nightmare." The controversy felt inescapable. Jackson felt inescapable. Overexposed. The tabloids were obsessed with him. After over twenty years of dominance, critics—and a good segment of the public—turned on Jackson.

"An air of desperate extravagance" is how the *New York Times* music critic Jon

Pareles described the "Remember the Time" video. "When Mr. Jackson's single 'Black or White' was released in November, Fox television followed the premiere of the video clip with a nearly wordless 'special' showing innumerable screaming Jackson fans. MTV followed the premiere of 'Remember the Time' with a Jackson 'rockumentary' called 'More Dangerous Than Ever,' including unenlightening glimpses of the making of the video clip. But most of the half-hour program was a similar montage of fans, celebrity endorsements, impressive dance bits and statistics about Mr. Jackson's record-breaking career, as if to remind viewers how very, very famous and important he is."

More of a concern: The emergence of hip-hop and grunge rock made Jackson's pop perfection look manufactured, hollow, and bloated. About a month before "Remember the Time" premiered on February 2, 1992, Nirvana's *Nevermind* supplanted *Dangerous* as the biggest album in the country.

★★★★★

On February 19, 1992, Singleton woke up in his Las Vegas hotel room a little before five thirty a.m. to find out if he had made history. In a few minutes, the Academy Awards nominations would be announced.

Over the past few months, Columbia had mounted an aggressive Oscar campaign for *Boyz N the Hood*, sending voters a package including a VHS copy of the film, the official soundtrack, and, in a nod to the Academy's very old and very white membership, a letter explaining hip-hop and its importance to the film.

Awards season had been quiet. Singleton didn't receive a Directors Guild nomination and the film had been shut out of the Golden Globes, typically an Oscar harbinger. For weeks, Oscar pundits predicted the five Best Director nominees would mirror the DGA selections: Barry Levinson (*Bugsy*), Oliver Stone (*JFK*), Barbra Streisand (*The Prince of Tides*), Jonathan Demme (*The Silence of the Lambs*), and Ridley Scott (*Thelma & Louise*).

At 5:38 a.m. the actors Karl Malden and Kathleen Turner revealed the nominees for Best Director.

Turner, in her deep, husky voice, then began, "In the category of best achievement in directing: *Boyz N the Hood*, John Singleton . . ." The assembled press gasped. Singleton also scored a nomination for Best Original Screenplay.

Back in Vegas, Singleton immediately called his mom. "Mom, your baby boy was nominated for two Oscars this morning," he said.

At twenty-four years and forty-four days old, he became the youngest person ever nominated for Best Director, eclipsing Orson Welles, who was twenty-six years and 279 days old in 1942, when he earned a nomination for *Citizen Kane.* Singleton also became the first Black person nominated for Best Director, which felt bittersweet. "I always felt like I got nominated because Spike was passed over for *Do the Right Thing,*" he said, citing the uproar that followed Lee's snub in 1990.

In any other year, Singleton's feat would've been the talk of the industry. Instead, the biggest story in Hollywood that morning was Streisand's omission amongst the Best Director nominees. Streisand, who had been overlooked in 1984 for her directorial debut *Yentl,* would've been the second woman nominated in the category. That *The Prince of Tides* received seven nominations, including Best Picture, elicited greater sympathy for her.

Later that day, Mark Canton, the new chairman of Columbia, released a statement denouncing the Academy's decision. "It is truly shocking Barbra Streisand was overlooked as a best director nominee," Canton said. "A film cannot be so distinguished in so many areas unless it directly reflects the vision of the director." Canton failed to congratulate, or even mention, Singleton in his remarks.

Columbia marketing president Paula Silver ended up as the scapegoat for the Streisand snub, amongst other things. "They blamed me for everything that went wrong," says Silver, who resigned in April 1992. "That year, I'd get blamed if the sun didn't shine." A source told the *Los Angeles Times* that Silver's "tempestuous dealings" with Streisand, Singleton, and director Barbet Schroeder (*Reversal of Fortune*) contributed to her ouster.

Later that day, Singleton moved across the floor at ShoWest, the annual Vegas convention that was equal parts trade show, Comic-Con, and Davos Forum, between filmmakers, exhibitors, and distributors, stopping every few steps to receive congratulations. He then came across one of his fellow nominees: Oliver Stone.

As a freshman, Singleton had approached Stone after a screening of *Platoon* at USC. "You're going to win an Academy Award for this!" Singleton exclaimed. Stone captured Best Director, and the Vietnam epic won Best Picture at the 59th Academy Awards. Three years later, Stone won another Best Director prize, this time for *Born on the Fourth of July.* Now they were peers, or so Singleton thought.

"I loved *JFK,*" he gushed, hailing Stone's three-hour-plus thriller. Stone had been pilloried in political circles for depicting the Kennedy assassination as a coup d'état to expand the Vietnam War. But as the son of Danny Singleton, John willingly embraced conspiracy theories. "You looked at history from a unique point of view. Hopefully, the country gets to a place where alternative points of view will be more accepted."

Stone looked directly at Singleton and shrugged. "Yeah," he said, "too bad about Barbra," and walked away.

"That fucking pissed me off," Singleton later said. "As if it's my fault Barbra Streisand didn't get nominated."

On March 30, 1992, Singleton, wearing a traditional tuxedo accented with an African-print bow tie, walked the red carpet outside the Dorothy Chandler Pavilion with his girlfriend, Tosha Lewis. "I tried to act nonchalant about it," he said. "But I was exploding inside with excitement to actually be there and be nominated for two Oscars."

He was featured prominently throughout the night, starting with being namedropped during host Billy Crystal's opening monologue. "We also have the youngest writer/director ever nominated, John Singleton" was the setup. Singleton stifled a smile as the camera cut to him. Then the punchline: "John, of course, directed and wrote *Boyz N the Hood—The David Duke Story*," Crystal said, referring to the former Grand Wizard of the Ku Klux Klan who ran for governor of Louisiana a few months earlier.

Singleton then presented Best Documentary and Best Documentary, Short Subject, with Spike Lee.

"I don't know that I was nervous," Singleton said years later. "But I felt like I was put on display. We just looked at each other like, 'Okay, let's go out and do this thing.' "

In the end, Singleton left empty-handed. He thought he had an outside chance at Best Original Screenplay, but the award went to Callie Khouri for *Thelma & Louise*. Best Director seemed like a long shot from the start. That window closed once it became apparent the night belonged to *The Silence of the Lambs*. The horror thriller became just the third film, and the first since *One Flew Over the Cuckoo's Nest* in 1976, to sweep the Big Five categories: Picture, Directing, Actor, Actress, and Screenplay, winning for Best Adapted Screenplay.

Singleton punched the air and pumped his fist when presenter Kevin Costner announced Demme as the winner.

They had stayed friends since Demme tried to produce *Boyz N the Hood* and Demme acknowledged Singleton during his acceptance speech when he called attention to the Black and female directors who had burst onto the scene in 1991.

"I want very much to salute John Singleton and Matty Rich and Jodie Foster, and Ernest Dickerson and a bunch of new people that in the last year that have come on with very exciting, wonderful visions, and really breathed tremendous important new life into our whole cinematic landscape—and I really want to salute those people, very strongly," Demme said.

Earlier in the evening, Singleton watched another familiar face honored when the Rob Fried–produced film *Session Man* won Best Live Action Short. Though it had been nearly two years since Fried missed out on producing *Boyz N the Hood* it was at the top of his mind when he accepted his Oscar. "John sat in the first or second row," Fried says, "and I stared right at him as I made my speech. I made my acceptance speech to John Singleton because I felt he wronged me after I had taken care of him."

Singleton felt somewhat relieved when the night was over, once he had departed Irving "Swifty" Lazar's Oscar party at Spago. He was deep in pre-production on his new film, *Poetic Justice*, but a slew of challenges lay ahead. In a few hours, he'd attend the first read-through. Principal photography started in just over two weeks, and his script still needed work. Singleton would also have to manage his new leading man, a volatile twenty-year-old rapper turned actor named Tupac Shakur.

# CHAPTER NINE

In the fall of 1990, while Singleton was still in production on *Boyz N the Hood*, one of his childhood friends deployed to the Middle East as part of Operation Desert Shield.

As war became more and more inevitable, Singleton grew upset. He concocted an idea for a script about a young soldier and his wife, a nineteen-year-old poet named Justice, living on an army base somewhere in Japan . . . or the Philippines . . . or maybe the Pacific Northwest.

Quickly, he realized he didn't know much about the armed forces or life on a base. He'd have to conduct research. But he didn't have enough time for that. He wanted to start writing immediately. So he stuck to what he knew and moved the story to a beauty salon on Crenshaw.

Switching locations was the first in a series of shortcuts Singleton made on *Poetic Justice*, an unfocused, meandering film that slowed his career momentum and chipped away at his reputation.

"I always felt like he got lazy on the script and was sort of bored on set," says Steve Nicolaides, who coproduced the film with Singleton. "This movie really disappoints me because he had everything. He could have done anything. I think that celebrity and wealth—but mostly celebrity—sort of got in his way."

In the end, he couldn't escape the sophomore jinx. He started writing the screenplay while still working on *Boyz N the Hood* but never devoted his full attention to it amid his *Boyz* commitments (postproduction, Cannes, and press) and the distractions that followed.

Throughout the spring and summer of 1991, Singleton tabled *Poetic Justice* until finishing the script in a three-week burst that lacked the creative verve that guided *Boyz N the Hood* to the finish line within a similar time frame. "I just wanted to get another movie out as quickly as possible," he said. Later in life, he regretted rushing the film into production. But in the moment he felt obligated to push forward.

On January 7, 1991, the morning after his twenty-third birthday, he woke up at four thirty a.m. His brain refused to rest. He couldn't shake the thought: *What happens after a gangbanger gets killed? What's the fallout for his girlfriend? Where does she go from there?* He opened his notebook and jotted down his main character's new backstory: *The whole story will spring forth from the effect of her boyfriend getting killed in front of her. The movie will be about how she learned how to love again.*

He recalled a story that Dedrick D. Gobert, Dooky from *Boyz N the Hood*, told him about his job at the post office. Sometimes, when he drove his mail truck from Los Angeles to Las Vegas for work, he'd bring along a friend and two girls and make it a road trip.

*What sort of girl would do that?* he thought. *They'd have to be straight-up homegirls.*

From there, the plot took shape with the story moving from South Central to State Route 1 to Oakland. Along the way, Justice and the postman driving the truck fall in love. A classic road picture where the leads are transformed during their journey.

From the start, though, he struggled with writing from a woman's perspective. He asked for help. Sometimes he'd flesh out scenes on the phone with Stephanie Allain or Tyra Ferrell. He'd often talk it out with his female friends.

They were concerned he wasn't mature enough to handle the subject matter. As a twenty-three-year-old man, he had blind spots. He relied too much on his own experiences with women. "Who are you talking to, to draw on these things?" his friend Adrianne Shropshire asked after he came to her for advice.

"Girls," Singleton said. "Girls I know. Girls I'm friends with. Girlfriends."

"If you're going to do a composite of the struggles of Black women in LA, you have to talk to a wide range of people."

"I know what I'm doing."

"This is not your experience," she stressed. "You have to be careful about projecting your shit—your perspective of women onto these characters. Besides, aren't there any women writers or directors who can tell this story?"

"I can tell this story."

He marched forward and weighed casting options. Initially, he considered Monica Calhoun for the role of Justice. A young actress best known for the indie film *Bagdad Cafe*, Calhoun came close to playing Brandi in *Boyz N the Hood*.

Then one day when visiting the set of *Hook*, he ran into Janet Jackson; TriStar president Mike Medavoy regularly gave tours of the set to A-listers such as Jackson,

Prince, Warren Beatty, Kevin Costner, and Singleton, who dropped in a few times.

"I'm writing a movie for you, and I think you'd be good for it," Singleton said to Jackson. He told the press that they had briefly met a decade earlier when they both attended Portola Junior High in Tarzana.

"Oh, really?" she said. "What is it?"

"It's called *Poetic Justice*. It's a street romance," Singleton said, launching into his pitch. "This is what we're going to do: You're going to give me your number and I'm going to call you when I finish the script."

They exchanged numbers. With a spring in this step, he got back to writing.

He finished the script in August. Jackson read it and loved it, just as she loved *Boyz N the Hood*. But it wasn't a done deal. "I was warned by powerful forces in Hollywood that an all-Black movie was the wrong move," she told *Rolling Stone*. "Conventional wisdom said I should make a musical. Go for the mainstream white market. Play it safe."

Singleton then met with Jackson and her representatives. "Janet has to do this movie," he said.

"Why should we listen to you?" one of her reps said. "What do you think you can do for her career?"

"Listen," Singleton said. "When Janet comes out with her next album it'll sell a couple million, no question. But what if she comes out with a movie at the same time? What do you think she'll sell then? Also, if you do a song for it, you might get an Academy Award nomination for Best Original Song."

Jackson wasn't a natural fit for the role of Justice. What did she know about hardship and trauma? She grew up rich and famous in Encino as the baby of the royal Jackson family. Supporting roles on the sitcoms *Good Times* and *Diff'rent Strokes* helped turn her into America's Sweetheart. All the while, she dabbled in music. But her career languished until linking with the producers Jimmy Jam and Terry Lewis. Together they collaborated on the five-times-platinum album *Control*. Jackson's most recent effort, *Janet Jackson's Rhythm Nation 1814*, was an artistic leap forward that sold another six million copies. She spent all of 1990 crisscrossing the globe on the most successful debut tour ever for an artist, playing to over two million fans. Shortly after getting off the road, Jackson signed the largest record deal in history, a three-album $40 million contract with Virgin Records.

Singleton had no concern about her ability to handle such a dramatic role. He knew Jackson had depth she could pull from. As Joe Jackson's daughter, she endured hardship and trauma. At the age of eighteen, she married the singer James DeBarge, a childhood friend, in an attempt to abscond from her dad's domineering presence both in her personal and professional life. Marriage was no picnic either, though. DeBarge had a serious drug problem. It was not uncommon for Jackson to roam the streets of Los Angeles searching for him when he disappeared on one of his binges. She soon got an annulment. In March 1991, a few weeks before running into Singleton on the Sony lot, she secretly married her creative adviser René Elizondo Jr.

Immediately, Singleton set out to transform the rich pop star into a hairdresser from the hood.

"You have a homework assignment: Rent Vittorio De Sica's *Two Women*," he told her. "It's an Italian film about a widow and her daughter in World War II."

Sophia Loren's portrayal of Cesira in the neorealist classic was his lodestar for Jackson's Justice. "She was a really glamorous woman. But this is an unglamorous role," he said to Jackson. "She doesn't wear any makeup in it. It was great for her image and she won an Oscar for it."

Singleton asked Jackson to gain about ten pounds for the role and suggested she spend time in a South Central salon observing the stylists. He tapped his friends, the dancers Fatima Robinson, Leslie Segar, Jossie Harris, and Tish Oliver, to tutor Jackson in hood etiquette.

"We were just so rough, rugged, and raw. John was like, 'You bitches are crazy. You need to hang with Janet, because that's the kind of essence I need,'" Segar says. "We moved in with Janet for about a month and got her to come out of her shell."

Singleton needed someone who could hold his own opposite Janet's star power and sexuality. Someone who wouldn't be intimated. He turned to Ice Cube.

"I can't do no romance," Cube said when Singleton offered him the role. "I'm no sex symbol, man."

"Don't you know bitches like you?" Singleton said. "You're a good-looking dude."

"I can't do that shit, man. Not at this point in my career."

"That's exactly why you should do it!" he said.

Cube didn't budge, leaving Singleton still in search of a leading man.

Singleton was eating a bowl of Honey Smacks when he found him.

One night in early 1992, he was in his Baldwin Hills home channel surfing when he flipped to BET. *Live from LA with Tanya Hart.* Tanya's guest: Tupac Shakur, promoting his new movie *Juice.* Singleton had met the rapper a few months earlier at a party for Queen Latifah at Big City Diner, a club on the west side of Manhattan.

He turned up the volume. Singleton's eyebrows arched as Tupac fired shots at the most famous entertainers in the world.

"I'm talking about Spike Lee, Arsenio Hall, Eddie Murphy, and the rest of them—Michael Jackson, Randy Jackson, Janet Jackson, all of them. Paula Abdul, she wants to not be Black, but she wants to sell to Black folks," Tupac said. "I don't appreciate that. I don't appreciate her going out of her way to say she's not Black."

Hart cut to commercial. "Whoo," Singleton shouted, pacing his living room. Tupac continued his rant after the break.

"All the ghetto people that want to know if Spike is down. No, he ain't down. Not to me. He need to check himself because he needs to stop disrespecting Black women in his films," Tupac said. "Eddie Murphy, with all that dough he's making, has done nothing for us."

He went on. "I want them to check they self. I want them to hear this young Black male checking them and then they can check they self. It's not a diss thing."

Singleton dropped his spoon into the bowl of milk and gawked at the television. Tupac lounging in an unzipped velour sweatsuit, black backward hat, gold chains shining against his smooth chest. Relaxed. Confident. Sexy. Provocative. *Where is this coming from?* Singleton thought. When he caught a sneak preview of *Juice* a few months back, he left thinking Tupac had a future as a leading man. But this interview—*phew!* This was Pac's true breakout performance. *That's who I need to fucking work with*, he thought.

"He could be dangerous. He could be romantic. Tupac was the perfect embodiment of young Black manhood at that time," Singleton said years later. "When I'm casting brothers, I'm always trying to find people who are men. A lot of these actors are so actorish. They preen just as much as actresses. I want the men in my movies to be men."

Singleton considered Shakur, who was born in 1971, a fellow "revolutionary baby," his term for Black men born in the late '60s and early '70s, in the immediate aftermath of the Civil Rights Movement. "We were built for the betterment of our people," Singleton said.

Rebellion flowed through Tupac, a Panther Cub, whose parents were both members of the Black Panther Party; Afeni Shakur was eight months pregnant with him when she was acquitted in the Panther 21 trial. Born in Harlem, Tupac grew up around revolutionaries who had a specific way of looking at life and dealing with the world. Assata Shakur and Geronimo Pratt were his godparents. His stepfather was Mutulu Shakur.

Afeni struggled with drug addiction. The family became homeless. In 1984, they moved to Baltimore, where Pac attended the prestigious Baltimore School for the Arts, and he gravitated toward acting. From a young age, he took the craft seriously. In one of his early plays, a school performance of Sam Shepard's *Fool for Love*, he smuggled a real gun onstage and swigged tequila from a bottle.

Once he moved to the Bay Area in 1988, he focused more on rapping than acting. Eventually, he hooked up with the eclectic hip-hop group Digital Underground. He contributed any which way he could. Store runs. Carrying records. Hauling equipment. Putting on a Speedo and humping a blow-up doll onstage. Roadie work, basically. He was game as long as he progressed. Soon, Shock G, the leader of the collective, gave him a shot on the mic. "Same Song," off the *Nothing but Trouble* soundtrack, announced his arrival as an MC in the summer of 1991.

Around this time, Spike Lee's cinematographer Ernest Dickerson was auditioning rappers to fill out the cast of his directorial debut *Juice*, a gritty drama about four Harlem teens. One of the first people brought in was Digital Underground's Money-B to read for the role of Steel. Tupac had helped him run lines and tagged along on the day of his audition. While sitting in the waiting room, Pac flipped through the sides. *I need to do this*, he thought. Once casting director Jaki Brown emerged, he made his move, and asked to read for Bishop, the film's hothead with heart.

Though *Juice*'s co-writer Gerard Brown had pictured Bishop as someone "physically bigger and more imposing," Tupac embodied the character from the moment he walked in the room. "I was blown away," Jaki Brown said. "He was so perfect that it was scary."

"Bishop is damaged," Dickerson said. "It was easy to get the more dangerous aspects of Bishop's personality, but there had to be a vulnerability in the middle of that. Bishop's whole deal was coming from the great deal of pain he had on the inside. I think Tupac understood that."

He stole the movie with his portrayal of Bishop, one of the great cinematic villains of that era.

*Juice* was a modest hit when released in January 1992. Afterward, the lines between fact and fiction, real and make-believe, started to blur for Tupac. Some people close to him at the time believe he lived the gimmick, suddenly taking on the guise of Bishop in a way that fundamentally changed both his public persona and who he was at his core.

"I took him to the Paramount lot to go see *Juice*. He came out of that theater and was never the same again," said Allen Hughes, who along with his twin brother, Albert, directed Tupac's earliest music videos. "He became utterly obsessed with thug life and with anything that related to becoming that Bishop character. Whether it was getting more tattoos, getting in altercations. He wanted to be that character. He saw in that moment, *This is how I'm going to be a star.*"

Tupac always had a little Bishop in him, though. While on the set of *Juice*, he carelessly shot full-charged blanks into the air, endangering his costars. He walked off the movie on multiple occasions. Once, while on a break, he flirted with a woman even after her boyfriend showed up. After an extra broke into his trailer and stole his jewelry, he recruited his friend, a six-foot-eight-inch bruiser named Randy "Stretch" Walker to find the perpetrator. A few hours later they stomped out the thief at an intersection in broad daylight.

"Tupac had the hottest temper I'd ever seen," says *Juice* producer Neal H. Moritz. "I said to him early on, 'If you don't get that temper under control you're going to die.'"

Singleton had heard all the rumors. Before offering Shakur the role of Lucky, *Poetic Justice*'s sensitive romantic lead, he reached out to Dickerson to kick the tires on him.

When he finally met with Shakur, they instantly hit it off. "I'm not looking at this as a one-off. We're going to grow together. I want us to make multiple movies together," Singleton said. "You're going to be the De Niro to my Scorsese."

"I'm with it," Tupac said. He recognized the opportunity before him. Janet Jackson. John Singleton. A leading role. An opportunity to flex his acting chops, to show the world he could be more than Bishop.

"I have to tell you, though, man," Singleton said, "fuck all the rapping shit."

"What?"

"You're better at acting than rapping," Singleton said. "I mean, you're an okay rapper. You're all right. But as an actor—fuck, man, when I say you can be Robert De Niro I ain't playing."

"I appreciate it," Pac said. "But fuck you. Music is my heart."

Once Pac aced a screen test with Jackson, Singleton had his leads for *Poetic Justice*. He filled out the cast with *Boyz N the Hood* alums Regina King and Tyra

Ferrell. Lloyd Avery II was once again Singleton's Angel of Death—Avery's character, Thug #1, kills Justice's boyfriend (played by Q-Tip of A Tribe Called Quest) in the film's opening scene. For the role of King's boyfriend, Chicago, he turned to Joe Torry.

His greatest casting coup was recruiting the poet Maya Angelou to contribute her poems to the film; Angelou also appeared in a cameo as Aunt June, one of three wise old ladies, at a family reunion scene.

Once Singleton realized he couldn't write poetry, he reached out to Angelou. Brad Smith then set up a screening of *Boyz N the Hood* in Winston-Salem for her and a group of friends. Angelou loved the film. A face-to-face meeting was arranged through Congresswoman Maxine Waters. Per Sheila's suggestion, Singleton gifted Angelou a single rose upon arriving. The charm offensive worked. "I saw at once the intelligence of the man," Angelou said. "It's the rare person who has the intelligence, the discipline, the forthrightness, and the perseverance to architect a dream. I could sense this in him."

With his dream cast assembled, he turned his attention to rehearsals. The first read-through was scheduled for the morning after the Academy Awards in a warehouse down the block from the production office. The cast arrived, shared hugs, and congratulated each other.

Singleton, shoulders slumped and his voice a little softer than usual, stood in front of the cast. "Since I didn't win last night, I'm going to give y'all the acceptance speech I had prepared," he joked.

After the laughter subsided, he continued, "Filmmaking is not an exact science. There's no set path to follow. All I'm going to ask of you is that each and every one of you get into who you are as characters and don't worry about what other people are doing. If you come up with something that you think is integral to the scene, don't be afraid to come up to me. I'm open to suggestions—I think only fools are not. I just want to cut through all that mire. We're going to have a great time, and in the end, I think you'll all be satisfied with the work we've done."

Singleton's pep talk inspired the actors, yet Nicolaides and Allain felt the script needed more passes. With principal photography scheduled to begin in two weeks, it was too late to hit the brakes. Columbia wasn't pushing its start date to doctor the script.

The studio had undergone more turnover since *Boyz N the Hood* was released the previous summer. In October 1991, Mark Canton, a former Warner Bros. executive, replaced Frank Price, who had overseen the studio's comeback. Price's drawn-out public ouster was an embarrassment to the company and, once again, it slowed down the production slate. But Canton, a fast-talking well-dressed executive from Queens, was hired, in part, to be the anti–Frank Price. "I'm not slow-moving," he said at the time. "I'm not going to come in walking, but I won't drive the car off the road, either."

The result?

"John got a blank check," Allain says. "He didn't want to work on the script much more and once he got Janet and Tupac he didn't have to. Mark was like, 'Great, let's make the movie.' When I complained that we needed to give John more notes, it was like, 'Eh, I think he's earned the right to just go do it.'"

Singleton had built enough capital with the studio to do whatever he wanted, and what he wanted was to rush *Poetic Justice* into production—even though he knew the script needed work. "The movie wasn't ready to go," he admitted years later. "But I could've turned in the phone book and they would've told me, 'Here's fifteen million dollars. Go make the movie!'"

This was John 2.0.

Everything felt a little more polished, a little more Hollywood. Singleton now wore a beret and dark round sunglasses like the specs John Lennon rocked. On the set, the backs of everyone's chairs read *POETIC JUSTICE: BACK TO THE HOOD*. Whereas Columbia executives didn't dare visit the South Central set of *Boyz N the Hood*, *Poetic Justice* was the place to see and be seen. Canton and Michael Nathanson dropped by, trailed by a photographer, no less, to shoot them for a book titled *A Day in the Life of Hollywood*. Oprah Winfrey even came to film an episode of her daytime talk show.

"A month into shooting, the barrage of visitors continues, press, industry, and financial-types, hangers-on and hopefuls, most of them gunning for Singleton" is how reporter Veronica Chambers framed the scene in an article that ran in the test issue of *Vibe*, Quincy Jones's new magazine covering Black culture. Chambers shadowed Singleton throughout the film's lifespan for the book *Poetic Justice: Filmmaking South Central Style*.

Singleton made a few changes in his crew from *Boyz*, most notably replacing Charles Mills with Peter Lyons Collister, his director of photography on "Remember the Time." He felt Mills was a bit too traditional compared to Collister, who cut his teeth on flashy commercials and music videos.

Before production started, Singleton shared his vision for the film. "I don't want it to look like a Hollywood movie. I don't want you wetting down the streets on set," he said. "I don't want that shit. That's Hollywood. This film isn't going to be any good if it looks like some glossy Hollywood movie."

Once he arrived on set, it was a new Singleton. A sign posted on his trailer read DO NOT DISTURB, KNOCK, OR NONE OF THAT SHIT.

"Everything about him was different," says the actor John Cothran (*Boyz N the Hood* and *Poetic Justice*). "John suddenly had money. He had glasses that fit. He had clothes that fit. He had someone there with his orange juice, and he had taken on the façade of this place."

After Singleton set up a shot, he'd retreat out of sight or find a corner and crack open a book, like *Rising Sun* by Michael Crichton.

Once, before a scene in the salon, the actor Roger Guenveur Smith had questions about timing, when to turn and give Tyra Ferrell a certain look.

"Where's John?" Nicolaides fumed.

"He's in his trailer," said Peter Ramsey, the storyboard artist and second unit director. He found Singleton on his couch playing video games.

"John, if you have some time, can we talk this scene over?" Ramsey said.

"No, I think they got it," he said, not looking up.

"Are you sure?"

"It's all good."

Singleton had other things on his mind. He recently learned his that his girlfriend, Tosha Lewis, was pregnant.

He'd met Lewis, a sophomore in college, through her cousin a few months earlier. It wasn't love at first sight for Tosha and John. On their first date, he squired the journalism major to a newsstand on Robertson Boulevard. He picked up a magazine and flipped through it until finding the article on him. "Read it," he said.

Decades later, in an Instagram post, Lewis recalled their first date as a disaster. She said she found Singleton's ego repellent. But eventually it was what made her fall in love with him.

Singleton later said he fell in love with her in part for her taste in movies. One night, at his house in Baldwin Hills, he asked her to pick a movie from his hundreds of laser discs. She selected *Citizen Kane*; Lewis had recently finished an autobiography of Rita Hayworth, Welles's ex-wife, and was curious about the film she'd read so much about.

He invited her to the set of "Remember the Time" and put her in costume as one of the ancient Egyptians. Two months later, Lewis, radiant in a pink gown, would be his date to the Oscars.

From the start though, they had a volatile relationship. Friends remember seeing them argue in public. "We all met Tosha. She was standoffish," says a friend. "He liked bad girls. John thought it was cute when she was being a bitch to us." When approached during the making of this book, Lewis did not respond to requests for comment.

In the spring of 1992, Singleton learned that she was pregnant.

On the set of *Poetic Justice*, he shared the news. One day, his friend Adrianne Shropshire visited him. "I got to tell you something," he said when he saw her. "Later."

When the crew broke for lunch, they went to a secluded spot between trailers, and he shared his secret.

"Dude, you have a job to do," she exclaimed. "Just tell me what you need to tell me, because you have to focus on this film."

"I'm having a baby," he said.

"What? Really? Now?" she said. "All of this in the middle of everything that's happening? You are just adding pressure to your life. We should talk about this later because you're directing a film right now. Also, congratulations."

He had already told members of his crew. "I want to have as many kids as I possibly can," he told Collister and Don Wilkerson during a location scout. "I want twenty to thirty kids."

Wilkerson scowled at him. "John, that is the dumbest thing I've ever heard," he said. "That's not a reason to have kids."

His work suffered, and Columbia noticed. "The studio was questioning what was happening. The dailies didn't look so great," says Columbia marketing executive Sid Ganis. Jackson's performance was of particular concern. "It was soft. It was not dynamic."

Singleton didn't waver in his support for her. Tupac was his main concern. He admired Tupac's talent and was drawn to his charisma, on and off camera. Yet Singleton moaned about his professionalism. According to crew members, Tupac smoked blunts on set and had loud sex with extras in his trailer. On more than one occasion, he threatened to quit the film. When he learned that Jackson had a private chef on set, he demanded one too.

"Pac, she's paying for it out of her own pocket," Singleton told him.

Singleton supported and defended Tupac in front of the cast and crew. But the rapper's nihilism confounded him. "Janet's an actress. She's given me no trouble. She gives me exactly what I want," he said one day on the set. He then glanced at Shakur. "I'm always looking for a young De Niro, and it always gets fucked up. I don't think a lot of young people respect what it takes to do great work. When you have things handed to you so easily, you don't respect it."

One day, while filming the family reunion scene at Griffith Park in Los Angeles, Tupac took a swing at an extra, who'd been calling him names. People scattered across the set, fearing gunfire could erupt. Security separated the fight. Tupac felt a hand on his shoulder. He turned around and saw Maya Angelou. "Young man! Young man!" she said with power. "Let me speak to you."

"This motherfucker thinks he can run his mouth on me," Pac screamed.

Angelou carried a significant presence on set. In *Poetic Justice: Filmmaking South Central Style,* Chambers described her as "a tall, big-boned Black woman with a regal posture, a definite grace in her gestures. At the same time, her gaze is so intense, her husky voice so cutting, that nobody dares cross her."

She moved with swiftness to break up the fight, steering Tupac away from the throng. Angelou wore a navy blue dress with lace trim, pearls, and a wide-brimmed pink floppy hat that made her look like she was on her way to the pews.

"This motherfucker—"

"Young man, calm down," she said louder. "I want to speak to you, please."

Tupac took a breath. "Do you know how important you are?" she asked him. "When was the last time anybody told you or reminded you that our people stood on auction blocks so that you could live today? Somebody in your background decided they would stay alive despite this. They lay in the filthy hatches of slave ships to stay alive so that they would have some descendants. And here you are. You're more valuable than you can imagine."

She put her arm around him and he began to weep. Angelou turned him away from the crowd and used her hands to wipe the tears off his cheeks.

Predictably, Shakur's relationship with Janet Jackson took several turns during production. Early on, Jackson agreed to appear in the "If My Homie Calls" video, which Tupac shot on a day off from the movie. A few days later, Pac's camp delivered the edited clip to René and Janet. They went back to their trailer and watched it. René came back out and said, "There's too much of Janet in it."

Tupac seethed afterward. "We don't fucking need her. Just take her out of the video."

By this point, Shakur had fallen for Jackson. But their personalities mirrored that of their characters: Shakur was personable and outgoing, Jackson wary and reserved. "I don't think there was any natural chemistry between them," Collister says.

A sex scene between them was scrapped. But they still had to share a kiss.

A day or two before filming the scene, Elizondo and Jackson called Singleton into their trailer. "We know the kiss is coming up," Elizondo said. "We want him to get an AIDS test." They stressed they were just taking precautions. Jackson had caught a cold after kissing Q-Tip earlier in the production. Why take the chance?

Singleton tasked Nicolaides with communicating this to Tupac.

"I'm not taking a test," Pac said.

"Look, they were really uptight about it," Nicolaides said.

"I don't give a fuck. She kissed Q-Tip no problem," Tupac said. Then he grinned. He had an idea. "Wait, are we fucking for real?"

"What do you mean?"

"Am I fucking Janet for real? Because I will take four AIDS tests if I'm making love to Janet Jackson for real."

"No."

"Then I'm not taking a test. Now get the fuck out of my trailer."

Nicolaides found Singleton. "He's not going to do it and I'm not going to make him do it."

In the end, Shakur and Jackson kissed as planned.

Shakur's outbursts became more frequent as production moved up the coast toward his adopted hometown of Oakland. On June 16, the day of his twenty-first birthday, he almost crashed his Jeep Cherokee on the set. A week later, he punched out a window in his trailer after getting called in on a Saturday. "I feel like a fucking slave in this dungeon," he cried.

July 3. Last day of production. Shooting was scheduled to start at five thirty p.m. By this point, three months into filming, everyone was ready to move on. The final call sheet contained a message. *Thank you, everybody. Have a great life,* Nicolaides had scrawled on the bottom of the page.

"I was just tired," he says. "I felt a little bit like a second-grade teacher on the last day of class."

On the set, Singleton mused about his upcoming plans: a trip to Pageland, South Carolina, for a family reunion. But first he had to get through one last night shoot.

The scene called for Lucky to weep after blaming Jackson for his cousin's murder. Tupac had previously cried on command but Singleton took one look at him, weary, distracted, and opted not to push his actor. The head of makeup fetched a bottle of fake tears.

At around three thirty in the morning, Tupac's job was done. Singleton raised his arm, pointed to him, and declared, "Ladies and gentlemen, say goodbye to Tupac Shakur."

The announcement was met with muted applause and a few cheers. A voice shouted, "Get lost!" And he did.

Over two months prior, he was was heading north on the 405 when the verdict came in.

It was Wednesday, April 29, 1992. Filming on *Poetic Justice* had moved to Simi Valley, a suburb about forty miles northwest of Los Angeles. Despite the presence of Janet Jackson, the movie wasn't the biggest show in town. The nation's eyes descended on the Simi Valley County Courthouse, where four white LAPD officers accused of assaulting Rodney King were on trial. A product of white flight, Simi Valley was home to an inordinate number of law enforcement officers, as well as the recently opened Ronald Reagan Presidential Library. Out of a population of 103,288, less than 1.4 percent was Black.

"Not guilty," said the voice on the car radio.

Singleton smacked the dashboard. He took off his white baseball hat and rubbed his forehead.

"This can't be real. This is bullshit," he said. He turned to his six-foot-seven, three-hundred-pound bodyguard Richard "Big Shorty" Alexander. "Let's go there."

"Go where?" Shorty said.

"To the courthouse."

"What about the movie?"

"Fuck the movie," Singleton said.

Once they arrived, Shorty cleared a path to the scrum gathered on the courthouse steps. Singleton's eyes darted from side to side in search of a television camera.

Suddenly, three white men in suits and sunglasses advanced toward him. "Watch what you say," they warned him.

*Clearly Feds*, he thought. Later in life, he told people that his words on that day compelled the FBI to open a file on him.

He didn't have to look hard to find a microphone. When he spoke, he squeezed everything he had to say into a thirty-second sound bite.

"If this was in Los Angeles, do you think the jury would have the demographics that it had?" he said, his voice cracking. "I'm not a lawyer, but it says you're supposed to go before a jury of your peers. Those people are not [Rodney King's] peers. The people that indicted Mike Tyson were not his peers. Listen, it's just like a bomb. It's a bomb. We're sitting on a bomb."

The fuse had been burning since the Watts Riots in 1965. Since then, the social and economic conditions had further deteriorated. Black communities such as South Central were hit hardest once the post–World War II economic boom subsided. They endured one body blow after another: 1970s-era stagflation. A crippling recession in the early 1980s. Reaganomics. Government austerity on social services. The crack epidemic. A biased court system. The occupying army known as the LAPD. In the rare moments when juries ruled favorably, a judge interceded to pervert justice. In November 1991, Latasha Harlins's killer received five years' probation and a $500 fine following her manslaughter conviction. Los Angeles inched closer to the brink.

At 4:17 p.m., about eighty minutes following the Rodney King verdict, violence erupted on the corner of Florence and Normandie.

Now back on the set in Simi Valley, Singleton had no use for his shot list. His attention wandered. Most of the night, the cast and crew huddled around his small portable television watching the images: arson, looting, chaos in general. Sheila soon arrived with tears in her eyes.

"It's like *Apocalypse Now*," Singleton said. He worried his house might burn down.

Over the next six days, sixty-three people were killed and over two thousand were injured. Police made over twelve thousand arrests. Property damage reached over $1 billion, making it the most costly episode of civil unrest in United States history.

A year earlier, *Boyz N the Hood* had shed light on the conditions in South Central, a subject white America had either taken for granted or ignored. "I remember being at the Hamptons in this rich white dude's house, Larry Gagosian—he owns the largest art galleries—and all these rich white people are watching *Boyz N the Hood*," says the director Brett Ratner. "They were like, 'Oh my God.' They were horrified."

So naturally, in the aftermath of the riots, rich white people turned to the film's twenty-four-year-old director for answers.

*Why did this happen? Who's to blame? What needs to change moving forward?*

(On the other hand, some rich white people, like the actor Mickey Rourke, blamed Singleton for the riots. "The blood of Los Angeles falls on those who instigated this revolt, the malicious prophets of Black cinema and rap music, the movies such as those of Lee and Singleton," Rourke said.)

Singleton embraced the role at first. "If I don't say something, who is gonna say something?" he told the *Los Angeles Times* about a month afterward. But in the end, it wore on him.

"There was a lot of pressure on John to represent himself, while trying to be a spokesman for the entire Black community," says writer Kevin Powell. "It was a heavy, heavy burden to carry."

While Singleton was in production on *Poetic Justice*, he took on the role of citizen journalist, filming interviews with South Central residents for ABC's *Nightline* and writing an essay for *Premiere* magazine titled "The Fire This Time," a heavy-handed play on James Baldwin's famous piece for the *New Yorker*. (In the end, the *Nightline* footage never aired; network producers told him the material was "too dated.") Later, he appeared on *Straight from the Hood*, an MTV documentary that Powell hosted.

Corporate America and both ends of the political spectrum used *Boyz N the Hood* as a teaching moment. The Nordstrom department store chain screened it for its employees to educate them on race relations. California's Republican governor Pete Wilson said the film's father-son relationship set a good example for inner-city youths. Later, President Bill Clinton praised *Boyz* in a *Rolling Stone* interview. When asked about proposed government regulation of violence in entertainment (a hot topic in the early 1990s), Clinton expressed concern it could stifle artists.

"For example, I watched *Boyz N the Hood* very carefully," he said. "While it was very violent, it had no romance about the violence. That is a movie I would've wanted a lot of elementary-age kids in the inner city to see, because there was no romance. It was a mean, ugly, sad, heartbreaking tale of basically good kids who wanted to have a decent life who had it taken away from them."

(Politicians continue referring to *Boyz N the Hood*, over thirty years since its release. In October 2024, then Republican vice presidential candidate J. D. Vance called the film "extremely influential to my entire political worldview," citing Furious Styles's speech against gentrification and the film's message about the importance of fatherhood. "It spoke to me when I was a kid because I grew up at the time and I didn't have much of a relationship with my dad," Vance said on the *Joe Rogan Experience* podcast.)

Singleton soon appeared on C-SPAN. In August 1992, he testified on Capitol Hill during a Senate labor subcommittee hearing on "Violence and America's Youth."

"Why does more federal and state funding go toward prisons than education," he asked the senate panel. "Isn't it common sense to understand that we can't put everybody in jail and that it would be more positive if we work toward raising a population of citizens to be assets to this country rather than dependents?"

Singleton's politics weren't radical by any means. But he was young and Black and America was in the twelfth, and final, year of its Reagan/Bush experiment, so he came across as one. Nowadays he'd be dragged online for uttering the words "Black-on-Black crime."

He wasn't an abolitionist. He pressed for better, more community-based policing. He liked Clinton, the neoliberal standard-bearer. He believed that frequenting Black businesses could ease capitalism's ills. His suggestion to create federal tax incentives for major corporations to promote investment in inner cities was strikingly similar to the later Trump/Kushner Opportunity Zones plan, which, in the end, was ineffective and a vessel for graft and government corruption.

He held firm political and economic perspectives based on his own life experiences and could articulate the failures of both the War on Drugs and trickle-down economics—the policies that removed over half a million families from welfare rolls, stripped one million Americans of food stamp benefits, and allowed 2.6 million children to lose their school lunch programs. In 1992, Singleton founded the Dakar Foundation, which supports disadvantaged elementary school students and increases opportunities for Black people.

But at twenty-four, Singleton was an imperfect messenger. During this time, he shared views that eclipsed his more salient points. He said the four Black men who attacked the white truck driver Reginald Denny during the riot shouldn't be prosecuted. He referred to Mike Tyson as a political prisoner. He spouted conspiracy theories.

"If AIDS was a natural disease, it would have been around thousands of years ago," he told the *New York Times*. "I think it was made in order to kill undesirables. That would include homosexuals, intravenous drug users, and Blacks."

Shortly after attending Clinton's inauguration in January 1993—where Maya Angelou read her original poem "On the Pulse of Morning" at the US Capitol building—he abruptly retreated from activism. "I don't speak for nobody but John Singleton," he told *USA Today* in 1993. "I'd be a fool if I tried that and I'm not a fool."

Activism wasn't his true calling. He was a filmmaker with a film still to complete. And *Poetic Justice* needed work—a lot of work.

★★★★★

During postproduction, it became clear to everyone but Singleton that *Poetic Justice* had serious third-act problems. His rough cut ran over two and a half hours. Yet somehow the movie ended abruptly. And what was with that herd of zebras?

At first, he refused to go back into the cutting room. "I'm done. That's it. We're locked," he said to Steve Nicolaides after showing him the film.

Singleton's associates sensed that all the recent changes in his life—the women, the celebrity, the famous friends—had sidetracked him. The biggest life change was the birth of his child Justice Maya Singleton on October 17, 1992.

Singleton's relationship with Tosha Lewis, which had never been calm and cordial, became even more unstable after Lewis gave birth. Police were called to Singleton's house several times to quell disputes between the two of them. In late 1992, Singleton asked Lewis to move out of his house. He had rented an apartment for her and Justice and had paid the first six months of a one-year lease. She refused. Cops were summoned to Singleton's Baldwin Hills home following an argument once again on December 21, 1992, which resulted in Lewis being arrested and taken to jail.

They entered a custody and visitation dispute that ended with both awarded joint legal and physical custody.

Singleton wasn't ready to settle down or be a full-time dad. Although birth control was readily available to him, he told friends that Lewis, Justice's mother, had "trapped" him. He later took vulgar shots at her in the press. "Two years ago, I didn't have to worry about bitches trying to get pregnant by me and shit," he told *Playboy*. "But that's the kind of shit I worry about now."

*Poetic Justice* was also a major worry. But he still had time to salvage the film before its July 1993 release date.

Rumors of *Poetic Justice*'s troubles circulated before Columbia held its first test screening on October 5, 1992. On that morning, during the celebrity gossip segment on her nationally syndicated television show, Joan Rivers mentioned both the test screening and the studio's concerns about the film's running time.

Over the next nine months, the bad buzz only intensified.

Columbia tested the film in Sacramento in hopes of attracting less of an industry crowd and to diminish the likelihood of a media member crashing the screening. After the audience was seated, Singleton and a group of Columbia executives slinked into the theater's back row.

Singleton paced in a hallway waiting for the audience survey results afterward. From what he could tell, the young people loved Janet and couldn't stop laughing with (or at) Joe Torry's character, Chicago. But there were some disconcerting moments. During the third or fourth poem, someone in the audience groaned, "Another poem?"

Then there were the zebras.

Singleton shot the scene near Cambria, a seaside village up the California coast. In the dream sequence, Justice wanders in a grassy field on a hill as she reads the poem "Phenomenal Woman." A herd of zebras then walk past her. Why? Symbolism. The four-minute scene established Justice's connection to Africa and how interacting with nature helped her cope with loss. But it slowed the film and the test screening audience responded with laughter.

Singleton knocked on the door to the room where an independent marketing group evaluated the response cards. A few seconds later, Michael Nathanson, Columbia president of worldwide production, appeared.

"They liked it," he told Singleton. "But the zebras have to go."

Still, Singleton resisted cutting it. Cannon screened the movie for him: once with the zebra scene and then without it. "He was open-minded," Cannon said. "Sometimes he could feel it. Sometimes he couldn't. That one he did."

"It was one of the most difficult things I had to do," Singleton said of the edit. "But it kept going above people's heads."

They shaved down more scenes, eventually cutting the run time to 109 minutes. But that didn't solve the film's weak ending. How could they create a beat between Lucky cursing out Janet and their big, climactic kiss in the salon?

Late that fall, Nicolaides secured funding allowing for two days of reshoots. In the first scene, Justice selects a white sweater from a closet full of black clothes, signaling she's no longer mourning; the second had Tupac, as Lucky, fiddling with his late cousin's DJ equipment and looking at his fingernails, making him reflect on Justice.

"They didn't think it through," Cannon says. "It wasn't the right scene."

At the end of postproduction, Jackson and her husband screened the film. They called Nicolaides in a state of angst afterward. "We need to reshoot," Elizondo said. "The movie needs an ending like *An Officer and a Gentleman* where he goes in and claims his woman."

"Well, yeah, you're probably right," Nicolaides said. "But that ship has sailed."

★★★★★

One of the first things Singleton did after finishing his cut of *Poetic Justice* was take his first trip to Africa.

In February 1993, Singleton, along with the musician Tracy Chapman ("Fast Car") and *The Color Purple* author Alice Walker, led a US delegation of over a hundred artists to the Pan-African Film & TV Festival, also known as FESPACO, in Ouagadougou, Burkina Faso.

Some people close to him tried talking him out of going. Better to focus on work. But he insisted. He'd always been enthralled with the continent. When he arrived in the west African nation, the first thing he noticed was that all the people he encountered were Black. The pilots. The flight attendants. The taxi drivers. Workers. Rich people. Poor people. Singleton was a tourist. He wrote in his journal daily. Snapped pictures. Away from the festival, he was anonymous. People left him alone. No one knew him as director John Singleton, yet they treated him with grace and dignity.

"I've come home," Singleton said of his trip.

FESPACO 1993 reportedly attracted over four hundred thousand spectators and cost $1.2 million to put on. Over 350 features and shorts were screened. Singleton, one of the festival's guests of honor, watched as many films as possible. *Kasarmu Ce: This Land Is Ours*, the debut feature from Nigerian filmmaker Saddik Balewa, stuck to his bones.

"He's, like, the African Kurosawa," Singleton gushed in an interview a few months later. "You know how Kurosawa does stuff from feudal Japan? This guy does the feudal system of Africa. Like murder mysteries. Blew me away!"

Singleton also walked away impressed with another artist he met in Burkina Faso: the Ghanian screenwriter and actress Akosua Busia. In April, *Variety* reported that he planned to direct Busia's screenplay *Seasons* and had already done location scouting for a potential film. "She couldn't tell whether he liked her or the screenplay," says Michael Hubbard, Busia's manager at the time. "Probably both."

Busia was born a princess into the Royal House of Wenchi in Ghana. Her mother was a fashion designer. Her father, Kofi Abrefa Busia, served as prime minister of Ghana from 1969 until the military overthrew his government in January 1972. He then fled to England. As a teenager, Busia pursued acting. She studied at the Royal Central School of Speech and Drama and landed the lead in the Oxford production of *Romeo and Juliet*. Later on, she moved to Los Angeles. She bounced around Hollywood until Spielberg hired her to play Nettie Harris in *The Color Purple*. In addition to acting, Busia was an accomplished painter (her work was displayed at the National Museum of Art in London) and screenwriter. At the behest of Oprah Winfrey, Busia had recently completed an adaptation of Toni Morrison's *Beloved* for the screen.

For Singleton, the appeal was obvious. Ken Sagoes, an actor who appeared in the 1986 TV movie *The George McKenna Story* opposite Denzel Washington and Busia, calls her "the most beautiful chocolate goddess that I had ever seen." But Singleton was infatuated with more than her beauty. Busia was different from the women he'd been with. He viewed her as a prize. From the moment they met, he wanted marriage—and more.

Later that spring, he told reporters that he intended to return to Africa once he finished his obligations on *Poetic Justice*. "I may just stay there," he said, "and in about twenty years, you'll see a bunch of young African filmmakers hitting the scene and you'll know why."

*B*oyz *N the Hood*'s success spurred a frenzy to find the next John Singleton. Inevitably, he'd be replaced as the industry's hot new Black filmmaker. Singleton wasn't surprised when it happened. But he didn't expect to be feuding with the new kids on the block during the run up to *Poetic Justice*'s July 1993 release.

As much as Singleton disliked rumblings of "the next John Singleton," the comparisons bothered the Hughes brothers even more.

"People were like, 'Spike and John. Spike and John.' That's all we kept hearing about," Allen Hughes said in a 2009 interview with *Vibe*. "It was like, 'Damn, that's the grading curve for the whole class? It's not Spielberg or Scorsese? It's Spike and John? You guys are grading us on that curve? Cool, I guess we'll get a straight A.'"

Allen and Albert Hughes were les enfants terribles of Black cinema in the 1990s. Born in Detroit in 1972 to a Black father and an Iranian Armenian mother, the twins moved to Pomona, a city about forty-five minutes east of Los Angeles, at the age of nine. The dark underbelly of society mesmerized them, and their taste in films reflected that fascination.

"We liked *Star Wars* as much as the next kids, but we weren't fanatical [about] that shit," said Allen, the more extroverted of the brothers. "We were more blown away by adventure and mayhem and blow and bitches."

The twins didn't attend film school. They became proficient in the technical aspects of filmmaking as kids after their mother bought them a camera. By the age of fourteen, they had experience in sound design, scoring, and film editing. With the advent of public television, they found an outlet for their home movies. At first, they made spoofs of their favorite TV shows. Soon, their work evolved into grittier fare.

In 1990, they directed an eight-minute short, *The Drive By*, which scored them an agent and a contract with Hollywood Records. Over the next nine months, they'd shoot thirty music videos for hip-hop artists such as KRS-One, Too $hort, and their closest collaborator, the Interscope Records recording artist Tupac Shakur.

"First time we met we were at a Waffle House in the Bay Area," Allen said. "I went to the bathroom and then Tupac came in and we were taking a piss the way gentlemen do. He says, 'Your short films are dope. I'm going to get y'all to do my first music video.' I was like, 'Yeah, whatever.' Three weeks later [Interscope chairman] Jimmy Iovine's office calls asking us to direct Tupac's video."

The Hughes brothers directed all three music videos from Tupac's debut album *2Pacalypse Now*: "Trapped," "Brenda's Got a Baby," and "If My Homie Calls," which they shot on Tupac's day off from *Poetic Justice* and which features a cameo from John Singleton.

They felt each other out that first time meeting. "Are you guys really just twenty years old?" Singleton said.

Albert passed Singleton his license. When he examined it, he noticed something in addition to the date of birth. "Claremont, huh?" Singleton said with a wry smile before handing it back. From that moment on, he questioned the Hughes brothers' authenticity.

"Claremont is a real white area next to Pomona where I grew up," Albert said in an interview with the *New Yorker*. "[John] made a mental note."

Feature films were the next step for them, and the twins brainstormed ideas with their friend's older brother, an aspiring screenwriter named Tyger Williams. They were interested in exploring how kids are a product of their environment, how their fates are already written. The film would be set in Watts. Stylistically, it would have voiceover elements like *Goodfellas*. They based their main characters on a twenty-three-year-old from the Jordan Downs housing project—a gang-banger, crack dealer, and known shooter.

Williams had recently ceded a football scholarship at the University of Utah to study film at Cal State Long Beach. He took Singleton's success as a sign the industry might be receptive to more Black stories. When he solicited agents during the fall of 1991, he wrote in his query letters, "With the success of Spike Lee and John Singleton, I'm sure you want to read another African American writer."

"I put that right there—shamelessly," Williams says.

Williams wrote the script for *Menace II Society* in December 1991. An independent producer shopped it around town, where it garnered interest from executives looking to capitalize on *Boyz N the Hood*. But there was a catch. The studios wanted the Hughes brothers to work under an established Black director who'd serve as their executive producer. Universal suggested Spike Lee. Tri-Star proposed Reginald and Warrington Hudlin; Columbia had Singleton in mind.

Instead, they signed a deal with New Line Cinema in July 1992. The Hughes Brothers balked at "the idea of a Black overseer," wrote Henry Louis Gates in the *New Yorker*. "They didn't want to be controlled by somebody who might perceive them as a threat."

So much and so little had changed for Black filmmakers since *Boyz N the Hood*. The year 1991 had been a watershed moment in the industry. Black directors were at the helm for nineteen films released in theaters that year alone—more than the entire decade of the 1980s combined. And many of them were extraordinarily profitable. Produced for $8 million, *New Jack City* grossed over $47 million. *House Party 2* almost quadrupled its $5 million budget. Even Spike Lee's *Jungle Fever*, which at $14 million was considered a mid-budget feature, generated profit after banking over $43 million worldwide.

Budgets for Black directors increased overnight. Warner Bros. put up $28 million for Lee's *Malcolm X*. (Lee ended up going over budget and raising $5–7 million to complete the film.) For his follow-up to *House Party*, Reginald Hudlin directed Eddie Murphy as a womanizing advertising executive in *Boomerang*. Paramount green-lit the R-rated romantic comedy at $42 million, at the time the biggest-budgeted film ever directed by a Black filmmaker.

Black filmmakers still viewed one another as competition. The media stirred the pot. A knee-jerk reaction to pit them against each other persisted, and a *Highlander* mentality formed: There can be only one.

"Spike Lee can take a rest. Matty Rich can go attend film school, and Mario Van Peebles had better start worrying. John Singleton is here, and if there really is a black American film renaissance afoot (the sheer number of films this year feels like more than a fluke), *Boyz N the Hood* may be its finest offering yet" is how the *Seattle Times* review of *Boyz N the Hood* opened.

Black filmmakers of that era were ambitious. They all had egos. But they all rooted for one another.

"There was almost this shared responsibility in this weird way," Mario Van Peebles says. "We looked at it like a relay race, where I'd have to run a leg and John ran a leg and Spike ran a leg and if we ran that leg successfully, the next guy or gal got a shot."

So, when Keenen Ivory Wayans's blaxploitation parody *I'm Gonna Git You Sucka* turned a nice profit for MGM, New Line green-lit *House Party*. When the $2.5 million–budgeted *House Party* grossed over $26 million, Warner Bros. moved forward on *New Jack City*. And when Columbia struck gold with *Boyz N the Hood*, New Line entrusted two twenty-year-olds with a $3.5 million picture.

Does *Menace II Society* get made if not for Singleton's film?

"Probably not," Williams says. "*Menace* was hard enough to get made as is."

During this time, Van Peebles and Hudlin took turns hosting big dinners for their peers where they'd dish on the state of the industry and about who was up and who was down amongst them. Within this circle, Singleton was perceived as the baby of the bunch. Sometimes he played nice with others. Other times he didn't, such as when he took shots at *New Jack City* during a 1991 interview with *Empire* magazine. "I just think that there are people who make films that rise above the ordinary and there are others who just make films," he said. "*New Jack City* was pure entertainment. It was not a quote, serious film. That's all."

"John came up to me and apologized," Van Peebles says.

The Hughes brothers had taken the Black filmmaker archetype—the one Spike created and John assumed—to a new level. More audacious. More controversial.

While Singleton revered those who paved the way for him, particularly Spike Lee, the Hughes brothers took aim at their forebears. In the June 22, 1992, issue of *Daily Variety*, Albert Hughes said *Menace II Society* would make *Boyz N the Hood* look like *Mary Poppins*.

From there, a rivalry ensued.

"We never had real beef with John Singleton or Spike Lee," Allen Hughes said. "I never felt really competitive with them because we were not making the same kind of movies. *Boyz* and *Menace* seem to be similar, but they are not at all. They are not even the same genre really. *Boyz N the Hood* is a coming-of-age story that takes place in the hood. I hate to say this because I don't like this term, but *Menace* is a hood film where niggas are trying to come of age. Our protagonist would be the bad guy in *Boyz N the Hood*. I think it was a disservice to John and to us."

Though *Menace II Society* is a bleaker, almost nihilist film, comparisons to *Boyz N the Hood* were inevitable once it too debuted to rave reviews at Cannes.

"If *Boyz N the Hood* was the story of a young man lucky enough to grow up with parents who cared, and who escapes the dangers of street culture, *Menace II Society* is, tragically, about many more young men who are not so lucky," Roger

Ebert wrote in his four-star review. "*Menace II Society* is as well-directed a film as you'll see from America this year, an unsentimental and yet completely involving story of a young man who cannot see a way around his fate."

*New York* magazine's film critic David Denby called it "perhaps the most striking debut in the history of black cinema." One reviewer said *Menace II Society* was "the movie John Singleton wanted to make when he directed *Boyz N the Hood.*"

*Menace II Society* was also a hit at the box office, taking in $27.9 million against a $3.5 million budget. In terms of a cost-to-return ratio, it was the fifth most successful film of 1993.

Singleton wasn't as impressed. Sure, he liked the film. But he spotted certain elements derivative of *Boyz N the Hood*: a shooting at an outdoor fast-food spot; characters plotting a move out of the hood in search of a better life—to Atlanta, no less; dominoes; barbecues; casting rappers as gangbangers. He viewed *Menace II Society* and the wave of hood films that emerged in the wake of *Boyz* as imitators cashing in on his success—similar to how *Jaws* spawned *Orca, Piranha, Grizzly, Alligator,* and *Mako: The Jaws of Death.*

He also didn't find it authentic. How could two guys *from Claremont* make a movie about the hood? "These *Boyz N the Hood* copies . . . people are making films about what they heard or read about instead of what they've seen or felt," Singleton said. He didn't mention the Hughes brothers, but it was clear who he was referring to. "Then they have to get somebody, a real street nigga like Tupac, to have some true flavor in it."

Shortly after wrapping on *Poetic Justice*, Tupac Shakur accepted a small role in *Menace II Society* as the conscience of the film, a devout Muslim named Sharif. His participation had been crucial for the project to get financed as New Line wanted to shoehorn a rapper into the cast. Tupac was one better: a rapper and an established actor. He insisted on taking a *supporting* role.

"I'm not starring in anyone's movies but John Singleton's," he told Allen Hughes. "We're going to be like Scorsese and De Niro."

Tupac picked up where he left off on the set of *Poetic Justice*.

"Every day he'd throw a tantrum about something," Allen Hughes said. "He would start this macho thug performing act—just arbitrary stupid shit."

Hughes fired him. A few months later, Tupac confronted the brothers on the set of a music video they were directing. Backed by about a dozen suspected gang members, Tupac punched Allen and ran off Albert.

By this point, Singleton and Shakur had become more than mere allies. They forged a friendship early on while filming *Poetic Justice*, bonding over their rough childhoods. One day Singleton went out on a location scout with Tupac. They spent the afternoon driving in Singleton's Nissan Pathfinder listening to a mixtape of classic soul songs, singing along to "O-o-h Child" by the Five Stairsteps.

Singleton became enraptured with him, and not merely as an actor. In a way, Tupac was everything he wanted to be—and everything he feared. He envied the ease with which Tupac carried himself, his magnetism and charm, his way with women. An alluring man, he had long, thick eyelashes and expressive eyes. His body was awkward but beautiful—lithe and lanky with sinewy muscles.

"When we went to Freaknik, twenty, thirty girls came running toward [Tupac] screaming his name and letting him rub on their titties," Singleton said.

When he was with him, he loosened up a bit; Singleton says Freaknik was the first time he got drunk in his adult life. "I'm running up and down the streets screaming, 'It's Black World! We're in Black World!'" Singleton said.

He found Tupac endlessly entertaining. But he also recognized that Tupac lacked impulse control and made poor decisions—like assaulting famous movie directors. They were both fascinated with "thug life," but Tupac succumbed to those callings. Singleton did too, in a way. During this time, he sometimes carried a Glock, usually in a holster strapped across the small of his back.

"He kind of admitted to me that it was almost a performative thing, like all of a sudden, he was trying to be this hard, tough guy, and that's not who he was," Kevin Powell says.

He couldn't help but try to act hard around Tupac. During an appearance on *Yo! MTV Raps*, during which Ed Lover introduced them as "two of the most controversial Black brothers there is in the music business today and film," Singleton played the sidekick as Tupac talked smack about the Hughes brothers. "They fired me but did it in a roundabout punk snitch way, so I caught them on the streets and beat they behinds," Shakur said, incriminating himself in the process.

"I was a menace to the Hughes brothers—and it ain't over!"

Singleton joined in doing a bad rendition of a tough-guy act. "Don't jump through the TV," he shouted repeatedly while pretending to hold Shakur back.

Later on, the Hughes brothers used the footage as evidence during criminal proceedings against Shakur. In May 1994, he was sentenced to fifteen days in jail for battery.

In the spring of 1993, Singleton had one last task on the film: Curate its soundtrack. *Music from the Motion Picture Poetic Justice* would also be the first release on Singleton's new label, New Deal Music.

Record labels were soaked in cash following the CD boom in the early 1990s. Over the next few years, they handed out joint ventures to any filmmaker who knew the difference between a kick and a snare. James Cameron had a record label. So did Spike Lee. Robert De Niro set up Tribeca Music at Epic. In early 1993 Singleton formed New Deal Music through the Sony subsidiary Epic Soundtrax and 550 Music.

As a self-proclaimed hip-hop filmmaker, he considered a record label the next logical step. Instead, he learned that the music business is a much different, more volatile, at times more dangerous industry than moviemaking. More politics. Less money once the advance dried up. More risk. Frustrated artists were a headache unlike anything he encountered on a movie set.

One of his first hires was a white guy from Baldwin Hills.

Paul Stewart was one of the most plugged-in people in the Los Angeles hip-hop scene when Singleton met him at a TV taping of the short-lived Patti LaBelle and Morris Chestnut NBC sitcom *Out All Night*. He DJed parties and worked at a record store after returning home from college. Soon, he scored an internship at Arista Records and became a correspondent for *The Source*. Then he started an artist management company. He connected the Pharcyde with Delicious Vinyl and brought House of Pain to Tommy Boy Records. Shortly after that, Ice Cube's label Street Knowledge hired him to run street promotions and marketing.

Singleton made him an offer on the night he attended an artist showcase Stewart set up at the Roxy. "Hey, so, I'm not sure if you heard, but I got a label through Sony," Singleton said. "I want to bring in my own guy to run it and was wondering if you wanted to be that guy."

One of their first conversations involved Stewart's management company, a glaring conflict of interest for a record label executive, as Singleton later learned.

"I was wondering if I could keep doing what I'm doing," Stewart said.

"Yeah, I know we're not paying you a lot," Singleton acknowledged. "How about we become partners in the management thing?"

"You're asking me to give up half of my commission?" Stewart said.

"Yeah, but now you can say you're partners with the director of *Boyz N the Hood*," Singleton countered. "Seems like a fair deal."

Immediately, Stewart got to work obtaining songs for the *Poetic Justice* soundtrack.

Singleton wanted the album to sound like Los Angeles, and in early 1993, that meant Death Row Records. He became obsessed with landing a song from the label's centerpiece, Snoop Doggy Dogg. Over the past year, the Long Beach rapper had gone from small-time drug dealer to the hottest artist in the game after costarring on Dr. Dre's triple-platinum album *The Chronic*.

Stewart faced headwinds from the start. With Snoop's debut album set for the fall, Death Row CEO Suge Knight wouldn't clear a solo song for the soundtrack. But he approved a request for Snoop to rap the chorus on "Niggas Don't Give a Fuck," by Tha Dogg Pound.

One day, Stewart arrived at Larrabee Sound Studios in West Hollywood with bad news for Dr. Dre, the song's producer. Stewart couldn't clear the Bobby Womack sample. While Dre got to work, revamping the beat without the sample, Stewart struck up a conversation with Dre's stepbrother, Warren Griffin.

"Hey, I got my own shit, cuz," said the producer known as Warren G. He pulled a cassette tape from his pants pocket.

They went to Stewart's truck to listen to beats. Stewart immediately recognized the bubbling bass as a sample of "Rapp Dirty," the 1980 gangster rap forerunner. After twenty seconds or so, Stewart ejected the tape.

"What are you doing?" Warren G said.

"This shit is hot," Stewart said. "Can I keep the tape? Let me roll with it. Trust me."

Later that day, he found Singleton and played him an early version of "Indo Smoke." "Whooo," Singleton exhaled, bobbing his head to the G-funk bounce. "We need that."

Warren G gifted the song to the West Covina rapper Mista Grimm. Peaking at #56 on the *Billboard* Hot 100, "Indo Smoke" would be the second single off the gold-selling *Poetic Justice* soundtrack.

The album also featured songs from Tupac (the Warren G–produced "Definition of a Thug Nigga"), TLC, Babyface, Naughty by Nature, Pete Rock & CL Smooth, and the debut single from a fourteen-year-old Usher. But the star of the film was missing from its soundtrack. How did this happen? Virgin Records wanted to protect their $40 million investment and not risk cannibalizing sales of Jackson's new album *Janet*, which was released five weeks prior to the soundtrack.

So, the label prevented Jackson from contributing to it despite her song "Again" appearing throughout the film.

"Things like that burned John on the music business," Stewart said. "He has Janet Jackson starring in his movie and can't get her song on the soundtrack?"

There was still a lot to celebrate. New Deal Music had its first hit. Slowly, Singleton built its roster, signing Mista Grimm, the reggae group Ruff Endz, and Cultural Revolution, a collective in the Soul II Soul or Arrested Development mold. He also signed Warren G to the management company he shared with Stewart just as the rapper became one of the most sought-after free agents in the music industry.

Spike Lee had warned him it was coming.

In the foreword to *Poetic Justice: Filmmaking South Central Style*, written in the form of an open letter to Singleton, Lee explained what he'd be up against on his sophomore film. "The same critics and people who championed you are gonna be after your ass. Why!? Human nature," he wrote. "The same people who said you were the second coming of Orson Welles will now say, 'What happened?' They'll feel it's their duty to 'knock you down a peg.' So, if you can understand that going in, you'll be prepared. Just let that stuff slide right off your back and keep on keeping on."

Singleton was unable to just let that stuff slide right off his back. Instead, he turned combative. Throughout the spring and summer of 1993, he spent the majority of his publicity tour dispelling negative rumors about the film.

He sparred with reporters and critics: sighing at a *Village Voice* writer's questions, debating a *Washington Post* journalist on the validity of Mike Tyson's rape conviction. "I just didn't think she was telling the truth," he said of Tyson's victim. An interview with the New York *Daily News* ended abruptly. "He stands, signaling the end of my not-so-confrontational questions. We don't shake hands. But he checks out my rear," wrote Monte Williams.

An *Esquire* profile caught him and his team off guard. In the piece, the writer, Joe Wood, referred to the *Poetic Justice* script as "a silly balance of adolescent sexuality and literary stargazing" with "heavy-handed references to films such as Fellini's confessional *8½*." Wood also made note of the "loneliness" and "sadness" in Singleton's eyes and questioned his origin story he repeated to reporters during his *Boyz N the Hood* press run.

For the first time, Singleton was publicly accused of losing touch with his roots. "He's still starstruck," Nicolaides was quoted as saying. "In a way it is sad, but those are kind of the choices that he makes. He'd rather hang with Eddie Murphy, which means being in the same room as Eddie and fifty bodyguards, and talk superficially about whatever superficial people talk about than sit down with his true homies. Seems like."

The highlight of his press run was a long interview in early July with Roger Ebert in Chicago. Over lunch, the two filmic soldiers spoke for hours about the industry, the art form, and their love of cinema. "It was like meeting with the chairman of the campus film society," Ebert wrote in the *Chicago Sun-Times*. "[Singleton] talked about Truffaut's *The 400 Blows*, Coppola's *Apocalypse Now*, and Bunuel's *Belle de Jour*. He talked about *Juice*, *Menace II Society*, and *Last Action Hero*. And he was exploding with enthusiasm for a new film he had just seen in Africa."

Ebert had been transfixed with Singleton from the moment *Boyz N the Hood* premiered in the Grand Palais at Cannes. He was the film's biggest booster in the press and would go on to become a staunch advocate of Singleton and his films even when it contradicted critical consensus. Eventually, they became friends outside of the industry. As much as he admired Singleton's talents as a filmmaker, he seemed to be just as impressed with his ethos about filmmaking and Hollywood. Ebert saw him as an old soul, a throwback.

"[*Poetic Justice*] isn't tightly plotted like a lot of 1990s movies. It's not 'high concept,' which means it can't be summed up in one sexy sentence for a TV commercial. It's more about character than about action. And it is unabashedly romantic," Ebert wrote. "Those are some of the reasons I think it is a brave film. *Poetic Justice* isn't the kind of film Hollywood is making right now. It's the kind of film that was made in the 1970s, when the best directors were aiming for artistic home runs, not box-office hits."

Tupac Shakur was a wild card while promoting the film. As always, he didn't mince words. He openly discussed rumors that Singleton and the studio would have preferred he didn't—namely, the AIDS test. "It was disrespectful to me," he said on *The Arsenio Hall Show*. "It made me look at [Janet] like, 'What?' Her people said I was lying about the test. I don't lie. I'm real—too real. She need to check that. Check her people and check who said that."

Even when Shakur praised Janet, it raised questions. "We had a good experience on the set. I really thought I made a friend," he said. "But as soon as the movie was over, her phone number changed. I thought I knew Janet. I guess not."

Singleton didn't want to make Jackson look bad. Yet he felt the need to protect Shakur. As a result, he concocted a bizarre lie, one he'd repeat for the next twenty-five years: He said the AIDS test was a publicity stunt.

"Me, Janet, Tupac, Regina King, and Joe Torry were sitting on the set. Everyone was trying to impress Janet," he said. "I was like, 'Man, I don't know about this love scene. You've been hitting all this shit. I don't know if I want you touching my actress. You need a test. You need an AIDS test.' You do shit like that and you know everyone is going to be talking about our movie."

Everyone but Janet Jackson. On July 16, the New York *Daily News* reported that she had pulled out of promotion out of fear of "overexposure." She no-showed the film's New York premiere, but attended the one in Los Angeles.

*Poetic Justice* received mostly negative reviews. "A disappointment," wrote Kenneth Turan of the *Los Angeles Times*. "While *Boyz* was all of a piece, this film feels thrown together, an unfocused compendium of conflicting impulses and moods." *Time* magazine's Richard Schickel branded it "simply awful: poorly structured, vulgarly written, insipidly directed, monotonously performed."

*Entertainment Weekly* named *Poetic Justice* the fourth worst film of the year behind *Last Action Hero*, *Kalifornia*, and *Flesh and Bone*. "John Singleton followed up *Boyz N the Hood* with a chaotic road movie about a verse-spitting South Central Los Angeles hairdresser (Janet Jackson) and her very loud friends. It's depressing to see Singleton abandon the storytelling verities that made him a success in the first place."

While Shakur's performance in the film was praised across the board, Jackson's work polarized critics. Ebert stood in the pro-Janet camp: "You'd think she'd be all flash and surface, but she's convincing as the no-nonsense working woman from South Central LA." Vincent Canby of the *New York Times* was less impressed: "Nothing in the character of Justice, as written by Mr. Singleton or as passively played by Ms. Jackson, remotely suggests that she's the repository of ideas and emotions attributed to her by Ms. Angelou's poetry."

Singleton himself had mixed feelings about the film. In a way, he accomplished what he set out to: a character piece about everyday people—the mailman who falls in love with the hairstylist—that proved he wasn't a one-trick pony. In later years, he acknowledged its flaws. How he poorly elucidated Justice's trauma. How Lucky takes center stage in the picture. How it's technically about women but unmistakably told through a man's perspective, much as his friends had warned him.

"It ain't a perfect film, but it got heart," he said. "What it lacks in perfection it more than makes up for it in heart and soul, and I think that that's really what great films are measured by—whether or not you feel something for the characters."

Despite the critical beatdown, *Poetic Justice* felt like a big moment when it opened on July 23, 1993. Jackson was at the peak of her powers—she was the biggest pop star in the world that summer. Shakur had made the leap from budding star to genuine superstar. "I Get Around," the second single off his sophomore album *Strictly 4 My N.I.G.G.A.Z.*, was the unofficial song of the summer. They were both everywhere—MTV, BET, pop radio, rap radio. Then the movie opened. It felt like a letdown.

*Poetic Justice* debuted at $11.7 million, a slight uptick from the $10 million *Boyz N the Hood* banked on its opening weekend. But it faded fast, tumbling 57 percent in its second weekend, and then another 58 percent, after which it exited the top ten. It topped out at $27.5 million, less than *Menace II Society*. Though profitable for Columbia, the studio and the town considered it a disappointment.

Three weeks after the film opened, the *Los Angeles Times* ran a postmortem titled "The Rise and Fall of *Poetic Justice*." It attributed the film's lackluster performance to an array of factors—the end-of-summer glut at theaters, poor reviews, and the lack of a draw for white filmgoers. The writer predicted Singleton would likely face more scrutiny from the studio next time around.

Singleton was a little down afterward. He worried that the aura he crafted had been shattered. But he didn't dwell on it. He had completed the script for his next film. He also started dating someone new. At the afterparty for *Poetic Justice*'s New York premiere, a photographer snapped him arm in arm with a nineteen-year-old model named Tyra Banks.

n the summer of 1993, Christopher David Fisher managed a Subway sandwich shop in Long Beach, California. He was also the head of the Fourth Reich Skinheads, a hate group, around thirty members deep, based in Long Beach and Orange County. They often worked out at a church in Newport Beach outfitted with weightlifting equipment, Nazi flags, and a grenade launcher.

For fun, the twenty-year-old psychology student and his friends built bonfires on the beach and loitered in a McDonald's. They also planned to start a race war.

Now, how would they do that? According to reports, the Fourth Reich Skinheads plotted to mail a letter bomb to a local rabbi, bomb the First African Methodist Episcopal Church in Los Angeles, and murder Rodney King, Al Sharpton, and several Black celebrities, including John Singleton.

(Fisher pleaded guilty in October to arson and conspiracy and was sentenced to eight years and one month in federal prison after turning state's evidence.)

Authorities later stated the threats against Singleton, Arsenio Hall, and Eazy-E weren't credible. But on July 16, the day after the arrests, it was the topic of conversation at the infamous *Yo! MTV Raps* taping where Tupac went on his rant, berating the Hughes brothers.

"Look at this," Singleton said, pointing at the front page of the New York *Daily News*. "Sharpton Death Plot," screamed the headline.

*Yo!* cohosts Ed Lover and Doctor Dré (not the same Dr. Dre from N.W.A. and *The Chronic* fame) referred to the story during a segment, and Tupac could be seen reading the *Daily News* article: "Feds bust neo-Nazis in race war terror plot." They revisited the topic toward the end of the show.

"We want to say something to all of y'all little neo-Nazi guys out there who think y'all got the guns," Ed Lover said. "We on point. We on point. We know what's going on and it's on."

Singleton, who loved to play the giddy troublemaker around Tupac, then sprang from his chair and snapped a right cross toward the camera.

The story didn't surprise him. Lately, he'd noticed a certain kind of white male angst on the rise—one rooted in racist and sexist resentments and fixated on the idea that straight white men were losing power in America. Michael Douglas in *Falling Down* was their archetype.

He found it laughable. What were *they* so angry about?

Singleton channeled his own post-riots rancor into his most ambitious screenplay to date. He felt like stepping up from character-driven pieces and making a statement film addressing third-rail issues like race, gender, sexuality, class, and Nazis.

Back in 1990, over tiramisu at a Midtown Manhattan trattoria, the director Jonathan Demme had pitched Singleton a film about racism on college campus. The idea stuck with Singleton. Over the years, he fleshed out the concept, developed it, made it his own. He hatched a title, *Higher Learning*, and a premise: a multicharacter drama with interconnecting storylines about three freshmen navigating their first semester on campus.

"In some ways," Singleton said, "*Higher Learning* is my whole answer to the experience of being a Black student going to a predominantly white university and me wanting to look back on that time."

He perused his old notebooks to unwrap memories. Black Pack parties at BPHQ. Frat parties on the Row. Take Back the Night rallies and the blue-light system. Conservative professors. Campus security. The alienation he felt in some classrooms. The fashion. The trench coats and Africa medallions. The segregated cliques on campus.

*Remember when that white boy called me a reverse racist for wearing a Black Panther T-shirt?*

*Remember when Yon beat up that guy up on Fraternity Row for calling his friend a Black bitch?*

*Higher Learning* was a necessary pivot for him. He never wanted to stop writing stories about South Central but felt a need to diversify.

Singleton got a taste of big-budget filmmaking that fall when he filmed a walk-on as a fireman in Eddie Murphy's $50 million sequel *Beverly Hills Cop III*.

Eventually, he hoped to work with bigger budgets and bigger stars, which pleased Columbia.

Prior to green-lighting *Higher Learning*, the studio nudged Singleton toward more commercial fare. They acquired a script-in-progress for an action-thriller

*Burnout* with him in mind to direct. He also developed *Drumfire*, a Western about a Black cowboy's quest for hidden gold. He had a writer in mind for it too. After meeting Quentin Tarantino at the *True Romance* premiere in September 1993, he discussed *Drumfire* with him during a two-hour phone call. But Tarantino was starting production on *Pulp Fiction* and unavailable.

Singleton's relationship with the studio changed in the aftermath of *Poetic Justice*. He felt Columbia bungled the film's ad campaign ("It's two weeks before the release and the advertising hasn't kicked in," he complained to Roger Ebert in the *Sun-Times*) and felt it contributed to the film underperforming at the box office. The bad press also made him think they didn't have his back.

Then there were the edits. The notes. The suggestions. The bullshit. Why didn't they embrace his vision? They trusted him on *Boyz N the Hood*. What changed?

Columbia, of course, saw it differently. There was a perception at the studio that Singleton's recent scripts lacked the same arduous care with which he'd crafted *Boyz N the Hood*. If anything, they coddled him, tiptoeing around his tantrums.

"I don't remember people really coming down hard on John, because he was so formidable in his opinions," Stephanie Allain says. "It was hard to have those note conversations either about the script or the film."

Singleton alternated between shouting matches and the silent treatment when challenged. Once, he burst into a Tuesday morning marketing meeting for *Poetic Justice*, barking demands, making people squirm. He yelled at executives who'd been in the game since before he was born. After getting his way like that once or twice, he leaned into it. He acted out because he could. As Columbia's golden goose—the auteur responsible for their most profitable film of 1991—he faced no consequences. Who was saying no to John Singleton? Studios permitted this kind of behavior all the time from older white filmmakers. Now they had to endure it from him.

From the start, he envisioned Tupac Shakur as one of his leads, the freshman track star Malik Williams. They fleshed out the character together and brainstormed ideas for the film. Sometime that fall, Singleton flew to New York City, where Tupac was filming *Above the Rim*. One night, they listened to old soul records in Tupac's hotel room until late.

At one point, Aretha Franklin's cover of "Young, Gifted, and Black" by Nina Simone played. Pac jumped from the couch. "Did you hear that?" he asked Singleton.

He hummed the piano melody and pumped his arms like a sprinter.

"We gotta use Aretha for the track sequences," Tupac said.

Singleton nodded.

But shortly thereafter, Tupac got indicted in Georgia for shooting two off-duty cops and then again in New York on sexual assault charges. In November 1993, about two months before production started, Columbia told Singleton he couldn't hire him.

"Do you want your movie held hostage if he does something crazy and can't show up to work the next day?" Allain told him. Singleton reluctantly agreed.

Tupac felt betrayed. He believed Singleton caved easily to the studio's demands and then twisted the knife in his back by "stealing" his ideas for Malik. Singleton also slimed Tupac while promoting the film. "I didn't know if he was going to be up to working out and becoming a track runner, cause, you know . . . a lot of blunts," Singleton said in a January 1995 radio interview with Hot 97. "You got to be able to have a good cardiovascular system." From their first meeting for *Poetic Justice*, Tupac bought into Singleton's vision for him: to develop into the De Niro to his Scorsese. Instead, their partnership fizzled after one film, and their personal relationship would never recover.

★★★★★

So, he couldn't hire Tupac Shakur. Leonardo DiCaprio dropped out to do the Western *The Quick and the Dead* opposite Sharon Stone and Gene Hackman. Juliette Lewis opted instead for the Steve Martin comedy *Mixed Nuts*. Sidney Poitier deemed the script too controversial for his taste and passed. And days before filming started, Gwyneth Paltrow exited, citing a commitment to the Merchant Ivory period piece *Jefferson in Paris*.

"Gwyneth Paltrow's daddy told her not to do *Higher Learning*," Singleton later clarified.

By the top of the year, he'd found his cast, starting with Omar Epps for the role of Malik. Since his debut in *Juice*, Epps had fallen into playing athletes for a living. First, a college running back in *The Program*, then a center fielder in *Major League II*. *Higher Learning* would stitch another letter onto his varsity jacket. Epps earned the role over Bokeem Woodbine and Will Smith, the rapper turned sitcom star, who, on the heels of *Six Degrees of Separation*, openly lobbied Singleton, Scorsese, and Spike Lee for dramatic roles.

Singleton had already hired Kristy Swanson, Epps's costar from *The Program*, as the female lead Kristen Connor. Early on, he met Swanson at a Los Angeles restaurant. "We had an amazing lunch," Swanson says. "We talked about LA. He had a lot of fun poking fun at me for being from Orange County. 'Ooh, you're from behind the Orange Curtain.'"

Throughout the meal, Swanson couldn't stop staring at the medallion around his neck.

"He was wearing this necklace," Swanson says. "It looked like a sculpted face, but it was three-dimensional. I couldn't tell who it was. It was so small."

She blurted out, "Is that Sammy Davis Jr.?"

Singleton burst into laughter. "Sammy Davis Jr.? What? No!"

"I'm sorry! I'm sorry!" she cried.

He shook his head. "You don't know who this is?"

"No," she said. "I can't tell."

"Oh my God," he said, panting. "This is Malcolm X. You've heard of Malcolm X, right? Please tell me you've heard of Malcolm X."

Swanson nodded.

"Do you know anything about him? Do you know his history?"

She shook her head.

"I'm giving you a homework assignment."

"He said I had to read *The Autobiography of Malcolm X*," Swanson says.

In the meantime, he made some tweaks to the role of Kristen. "He'd written this character and it was perfect," Swanson says. "It fit me perfectly."

She read with Paltrow, who was set to play the upperclassman Taryn, a lesbian Kristen ends up falling for. Suddenly though, Paltrow was replaced with Jennifer Connelly of *The Rocketeer* fame.

DiCaprio's exit opened the door for Michael Rapaport to play one of the leads—Remy, the freshman who falls in with a group of neo-Nazis. Rapaport had initially been cast as Scott, the leader of the campus gang, before moving up the call sheet; Cole Hauser ended up as Scott.

An actor from New York known as White Mike to his Black friends, Rapaport got his big break in the 1992 indie film *Zebrahead*. The role wasn't much of a stretch. He played a teen obsessed with hip-hop and crushing on a Black girl. Singleton loved him in it and called Rapaport in for a meeting before *Poetic Justice* went before cameras. Eventually, he gifted him a small part in the film. The two became fast friends.

The part of the professor changed hands throughout the film's development.

Poitier wasn't even the first actor Singleton considered. Initially, he envisioned Dustin Hoffman in the role.

Whenever they'd cross paths in the Sony commissary, one of them would say, "Hey, we should do something together." But when they formally met about the film, Hoffman requested big changes to the script. He wanted to turn it into a two-hander about the professor and Malik. "I just wanted him in it for a hot second," Singleton said.

The character morphed into a Black conservative named Maurice Phipps. Once he thought of Poitier, he wrote the political science professor as Bahamian as a way to explore tension between West Indians and African Americans. He had Samuel L. Jackson read a few days after the actor finished filming his breakout role in *Pulp Fiction* and leaned toward hiring him. But Columbia chairman Mark Canton remained fixated on reuniting Singleton with Laurence Fishburne and steered him in that direction.

Singleton thought the actor, at thirty-two years old, was too young for the role, and spelled it out for him when they met. Fishburne explained how he'd age himself for the part and started experimenting with an accent.

Singleton added more *Boyz N the Hood* alumni to the cast, including Regina King as Kristen's roommate, Monet, and Ice Cube as Fudge, the super senior Black nationalist who takes Malik under his wing. Dedrick D. Gobert had a small part as Fudge's friend. Morris Chestnut and Malcolm Norrington both appeared uncredited in cameos during a track meet.

Lloyd Avery II did not return for *Higher Learning*. Singleton's relationship with him had taken a turn following an incident at a screening of *Poetic Justice*; Avery stood and hollered, "That shit was wack, John," as the closing credits rolled. But Avery's descent into the streets was of greater concern to Singleton and is what pushed them apart. "John had to distance himself from it," Norrington says. "Lloyd, at one point, threatened John like, 'I'm going to fuck you up' . . . It got to a point where John stopped taking Lloyd's calls."

In September 2005, Avery was murdered in Pelican Bay State Prison, where he had been serving a life sentence for a double homicide.

Singleton's most controversial casting decision involved the role of Malik's love interest Deja. From the start, he insisted on casting his new girlfriend Tyra Banks.

He met Banks after his publicist, Cassandra Butcher, spotted her on the cover of the June 1993 issue of *Essence* magazine and reached out to Banks's team. "I saw her and said, 'Let's set up a lunch. I think this is Deja,'" Butcher said. "[Tyra's] mother and Tyra and John met and talked."

Soon, they were seen dancing together at Club USA in New York.

Banks was a nineteen-year-old supermodel on the cusp of stardom when they started dating that summer. Born in Inglewood, she famously booked twenty-five runway shows at Paris Fashion Week her first time in Europe. She later earned a CoverGirl contract. All along she dreamed of working in the movies. Before her modeling career took off, she'd planned on attending Loyola Marymount film school. Two weeks before classes began she deferred her admission and headed overseas.

Banks's initial objective was to write and direct. But once she became a famous face, she understood her future lay in front of the camera. In the summer of 1993, she scored an eight-episode arc as Will Smith's girlfriend on the NBC sitcom *The Fresh Prince of Bel-Air*. Singleton cast her as Deja, despite much consternation from the studio.

He knew what it looked like but didn't care. When friends tried reasoning with him, he blew them off, huffing and puffing about his eye for finding new talent. Columbia begged him to consider other actresses, like Vivica A. Fox. He refused. The studio dispatched multiple envoys in a last-ditch effort to save Singleton from a bad decision of his own making.

One afternoon, Stephanie Allain knocked on his office door.

"John, you can't cast your girlfriend in the movie," she said upon entering.

"Well, I'm going to and I did," Singleton said. "She's cast."

"Dude, you're asking her to do a death scene," she said, concerned. "This is serious acting here."

"Look, she's Deja, period," Singleton yelled. "You know what? Don't say shit to me. This is gonna work. She's gonna be great. It's gonna be good for her. It's gonna be good for the movie. She's gonna be on the cover of *Vogue* or *Elle* when the movie comes out."

Allain tried one more time. "I don't think she can handle the role. She hasn't done anything like this."

"If you mention it again," he said, "I'm going to sock you in the face."

Allain never brought up the subject again. Looking back at the argument, she laughs. "He never would have done it. But he was so mad," she says. "I did try to talk him out of it, and he was not having it. That's one of the ones where he was like, 'No, fuck all of y'all, I'm doing it.' When he gets to that place, you just say, 'Okay.'"

By the time the film started shooting in January, Banks had survived rehearsals and a rigorous training regimen. She endured daily workouts with a track coach to lose twelve to fifteen pounds in order to look like she ran hurdles at a champion level. Still, there were nerves. Singleton could've eased her into the film. Instead, he scheduled her sex scene with Omar Epps for her first day on set. There she was naked, licking a strange man's nipples with her boyfriend looking on, directing her movements in a cold, meticulous manner. Later on, she'd admit that the scene made her feel "weird."

Once it was over, Singleton retreated to his trailer with Banks stepping not far behind. He slammed the door.

"You didn't act like you cared," she shouted.

"What are you talking about?"

"It didn't seem like you were affected by it one bit."

"Of course I was affected. I was, like, dying inside," he said later on in an interview. "But I'm not going to let the whole crew know that I'm pissed off that you have to do this scene with this dude. I'm fighting a war now."

He hadn't foreseen the problems that could arise from casting his significant other—either that, or he naïvely believed in his ability to sidestep them. But the decision to intertwine his personal and professional life added stress to an already tense situation.

"We were kind of living together and working together and we were both young," he said later on. "Her mother is nervous. My mother is nervous. She's nervous about acting. I thought she did a great job, but she was nervous every day. She knows the pressure I'm under from the studio, like, 'You're putting your girlfriend in the movie!'"

Singleton hit his stride as a director on *Higher Learning*, growing more confident on set and more confident in his abilities. He suffered from imposter syndrome on *Boyz N the Hood* until his success made him his own biggest believer. Now, working on his third film, he was as decisive as could be. There was an intention behind every shot. He knew what he wanted from his actors and from his crew, everything from how to light a scene to how much mayonnaise he wanted on the sandwiches his assistants fetched for him.

He handpicked his coproducer on the film. One night during preproduction, he called Paul Hall, who he knew from doing the electronic press kits for *Boyz N the Hood* and working on a behind-the-scenes feature on *Poetic Justice*. "Come over to my place," Singleton said. "I want to talk to you about some things. Pick up some pizza on the way."

Singleton laid it out for him. "So, you're going to produce *Higher Learning*."

Hall was stunned. "No, I'll produce the doc on it," he rebutted.

"No, no, no, you need to produce this film. I talk cinema with you. I talk story with you. I need you to help me make this movie."

Hall hesitated. He had a company and partners.

"You should be doing this," Singleton prodded. "You should be producing features."

Hall came on board to do the film. He'd go on to become Singleton's long-time producing partner and one of his closest friends.

"John would see things in you that you wouldn't see in yourself," Hall recounted years later. "It was wonderful to be introduced to filmmaking through him. His enthusiasm just pushed you forward in every aspect of the process."

Singleton loved the cast. By now, he'd developed a shorthand with Fishburne, King, and Ice Cube. Cole Hauser became one of his favorites, and he'd go on to work with him again. He also found collaborating with Michael Rapaport extremely fulfilling. Together, they shaped Remy into a sad, disturbed creep, much more nuanced than the typical Nazi villain.

On the set, they'd sidebar often and unearth little things to add to the character, like a quirky line reading. Singleton would suggest Rapaport move his torso side-to-side sporadically, anything to make Remy come across as a pitiful weirdo. He ostracized Rapaport to some point. While the young cast bonded between setups, listening to Omar Epps's bootlegged copy of Nas's *Illmatic*, Singleton banished Rapaport to his trailer where he'd read *Mein Kampf*. He wanted the energy to feel real when the Nazis and the Black students came face-to-face. And so, he asked Rapaport to ad-lib during scenes and call the Black actors the n-word in places it didn't appear in the script.

"We did one take and I went off just riffing, saying wild shit," Rapaport said. "You couldn't hear a word afterward."

But there were moments on *Higher Learning* when the cast became irritated with Singleton and the habits he'd developed over three films. His penchant for quiet observation became mistaken as aloofness. First-time collaborators weren't prepared for how he'd pick up a book while waiting for the next setup.

One morning, he showed up over an hour late. Upon arriving, he nervously chuckled the way he did when he felt guilty. Ice Cube put his arm around him.

"Let's go for a walk, John."

Singleton had escorted Cube into the movie industry. For a spell, they were neighbors in Baldwin Hills. Sometimes Cube would ring his doorbell unannounced and they'd spend the afternoon watching Kubrick flicks on Singleton's big screen. Slowly, Cube learned how to differentiate a bad movie from a good movie and a good one from a great one. One day, Singleton asked him, "When are you going to write your own script?"

"Write my script?" Cube said, pulling his head back. "What do you mean write my script? I'm no writer."

"If you can write records the way you do, records that are so vivid I can close my eyes and see the characters, you can write a script."

A few minutes later, they were in Singleton's Pathfinder driving to an electronics store in Santa Monica, where Cube bought the laptop and screenwriting program Singleton recommended. Later that night, he started writing *America Eats Its Young*. Over the weeks and months after that, Singleton shared tricks of the trade he learned in film school. That first script, Cube said, was "terrible." But he completed it. He then wrote a prison movie, *For Life*. From there, he moved on to a stoner comedy called *Friday*. In early 1994, he secured funding for it at New Line Cinema.

By the time of *Higher Learning*, Cube had morphed into a triple threat: writing, acting, and producing. Soon, he'd add directing. Once dismissive of the industry, he now took the business seriously. Seeing Singleton, his mentor, show up late didn't sit well with him. They stepped away but remained within earshot of the crew.

"John, all these people are here to make your movie," Cube said. "We've been here since the morning waiting for you. By being so late, you're disrespecting me, you're disrespecting all of us, and you're doing your movie a great disservice. What are you thinking?"

Singleton regrouped, and on the last night of shooting, at around four thirty in the morning, he asked the crew to gather around him. "I don't want this moment to end," he said as the lights around him shut down one by one. "I just want you to know how much I love all of you. This thing we do, making movies, is all about human connections. I recognize how lucky I am to do this. Being able to express yourself creatively is so therapeutic and so cleansing to the soul. And this film was me purging the angst that's been nestled in my soul for some time now."

★★★★★

During the early days of Singleton's relationship with Banks, he learned that the curvy old flame he'd originally met on USC's campus was pregnant with his son.

Singleton had started seeing Barlow after having reconnected with her. They ran into each other at a nightclub on Sunset and started dating around the spring of 1993. He liked showing her off. When it came time to film his cameo in the music video for Mista Grimm's hit single "Indo Smoke," Singleton lifted Barlow onto his shoulders in a chicken-fight position and walked through the shot. Barlow, in an off-shoulder tube top and miniskirt, looked at the camera and smiled.

"John was infatuated with her. She was young and beautiful," says his assistant at the time, Joe Doughrity. "There was a streak, though. It was more of a volatile relationship."

As their relationship intensified, Singleton expressed a desire to add to his family even though he wasn't ready to be a father to one child, let alone two. That he was also publicly dating a famous model wasn't much of a concern to him either. But he wanted a lot of kids and he hounded Barlow about it. "I'm going to get you pregnant," he'd tell her. "It's going to be a boy and he's going to be born on Easter."

But while pregnant she learned about the supermodel on the side. "I probably read about it in a magazine," Barlow says. "He wouldn't tell me about it." She also wanted children. In Singleton, Barlow saw a rich, successful nerd who made her laugh. His activist streak impressed her. Together, she envisioned, they'd do "revolutionary work" for their community and raise highly educated Black babies.

Singleton urged her to move closer to him from where she lived in Redlands, a city about an hour east of Los Angeles. He paid for her apartment in Culver City, where she'd raise their son.

One night in early April 1994, while Singleton was filming *Higher Learning*, Barlow called him to let him know she was being induced. He soon arrived at Cedars-Sinai on Beverly Boulevard.

"John came in with candy and popcorn," Barlow says. "He acted like it was a movie while watching me in labor. It was just his personality. He was so quirky." At one point, Singleton donned a surgical mask and gown and filmed Barlow's

C-section with his camcorder. "I got your guts and everything," he later told her.

They named their son Maasai Mohandas Singleton. "I named him Maasai because they are great warriors," Barlow says. "John picked the middle name. He wanted it to be balanced. So he named our son after Gandhi."

Meanwhile, Singleton's relationship with Banks had propelled him to another level of fame just as the sheen from *Boyz N the Hood* started to diminish. Some friends didn't approve of her. Quite a few people close to him took him aside and shared their thoughts: how they felt Banks was using him to benefit her film career. He knew Banks wasn't with him for his looks. But he liked the idea of dating a supermodel and the attention that came with it.

Their courtship played out in the press. Stories about Singleton organizing a surprise party aboard a chartered yacht for her twentieth birthday in December 1993, and how he bought her a large sapphire-and-diamond "friendship" ring the next year. When *GQ* magazine asked Banks for the most romantic thing anyone had done for her she mentioned the time Singleton "picked me up from the airport when I came back from Paris. We got back to the house and there were candles leading all the way up to the bathroom. He gave me a bath, dried me off. I walked downstairs and there was a chef and table laid out with all my favorite foods. For dessert there was a big basket of perfectly cut watermelon. I really love watermelon. Of course, I started crying."

Banks told reporters that she hadn't intended to rush into a relationship. But then, one night, during a long walk in Manhattan, where Banks lived part-time, she took the plunge. Standing in front of the Empire State Building, she told him she wanted to be his girl.

"It sounds so corny," Singleton said to the writer from *People* magazine. "But it's real."

*People* interviewed Banks and Singleton, a "lavish romantic" who turns into "a soft and cuddly fellow" at the mere sight of his "main squeeze," inside his Baldwin Hills home. Titled "Higher Yearning," the article captured them playing house for the magazine's Couples column.

"Moments after the green-eyed, 5'11" beauty enters the director's L.A. home, she begins her affectionate ritual of squeezing bumps on his shaved head," the article read. "Instantly, the macho man melts, becoming giggly and tender as they snuggle together on his black leather couch."

Banks said she wasn't interested in cohabitation ("Not until I get married," she said. "I'm old-fashioned."), while Singleton revealed they weren't thinking marriage—yet. "We are both pretty young to consider that," he said. "We are just taking it as we go along."

In the accompanying photo shoot, Singleton and Banks posed with their bodies pretzeled together on his living room floor. For someone once so protective of his personal life, it all felt performative and out of character for him. "My guess is that was Tyra's idea," Yon Styles says. "That was some fake Hollywood stuff and John wasn't a fake Hollywood guy."

They broke up shortly after *Higher Learning* opened; in the May 1995 issue of *GQ*, Singleton was referred to as Banks's "ex-boyfriend," which dates their split to before the issue went to print, sometime in February or March of that year.

How did he look back on the relationship? Some friends considered her one of his great loves, while others describe it as "a relationship of convenience."

After it ended, he spoke bitterly about her, telling some friends she dated him to launch her acting career. But with others he took responsibility for the end of the relationship.

He said that he cheated on Banks once while out of town for work. Singleton became conflicted right before he went through with it. He actually stopped what he was doing and debated what to do next. "What am I doing?" he said. "Why am I here?"

Then the other woman looked at him and said, "Boy! Come over here and get this pussy!" And he did.

"Whether he told Tyra about it or she found out, I don't know," one of his friends says. "But it was a story John talked about and one that he re-created for *Baby Boy.*"

Through her reps, Banks declined to comment.

★★★★★

Singleton's first cut of *Higher Learning* ran over three and a half hours, and he struggled whittling it down to an acceptable length.

Columbia had no plans to release the film at that run time and proposed big lifts along with the nips and tucks needed to cut at least an hour from the film.

"No. No. No. I'll look at this one. No. Maybe. No" is how he responded to their notes.

At one point, he called Brad Smith at CAA and said, "Tell these people not to call me or come around me. If you think I'm joking, know this: I brought my gun to the cutting room." Whether he was aware of it or not, making a threat with a deadly weapon could warrant a potential felony charge. But Singleton's chutzpah was both his gift and his curse. It was what drove him to turn down six figures for the *Boyz N the Hood* script and hold out for a directing gig. It could also account for his unacceptable behavior, such as mentioning his gun as a way to "preserve his vision," as he put it.

In a way, Columbia was also to blame. They created this monster. The studio had enabled him from the moment they entered into business with him. They looked the other way while he played his Nintendo Game Boy on set. They let it slide when he bullied marketing executives. They allowed him to cast his girlfriend, a nonactor, in a major dramatic role! They did everything possible to acquiesce to the talent—and then acted surprised when the talent walked all over them.

Singleton intended for the film to push buttons. From the start, he felt the studio had gone soft—that it tried to scrub anything it deemed risqué or controversial: the rumble between the Nazis and the Black students; Busta Rhymes, fist in the air, shouting Five Percenter creed; Ice Cube taunting campus security.

"Why does Cube have to go after the police like that?" he was asked.

"Because that's what a certain segment of the audience is going to respond to. Brothers love to see Ice Cube talking shit to police," he said. "Look, I'm just trying to make you some money. Trust me. Just sit down."

The biggest battle involved the lesbian relationship between Kristen and Taryn. In his initial cut, the sex scene ran longer. Singleton hesitated to cut it. Without the scene, he thought, it remained unclear whether Kristen had sex with Taryn or just fantasized about her while with her male love interest played by Jason Wiles. Singleton agreed to cut the scene. Then, days away from locking the film, he had second thoughts. He called his editor, Bruce Cannon.

"Bruce," he said, calling from the Caribbean where he was vacationing, "put it back in."

Cannon phoned Paul Hall. On the set, the crew viewed the first-time producer as a rubber stamp for Singleton. But in the most crucial moment he convinced him to stand down.

*Higher Learning* got down to two hours and eight minutes mostly through sacrificing Kristen's storyline. From the start of rehearsals, Singleton felt uneasy about Swanson's performance. Later on, he said that "her insecurities really got in the way" during her sex scene with Connelly, and that at other times, "it was difficult to pull that emotion out of her, that performance out of her." As a result, many of Connelly's, Wiles's, and King's scenes were also cut from the film.

At the film's New York premiere, Connelly turned to a crew member while the credits rolled and said, "Why am I even here? I'm not even in the movie."

*Higher Learning* had its fans. Roger Ebert praised the film's performances in his three-star review, while Todd McCarthy at *Variety* and *Rolling Stone*'s Peter Travers complimented Singleton for his ambitions. "Singleton has a goal most of his contemporaries have given up on: He wants to make a movie that makes a difference," Travers wrote.

Owen Gleiberman at *Entertainment Weekly* called it "a demagogic rabble-rouser" and decried the film's climactic fight scene between Malik and Remy. "During the final battle, in which the campus security behave in nearly as racist a fashion as the skinheads (the key moment is staged beneath a painting of Thomas Jefferson), Singleton's threadbare hatemongering becomes loathsome, a way of pandering to the most apocalyptic fantasies of black victimization."

Critics found it overly moralizing and lacking nuance. "Too many of the people in *Higher Learning*, like Taryn the feminist, tend to come off as billboards more than people," wrote Kenneth Turan of the *Los Angeles Times*. Janet Maslin at the *New York Times* said that "there are enough little lectures to warrant course credit before the film is over."

At the time, critics slammed him for depicting Nazis and white supremacist ideology as a current menace. "The film's least convincing character is Remy, the born-again skinhead," Gleiberman wrote. "Aryan youth groups, after all, don't exactly constitute a towering threat to our universities."

But Singleton sensed the moment: the ascendance of white supremacist and antigovernment ideology that accelerated following the election of Bill Clinton. Ruby Ridge. Waco. The upsurge of militias in the Midwest. The raggedy bunch of skinheads in Long Beach. Three months after *Higher Learning* opened, Timothy McVeigh, an avowed white supremacist, bombed a federal building in Oklahoma City, killing 168 people. A year later the fundamentalist Christian terrorist Eric Rudolph bombed the Olympic Village in Atlanta.

"A lot of people don't really want to get into the whole issue about how to kill racism. Whenever they bring up a discussion about how to kill racism, they never bring up the subject of killing white supremacy to kill racism," Singleton said while promoting the film. "You might not think that we live in a country that is white supremacist in nature. Or when you hear *white supremacy*, you think I'm speaking of Nazism or whatever. It's on different levels. It's an institutionalized belief that if you are not white, male, and rich, you shouldn't be here."

Looking back, he accepted the film as flawed. "Some of it is kind of didactic," he said. "Hey, man, I was twenty-four years old writing this stuff. It worked. It made money. I guess that's what counts in this business."

*Higher Learning* was released on January 11, 1995, ahead of Martin Luther King Jr. weekend. Once considered a dumping ground for new films, Columbia staked out the January date to avoid the crowded Christmas season, and it worked. The film took in $17 million over its first six days in release (good for second place behind the Brad Pitt vehicle *Legends of the Fall*) and ended its run at a respectable $39 million.

The film marked the end of the beginning of his career, as it fulfilled his three-picture deal with Columbia. Over that time, Singleton learned a series of hard lessons about the business, some of which he refused to absorb.

# CHAPTER THIRTEEN

Late January 1995. John Singleton was in Orlando, Florida, to interview survivors of the 1923 Rosewood massacre. When he stepped off the plane, he met Arnett Doctor, a retired Tampa businessman with deep familial ties to Rosewood, and his lawyer, Greg Galloway.

They drove two hours northwest through the pine swamps and overgrowth until reaching a sign announcing the town of Rosewood.

"Where's the town?" Singleton asked as the car stopped.

Scattered across the terrain stood a few small trailer homes. Luckily, Doctor knew his way around the grounds. He scrambled down a dirt road, past rows of cages filled with snarling pit bulls, until arriving at a rickety house.

A middle-aged white man clutching a pump-action shotgun walked onto the porch.

"Whadda y'all want?" he said.

"We spoke last week," Doctor said. The dog pens rattled with fury as he approached.

This is exactly what Singleton, who had a deep contempt for the South, feared.

Now here he stood in rural Florida—Klan country—opposite some strange cracker packing a goddamn shotgun.

Doctor waved the group forward.

A few hundred yards or so past the house, he stopped. "This is it," Doctor said, arms outstretched. "This is where my family is buried."

For the next thirty minutes he narrated the history of the mostly Black town of Rosewood, from its founding in 1845 to the events of January 1923. How a racist mob burned it down after a white woman named Fannie Taylor lied about a Black man assaulting her. The estimated death toll ranged from six to 250.

"It was cold—colder than this now," Doctor sermonized. "Imagine children and mothers hiding in the swamps. No food. No water. Shivering. Praying to be rescued."

Singleton closed his eyes and filled his lungs to the brim. He exhaled, looked up, and then wobbled a bit from the spirits at work.

They all marched back to the house, where the man's wife had now joined him.

"I'm sorry what happened to your ancestors," she sneered. "But you niggers need to get off our land."

Singleton turned and stepped toward them until Howard Hobson, his new director of production at New Deal, put his arms up. "Dude, we need to go," he said. "Now."

They all piled into their rental van, except for Doctor, who hopped into a red Mustang, vanity plate spelling out some abbreviation of Rosewood, and zipped back to Orlando.

Singleton remained quiet during the drive to the hotel. Every so often, he'd mutter, "Fuck that cracker," and then return to his thoughts. How much had really changed in seventy-two years?

Later that weekend, in a hotel conference room, he met people who could answer that: the eight living Rosewood survivors. He sat opposite Minnie Lee Langley, who was nine at the time of the massacre. Singleton leaned in. Held her gaze. Though her memories were from childhood, she painted a vivid picture. One tends not to forget what it's like to be hunted.

Langley was inside her uncle Sylvester's house when the mob attacked. Before fleeing into the swamp, she witnessed him shoot and kill two white assailants. For the next three days, she took cover in the cold Florida muck until a train lifted her to safety. She didn't speak of Rosewood for decades.

"Son, you were chosen to do this movie by God," she told him. "So don't try to take anything from it or add a whole lot to it. Just do the movie. It'll take care of itself."

He lowered his eyes and swallowed hard. He looked away. He then made his way toward the exit. Suddenly, one of the descendants of the Rosewood survivors—Singleton described her as a "big, thick woman with thick arms"— muscled him into a corner.

"Baby, you have to make this movie," she said.

"Ma'am, I'm going to try," Singleton whispered, his eyes welling up.

"No, baby, you *have* to make this movie."

"I'll figure it out once I'm back in LA," he said. "And I promise I'll be in touch."

"Listen, baby, either you're going to make this movie or Steven Spielberg's going to do it," she said. "And we don't want him."

★★★★★

Singleton had become familiar with Rosewood on a restless night in the summer of 1994. Sometimes when he couldn't sleep, which happened often, he'd drive to the newsstand on Robinson and Beverly and flip through magazines. On this night, he picked up the July issue of *Esquire.*

"The Rosewood Massacre" was the headline. "Seventy-one years after a rampaging white mob lynched a small black town in the Florida swamp, the survivors have finally told their story. A gothic drama of race wars, justice delayed, and the ultimate TV tie-in."

Singleton didn't think much of the article. He certainly had no intention of making a movie from it.

Rosewood was one of many pogroms against Black Americans post-Reconstruction and into the early twentieth century. Over the next sixty years, the massacre lapsed from the public view until Gary Moore, a reporter with the *St. Petersburg Times* unearthed the story in 1982. A year later, *60 Minutes* aired a report featuring interviews with the survivors, including Minnie Lee Langley. When the journalist Ed Bradley asked what she'd say to children today, Langley didn't mince words: "Don't ever stay in a place where white folks can surround you, because if anything happens, they'll run you out just like they did us."

About a decade later, the Rosewood families initiated a targeted campaign with Arnett Doctor leading the effort. Doctor, as chairman of the Rosewood Advisory Committee, had two objectives: to secure monetary compensation for the victims, and sign a movie deal. To attain the latter, he hired Greg Galloway, a white entertainment lawyer out of Orlando.

Doctor gave him specific instructions for the negotiations: He could only pitch Black filmmakers. "I cautioned him against that," Galloway says. "Then I sent out solicitations to every Black production company I could think of: Oprah Winfrey, Wesley Snipes, Bill Cosby, Spike Lee. We didn't get anywhere."

The Rosewood Advisory Committee had more success winning reparations from the state. In April 1994, the Florida State Legislature awarded $2.1

million to the nine survivors and the descendants of the massacre. The legislature explained that state officials "had sufficient time and opportunity to prevent the tragedy, and nonetheless failed to act to prevent the tragedy."

Following the decision, the national media rediscovered Rosewood. *Esquire* sent a reporter to Florida. And in June 1994, *60 Minutes* aired an update to the original segment.

Somewhere in Los Angeles, Jon Peters was watching.

Peters, the former Sony cochairman, had regrouped since his public sacking in April 1991, with twin production deals at his former studio and at Warner Bros. The "street fighter" remained ferocious and a little nutty. Around this time, he got into a fistfight with Steven Seagal while developing *Under Siege 2*, or so he claimed. But more important to Doctor, Peters still possessed enough clout with Warner Bros. cochairmen Bob Daly and Terry Semel to get a film like *Rosewood* into production. Warner Bros. focused on tentpole films: big, special-effects-heavy action-adventure romps and star-driven comedies, not period pieces about racist massacres.

Doctor and the families approved of the producer thanks to his involvement with *The Color Purple*. But Galloway maintained to him that *Rosewood* must be a "Black film" and as "Afrocentric as possible." The conversation turned to directors.

"Well, I got a director," Peters said coyly, "and I think you're going to like him."

★★★★★

Singleton hadn't selected his next film, and it was shaping up to be the most crucial decision of his career. Though *Poetic Justice* and *Higher Learning* were both profitable, they lacked the focus and impact of *Boyz N the Hood*. He could pivot in any direction. Action. Drama. A period piece. A cartoon. He could play it safe or take a risk. He orbited five projects. *Makes Me Wanna Holler* was the front-runner.

Columbia optioned the book in September 1993, before it was published, with Singleton in mind to direct. On the surface, it appeared a perfect match between filmmaker and subject matter—*Washington Post* reporter's Nathan McCall's memoir detailing his hardscrabble years growing up in Portsmouth, Virginia. But Singleton struggled with the screenplay. He was unsure about what to cut from the book. Structure was a problem, as was how to depict the violence. He completed a draft, and the project gained enough momentum that he hosted a reading at his home, soon after which he tabled the script.

He also weighed adapting *This Side of Glory*, the memoir from former Black Panther chief of staff David Hilliard, to which Paula Weinstein held the rights. Weinstein, who'd produced *The Fabulous Baker Boys* and had a deal with Warner Bros., was an outlier in Hollywood. "Paula was sympathetic to the Black experience," Hobson says. She'd admired Singleton since *Boyz N the Hood* and pursued him upon optioning the rights to Hilliard's inside look at the Black Panther operation. By this point, however, Mario Van Peebles had moved forward on *Panther*, and although the two projects differed in both scope and story—Van Peebles's movie centers around a fictitious composite character—any prospect for Weinstein's film ended when *Panther* earned a disappointing $7 million at the box office in the spring of 1995.

The challenge of tackling a different film genre also appealed to Singleton. He tried developing a computer-animated film based on the popular Sega video game *Ecco the Dolphin*.

"When I got the call, I said, 'Wait a minute, John Singleton wants to do an animated film?'" says Stu Krieger, who'd written *The Land before Time* for Spielberg and Lucas. But Singleton loved video games and perceived *Ecco* as a true about-face. He wanted people to say, *Wait a minute, John Singleton is directing an animated film?*

They worked on it for about a year, but the technology hadn't developed enough, and everyone moved on.

An adaptation of his favorite comic book, *Luke Cage*, was another possibility. In the 1990s, Marvel Comics arbitrarily sold off the film rights to its iconic characters with the veteran producer Ed Pressman (*Conan the Barbarian* and *Wall Street*) controlling *Luke Cage*. Singleton and his cowriter, his assistant Joe Doughrity, had a bold vision for the Hero for Hire. In addition to transporting Luke Cage from the streets of Harlem to Africa, they also proposed teaming him with his occasional partner from the comics Iron Fist.

Pressman dismissed the idea. "You can't have more than one superhero in a movie," he told Singleton during a development meeting.

Singleton turned to Doughrity and smirked.

"We had the Avengers showing up. We had references to S.H.I.E.L.D.," Doughrity says. "We acknowledged this greater Marvel universe."

"It was a radical change, which probably showed a lot of foresight," Pressman said, shortly before his death in 2023. "But I was stuck on the original Hero for Hire here in the States. After working on it for a while, we parted ways on a friendly basis."

That left *Rosewood.*

"We had a similar background," says Peters, who is of Italian and Native American descent, about Singleton. "I grew up in San Fernando in a Hispanic/Black neighborhood and I did *The Color Purple* and later *Rosewood, Ali,* and *Wild, Wild West.* I've always been kin to the underdog and people of color as well."

Singleton had got along fine with the mercurial producer when he ran Sony, yet remained wary of working with him. He'd heard all the stories about Peters—the outbursts, some of which Peters embellished, and all the impulsive, rich-guy quirks he'd have to deal with. Peters once sent the Sony corporate jet to deliver flowers to a supermodel he was courting. He liked to have scripts read to him. "I just, you know, just lay back and listen and I run it on my screen in my brain," he said in the 2015 documentary, *The Death of Superman Lives: What Happened?*

For all his flaws, Peters produced big hits like *A Star is Born, Caddyshack*, and *Flashdance.* His work on the $400 million–grossing *Batman* earned him the reputation of a marketing genius. And he was a great salesman. Peters "talked like a young boy excited about a new bike," when pitching a project to talent, says Kim Pucci, his former assistant. Singleton received the full Jon Peters charm offensive.

"I really want to make a movie that's about something," he told Singleton during one of their initial meetings. "*Rosewood* is about right and wrong and cheering for the marginalized as they fight back."

Peters also believed *Rosewood* could be an Academy Awards contender, and nothing motivates Hollywood creatures like Jon Peters (and John Singleton, to an extent) like the thought of cradling little gold men on Oscar night.

"You can make something important, John," Peters said, his voice growing louder. "You can make something historical! It's going to be amazing! And we're going to take it all the way! We're going all the way to the Oscars! And it's going to be John Singleton bringing this story to light!" Soon after the meeting, Singleton signed on to direct.

*Rosewood* would be his first film outside of Columbia and his first time working with another writer. "John was a little tired of writing," Hobson says. "He wanted a writer where he could do the Spielberg thing—talk through the story points and beats and collaborate on the script."

Gregory Poirier was a thirty-three-year-old former would-be actor when the studio hired him to write *Rosewood.* A Hawaiian native with an affinity for tattoos and Hawaiian shirts, Poirier graduated from USC with a BFA in theater and earned an MFA in screenwriting from UCLA. While in film school, he made a living writing adult films. He sold a script to HBO about kickboxers. A Western called *The Iron Horseman* then made him a player. After Warner Bros. bought the script, names like Arnold Schwarzenegger and Harrison Ford circled the film. But that wasn't enough to drive the film into production. Warner Bros. executives were still high on Poirier though and recommended him to Peters, who passed *The Iron Horseman* on to Singleton.

They felt each other out before collaborating. Singleton brought Poirier to the premiere of *Higher Learning* and took him to his favorite bookstore, Esowon Books.

They'd sit in front of Singleton's big screen, a TV "the size of Guatemala," as Poirier remembers it, watching laser discs. Singleton once spent an entire afternoon with him playing nothing but his favorite sound cues from movies.

Throughout the spring of 1995, they met about the script. Early on, they realized that *Rosewood* lacked a main character. So they created Mann, a Clint Eastwood Man-with-No-Name archetype.

With *Apocalypse Now* on in the background, they spitballed ideas. "This guy, whatever his name is, rides into Rosewood just as the events of the film unfold," Poirier told Singleton. "He's this arbiter of change."

Singleton insisted on two points: depicting the savagery of the lynch mob and showing Black people fighting back.

"We just got our ass kicked and took it and then started singing to Jesus, right? No. We fight back," Singleton said. "We're gonna have brothers doing stuff in this movie that they've never done in the history of American cinema."

Initial drafts of Poirier's screenplay were brutal. Some of the survivors' stories were too grisly to film.

"There was one scene they told us," Poirier says. "A woman, a man, and a baby were hiding in the swamp when a stray bullet killed the woman. The baby was screaming as the mob approached. The father then attached the baby to the dead mother's breast, so that the baby could suckle and stop crying. Singleton just looked at the script and was like, 'I can't shoot this.' We ended up cutting it out."

Singleton tweaked Poirier's drafts, as any director would: naming Mann's horse Booker T., adding a morbid joke here and there, beefing up a father-and-son story. In his mind, though, he wasn't just giving notes. He had cowritten a screenplay. Now he wanted credit.

As *Rosewood* marched toward an early 1996 start date, Singleton chased more work. He burned to be prolific like his heroes Spielberg and Spike Lee, and the money was too good to turn down—$450,000 to write *Makes Me Wanna Holler*; $1.5 million to direct *Rosewood*; $600,000 to write *Band of Assassins*, a *John Wick*–like action film with Laurence Fishburne, Chazz Palminteri, and Chow Yun-fat attached to it.

Some projects never stood a chance, like an adaptation of *The Confessions of Nat Turner*, which he pitched to Disney. He also attempted to get August Wilson's *Ma Rainey's Black Bottom* off the ground. A few years earlier, he'd been floated as a potential director for *Fences* when Eddie Murphy held the rights at Paramount. But Singleton was still locked into his three-picture deal at Columbia at the time.

One afternoon in 1995, he toured through the town with Wilson for pitch meetings at Disney, United Artists, and Fine Line. Afterward they shopped for laser discs at Laser Blazer and played pinball at an arcade near the Westside Pavilion. Now back in the New Deal offices, Singleton had an idea for the screenplay.

"We need to do this together," he said.

Wilson shook his head. "John, you know I don't work that way," he said. "Let me do my thing and then you can take a look at it."

*Ma Rainey* came close at United Artists but didn't get made until 2020 at Netflix.

He also took another crack at directing a comic-book movie. In early 1995, Columbia held the rights to *Black Panther* with Wesley Snipes locked into the lead. In a little over eighteen months, Snipes had starred in *Mo' Better Blues*, *New Jack City*, *Jungle Fever*, and *White Men Can't Jump*. *Boiling Point* and *Demolition Man* then turned him into a bankable action star, though a rung below the Schwarzenegger/ Stallone/Willis tier. A comic-book adaptation was the sensible next step for him.

Singleton and Reginald Hudlin were on Columbia's short list to direct—the studio wanted to pair Snipes with a Black director—and both wanted the job.

"Once we realized we were in competition with each other, it made for an awkward moment," Hudlin says. Then, one day, they bumped into each other at Golden Apple Comics on Melrose. Singleton smiled and stuck out his hand. "Let the best man win," he said.

Snipes had other filmmakers in mind. "I knew Wesley from my New York days and from the martial arts community," Hudlin says. "We went to him about

*Black Panther* and he was like, 'Nah man, I'm trying to get Ridley Scott to direct.' I was like, 'Ridley Scott is never going to direct this!'"

Snipes rebuffed Singleton as well. A planned meeting between them on the New York set of *Money Train* was scrapped. That followed a missed connection at the CAA offices where Snipes seemingly blew him off. Singleton was perplexed. He'd had a good relationship with Snipes since meeting during his whirlwind post-*Boyz* period; they'd even partied together recently in Vegas. But Snipes's cold shoulder wasn't personal. He just hated Singleton's pitch: a father-son story set against the Civil Rights Movement.

*Dude, where are the toys?* was the actor's first thought. With *Black Panther* languishing in development hell, Snipes moved on to *Blade* for his comic-book movie fix.

During this time, Singleton aimed to transform New Deal into a hitmaking production company in the mold of Steven Spielberg's Amblin Entertainment. Spielberg didn't direct every Amblin picture but every Amblin picture felt Spielberg-esque—*Gremlins* (directed by Joe Dante), *The Goonies* (Richard Donner), *Back to the Future I, Part II,* and *Part III* (Robert Zemeckis), and *Who Framed Roger Rabbit* (Zemeckis again).

Similarly, Singleton envisioned New Deal producing films that reflected his brand: hip, provocative stories from the young Black filmmakers emerging in his wake.

In May 1995, New Deal purchased *Brushback* from rookie screenwriter Eric Daniel for a six-figure sum. A former PA for Spike Lee, Daniel was a product of the Disney Fellowship Program. *Brushback* was more high-concept than the typical Singleton film. It featured a great elevator pitch: *Field of Dreams* meets *Back to the Future* set in the Negro Leagues. An arrogant modern-day slugger (think Barry Bonds) is plunked with a beanball and wakes up in 1945 wearing a Kansas City Monarchs uniform. Now teammates with Jackie Robinson and Satchel Paige, he must rekindle his love of the game—and get the girl.

With the right star, *Brushback* read like a potential tentpole film. And who was that star? Daniel wrote the lead with Will Smith in mind.

Initially, Singleton felt ambivalent about the actor. He recognized Smith's colossal marketing potential, but it left him uneasy. "He got what Will represented—that wholesome all-American guy," says Joe Doughrity. "But he also thought he was corny and that his image was corny. He thought Will was doing this sanitized Black man act."

Singleton first met the star of *The Fresh Prince of Bel-Air* during the summer of 1990 shortly after signing his *Boyz N the Hood* deal. He was at the Roxbury on the Sunset Strip, celebrating with a group of friends he'd known for years—and picking up the tab for the first time—when Smith and his manager Benny Medina approached his table to offer their congratulations.

In late 1993, Singleton considered Smith for the Omar Epps role in *Higher Learning*. But he sensed he'd bring too much small-screen baggage with him to the film. Eighteen months later, he encountered a much different Will Smith. *Bad Boys* had just topped the box office and grossed $65 million and *Independence Day* was on a fast track for a summer and fall shoot. *Brushback* had to wait. Singleton thought the script needed work anyway.

He perceived *Brushback* as more than a sports film, and certainly not a lighthearted one at that. In edit meetings with Daniel, he urged him to explore the discrimination Negro Leaguers faced during the World War II era. Daniel pushed back.

"I feel like we've seen that already," he told Singleton. "Don't we want the audience to feel positive?"

"Black people can't really look back at any time in history and say, 'Oh, this was a fun time! These were the good old days!' It doesn't work like that," Singleton said. "I've seen *Bingo Long* and I want this to hit harder."

With Daniel off rewriting *Brushback*, Singleton turned his attention to *Magic Markers*.

Originally a twenty-three-minute sixteen-millimeter film by an NYU graduate student named Geoffrey Fletcher, the quirky love story reminded Singleton of Woody Allen's work. New Deal bought the rights with the intention of producing a feature-length version Fletcher would write and direct. Despite being two years his junior, Fletcher, a shy, likable kid, looked at Singleton with awe.

"It was surreal that I knew him. I mean, I'd seen him on *Oprah*," Fletcher says. "For me, it didn't feel like we were so close in age. Here's a man with money, a career, a cool car, and had dated Tyra Banks."

Singleton flew the Harvard graduate out to Los Angeles for meetings with studio executives. He put him up in the Chateau Marmont. One morning, he called and told Fletcher, "I'm on the way—be ready. By the way, that means downstairs out front." About thirty minutes later, Singleton arrived. They drove off under the California sunshine with "Maybe Tomorrow" by the Jackson 5 on the radio.

He turned down the volume before Michael finished the chorus. "Man, Michael knows the business through and through," Singleton said. "Ten years ago, he bought the Beatles catalog for forty-seven million dollars. He just sold fifty percent of it for a hundred million."

Later that day, they sold *Magic Markers* to Fine Line Features, the cool, indie division of New Line Cinema. As it was known for its auteur-driven projects and its good taste (*Hoop Dreams* was Singleton's favorite film of 1994), Singleton considered the studio a good fit for the film. He left Fletcher alone to develop his feature-length script.

That summer, Singleton was also in negotiations with Miramax, the pioneering indie studio that Disney had recently devoured for around $100 million. For a few more months, he was locked into a nonexclusive first-look deal with Columbia. He could bring projects to other studios only after Columbia passed on them. Singleton pictured Miramax as the perfect home for a second-look deal—a place where he could funnel the small, low-budget features he thought New Deal should produce between his films and commercial fare like *Brushback*. He prepared to move fast. He already had a film in mind for the proposed New Deal/Miramax partnership.

Lee Davis was another former Spike Lee PA that Singleton took an interest in. Through the Sundance Lab, Davis developed a screenplay, *Running Meters*, about a night in the life of New York City cab drivers. Singleton heard about it, pursued it, read it, and liked it so much he flew Davis to Los Angeles and put him up in his guest bedroom for a week to work on the script.

"I felt like I was at my cousin's house," Davis says.

Singleton didn't have many edits for him other than cutting the amount of direction in the screenplay—"Nobody reads that shit," he said. Once Davis finished the script, Singleton told him he wanted to produce the film and would do so at Miramax. Enter Harvey Weinstein.

The Miramax cofounder was infatuated with auteurs like Quentin Tarantino and Robert Rodriguez and had wanted to get into business with John Singleton since meeting him at the 1991 Cannes Film Festival. He bought *Running Meters* and discussed the framework of a production deal with Singleton.

That Singleton even negotiated with Weinstein was further evidence of the rift with Columbia, which first emerged following *Poetic Justice* and had yet to heal. Singleton felt the studio didn't support New Deal. In a way, he was correct. Columbia wasn't interested in any New Deal project that Singleton wasn't directing. It got to the point where Hobson would pitch Stephanie Allain and say, "I'm sending this to you. Give me your fast pass."

"John was known as a filmmaker, a writer-director, and we were more interested in him as a director," Allain says. "I just don't think he was taken seriously as a producer."

When the love and attention he craved vanished, he sought it elsewhere, whether it was with Weinstein or a rival studio like Warner Bros. Both Columbia and Singleton agreed it was time for a divorce. "*Rosewood* was a period piece, dark, a hard movie to make," Allain says. "So, it was like, *Great, let him go make that with someone else.*"

On December 3, 1995, *Variety* reported that New Deal had signed a two-year first-look deal with Universal for $350,000 annually.

Singleton's proposed deal with Miramax collapsed around this time as well. All along, Weinstein wanted New Deal's big-budget features, not just art house films aimed at niche markets like *Running Meters*. Singleton had second thoughts as well and it had nothing to do with budgets or anything involving the multiple rape charges that later sent Weinstein to prison.

Deep into negotiations, Singleton learned the studio would be releasing *Don't Be a Menace to South Central While Drinking Your Juice in the Hood*, a spoof of so-called hood films, which took aim at *Boyz N the Hood*. The lead was named Ashtray. Lines of dialogue were lifted ("We got a problem here?") and key scenes from *Boyz*, such as the one where Reva drops off Tre at his father's house, were lampooned.

Singleton didn't find it funny. His life story wasn't ripe for parody. "Fuck them," he fumed. "Fuck Miramax."

And like that, he walked away from the deal.

Singleton could be like that. He could make irritational decisions and walk out on deals. He could, because studios still killed to work with him. They sweated him because he had built something powerful in a flash.

*The first Black nominee for Best Director.*

*The youngest nominee for Best Director.*

*The auteur behind a trio of profitable films.*

*The kid who changed the game.*

He had built something powerful and he knew it. He always had a healthy ego. He always thought he knew better. Always thought he knew best. He handled his business, sitting there in his office behind his desk making big decisions. What movie to direct. What party to attend. What laser disc to watch. Which woman to call.

He was now a fully formed creature: a film nerd from South Central Los Angeles, with talent, love for his people, a big bank account, and one weak spot. Not drugs. Not drink. Not fast cars. Not the streets. Nothing illegal. He loved women. Pursuing women. Dating women. Being with women. But the more he indulged, the deeper he plunged into a web of toxic relationships that simultaneously exhausted him and captivated him. He was usually going through a rough patch with at least one girlfriend or ex-girlfriend or coparent. Then he'd seek refuge in the arms of a different girlfriend, ex-girlfriend, or coparent.

He started seeing Barlow more often after he split from Tyra Banks. Barlow and Maasai had moved to La Brea, about ten minutes from the Baldwin Hills house. Singleton referred to the boy as "the tie that binds us." One day Barlow went to her parents' house to pick up Maasai and there he was: Singleton playing with the baby, sitting on the couch chatting up her mom, asking about her church. *True Gospel Missionary? That's on Seventy-Eighth and Hoover?*

He made fleeting attempts at domesticity. Family reunions. Barbecues. They spent a weekend at Skywalker Ranch as George Lucas's guest. Picnics in Kenneth Hahn park on La Cienega. Maasai's first birthday party at Knott's Berry Farm, an amusement park in Buena Park, California. They attended family counseling together. They also got into silly fights. One time while waiting for their strawberry shakes at a drive-thru, Barlow presumed the cashier had flirted with Singleton and that he was a little too receptive to her overtures. They had it out right there.

Still, Barlow looks back on that time as the happiest point in their on-again, off-again relationship.

"That was his most stable, family-oriented era," she says. "The *Baby Boy* era."

The era would not last long. He was always on the go. There were deals to close. Women to see. Movies to make. He was living his best life.

He'd fly cross-country to attend a lavish benefit event on June 8, 1995, the Fresh Air Fund's "Salute to American Heroes" gala at Tavern on the Green in Central Park. There, he'd appear onstage with his "Remember the Time" star Iman, catch up with Russell Simmons, socialize with the top one percent of the one percent. San Francisco 49ers quarterback Steve Young. Model Veronica Webb. *Vogue* editor Anna Wintour. Fashion designers Ralph Lauren and Tommy Hilfiger.

He'd outgrown his awkward phase. He looked sharp and cool, handsome in fact. Shiny bald head. Clean shaven face. Rimless glasses. A surprisingly strong jawline. He wore a classic mid-'90s look: a tan summer suit with three buttons, a little baggier than Ralph would rock. But Singleton was a twenty-seven-year-old member of the hip-hop generation. What did they expect?

Less than twenty-four hours later he'd be back on the coast for the *Batman Forever* premiere at Mann Village Theater. Then, in three days, on June 12, he'd make an appearance at the VH1 Honors at the Shrine and get a close-up look at Whitney Houston bringing down the house with a performance of "This Day." He was out there doing it. Living out his dreams every which way he could.

"I'm not a star," he liked to say once he got older. "I make stars." But in the summer of '95 he remained a star.

At the end of July, he was back in New York checking in on Geoffrey Fletcher. Their script meetings could devolve from conversations about *Magic Markers* to debating film theory to exchanges about whatever was in multiplexes.

"Let's go see *Waterworld*," Singleton would say.

Then they'd troop to the Village East on Twelfth and Second and buy tickets. His treat. He was familiar with Kevin Costner's troubled production. *Waterworld*: the $175 million guaranteed bust. The town called it *Kevin's Gate* after *Heaven's Gate*, that legendary flop. Singleton, a ravenous consumer of print media, read all the articles about *Waterworld*. The gossip. The breathless updates in *Variety* and the *Hollywood Reporter*. The big feature in the recent *Vanity Fair*. But he could set aside the negative chatter and evaluate the film both as a filmmaker and a fan.

Afterward, they'd step outside into the thick air covering the city on this dog day afternoon. Singleton would look at his watch. He'd make phone calls. When he learned he had time to kill, he'd improvise plans. "Let's go see *Kids*," he'd say. Then they'd head south toward the Angelika. Mr. LA learning to walk the streets of New York to indulge in his one-, sometimes two-movie-a-day habit.

"If you're going to call yourself a screenwriter or a director, you have to watch movies every single day," he always said. "You are constantly watching movies and learning."

"It seemed like he was always thinking. He had a great bandwidth," Fletcher says. "He was busy with meetings and projects. It seemed like he could keep all of those pots spinning but also compartmentalize. But it was remarkable how he could always make time to watch films. I was in awe of just how professional he was. There was a great flow to it. It looked as if he had been in the business for decades."

Fletcher wasn't on Singleton's level yet. He struggled expanding his screenplay for *Magic Markers* from its original short format to a feature length. Singleton felt it needed a few more passes before turning it over to the studio. But Fletcher submitted the draft anyway. He was inexperienced and full of hubris. Fine Line canceled the deal afterward just as Singleton had warned. Shortly thereafter, UTA dropped Fletcher as a client.

"John was trying to give me the chance he had," Fletcher says. "I think I was too young to capitalize on the opportunity. I sometime feel like that first encounter with Hollywood was like when Luke went off to face Darth Vader for the first time. He wasn't ready. And I wasn't ready."

★★★★★

By this point, New Deal Records had collapsed.

Singleton took an active interest in the label at the start. He made the rounds as a record executive—late-night studio sessions; industry parties; artist showcases in Arizona; Thursday nights at the Good Life Cafe, the famed Los Angeles venue known as a hotbed of unsigned talent. But then his film commitments surfaced and his interest shifted. The label could never be more than a side hustle.

In a strange twist, New Deal's greatest success sparked its decline. On the strength of "Indo Smoke," Def Jam VP of A&R Chris Lighty encouraged Russell Simmons to sign Warren G. Simmons then called Paul Stewart, floating a six-figure deal for the artist. As his comanagers, Singleton and Stewart could reap a potential windfall if Warren G blew up. Though Def Jam had declined since its late 1980s heyday, the label stood better positioned to break a new artist than New Deal.

Instead, Singleton demanded that Stewart turn down Simmons and steer the rapper toward signing with New Deal/Epic.

Stewart knew that would be a nonstarter for their artist. The math didn't add up. He broke it down for Singleton: New Deal offered artists around $40,000 to sign. Once Warren G learned they'd turned down $350,000, he'd fire them on the spot.

Simmons didn't just want to sign Warren G. All the while, he was also recruiting Stewart to run Def Jam West, a Los Angeles–based sub label dedicated to West

Coast hip-hop. Stewart called in sick one Friday afternoon and flew to New York to meet with Simmons. Somehow, Singleton found out. He fired Stewart when he returned to the office on Monday. A security guard confiscated his Rolodex and bounced Stewart off the lot.

Warren G's triple-platinum debut album, *Regulate . . . G Funk Era*, would be released in June 1994 and led the label's mid-to-late-1990s renaissance.

Stewart hadn't finished poaching artists associated with New Deal.

Sometime in 1993, Singleton's frat brothers brought the R&B singer Montell Jordan to the label for a meeting. Jordan, a six-foot-eight-inch Kappa from Pepperdine, had a style a little more street than the typical R&B dude. Stewart told him he'd sell millions of records. But the line went cold for Jordan at New Deal following Stewart's dismissal. He then reached out to him at Def Jam where Stewart was now VP of A&R.

Following a brief courtship, Jordan signed with the label. Released in February 1995, his Slick Rick–inspired single, "This is How We Do It," spent seven weeks at number one on the *Billboard* Hot 100 and sold over a million copies.

Mista Grimm, New Deal's best chance at a breakout act, never fulfilled the promise of "Indo Smoke." There was talk of writer's block. He couldn't replace Warren G's production. Couldn't craft another hit. His solo album landed with a thud. Finally, a dispute arose over money.

One day, Grimm and an associate showed up at New Deal and cornered Singleton in his office. Details of what happened next are sketchy. But Singleton emerged with a swollen eye and his shirt pulled over his head. He could be heard shouting about his gun. But it's unclear whether Singleton actually had a gun on him at the time. Afterward he felt a combination of anger and shame and didn't return to the office for about a week.

Singleton still loved hip-hop, and wanted to be down any which way he could. On August 3, 1995, he attended the Source Awards, hip-hop's version of the Grammy's. Already in New York for meetings, he wouldn't miss it for the world.

Singleton was long connected to *The Source*, aka the Magazine of Hip-Hop Music, Culture and Politics, aka the Bible of Hip-Hop. As a USC student, he cold-called *Source* founder David Mays, to tell him how much he loved the magazine. "John was one of our first subscribers," Mays says. He remained a fan even after *Boyz N the Hood* blew up, and he was profiled in the September 1991 issue featuring Ice Cube on the cover. Singleton was the one director in Hollywood who could moonlight as a hip-hop journalist. In the spring of 1992, he was named a contributing editor.

There was something in the air when Singleton arrived at the Paramount Theater at Madison Square Garden. The 1995 Source Awards would be remembered as one of the most consequential nights in hip-hop history. An industry-altering event that made an immediate impact and left a devastating fallout. Big Gipp, a member of the Atlanta rap group Goodie Mob, later compared the energy in the building to that found in a prison yard.

For months, a cold war had been brewing between Death Row and Sean "Puffy" Combs's Bad Boy Records, which was based in New York. Not surprisingly, Tupac Shakur was at the center of it. In a prison interview with *Vibe* magazine's Kevin Powell, he blamed Puff Daddy and his artist the Notorious B.I.G. for the November 1994 attempt on his life at a New York recording studio. Behind the scenes, Death Row CEO Suge Knight plotted on getting Tupac released from prison and then signing him to his label. Battles lines had been drawn.

Death Row's show-opening set seemed to win over the partisan New York crowd. But the rank and file in the audience had other plans and were determined to make their presence felt. They booed OutKast so viciously after the Atlanta rap duo won Best New Artist, Group, that the normally reticent André 3000 pushed back. "I'm tired of closed-minded folks," he said in his acceptance speech. "But it's like this: The South got somethin' to say. That's all I got to say."

Puff raised the temperature in the room at the start of Bad Boy's performance, proclaiming from the stage, "I live in the East, and I'm gonna die in the East." (At the end of the set he pulled back, saying, "Big shout-out to the West Coast people that came out. Big shout everybody from the East. We all together. Congratulations to all the winners.")

Minutes later, Suge Knight, wearing a red button-down shirt, accepted the award for Best Soundtrack for the Death Row release *Above the Rim*. A smattering of boos rained down as he climbed onstage. He shouted out Tupac, then paused, milking the moment like the showman he is, and took aim at his archrival, Puff.

"Any artist out there that want to be an artist and want to stay a star, and don't have to worry about the executive producer trying to be . . . all in the videos, all on the record, dancing, come to Death Row!"

Slowly, the murmurs turned to loud boos as Knight walked off stage triumphant.

Knight's speech stopped Singleton in his tracks. Prior to that, he was chit-chatting with Sam Cassell of the two-time NBA champ Houston Rockets. They were backstage set to present the next award. His demeanor immediately changed. "John looked at me like, 'Oh, shit,'" Cassell remembers.

The night's hosts Ed Lover and Doctor Dré tried easing the tension. "Everybody's got it going on tonight. Don't you think?" Dré said. "Give it up to everybody y'all. Give it up."

The crowd remained stunned as Singleton and Cassell walked to the podium. Loud chatter, oohs and aahs, and some heckling could still be heard as Singleton fiddled with the microphone. He tried lightening the mood with some sports trash talk. "Do you want to say something about the Knicks?" he said to Cassell, who tormented the Knicks in the 1994 NBA Finals. When that failed, he got serious.

"Before we pass out this award, we got, to say something, all right?" Singleton said. "We got to kill all this East Coast/West Coast/South/Midwest dissention in rap because, you know, there's a lot of devils out there that will be damned if they could ban it, and we wouldn't be having no show, and a lot of y'all wouldn't be making no money. So, um, with that, we're gonna pass out this award for Producer of the Year."

He recognized what was at stake. He could see forces using this in an attempt to destroy his culture. But on a personal level he knew where this could lead. He had seen it growing up. The petty disputes ending with the violent deaths of young Black men. He tried squashing the beef before it started. But it was out of his hands.

He announced the winner. "Uh-oh, we're gonna have some trouble here, Dr. Dre." (Not the Doctor Dré hosting the show.)

Cheers turned to jeers when Dre took the stage and said, "West Coast, baby, yeah! In the house!" When Singleton tried handing the award to Dre, Snoop Dogg, wearing a blue bandana, brushed past Singleton and snatched the microphone.

"Wait, wait, wait, wait, the East Coast don't love Dr. Dre and Snoop Dogg? The East Coast ain't got no love for Dr. Dre and Snoop Dogg, and Death Row? Y'all don't love us?" he said, sounding equally angry, heartbroken, and confused. "Y'all don't love us? Well, let it be known, then: We don't give a fuck. We know y'all East Coast. We know where the fuck we at."

Singleton waited for Snoop to end his rant. Then he turned and walked off the stage ahead of the rappers.

★★★★★

When it came down to it, Singleton couldn't wait for Denzel.

Through the summer and fall of 1995, as Singleton cast *Rosewood*, Denzel Washington remained everyone's first option for the crucial role of Mann. Warner Bros. even prepared to open their budget to meet the Oscar winner's eight-figure quote. But Washington had committed to shoot the 20th Century Fox Gulf War drama *Courage Under Fire* and *The Preacher's Wife* for Disney back-to-back, rendering him unavailable until late spring 1996. Washington had been on the fence anyway, questioning whether Mann was a genuine leading role.

Laurence Fishburne and Wesley Snipes were also discussed before Singleton hired Ving Rhames, a brooding, intense actor who'd recently broken through with *Pulp Fiction*.

"John fought for Ving," says Tracy Barone, president of Peters Entertainment and a producer on *Rosewood*. "That was a big issue. This was a leading-man part, and you want that person to look like a leading man, and Ving wasn't your typical leading man."

Initially cast in a supporting role, Rhames claimed his first lead despite the knowledge he was, at best, the fourth choice for it. "Some of the actors considered for the part were . . . more palatable to certain audiences than me," Rhames said. "I mean, I'm a quote-unquote big, shaven-head nigger, where someone like a Denzel Washington is physically more acceptable to white America."

With Rhames cast as Mann, the role of Sylvester Carrier went to Don Cheadle, who'd recently upstaged Washington in *Devil in a Blue Dress*. Singleton desperately wanted Cheadle and stepped in when Warner Bros. balked at meeting the ascendant actor's price.

"There was some gap between what the studio wanted to pay me and what I wanted to make or needed to make or thought I should make," Cheadle says. "John said, 'I'll make up the gap. I'll write the check personally.' That doesn't happen often."

Filling out the cast on a tight budget proved challenging. After Warner Bros. couldn't match Ruby Dee's and Tommy Lee Jones's rates, Singleton pivoted to Esther Rolle for the part of Aunt Sarah, and cast Jon Voight as Johnny Wright, the white shopkeeper and reluctant ally to the town's Black residents. Casting director Marion Dougherty, who'd hired Voight for the 1969 Best Picture winner *Midnight Cowboy*, suggested he read for Wright. Now in the midst of a comeback following a near decade-long hiatus, Voight, the 1979 Academy Award winner for Best Actor (*Coming Home*), had momentum following roles in *Heat* and *Mission: Impossible*.

"I really wanted an actor of some type of authority and some kind of history behind him, someone who could be a rock and wholeheartedly take to this film and this subject matter," Singleton said. "Jon felt like it was a very important picture that needed to be made. He became kind of the soul of the film."

Singleton hired Elise Neal as Mann's love interest, Scrappie, and chose sharp character actors like Michael Rooker, Bruce McGill, and Paul Benjamin for supporting roles. He filled out the cast with locals selected during casting calls in Orlando. He assessed actors in a matter of seconds.

"Book him," Singleton said as soon as one actor entered the room.

"John, I spent two days finding actors," said Lori Wyman, the casting associate. "Wouldn't you like to see other actors for that role?"

"Nope, I want that face in my movie."

Singleton told Wyman he wanted "good Southern accents and interesting faces" for the townspeople. When an audition didn't move him, he'd zone out. Once, Singleton put his head down on his desk as soon as an actor walked in the door. The actor read and left quickly. Afterward, Penelope Foster, the film's line producer, said to him, "John, you didn't even look at him."

"He was boring and I didn't want him in my movie," Singleton said, revealing an appalling lack of social graces.

The cast was in place. Shooting was scheduled to start on January 22. And yet, he still had cold feet about *Rosewood*. In December 1995, soon after closing the Universal deal and with the industry preparing to shut down for the holidays, he considered pulling out of the film. Throughout the fall, his anger had been building. He felt duped out of a screenwriting credit and a producing credit. Suddenly, the $25 million budget seemed light. He wanted out. Friends tried reasoning with him. They mentioned the survivors. Didn't he feel a sense of responsibility to them?

Singleton carried a heavy burden on each of his films. *Boyz N the Hood* was his make-or-break moment. On *Poetic Justice*, there was anxiety to prove he wasn't a one-hit wonder. He felt external pressure from the studio on *Higher Learning*. Now, with *Rosewood*, he didn't want to disappoint the survivors. He couldn't make a bad movie about their story, especially after meeting them and crying with them.

Then, on December 16, 1995, Minnie Lee Langley died at a Jacksonville hospital following cancer surgery. She was eighty-two. Five days later, Singleton attended the graveside service in Jacksonville. There, standing amongst the mourners, he made his decision.

"It gave me energy because all these people were there talking about her courage," he said. "And I thought, 'I've got to keep going here. I've got to do it, just do it, and fight to do it, because this story should be told.'"

# CHAPTER FOURTEEN

**S**ingleton had little time to relax prior to *Rosewood*'s January 1996 start date. But in October, he attended the Million Man March in Washington, DC, a mass gathering of Black men that was the brainchild of Minister Louis Farrakhan, leader of the Nation of Islam.

The trip came together at the last minute. About two days prior to the event, Singleton called his assistant Joe Doughrity and simply said, "Let's go." Soon, they were checking into the Watergate hotel, scene of one of the most infamous crimes in American political history.

Before heading to the National Mall—the same location as the 1963 March on Washington and the 1969 Vietnam War Moratorium Rally—Singleton, Doughrity, and Singleton's security guard, a member of the Nation of Islam named Ezekiel, were on the lookout for violence, either from knuckleheads or outside agitators. Instead, they enjoyed a peaceful day.

He felt an amazing sense of brotherhood, standing near the stage, listening to the calls for responsibility, unity, entrepreneurship, political activism, and accountability coming from speakers that included Reverend Jesse Jackson, Maya Angelou, Martin Luther King III, Rosa Parks, Reverend Dr. Jeremiah Wright, and Minister Farrakhan.

Toward the conclusion of Farrakhan's speech, Singleton took the same oath as the rest of the Black men in attendance.

*"I, John Singleton, pledge that from this day forward, I will strive to love my brother as I love myself. I, John Singleton, from this day forward, will strive to improve myself spiritually, morally, mentally, socially, politically, and economically for the benefit of myself, my family, and my people. . . ."*

On the flight over, Singleton mused about meeting the women of Chocolate City. But after the march, he found himself in his suite, reflecting on the day's events with Doughrity and his Detroit friends late into the night. They felt they were a part of history.

Later that fall, Singleton took a trip to Miami, where he reconnected with a childhood love: the ocean.

One afternoon, Singleton met with Randall Batinkoff, whom he'd cast in *Higher Learning*, and about a dozen of the actor's friends, and they made their way aboard Batinkoff's friend's boat: the *Ticonderoga*, a seventy-two-foot clipper-bowed ketch built in 1936. She owned more racing records than any other boat afloat. When her racing career ended in 1967, the *Ticonderoga* became a luxury charter.

In 1993, L. Scott Frantz, an investment banker turned venture capitalist, and a lifelong sailor, saw a classified ad for it in *Yachting* magazine. Ultimately, he outbid twenty-two people, including Jimmy Buffett, for the boat he'd been fixated on since childhood.

The sun shone bright as Singleton boarded the *Ticonderoga* at a marina just north of Fisher Island. The vessel cruised up the shipping channel. About thirty minutes later, she raised her sails and headed east for a half mile until turning north along the beach.

"We were immediately having a good time and drinking beer. People were jumping off the boat and swimming around. I was like, 'You can't do that! There are cruise ships around!'" Frantz remembers. "John had this big smile on his face. He was very interested in everything. He was looking around and being observant. Occasionally, he'd ask a question. We put him on the helm once we got outside the shipping channel. He didn't want to give it up to anyone else. He was thinking, 'Maybe I can do this someday?'"

Singleton's fascination with the water stemmed from trips to Palos Verde with his dad. But the day trip on the *Ticonderoga* sparked a decades-long obsession with sailing. He found peace on the water. He needed it prior to the most stressful shoot of his career.

Singleton's problems on *Rosewood* began before the film went into production.

One day, before leaving for Florida, he had a lunch meeting at his favorite sushi restaurant, Matsuhisa on La Cienega. Across from him sat *Rosewood* producer Tracy Barone, and Peter Lyons Collister, his director of photography on "Remember the Time," *Poetic Justice*, *Higher Learning*, and, he assumed, *Rosewood*. Singleton had shared the script with Collister a few weeks earlier so he could create his lookbook—a collection of images expressing the cinematographer's visual blueprint for the film. The mood. The tone. What to expect on-screen.

Sometime during the meal, it became evident that Collister wouldn't get the job. Barone skimmed the book and changed the subject whenever Collister pointed something out in it.

Singleton sat silent, shoulders slumped, picking at his food.

"John didn't have to say anything," Collister says. "I knew I wasn't going to do the film."

"Warner's production department had their own people," Barone says. "That was part of the nervousness we felt about the production and about Singleton in general. We wanted to surround him with the best people. People we trust. People we know have done this sort of show before."

Singleton learned early on that *Rosewood* would be unlike anything he'd experienced. Over the next year or so, he'd be second-guessed, marginalized, and, in his eyes, disrespected.

"Before that, I was a golden boy," he said. "*Rosewood* was a whole different thing."

Though Peters Entertainment targeted Singleton for the job, Barone, and others, weren't sure he could handle it. She'd heard about his issues on *Higher Learning*. *Rosewood* was also unfamiliar territory for the twenty-eight-year-old director. His first three films were contemporary dramas shot in Los Angeles from his own scripts and based, in varying degrees, on his own experiences. Now he'd be filming a period piece on location in the Florida swamp with a large cast, scores of extras, and set pieces involving firefights and featuring a speeding train. There would be extensive night shoots. He'd work with child actors and livestock. At $25 million, it was the biggest budget he'd managed up to that point. Warner Bros. constructed an entire town just to burn it down.

"It was a long way from *Boyz N the Hood*," Barone says.

Why hire him in the first place? "We thought we'd surround him with really good people," Barone says. "I'll be on set. We'll have a really good line producer. We'll make sure he has a great DP. We're going to pick him up."

Over three months, the Academy Award–winning production designer Paul Sylbert and his team built replicas of Rosewood and the neighboring white town of Sumner in the middle of nowhere; they paved three and a half miles of road just to transport equipment to the set. Sylbert based the towns on architecture models, local archives, and the memories of the Rosewood survivors. He imported about thirty period buildings from across the state and constructed an additional fifteen homes using local raw materials. The crew also built over a mile of train tracks. And the train? A vintage locomotive airlifted in from Arkansas.

This was what Singleton wanted when he left Columbia: a bigger budget and a fresh start. "I had to get out of the whole ghetto-movie thing," he said to a reporter on set. But working with an unfamiliar crew heightened his anxiety about the film. Through three movies he had assembled a team he could trust and lean on. Now he had to grow accustomed to a new line producer, a new DP, a new AD, and so on and so on. He managed to enlist some familiar faces such as Cassandra Butcher, Dwight Williams, and Peter Ramsey. He also hired Spike Lee's go-to costume designer Ruth E. Carter, a future member of the Singleton Family.

The long prep period in Los Angeles allowed him to form relationships with the new members of his crew including the director of photography, Johnny E. Jensen.

"I immediately fell in love with John's commitment," Jensen says. "He had, like, a photographic memory. When we spoke about films he would say, like, 'Do you remember that shot in *Bridge on the River Kwai*?' He had recollections of shots from hundreds of movies. I don't remember shots."

Their collaboration got off to an inauspicious start. One day, Singleton walked into Jensen's office and dropped a two-inch stack of storyboards on his desk.

"Study that," he said.

"John, I'm not much of a fan of storyboards," Jensen responded. "Adhering to them is not precisely my cup of tea. I like to get inspired and figure it out while shooting."

Singleton soon realized their vision for the film aligned. *The Grapes of Wrath*, *The Ox-Bow Incident*, and *How Green Is My Valley*, early American films he deemed "big on emotion," served as inspirations for *Rosewood*.

Filming took place in the opaque swampland northwest of Orlando, about three hours from the original town. Various critters could be found in the woods and marsh. Ticks. Chiggers. Water moccasins. There were alligator spotters on set. A rattlesnake bit one of the second ADs. Mosquitoes traveled in thick herds. The most popular members of the crew were the PAs. At the start of each day, they'd emerge from base camp toting buckets of insect repellent. Nighttime temperatures dipped near freezing. Producers moved the start date back a week after heavy rain in early January prevented the crew from finishing the sets.

Upon arriving in Florida, Singleton assembled the cast for their first read-through. Bruce McGill, who played Duke Purdy—perhaps the most racist member of the racist mob—reported in character and tied and untied a hangman's noose throughout the reading.

From the start of filming, Jon Voight made his presence felt. "Voight was Voight," McGill says. "He was a load. He was always trying to tell everyone what to do. He always does. Keep in mind, I've worked with Jon several times and I like him a lot."

For Jon Voight, the script is a starting point. He absorbs it, workshops it, whether it's altering a word, a stitch of dialogue, or an entire scene, and then pushes his notes onto the director.

"I have to be collaborative," Voight says, defending his methods. "I don't know another way. I don't just come to set and read the lines."

Sometimes, his suggestions were innocuous, such as the night when Voight became fixated on a single word.

"I think the line should really be 'What do you all peckerheads want?'" Voight said.

"No one uses 'peckerhead' around here," said a member of the crew. "It's 'peckerwood.'"

"Historically speaking, 'peckerhead' is what people around here would've said."

Singleton, busy reviewing footage, ignored the debate until Voight's amateur etymology distracted him.

"'Peckerwood,' all right!" Singleton yelled.

Voight's ad-libbing was one thing. Then he started directing his costars. During a scene on a train, the actor Brett Rice went along with Voight without consulting Singleton.

"Cut, cut, cut," Singleton said, shaking his head. "Brett, I thought I told you that as soon as you see the guys on horseback you take off."

"Well, Mr. Voight told me not to," said Rice, whose résumé at that time consisted of roles like "High School Football Coach" in *Forrest Gump* and "Police Officer" in *Kalifornia*.

Singleton took off his glasses and rubbed his head.

"Who's directing this movie, anyway?" Rice shouted. "This John or that Jon?"

"Come here," Singleton said, pulling him aside. "Mr. Voight is a fantastic actor," he said, through gritted teeth. "But I'm the director of this movie, so if I tell you to do something, you do that."

A friendship eventually developed between the director and his star. But on the set in Florida, Singleton couldn't have been more annoyed with Voight. He kept his anger in check unless someone cost him time or money.

One morning, Esther Rolle showed up to the set sporting French-tip mani-cured nails. Nobody noticed until she had already filmed for the day. When he realized the oversight, Singleton paced back and forth, thinking about how far she'd set him back. Still, the seventy-five-year-old actress was beloved. Everyone looked forward to working with Florida Evans from *Good Times*. But she kept bun-gling her lines; *Rosewood* would be her final film.

"I can't do this," she said, after blowing her fourth straight take. "I have to go to the bathroom."

"Esther, you get this take right, you're gonna go to the bathroom," he replied. "You flub your line again, we're gonna have a problem and everybody gonna know."

She nailed it on the next try.

★★★★★

One Sunday afternoon, Johnny Jensen stepped into a bar in town for lunch. From the moment he revealed his Danish accent, he sensed he wasn't welcome. He took it in, all the hard stares and murmurs. Then a man approached his table.

"I can tell you're not from around here," he said. "What are you up to?"

"You are correct. I'm Danish," Jensen said. "I'm working on a film called *Rosewood*."

"*Rosewood*, huh?"

"Yes, it's about this town—"

"I know what it's about," said the man. "Enjoy your meal."

A few minutes later, the band returned to the stage for their next set. The lead singer grabbed the mic and announced, "We have a guest from Denmark shoot-ing a movie about Rosewood. Is there anyone here who wants to go up there and shoot some niggers?"

"We were given specific instructions that if anything happened to our car not to start knocking on doors. They said, 'People will shoot you. Get a phone and call someone,'" Don Cheadle remembers. "The KKK showed up to the set one day, not in hoods, dressed in regular clothes. 'Oh, what are y'all making? *Rosewood*, huh?' Then they looked at each other like, 'Oh yeah, some of our greatest hits.'"

Off the set, Singleton tried bridging the cultural divide with the local white people in the cast and crew. Early on, he invited everyone to happy hour. A few rounds in, one of the men working in construction stumbled toward him and said, "I wasn't going to tell you this because we're friends now but my great-granddaddy used to own slaves."

"That's funny as fuck," Singleton said.

"What's so funny about it?"

"Well, that's funny as fuck because you're my slave right now. You're working for me. You're mine. I own you. Let's do another shot!"

"It broke the ice," Singleton later said. "We became buddies."

On the set, Singleton wanted his racist white people as racist as possible and to sustain it even when cameras weren't rolling. When Arnett Doctor and Greg Galloway visited one day, extras peppered them with racial slurs. "The hell you doing here, nigger-lover?" someone shouted at Galloway.

One night, while filming the lynching of Sam Carter, the Black craftsman suspected of abetting the man Fannie Taylor accused of rape, Singleton abruptly called for a break. To him, the mob's bloodlust felt manufactured. He asked the posse of white actors to gather around.

"I need y'all to be real," he shouted. "Y'all are real crackers. I need y'all to be real crackers right now. If you feel differently about what happened then and it's not in your heart, that's fine. But I need y'all to go back to that time. Go back to your ancestors and make this real. The more real this is, the more impact the film will have."

He slapped their shoulders like a football coach motivating the defense before a goal line stand. "Go get that motherfucker," he seethed, pointing at Kevin Jackson, the actor portraying Sam Carter. "Hang that nigger! Hang him!"

"There were moments when it got frightening for me. It was very scary," Jackson says. "Things started to blend together. I remember how I thought they were actually having a good time lynching me."

But the material affected the white actors as well.

"I think it was the only film I've done where I've had nightmares that were clearly related to the subject matter," McGill says.

When McGill first read the script he thought, *Oh my God, this is tough.* He grew up in Texas in the 1950s, a time and place where hearing the n-word was common in white circles. To his character, Duke Purdy, it was just a word, though. For the next few weeks, while in the shower, shampooing his hair, he'd scream the n-word over and over just to get comfortable saying it.

Singleton praised McGill's commitment to the role and his performance. "Bruce McGill went to the depth of his psyche to play this despicable guy with some form of respect," Singleton said.

But for someone like Paul Benjamin, a Black man born in South Carolina in

1938, McGill's depiction of Duke hit different. Best known for his roles in *Across 110th Street* and *Escape from Alcatraz*, Benjamin played James Carrier, an animal trapper. On the night they filmed his death scene, Voight escorted Benjamin toward the rowdy, bloodthirsty posse.

Benjamin, wild eyed and confused, walked gingerly toward them, flinching from the bright burning torches some carried. The woods were quiet. Crickets chirped in the distance. The mob peppered Benjamin with insults.

*C'mon, nigger.*

*Dig a hole, nigger.*

*Let's go, nigger.*

The scene called for Loren Dean, the actor playing Fanny Taylor's cuckolded husband, to muscle Benjamin toward the ground. But Benjamin felt Dean had gotten a little heavy-handed with him. He popped up and started throwing punches until McGill grabbed him from behind in a bear hug.

"Let me go! Let me go!" Benjamin shouted.

"I will let you go when you calm down," McGill shouted even louder.

Benjamin struggled for a long time before submitting.

Singleton arched his eyebrows and smiled. He didn't want his actors to get into a fistfight, yet he pushed them until the emotion boiled over.

"It was tough for the Black cast to be emotionally open in the moment," Ramsey says. "Paul Benjamin was at an age where a lot of that shit was close to him, much more than even I or John could really appreciate. The lynching scenes were hard for people to get through. There were also the stresses you would have on any production, and that production was very stressful."

On another evening, while filming the firefight at the Carrier home, someone put the wrong caliber of blanks into the shotguns, resulting in deafening blasts. Afterward, a few members of the crew blamed Singleton for the mistake.

Singleton listened, shaking his head, and then returned fire. "Man, y'all were born in the suburbs and listened to the sounds of birds chirping. I grew up in the ghetto listening to gunshots all night."

At the beginning of the shoot, Singleton projected optimism despite still harboring concerns about the budget. But the pressure mounted as filming moved slower than what he had storyboarded.

For over six weeks, the cast and crew worked punishing night shoots six days a week from eight p.m. to eight a.m. Some actors in the film compared the shoot to *Lord of the Flies*. On some days, Singleton, visibly thinner than at the outset, carried a small snake in his shirt pocket. Bob Marley's "War" became his theme song. Friends who flew in to visit noticed a change.

"I remember him being tense, different from how he was on other sets," Adrianne Shropshire says. "Normally, I would have to hear about every scene that was shot before I got there. This time, we didn't talk about it much."

At some point, Singleton realized he wanted to make a different movie than the one he set out to. When he first started *Rosewood*, he imagined it as a Western with an action vibe. One of the reasons he wanted to work with Poirier was the big train robbery at the center of *The Iron Horseman*. Once he got down to Florida and started telling the story, his feelings changed. He confided in people that the studio was pushing him to emphasize the film's action.

During one of the many moments of downtime, Singleton approached McGill about it.

"Warner Bros. is leaning on me to go in a direction I don't think we ought to go in," he said. "I don't want to make that movie."

"You're gonna have to fight and you're gonna have to fight every day," McGill said. "You'll probably lose in the end."

"It wasn't lost on him that he was fighting an uphill battle from the beginning with the kind of movie he was trying to make," Cheadle says. "I think he was always trying to prove that he belonged in the chair."

For the studio, and for some members of the crew, it validated their concerns about Singleton going into the film. His maturity. His work ethic. His ability to marshal a production on the scale of *Rosewood*.

Some filmmakers lost their cool if a grip did a crossword puzzle during downtime. Then there were directors like Singleton. He stopped whatever he was doing when his shipment of comic books arrived. "John was one of our first subscribers," says Ryan Liebowitz, owner of Golden Apple Comics. "He'd subscribe to five to ten titles per week. When he wasn't in town we'd ship them to set. That's how much he wanted to read his comic books."

Sometimes, he'd hop in an ATV and retreat to his trailer no matter how long it took for Jensen to light the next scene. "It would drive the AD and the producers crazy," says a member of the crew. On more than one occasion he threatened to walk off the film.

"He was in over his head," Barone says.

"In over his head? I would kind of dispute that," Ramsey says. Still, Singleton managed to alienate even his staunchest allies. "We were joined at the hip through the whole thing," Ramsey says. "But after *Rosewood* it was like, 'I'll see you when I see you.' We were both like, 'I love you. But I don't know if I can take any more of you right now.'"

A lot of his difficulties involved the newness of it all. The new crew. New actors. Filming in the swamp. Producers who hadn't worked with him on a day-to-day basis through three films. An unfamiliar studio he hadn't made millions for. But he lacked self-awareness in this respect. He missed all the signals sent to him during the making of *Higher Learning*. It should have been a wake-up call when Columbia decided it wanted to get out of the John Singleton business. Instead, he continued with his ways. Reading comics on set. Stubbornly doing his own thing. Not adapting to the circumstances.

Some of the film's troubles were out of Singleton's control, like the lightning storms. But he also made unforced errors along the way. One morning, the cast and crew arrived on set to find *Story by John Singleton* added to the title page of the distributed script. He still felt aggrieved over the writing credits on *Rosewood*. In reality, he had two options: Discuss it with the producers or submit a complaint to the Writers Guild. Instead, he chose a passive-aggressive stunt that raised tensions on the set.

"It was just a shock," Poirier says. "I felt helpless. It was my first produced picture and I'm the least powerful person here."

Shortly thereafter, without an apology or explanation, Singleton changed it back.

"He deserved that credit," Joe Doughrity says. "I know for a fact that John wasn't just giving notes. He was in the Final Draft file, writing dialogue, slug lines. He wasn't just giving notes to the screenwriter."

Singleton reopened the wound while promoting the film. In an interview with the *Los Angeles Times*, he said, "This is the first time I haven't written the screenplay for a film I've directed. I just didn't have time with everything else that was involved. I did write the story, though. It was just easier to dictate it to someone else."

Poirier immediately called Singleton. "For whatever reason, John seemed genuinely surprised that I was upset," Poirier says. "I thought it was condescending and a bad choice of words." The conversation ended both their personal and professional relationship. "I don't think either one of us had a strong desire to speak to the other one after that call."

Singleton's relationship with Akosua Busia caused a greater stir.

"It was pretty hard to miss," Ramsey says.

Singleton never got Busia's screenplay for *Seasons* out of development, but he jumped at the chance to cast her as Johnny Wright's mistress, Jewel. From the start, he had been infatuated with more than just her beauty. Who does one date after a supermodel? Anything other than a real-life African princess would be a step down from Tyra Banks.

At first, no one thought much of the on-set romance. Then, to the surprise of the cast and crew, Busia's role expanded. "Everyone attributed it to John's attraction to her," Kevin Jackson says. On one instance, Singleton almost stretched a day into overtime to film a scene showcasing her. Busia didn't respond to requests for comment.

When production wrapped in late April, the director, the cast, and the crew were ready to go home. Bruce McGill shaved his beard and held a ceremonial burning. Ving Rhames, who had worked nonstop for over a year, going from *Mission: Impossible* to *Dangerous Ground* to *Striptease* to *Rosewood*, was off to Bali. Singleton returned to Los Angeles.

On the last day of filming, he hugged the film's costumer and whispered to him, "Thanks for enduring."

# CHAPTER FIFTEEN

**W**hile filming *Rosewood*, Singleton received a set visit from the talent agent known as the Dark Prince of Hollywood.

Singleton had been unhappy with CAA for some time now. In early 1996, he connected with Gavin Polone, a partner at United Talent Agency, a small, upstart outfit. With his long black hair and grungy beard, Polone exuded a rock-star vibe for a ten-percenter. He posed for *Vanity Fair* and spoke without a filter. Polone once described the cast of *Friends* as "six morons America loves." As an agent, his demeanor was more Ari Gold than Jerry Maguire.

"Any time anyone confronted me with anything, I just hit back harder," Polone says, making him the kind of fighter Singleton wanted on his team.

He flew in from Los Angeles to close the deal. When Polone arrived on the set, a production assistant led him to a trailer where he waited until a break in filming. Singleton walked in, plopped down on the couch, and turned the television on to the Lakers game.

Polone recited his sales pitch.

"I know how you feel about CAA. We all know their deal: CAA represents CAA. Everybody is just a cog in their machine. It's not about you. It's about what you can do for them," Polone said. "If you sign with me, I will represent you. I will fight for you. I will fucking murder for you. And I'll be there for you twenty-four seven."

Singleton agreed to sign with UTA there in the trailer.

The next twelve months marked the most turbulent time in Singleton's life. In the year that followed, he would switch agencies, switch agents, vacate his production deal, have a shotgun wedding, become a father again, get divorced, and endure the first outright flop of his career. How did he get here? What happened to the golden boy? He misread the business; ignored good advice; mixed business with pleasure over and over again.

The trouble with CAA started brewing in early 1995. Sensing his job was in jeopardy, Brad Smith left the agency in February to become Singleton's producing partner at New Deal. John Ptak replaced him as Singleton's agent. A nearly twenty-five-year veteran, Ptak started his career at ICM in 1971. His client list included Ridley Scott, Peter Weir, Wolfgang Peterson, and Costa-Gavras. At CAA, he specialized in the foreign financing market. Ptak was more of a deal/structure guy than a mentor and pal. Closing in on fifty, he was much older than Singleton. There was no acrimony between them. But there was not much of a personal relationship. Ptak dealt mostly with Smith.

CAA was also no longer the same CAA that Singleton had signed with back in 1990. By the summer of 1995, the agency had loosened its grip on the industry. In July, co-founder and president Ron Meyer assumed the presidency of MCA Inc., parent company to Universal Pictures. Five weeks later, co-founder and chairman Michael Ovitz departed to become president of Walt Disney; Ovitz lasted less than eighteen months as Michael Eisner's number two. Another co-founder, Bill Haber, left CAA soon afterward. With no succession plan in place, a free-for-all ensued. The sharks smelled blood. Over the next three months, rivals poached thirty high-profile CAA clients, including Kevin Costner, Sylvester Stallone, and John Hughes. A few months later, John Singleton joined the list.

Around this time, Singleton started dating a junior agent at UTA. He shared his frustrations with her. How he felt neglected at the agency. How he blamed CAA for not securing him a producing credit on *Rosewood*. How he wanted bigger budgets and more opportunities.

She introduced him to Polone.

Smith and Ptak ignored warnings about Singleton's intentions until it was too late.

His partnership with Polone wouldn't last long. In April 1996, with Singleton still on location filming *Rosewood*, UTA abruptly fired the Ferrari-driving rep. Publicly, the agency accused him of "inappropriate behavior" toward a female agent. Polone denied the charges and threatened litigation. A few days later, UTA issued a public apology and agreed to pay him a $6 million settlement.

Singleton seemed to be in a good place when he returned from Florida. He had a movie to finish. Deals to close; UTA cofounder Jeremy Zimmer now repped him. A fresh home for New Deal Productions. But his mood turned once he arrived on the Universal lot and noticed the small office space New Deal now occupied. Despite how it ended, he missed Columbia. After a while, he stopped showing up in the office other than for meetings. UTA was more than happy to feed Singleton's discontent with Universal.

Since Ptak had negotiated the two-year, $700,000 first-look deal with the studio, UTA urged Singleton to seek an agreement with another studio. Somehow, Singleton believed that Warner Bros. had interest in signing him.

"I don't think that was happening at Warner Bros. after *Rosewood*," Tracy Barone says.

Singleton trusted his instincts and defied the advice of his close colleagues. In June of 1996, he walked away from his deal at Universal. Without a studio covering his overhead, he laid off employees. He paid others out of pocket, bearing another financial burden. A narrative within the industry took shape: Singleton had grown dysfunctional.

But Singleton learned to thrive off dysfunction, particularly the dysfunction in his personal life. Two kids. Two different mothers. Two unpredictable and explosive coparenting relationships. A rotating cast of girlfriends and hookups. Singleton and Busia continued dating after *Rosewood*. By the end of the summer of 1996, she was pregnant. So too was Vestria Barlow. And another woman as well.

Singleton channeled what he knew about dysfunctional relationships into a screenplay that he titled *Fighting and Fucking*. Back in his comfort zone—an autobiographical film set in South Central—he'd eventually snap the two-and-a-half-year writing slump that had plagued him since completing *Higher Learning*.

Immediately, he knew who he wanted for the lead: Tupac Shakur.

When he started taking notes on the script, he'd yet to mend his relationship with the rapper. Tupac believed he'd been abandoned during his trial and the eight months he spent in prison for sexual abuse. He lashed out at anyone who wasn't there for him, which included Singleton.

"John Singleton is a coward," Tupac said in an October 1995 phone call, days after his release.

Tupac became the biggest rapper in the world once he set foot out of the Clinton Correctional Facility in Dannemora, New York. *All Eyez on Me*, his double album released in February 1996, sold ten million copies. Although the movie business wasn't as forgiving as hip-hop, he tried regaining his foothold in Hollywood. In the spring of 1996, he played a heroin addict in the indie film *Gridlock'd*. He started filming *Gang Related* on July 22, 1996.

Through it all, Singleton remained optimistic he'd eventually reunite with his De Niro. On July 23, he ran into him at the Baldwin Hills Crenshaw Plaza while

Shakur filmed the music video for "To Live and Die in L.A." It was the first time he'd seen him since Shakur went to prison.

"I got the movie that's going to get you an Oscar," Singleton told him.

"I'm with it," Tupac responded.

They never had a chance to proceed further. On September 7, Tupac was shot on the Vegas strip after attending a Mike Tyson fight. Six days later, he succumbed to his wounds.

The way Singleton told the story about the Crenshaw mall encounter raised questions: Did they reconcile? Did either apologize? Tupac exhibited manic behavior throughout the summer of 1996. Is it believable that Mr. Hit 'Em Up acted remissive toward one of his perceived enemies? Even some of Singleton's closest friends can't confirm the meeting. Recently released audio of Tupac potentially contradicts Singleton's yarn.

In the recording, Tupac lists his grievances with Singleton: He initiated Pac's beef with the Hughes Brothers. He didn't hold the line with Columbia. Then, instead of supporting him in the press, he smeared his name. He stole his ideas for *Higher Learning*. The Aretha Franklin placement. The headphones on the track. Malik's character and motivation.

This disappointed Tupac as much as it enraged him. All the while, he had admired Singleton for his talent. Now that feeling was gone.

Earlier in the recording, Tupac mentioned having wrapped filming on *Gang Related*, timestamping the audio to sometime between late August and September 7, 1996.

★★★★★

Singleton had high expectations when he screened *Rosewood* for the Warner Bros. brass.

Though the trend had shifted toward flashier, MTV-style edits, Singleton, working once again with Bruce Cannon, set a leisurely pace for the film. He modeled *Rosewood* after the old Westerns he loved—movies that took time establishing tone. *Rosewood* left executives feeling a little wobbly afterward.

"We didn't count on how hard it would be for the audience to experience," says Lorenzo di Bonaventura, then Warner Bros.' president of production.

They had notes.

"John, you can't show them cutting off an ear."

"But that's what the movie is about!" he said. "The movie is about the brutality of the lynch mob. You can't make it softer."

In the end, he went to a wide shot when the mob mutilated Sam Carter.

The film score produced greater unease. Warner Bros. had doubts from the moment Singleton enlisted jazz great Wynton Marsalis to score the film. "This generation's Duke Ellington," he called him. But in the eyes of the studio, Marsalis was merely a first-time film composer.

Early on in the scoring process, Singleton and Marsalis decided to move away from the sort of triumphant Wagnerian compositions that had become commonplace. This led to the music diverging from the action on-screen—somber music played during happy moments; triumphant harmonies were set to tense visuals.

One afternoon, the producers gathered on the scoring stage while Marsalis and his band played.

"No, no, no," Jon Peters said, shaking his head.

Singleton was reluctant to fire Marsalis. He had grown to distrust the executives on the film. He also thought the score worked in a way. But he couldn't ignore the growing chorus of voices urging him to make a change. Peters. Barone. Cannon. The sound editor. Even his friends recommended he move in a new direction, and so he did. (In November 1999, Marsalis released the unused *Rosewood* compositions on the album *Reeltime* to widespread critical acclaim.)

Peters arranged a screening for John Williams, Spielberg's go-to guy and the most decorated composer in movie history. "This looks like a Martin Ritt film," Williams told Singleton afterward; Ritt directed a trio of Westerns starring Paul Newman in the 1960s. Later on, they sat in Williams's office at Amblin Entertainment.

"John, you're a genius," Singleton said. "You've done these classic scores. But what do you know about the souls of Black people?"

Singleton continued. "This is different. This is the heart. This goes all the way back through emancipation to joy and pain and everything."

"Well, John," Williams said, "before I was a composer, I was an arranger. In the 1960s, I arranged several albums for Mahalia Jackson. You ever heard of her?"

"Okay, John," Singleton said with a smile. "I can't tell you shit."

Williams ended up writing three original gospel songs for *Rosewood*. His score did what a good score is supposed to: The music supported the emotional beats of the film and the images on-screen. But it came at a steep price. By replacing the score so late in postproduction, *Rosewood* wouldn't be ready in time to make its December release date. It would miss out on both the holiday box office rush and, more importantly, awards season. Holding the film for fall 1997, where it could rebuild buzz on the festival circuit, wasn't considered an option. Instead, Warner Bros. pushed the film to late February, a dead zone on the movie calendar.

In preproduction meetings, Jon Peters acknowledged *Rosewood* would be a hard sell. He stressed he had a plan. "We're going to caravan it and get it everywhere," he said. "We're going to march this film around the world and get everyone to see it!"

But there was no marketing plan that didn't involve the pursuit of Oscar gold. Test screenings didn't reveal much new information. It was a hard movie to sit through. It wasn't that audiences didn't like the film; they couldn't handle it. Too painful. Too real. At 140 minutes, perhaps too long. Some moviegoers were overwhelmed with emotion. "Oprah says that it affected her so deeply that she went into her bathroom and cried privately into a towel," a spokeswoman for *The Oprah Winfrey Show* said.

Others had no interest in reliving an ugly chapter of American history, one their ancestors may have contributed to. At one test screening, about fifty-five minutes into the film, when the Black residents of Rosewood start shooting back at the mob, several older white audience members walked out of the theater. Singleton turned to Gregory Poirier.

"There goes the Academy," he joked.

Singleton thought he could sell the film to Black audiences. He suggested taking *Rosewood* to Baptist conventions. Let the grassroots build word of mouth, he said. The studio nixed that idea. Warner Bros. had other plans. Time Warner CEO Gerald Levin screened the film for members of Congress. The event garnered some publicity but sold zero tickets.

Released on February 21, 1997, *Rosewood* debuted in eighth place, earning $3.1 million on just 991 screens during its opening weekend; it topped out at $13.1 million. Warner Bros. had sold Singleton a much different vision when they courted him during the fall of 1994.

"Once the film was done and they saw how powerful and strong it was, they basically got cold feet," Bruce Cannon says. "I feel like they abandoned it. Both Lorenzo and Jon Peters."

"We all were collectively brainwashed, I guess," di Bonaventura says. "We all believed that the story was so important and so powerful that it would drive itself. I think that was a mistake."

*Rosewood* fared better with critics than it did with audiences. "Rich in flavor and atmosphere, it represents an impressive change of artistic pace from the contemporary urban movie for which he is known," Jay Carr wrote in his four-star review in the *Boston Globe*. "Mr. Singleton is clearly a man with a purpose here. He means to make it stomach turning, and it is."

Jay Boyar of the *Orlando Sentinel* also awarded the film four stars. "Unlike most films on such topics, this one doesn't feel obliged to demonstrate that racism is evil. *Rosewood* simply takes that for granted. It's hard to overstate what a difference this makes. Where movies like *A Time to Kill* and *Ghosts of Mississippi* spend a lot of time making pious, obvious points about race relations, this one concentrates on telling its specific, shocking tale. Where many filmmakers shout their good intentions from every scene, director John Singleton allows his message to arise naturally, from the specifics."

*Rosewood* came and went in theaters and didn't receive a single nomination at the 1998 Academy Awards. Once forgotten, it became a hidden gem. In a 2001 essay for the *New York Times*, the cultural critic Stanley Crouch dubbed it "Singleton's finest work thus far." He wrote, "Never in the history of American film had Southern racist hysteria been shown so clearly. . . . *Rosewood* demonstrated what John Singleton can do when he has the freedom to explore the themes of personal identification and alienation that continue to tie our society in knots."

But that didn't relieve the sting from the box-office disaster. Later on in life, Singleton expressed great pride in the film. But in the moment, *Rosewood*'s failures deflated him. He thought it would be culturally significant. When that didn't happen, it deeply wounded him.

The lack of a production deal didn't slow Singleton's efforts to get projects off the ground. New Deal still held the rights to *Brushback*, the Negro Leagues film Will Smith had been circling. On the heels of the $300 million–grossing *Independence Day*, Smith was now one of the hottest movie stars in the industry. He had finished shooting his follow-up, *Men In Black*, a big-budget tentpole that Columbia slated for the summer of 1997. He remained enthusiastic about *Brushback*.

Around this time, Smith and Singleton had lunch together at a closed restaurant in Los Angeles to discuss the picture. But the meeting proved unproductive. Eventually, Singleton's option on *Brushback* ran out. Smith picked it up and tried to get the film made at Fox but was unsuccessful.

The husband-and-wife producing team of Michael and Beth Hubbard brought *Woo* to New Deal after Disney put it in turnaround. Singleton loved the script. He viewed the romantic comedy about a mismatched pair on a blind date as a potential *Breakfast at Tiffany's* meets *After Hours*. New Line Cinema committed to the film once Jada Pinkett became attached to it. Production started in the fall of 1996 in Toronto.

The Hubbards hoped Singleton would direct, but *Rosewood* was still in postproduction. New Line executives suggested Daisy von Scherler Mayer, the director of the 1995 cult classic *Party Girl*. Though the producers were skeptical of a white director, Singleton approved. He was a fan of *Party Girl*, which also revolved around a flaky young woman's romantic escapades.

Everyone seemed to be having a difficult time in Toronto. Pinkett, who had been high school friends with Tupac, was grieving his murder, which occurred a few days before production started. On the set, the producers and the director disagreed about the script. The Hubbards asked Singleton to help oversee production.

At first, Singleton's presence proved comforting. Beth Hubbard had just given birth to her first child a month premature. "He had breathing problems," she says. "I was just holding it together."

On one of his first nights in Toronto, Singleton and Beth Hubbard stood on a rooftop. He looked at her and said, "Beth, you know what? God doesn't give you anything you can't handle, girl. You're going to be fine. We're going to work all of this out." She burst into tears.

"I never expected that to come out of John's mouth, because he had never gotten that personal with me," she says. "That was the kindest, gentlest thing he could have said."

But Singleton quickly became a disruptive force on the set, insisting on sidebars with the actors and stepping on the director. "He would be all over the place," Michael Hubbard says. "He seemed distracted. We could tell he was distracted."

Shortly after learning Busia was pregnant, Singleton approached her mother in a traditional Ghanian betrothal ceremony. They were married in Los Angeles on October 12, 1996. Singleton reportedly answered his cell phone in the middle of the wedding ceremony. Two weeks later, they had a church wedding on Gorée Island in Senegal. He hosted a wedding dinner later that fall at the River Café in New York.

Singleton barely spoke of Busia or the marriage to some friends.

On October 18, Singleton went to see the new Spike Lee joint *Get on the Bus* at the Cinerama Dome with Cheo Hodari Coker, an *LA Times* journalist Singleton befriended following an interview, and the directors Reginald Hudlin and Rusty Cundieff. Afterward, they lingered on Sunset Boulevard discussing Lee's film about a group of men attending the Million Man March, marveling at how quickly he turned around the film; *Get on the Bus* was released on the one-year anniversary of the Million Man March. Then someone suggested going to Mario Van Peebles's house.

They all sat around his kitchen table until five a.m. talking film, the industry, their dream projects. During lulls in the conversations, Singleton kept returning to *Fighting and Fucking*, the movie he wanted to make with Tupac, who had been murdered six weeks earlier. He barely mentioned his wedding from earlier in the week, if at all.

Busia later said that her marriage to Singleton consisted of "emotional abuse, physical neglect, and total disrespect." While pregnant, she learned about the two other women he'd impregnated. One woman, who hasn't been identified, later miscarried. Vestria Barlow says she had an abortion. Around this time, a third woman told Busia that she'd been having unprotected sex with Singleton. He had hoped to get her pregnant as well.

When Busia raised the subject of his repeated infidelities, Singleton told her, "This is who I am. I've got to be me."

What did he mean by that? He wasn't the most upright boyfriend or husband. He was unfaithful. He strung women along. Instead of moving on from fading relationships, he didn't allow them to die. He called. He wrote letters. Later on, he texted. He asked for one more chance. He did what he wanted, when he wanted. He wouldn't allow anyone to slow him down. The business was always his top priority. Around the time he got married, Singleton decamped for New York to write his next film. He checked into the Mark Hotel on the Upper East Side where he hoped to bang out a first draft.

"He simply does not want to be committed to anyone or make any kind of sacrifice," Busia said in court papers. "In addition to this, in order to maintain his lifestyle, he has weaved a complicated web of lies and deceptions regardless of the price women in his life or his children have to pay."

They separated on March 12, 1997. On April 3, the same day that Singleton's son Maasai turned three, Hadar, his daughter with Busia, was born. On April 15, six months and three days after their wedding, Singleton filed for divorce.

Later on, he told friends that Busia had forced him to marry her. If he didn't, he said, she'd tell the press he raped her.

In court papers filed in spring 1997, Busia recounted their first time together.

"I have abstained from premarital sex," she declared. "It is a personal stand which I shared with John four years ago when I first met him, and which he abided by until one night in the summer of 1996, when he ignored my requests to 'stop' and proceeded to have sex with me anyway. Seeing the effect it had on me, he was afterward remorseful for what he had done and suggested I talk it over with the counselor with whom we had been having premarital counseling. I did, after which John and I continued together in counseling for our relationship. Sometime after that incident, I found out that I was pregnant. By John's admission weeks later, getting me pregnant was something he had deliberately set out to do, stating that he had been wanting to marry me for four years."

Singleton used the term "extortion" to describe the situation. He also told friends he'd been "cuckolded"—that Busia was in love with Stevie Wonder the entire time they were together. Wonder, who'd become Hadar's godfather, had known Busia since the late 1980s. They remained friends through the decades. On October 10, 1996, two days before Singleton and Busia married, Wonder read from Busia's novel, *The Seasons of Beento Blackbird* at Book Soup on Sunset Boulevard. In 2005, Wonder and Busia collaborated on the song "Moon Blue" off Wonder's *A Time to Love* album.

Following their divorce, Singleton went back and forth in the courts with Busia.

In September 1997, Singleton agreed to pay $2,500 a month in child support for their daughter, Hadar. Later on, the amount was raised to $4,000 a month. He was also ordered to pay Busia $40,000 in three installments before December 1, 1997, and to put $15,000 toward the purchase of a car by February 1998. Singleton had been giving Busia $4,000 a month while she was pregnant to maintain her property bills.

Busia claimed that Singleton rescinded his commitment to put $100,000 toward a down payment on a house for her and their daughter after she had opened escrow on it; she then borrowed the amount to close escrow and purchase the home. "I currently receive approximately $7,000 in borrowed funds from private concerns," she said in court papers.

Busia asked for sole custody of Hadar.

"While I do not believe John would deliberately harm Hadar, I am concerned by his lack of judgment and self-control," Busia said, "which cause him to lie and harm those he 'loves' for which he is later remorseful, only to repeat the same offenses, despite his apparent caring."

# CHAPTER SIXTEEN

**S**ometime in 1996 while still working on *Rosewood*, Singleton had an epiphany.
"I want to get away from real people, real events, real tragedy," he said.

He stepped back and contemplated the state of his career. Then he noticed the films his contemporaries were making. Brett Ratner, a longtime friend he met through Russell Simmons in 1990, had just directed the comedian Chris Tucker in *Money Talks*. Soon, they'd redefine the buddy comedy with *Rush Hour*. Michael Bay had transitioned from commercials and music videos to directing *Bad Boys* and *The Rock*, preposterously fun action movies that banked hundreds of millions of dollars. Bryan Singer, who graduated USC film school a year prior to him, had landed one of Singleton's dream gigs. In the summer of 1996, Singer became formally attached to *X-Men* for 20th Century Fox despite being unfamiliar with the comics.

Singleton feared the industry had pigeonholed him. "I was so serious that everyone thought of me as a serious-minded filmmaker and person," he said.

What could give them that idea?

His first four films were bold statements about race, gender, sexuality, the inner cities, America. The stakes were life and death. They often ended in heartbreak. A drive-by. A campus shooting. A racist pogrom.

He didn't like comedies, particularly Black comedies. They all felt silly to him. He rolled his eyes at *B\*A\*P\*S* and *Booty Call*, avoided watching *Martin* until years after the sitcom's run ended. But now, after two years of working on a film about one of the darkest chapters in American history, a revelation occurred: Not every film had to mean something. Not every film had to change the world. He could lighten up.

He had the perfect pivot in mind for the post-*Rosewood* phase of his career. *Shaft*.

The Black private dick that's a sex machine to all the chicks had always been his ace in the hole—a surefire idea he could turn to when in desperate need of a hit, which now was the case. The term *IP* wasn't part of the lexicon back then. No one spoke of intellectual property or brands. But Singleton understood that the title of *Shaft* alone resonated with a broad swath of the moviegoing public.

Gordon Parks's 1971 film was a huge commercial success. With Richard Roundtree in the title role, *Shaft* made over $12 million at the box office against a $1.2 million budget. In the process, it helped save MGM Studios. The film spawned two sequels and a short-lived television series. Along with Melvin Van Peebles's *Sweet Sweetback's Baadasssss Song*, it triggered the blaxploitation wave of the 1970s. The film's music also became a cultural touchstone. Isaac Hayes's score topped the *Billboard* album and singles charts, won three Grammy Awards, and the Oscar for Best Original Song. With its high-hat symbols and wah-wah guitar, the "Theme From Shaft" embodied the character: "always on the move, roving, prowling," as Parks put it.

Singleton was three years old when his father took him to see the film.

"You know, somebody saw me coming down Hollywood Boulevard in a leather trench coat and went ahead and made that movie," Danny told him later on.

Shaft was John Singleton's James Bond—the closest thing he had to a Black superhero growing up. As an adult, he dressed up as Shaft on Halloween. The character marked a notable shift in how Hollywood depicted Black manhood. During the 1960s, Sidney Poitier, the clean-cut, clean-shaven, respectful "hero of integration" represented Hollywood's archetype. Shaft signaled a new era. With his tight pants and mustache, John Shaft oozed machismo. He was a Black man kicking ass; talking back to police; making love to a white woman in the shower, then telling her to get lost.

"It was revolutionary," Singleton said.

MGM still held the rights to the film. One morning, Singleton pitched studio president Mike Marcus, an ally dating back to Marcus's time at CAA.

"Mike, I loved the original. I'd never disrespect the legacy of *Shaft*," Singleton said in a hushed, sincere voice. "I'm the only director who should be allowed to touch it."

Singleton proposed an ambitious film, comparing his script for *Shaft Returns* to *The Dark Knight Returns*, Frank Miller's inventive comic-book miniseries about an aging Batman coming out of retirement. Here, Shaft teamed with his adult children to take down a Hans Gruber–type European villain named The Artist. He envisioned Roundtree reprising the role of Shaft; Lauryn Hill of the Fugees as his expert-in-martial-arts daughter; and Will Smith playing his son, a by-the-book NYPD officer—Singleton still hoped to land the megastar despite failing to close the deal with him on *Brushback*.

He'd shoot in New York, Africa, and the Caribbean. The opening scene set the tone with modern-day pirates robbing a yacht party. Suddenly, someone in a pair of flippers climbs a ladder onto the boat. He thrashes the pirates and saves the day. Then a big reveal, similar to Indiana Jones in *Raiders of the Lost Ark*: John Shaft Jr. smoking a cigar.

Cue the theme music.

Singleton's projected $25 million budget proved a dealbreaker, though, for the studio. MGM hoped to cap the film at $20 million. They did, however, permit him to shop it.

With *Shaft* stalled at MGM, Singleton considered other projects. He briefly discussed adapting Octavia Butler's *Wild Seed* before setting up *Golddiggaz* at Universal. The idea sprang from "Love in the Time of Magic," an E. Jean Carroll article in the April 1992 issue of *Esquire* about NBA groupies. Originally, he tapped Kim Greene and Camille Tucker, the young, creative team behind the acclaimed short film *Sweet Potato Ride*, to write and direct *Golddiggaz*; Tucker had been an extra in one of the music videos Singleton directed as a USC student. But he got antsy once MGM shelved *Shaft*. He elbowed aside the duo and took over directing duties, to the surprise of everyone involved. In the end, he abandoned the project once the NBA denied permission to use its logos and likenesses.

He turned his attention back to *Woo*. After an initial cut proved disastrous, Singleton secured an additional $2.3 million for reshoots. He felt he could fix it in the editing room. In the end, the film sat on the shelf for close to a year. During that time, Barry Hankerson, the founder of Blackground Records and the father of Singleton's longtime friend Jomo, pulled music from the film; some of the songs, including Aaliyah's "Are You That Somebody" ended up on the *Doctor Dolittle* soundtrack. *Woo* quickly exited movie theaters in May 1998, earning slightly over $8 million.

By this time, *Shaft* had moved into preproduction. In June 1997, Singleton set up the project at Paramount with Scott Rudin producing.

Singleton's first encounter with the Long Island–born producer occurred in the summer of 1991, a few days before *Boyz N the Hood* opened.

"Well, the tracking this weekend says your movie is going to kill my picture," said Rudin, whose film, the Harrison Ford drama *Regarding Henry*, opened in seventh place on the same weekend as *Boyz*'s debut. "So, I wanted to meet you and see who you were." Before leaving, he added, "One day, I promise, we'll find a project together."

During their lunch meeting, Singleton learned they shared a love of theater, a love of film and had nothing else in common. "Like oil and water," he later said.

Rudin made his name as president of production at Fox in the 1980s. He was twenty-seven when he secured the gig, the youngest executive in that position in town. The *Los Angeles Times* profiled him under the headline "Baby Mogul Running Fast for Fox." Rudin's stint in the chair was brief. In February 1988, the studio fired him for "maturity" issues. But during that time, he worked on hits such as *Aliens, Wall Street, Broadcast News, Big*, and *Working Girl*. He later achieved greater success as a producer.

Rudin was a rainmaker for Paramount in the 1990s, producing hits as varied as *The Addams Family, The Firm, Clueless, The First Wives Club, In & Out*, and *The Truman Show*; he also produced the blockbusters *Sister Act* and *Ransom* for Touchstone. With four or five projects going at once, Rudin became known for his prodigious work ethic—and also for his volcanic temper.

An assistant from this time once described Rudin's tantrums as "super-explosive, hands shaking, face shaking, bright red, screaming at the top of his lungs, saying, 'I want to rip your fucking head out! I want you to jump out a window and kill yourself! I want to murder you!'" Rudin hurled phones and fax machines. He flipped desks. Snapped phones in half. And yet, A-list directors such as Mike Nichols, Sydney Pollack, and Peter Weir lined up to work with him because Rudin and his team were among the best in the business. They had smart ideas about everything from storytelling to marketing. He was a great champion for filmmakers. When a director needed extra days to shoot or to cast a certain pricey actor, they could count on Rudin to go toe-to-toe with the studio and come out on top.

*Shaft* appealed to Rudin for obvious reasons. He was an IP-driven producer and *Shaft* was existing IP. Though contemporary literary adaptations were more his domain, he previously turned *The Addams Family*, a black-and-white sitcom from the 1960s, into a $191 million worldwide hit.

"*Shaft* was a chance to do a franchise. There was talk about that at one point," says Adam Schroeder, then president of Scott Rudin Productions. "I think John being the director was also exciting to everybody. We loved *Rosewood*. Maybe it wasn't a commercial success but creatively and artistically it's a fantastic film. It seemed like a departure from what he was doing. His earlier hits were incredible as well but *Rosewood* showed his elevation as a filmmaker. There's a lot going on in that movie."

At first, Singleton resisted his overtures.

"I'm not making this movie with Scott Rudin," he told his producing partner Paul Hall.

Why work with another hard-nosed producer after *Rosewood*? Rudin's behavior was widely known around the industry. But *Shaft* would linger in developmental hell at MGM without him. Singleton needed Scott Rudin.

"You will get the movie made," Hall told him. "It will be awful. But you will get the movie made."

Rudin settled Singleton's $2 million developmental debt at MGM and put *Shaft* on the fast track at Paramount.

Singleton made his Faustian bargain. Now he braced for the fallout.

Rudin quickly took control of the film. He scrapped the international elements and jettisoned the father-and-son storyline from Singleton's script. "It made you feel like you were watching *Young Indiana Jones*," Rudin said. Singleton agreed to work with a cowriter on the rewrite. He turned to Shane Salerno, one of the hot new screenwriters in town.

Salerno, twenty-four, experienced a meteoric rise in the industry. As a high school senior, he directed a public access documentary called *Sundown: The Future of Children and Drugs*. *NYPD Blue* producer Gregory Hoblit invited him to be an apprentice writer/director on the ABC ratings smash when Salerno was just nineteen years old. By the age of twenty-two, he had a three-year contract with Universal Television and earned $200,000 annually for his work on the Fox series *New York Undercover*. He churned out a production rewrite on the Kurt Russell thriller *Breakdown*; sold a spec script; wrote a World War II submarine movie for Spielberg called *Thunder Below*; and rewrote *Armageddon* for Michael Bay.

Salerno had two attributes that appealed to Singleton: He could spin cop stories and had blockbuster filmmaking experience, making him the perfect collaborator for a blockbuster film about NYPD cops.

"John loved big, fat commercial movies," Salerno says. "I didn't get hired off of *My Dinner with Andre*. I was hired off *Armageddon*. John wanted *that*."

During their first meeting, Salerno expressed concern he might not be right for the job. "I am white, you know," he said.

Singleton rolled his eyes. "I'm interested in your writing, not the color of your skin. You do know that a white guy named Ernest Tidyman created *Shaft*, right?" he said. "But we got to take you to school. Put you through the paces."

For the next six months, Salerno doubled as Singleton's wingman around town. He accompanied him to bars, nightclubs, dance clubs, the movies, lounges, sushi lounges, sushi restaurants, Roscoe's Chicken and Waffles. He was his plus-one at industry parties and premieres and rolled with him to concerts and comedy clubs. Singleton went out six nights a week, minimum. He'd toss the keys to the valet, walk past the velvet rope, glide through security, bypass lines, and be escorted to a table. Drinks magically appeared. Throughout the night, an endless parade of waitresses and hostesses stopped by. "Hi, John. Hi, John. Hi, John. Hi, John. Hi, John." He could get into any party, anywhere in LA.

"I've worked for the biggest directors in the business," Salerno says. "I've worked with one rock star." Salerno counts Spielberg, Ron Howard, Michael Bay, Michael Mann, Oliver Stone, and James Cameron as collaborators. "It was just a different vibe with John," he says.

Singleton's enthusiasm for life and for the work seduced Salerno. They became fast friends, nicknaming each other Crockett and Tubbs. Singleton was the alpha in the equation. But he left all the writing to Salerno, even though they were credited as cowriters.

Salerno never shared his concerns with Singleton, but he brought them up to CAA. "I wouldn't rock the boat on this," his agent told him.

They'd talk out scenes and dialogue before Salerno went off to write. Singleton would then give copious notes. Sometimes he acted out precise details he wanted in the script.

"This is how Shaft walks," he'd tell Salerno, mimicking Richard Roundtree's stride from the opening credits of *Shaft*.

"This is how Shaft pulls his gun," he said.

Singleton took in the world and poured it into the script. One night, he called Salerno on his way home from a party.

"I'm coming over. I'm coming over. Can I come over?"

Salerno, in bed, looked at the time. It was after midnight. A few minutes later, the doorbell rang.

"C'mon, let's get to work," Singleton said. "I just overheard the greatest line ever!"

Salerno led him into his writing room. Singleton paced back and forth. He hovered over Salerno as he pulled up the draft.

Salerno wiped his eyes. He scrolled through the pages.

"Okay, stop—stop! This is so good," Singleton said, tapping Salerno on the shoulder. "Okay, at the end, Shaft looks at her and says, 'Well, you know me. It's my duty to please that booty.'"

"You're joking."

"Just write what I'm telling you," he said. "Trust me."

"Please tell me you're joking."

"That's the line they're gonna be quoting walking out of the theater. Trust me."

Now he had to find the right person to say the line.

Will Smith was both Singleton and the studio's first choice. After conversations with Smith's team (not necessarily with him, though), they moved on. Singleton advocated for Don Cheadle. But the studio vetoed the five-foot-eight-inch-tall actor.

"At the time, I was like, 'I don't see them saying yes to me playing Shaft for some reason,'" Cheadle says. "I wasn't too surprised when it didn't happen."

Rudin also shot down a pre-*Rush Hour* Chris Tucker (too clownish) and a post-*How Stella Got Her Groove Back* Taye Diggs (too young).

In the fall of 1998, Wesley Snipes appeared to be the frontrunner. Though past his box-office prime, he had all the necessary traits. Tough. Suave. Good-looking. Few actors talked trash and delivered one-liners as effortlessly as Mr. See-ya-and-I-wouldn't-wanna-be-ya. "Wesley Snipes is Shaft," Singleton told a friend over Instant Messenger. Rudin arranged a meeting.

According to people close to Singleton, Snipes walked in, trailed by four or five women and a cloud of marijuana smoke. He sat down, put his feet up, his hands behind his head, and leaned back. "I am Shaft, motherfucker," he said through a smirk. "But the script is a piece of shit. We're getting a new writer. We're partnering on this film: Scott Rudin and Amen-Ra."

Shane Salerno remembers the meeting a little differently. In his telling, the meeting took place in Rudin's office. Singleton and Salerno sat together on a sofa near the door. Snipes entered the room, oblivious to the pair, and dropped their script on Rudin's desk.

"I don't know who wrote this shit, but I'm not doing it," he said. "If I *do* do this, I'm bringing in my own team and it will be an Amen-Ra production."

Rudin looked at Snipes. Then he looked past him toward Singleton and Salerno on the sofa. Snipes turned around. Then turned back to Rudin.

"I'm a huge fan," Rudin said, extending his hand. "It was great to meet you. Thank you so much."

"Wait, what are—"

"It was great to meet you. Thank you so much for coming in."

"It was the greatest 'Fuck you' I've ever seen in my whole life," Salerno says.

Nevertheless, the meeting left a mark on Rudin. Snipes didn't get the role. He slammed the film upon its release. "There's only one Shaft—Richard Roundtree—but if you're going to do a remake, there's only one person that can do that—Snipes, period," he said. "I was offered the film and it was terrible, horrible. It was an insult not only to African American culture, but an insult to what the icon of Shaft was."

Samuel L. Jackson hadn't been mentioned for the role—and with good reason. Everyone, including Jackson, thought he'd aged out of playing Shaft. When approached for the film, Jackson thought, *Well, what character do they want me to read for?* Roundtree, a former model, first donned the leather jacket at twenty-nine years old. Jackson was fifty with bad knees. But he had the star power Rudin required for Shaft and the swagger Singleton coveted. In February 1999, after a nearly two-year search, he found his leading man.

The lengthy casting process drove the film's start date from spring 1998 to spring 1999. Jackson's commitment to *Rules of Engagement,* another Scott Rudin production shooting throughout the spring, then pushed production on *Shaft* into the fall of 1999. During that time, the script also underwent numerous changes.

The film's plot turned into standard detective fare—a twist on the "witness in jeopardy" storyline found in countless television shows, and movies like Steve McQueen's *Bullitt.* And the private investigator was now an NYPD detective, although Jackson successfully lobbied for the character to quit the force early in the film. Rudin felt the script needed more work. Sometime in 1998, he hired the screenwriter and novelist Richard Price to rewrite the film and handle rewrites on set. Rudin trusted Price. One of Rudin's first jobs as a casting director was the 1979 film adaptation of Price's debut novel, *The Wanderers*. More recently, Price had written the 1996 Mel Gibson kidnapping thriller *Ransom* for Rudin.

Soon after Price's hiring, Salerno left the film to work on a Sonny Liston biopic for William Friedkin. After "something like sixteen drafts" in eighteen months, he was eager to move on. Rudin handed him a note on his last day.

"It was brutal," Salerno says. "It said—and I'm paraphrasing here—'I'm still trying to unfuck what you guys did to the movie.' It was on his letterhead and everything."

★★★★★

Singleton's personal life spiraled as he worked on *Shaft*.

After filing for divorce from Busia, Singleton once again tried making it work with Barlow. They talked to a couples therapist starting in the summer of 1997 and attended industry events as a couple. But they reverted to old patterns, bickering over petty jealousies. They argued after attending Janet Jackson's album release party for *The Velvet Rope* in September. Barlow remembers Singleton feeling she had attracted too much attention.

"You haven't done nothing," Singleton told Barlow later that night. "You're not the star. Why do they care about who you are?"

The next night Singleton attended the premiere of the new Michael Douglas thriller *The Game* on Hollywood Boulevard.

Barlow still held on to a lot of pain. She resented Singleton for past slights—first in favor of a supermodel and then for an African princess. For his part, Singleton knew their relationship was doomed. But he couldn't let her go.

"I love you Ves. I have for a long time," he wrote to her. "But we have many problems. Big ones. The hard part is they are the same ones we've been having since the beginning of our relationship. There's been no growth. Our trust is wanting. Communication is abysmal. You don't call me. I don't call you. Sex? It's not as good as it used to be which is painful because I still love your body.

"I really wanted us to work because we are both from the same place. We grew up in the ghetto in LA and all that is cool. But we share that ghetto love. I [love] you Ves but I feel that we are holding each other down. I don't know what to do."

One night in the fall of 1997, while Singleton was prepping *Shaft*, he asked Barlow to visit him in New York.

Barlow dropped off Maasai with her cousin and flew east. Around nine p.m. the next evening, she arrived at the Mark on the Upper East Side. She waited in the lobby for what seemed like an hour. Singleton appeared, holding hands with a short-haired Latina.

"Hey, John," Barlow said. "You didn't think I was coming, huh?"

Singleton smirked. "I knew you were coming," he said.

He introduced the women. Barlow looked at her, then at him.

Singleton tapped his feet rapidly and giggled. They took the elevator upstairs to his room. Once inside, the women took off their coats.

Barlow glared at her. Then she called her cousin.

"This bitch isn't getting any of my clues," she said loudly about Singleton's date. "Like, 'Girl, stop talking to me.'"

She slammed the phone. "John, you need to tell her to leave."

He exhaled deeply.

As soon as his date left, Barlow erupted. "You got me to let my guard down," she said. "I can't believe I fell for all that shit you was talking the other night."

"Why are you being so insecure?" Singleton asked. "Why you being so insecure?"

"That's when I went off. I kind of tore up the room," Barlow says.

She picked up a glass, threw it at his face, and unleashed a barrage of hay-makers. Singleton ended the argument. He started kissing Barlow, then he went down on her. When the dust settled, Barlow says she caused about ten thousand dollars' worth of damages to the room.

They went on like this for the next year. Barlow got pregnant again toward the end of 1998. Early on, he accompanied her on prenatal doctor visits. But as the pregnancy progressed, his work on *Shaft* took him to New York.

One day, during the summer of 1999, Singleton returned to Los Angeles.

"Are you going to be with me after you have this baby?" he asked Barlow.

Barlow, eight months pregnant, looked at him. "John, I can't come back to you. I can't."

Barlow had been around Singleton long enough to know he couldn't commit. He loved her. He might want to "be with her." But it wouldn't be what she envisioned. Monogamy. White picket fence. Stable nuclear family. That wasn't him. At best, Singleton could do that for a quick spell. Besides, he'd soon be in New York working on *Shaft* for the next eight months.

Their daughter, Cleopatra, was born in September 1999 while *Shaft* filmed in

New York. Singleton refused to sign the birth certificate until a DNA test established paternity.

"He got this perverse thrill by putting me through that and degrading me," Barlow says.

Singleton's relationships with the mothers of his other children were equally contentious and complicated. He was engaged in almost nonstop litigation with Akosua Busia and Tosha Lewis.

On January 2, 1999, Singleton and Lewis got into an argument about visitation rights that ended with police arriving on the scene.

According to court documents, Lewis showed up to Singleton's house even though his custody time with Justice had not expired. When she arrived, she knocked on his door, rang his doorbell, and yelled. Singleton emerged through the garage, loudly asking her to leave. She then approached him in a "threatening manner." When they converged, Singleton grabbed her arms to restrain her and to steer her off his property. A friend of Lewis's, who witnessed the confrontation, later compared it to an episode of *The Jerry Springer Show*.

Lewis didn't receive any medical treatment. The small scratch she claimed to have suffered was not supported by evidence.

Singleton later pleaded no contest to one count of battery. A judge sentenced him to three years' probation, a three-hundred-dollar fine, and mandatory counseling. He was also ordered to make a fifteen- to thirty-minute short film about domestic violence.

"I'm a very passive guy. No one would ever think I was the one going through the abuse," he said in an interview with the *Washington Post*. "So that's what my short film is going to be about."

Lewis later filed suit against Singleton in Los Angeles Superior Court for the January 1999 incident. In the complaint, she alleged that Singleton had physically abused her in the past, detailing incidents in December 1992 and October 1993 that turned physical. He denied the past accusations, claiming "sometimes there are squabbles . . . and the man gets the short end of the stick."

Singleton, in turn, filed a cross-complaint alleging Lewis committed an assault and battery against him and had trespassed on his property during the January 2, 1999, altercation.

Following a short trial, the jury returned a verdict in favor of Lewis against Singleton—but also in favor of Singleton on his cross-complaint against Lewis. In both cases, the jury awarded an amount of zero dollars.

Singleton filed for full custody of Justice in March 2000; Lewis considered it "retaliation" for the lawsuit. By this time, they had mutual restraining orders against each other. Back and forth they went in the press. "This woman has been the bane of my existence because she's a scorned lover," Singleton said. "She hasn't moved on, and it's been ten years." He accused Lewis of raising Justice in an "unstable household" and claimed their child was at risk of repeating second grade due to frequent absences.

Lewis, who at the time worked for Benny Medina, denied the charges of neglect. "For him to say those things is ridiculous," Lewis said. She added, "He can't take care of himself, let alone a child."

★★★★★

Singleton's family continued to grow. About a month after Cleopatra was born, Singleton's girlfriend Massiel Selene Bueno gave birth to his fifth child, Selenesol. Singleton, who was shooting in Brooklyn, missed the birth; calls to his cell went straight to voicemail. He showed up to the hospital later that day with his camcorder in tow.

Selenesol recalls hearing the story of how they met. About a year or two earlier at an industry party in Los Angeles, Singleton overheard Bueno, an aspiring actress, lamenting to a friend that no one had asked her to dance. He took one look at her and promptly escorted her to the dance floor.

Later, when Singleton learned she was pregnant, he suggested she come to New York and stay with her family in Corona, Queens, and Washington Heights, while he worked on *Shaft*.

One Saturday afternoon during the summer of 1999, he met the entire clan. He climbed into the Cadillac Escalade he used on the weekend and made the long drive from his West Village apartment on Spring and Wooster to deepest, darkest Queens. When he got close, he called Bueno.

After hanging up, she went looking for her twenty-five-year-old cousin Francisco Taveras. She found him on the front stoop drinking beers with five or six friends.

She told him that her boyfriend was lost and asked if Taveras could find him and bring him back to the house.

Taveras, nicknamed Coqui, gathered his boys and set out to corral Singleton.

He found him parked a few blocks away standing next to his car. As Coqui approached the Escalade he realized that he owed his cousin an apology. He'd scoffed when she told him that her boyfriend—the father of her unborn child—made movies. "My cousin would say things like that, and I would not pay her any mind," Coqui says. "When I saw him, I thought, 'Holy shit, that's John Singleton.' She told me his name was John and I had read in the *Daily News* that John Singleton would be filming *Shaft* in New York. But I hadn't put two and two together."

Singleton followed Coqui's car back to the building where Bueno's family had gathered. He didn't know what to expect. There weren't many Dominicans in Los Angeles. As soon as he walked in the door, the mood shifted.

"Dominicans, we can be racist," Coqui says. "We share an island with Haiti but we don't admit that we come from African descent. We tend to call Spain the motherland. So, my grandmother, when she first met John, she was like, 'Ugh,' because he's African American. That bothered me. She was weird with him. He didn't sense it. But I could. I know my grandmother."

On his way out, Singleton stopped to talk to Coqui and his friends.

"I'm doing this movie called *Shaft* and the bad guys are a Dominican gang," Singleton said. "Are you guys in a gang?"

The stoop exploded in laughter. "Gangs aren't really a New York thing," Coqui said.

Singleton became instantly fascinated with them. He looked at their clothes. Listened to them talk—their slang. Noticed their demeanor and how they interacted with one another. They were the real deal, he thought. He started asking questions, which they reluctantly answered. Singleton held his gaze for an uncomfortable length of time. He laughed his signature laugh at odd moments. At one point, he walked outside the gate, crouched down, and made director hands as if he were framing a shot.

Coqui and his friends looked at one another. *¿Que le pasa a este tipo? (What's the matter with this guy?)*

"It was like he was making mental notes," Coqui says. "At first, I thought John was weird. It didn't dawn on me until I had known him for a month or two that he was just an artist. Everything was a scene to him."

Before departing, Singleton extended an invitation. "Hey, I really need some New York street dudes, real mean-looking guys. Why don't you come audition? Tell your friends."

Coqui had no plans to act. He loved to read. He loved the movies. He had a gift for memorization. But actors went to acting school. They trained. Honed their craft. He was a bartender. And yet, he couldn't turn him down. *Boyz N the Hood* was "life-changing," he says. He took his then girlfriend to see it during the summer of '91. "I thought I was Doughboy until I saw that movie. But I wasn't. I was actually Tre," he says. "My father had a good union job. My mother was a treasurer for the Brooklyn diocese. We weren't well-off but I was spoiled. I went to Catholic school—St. John's Prep in Astoria. I realized I'm not a killer. I'm surrounded by killers and criminals. But I'm not a killer. I'm not Doughboy. I'm Tre. One time, I told that shit to John. He just laughed, and was like, 'That's bugged out.'"

He switched shifts with a coworker to audition. He read some lines for Singleton, Adam Schroeder, and casting director Ilene Starger. Didn't think much of it until a few hours later when his beeper vibrated. He called the number. It was Singleton telling him he won the role of Lucifer, the little brother of *Shaft* villain Peoples Hernandez. Coqui took a deep breath. He had one question on his mind: *Why?*

"They loved you," Singleton hollered. "They say you're a natural."

"I don't know. I'm not an actor."

"Don't worry about it. I'm gonna be there on set. I got you."

Coqui quit his job at the Marriott about a week before filming started. He saw Singleton more and more throughout the summer.

"John was coming into Queens a lot," he says. "He wasn't coming so much to see Massiel. He was coming to hang with me and my friends and observe. He asked me to take him to the bad parts of my neighborhood."

They hung out in barbershops and restaurants. Street corners and stoops. Coqui told Singleton stories about his uncle, Bueno's father, a Dominican revolutionary who protested El Jefe, the Dominican dictator Rafael Trujillo, and spent a decade in exile for it.

Singleton already loved Dominican women. He came to embrace the culture as well. Soon, he was reading books on Dominican history and making plans to visit the island.

On August 15, 1999, Singleton met Coqui in midtown Manhattan for the Dominican Day Parade.

"John almost got me killed," Coqui says.

At one point in the afternoon, they stumbled into a dispute between NYPD officers and about fifteen guys in white T-shirts and Dominican flag bandanas. It escalated quickly. As the police called for backup, Singleton drifted toward them, squatted into a catcher's stance, and started taking pictures of the confrontation.

"Yo," Coqui thundered, "what the fuck are you doing, bro?"

Singleton could barely contain his excitement. "Oh my God, there's this scene where you guys come out of the apartment and confront Shaft and this is it! This is like a standoff!"

"You need to chill out. Now is not the time."

One of the Dominicans arguing with the police turned toward them. "Aren't you John Singleton?" he asked.

Singleton nodded.

"Yo, you knew Tupac?"

"Yeah, I knew Pac."

Singleton nonchalantly walked away, stopping to snap more pictures every few steps.

Later that day, they met with Jeffrey Wright, who'd be playing Peoples Hernandez. The Colombian American actor John Leguizamo (*Romeo + Juliet*, *Spawn*, Spike Lee's *Summer of Sam*) had originally been cast in the role. But he dropped out to shoot *Moulin Rouge!* for Baz Luhrmann in Australia. Singleton didn't seem to mind so much. He wasn't a fan of Leguizamo's scenery-chewing as Benny Blanco in *Carlito's Way* and happily swapped in Wright. A theater actor with a Tony Award on his résumé (Best Featured Actor in a Play, 1994, for *Angels in America*), Wright seemed poised for a breakthrough following his performance as Jean-Michel Basquiat in the 1996 biopic of the charismatic artist.

Despite Wright's credentials, Coqui couldn't envision him as a flamboyant Dominican drug lord—and it wasn't solely because Wright, an African American from Washington, DC, wasn't Latino. Wright was bookish and erudite. He had little swagger.

"This isn't going to work," Coqui told Singleton. "He's not believable."

Singleton laughed. "Jeffrey's a bad motherfucker."

When Coqui saw him again at the table read three weeks later at the Waldorf, he remained skeptical as Wright hadn't perfected his accent. But all the while he was spending a lot of time around Dominicans in Washington Heights. He also consulted with the Dominican manager of a social club in midtown Manhattan. "Rafi was the carillon bell for Peoples. He was the one who gave me the voice," Wright told *GQ* years later. "In fact, when I got the script, I said, 'Rafi, will you read some of these lines?' He came over and I recorded him."

Wright also ended up shadowing Coqui and his friends. They went to bars together in Washington Heights, the Bronx, and Corona, including Manny's, an infamous after-hours spot in Queens. Coqui realized he was hanging with a different guy than the one he met at the parade.

"Jeffrey went a little method with it," Coqui says. "He was Peoples for, like, a month straight. We would go out and almost get into fights because of him. He would not break character."

By the time he got on set, Wright, now rocking a Caesar haircut with sideburns shaped like daggers and a manicured goatee, had brought Peoples Hernandez to life.

Coqui approached Singleton. "Holy shit, John, you were right."

"I told you," Singleton said, snickering. "Jeffrey's a bad motherfucker."

★★★★★

Wright's transformation into Peoples Hernandez was a rare bright spot for Singleton. Though it had been his dream project, *Shaft* turned into as much of a slog as *Rosewood* and left him feeling just as disenfranchised.

Rudin asserted dominance early on during production. He fired actress Jennifer Esposito over a hair and makeup disagreement after her first day shooting. He dismissed Academy Award–nominated cinematographer Stuart Dryburgh about three weeks into filming. During preproduction, Singleton and Dryburgh planned to shoot John Shaft heroically, using a variety of low angles, push-ins, and crane shots. Once they got on set, though, Rudin nixed all that. "I sided more with John and that caused Scott to find an excuse to get rid of me, which he did," Dryburgh says. "John was apologetic. But he also knew it was aimed at him as much as me."

Singleton had few allies on set. The Singleton Family was mostly absent. His crew was filled with Rudin's people. They were a New York- and London-based crew that Rudin returned to over and over again. Competent. Loyal. Older. Very white.

In August 1999, a story ran on the gossip pages of the New York *Daily News*. "*Shaft* Bigs Lock Horns over Few Black Hires." According to the piece, six of the 125 crew members working on the film were Black. Singleton was "miffed" over the demographics of the crew. "There's enough quality people in New York to fill three or four film productions," Singleton's friend Spike Lee said in the piece. DGA Eastern Council chair Roni Wheeler called the lack of Black crew members "a slap in the face to the African American community." Following the report, the Alliance for Stunt Performers of Color called for a boycott of Paramount parent company Viacom. Singleton defended Rudin to the *LA Times*—even though he quite possibly planted the initial *Daily News* story.

"I've hired the best people possible and I've assembled a great crew," he told the paper. "The allegations that anyone is being hired on a racial basis is unfounded, totally erroneous and offensive to me."

The script was his primary concern.

Adding Richard Price to the team seemed like a good idea. A native of the Parkside Houses in the Bronx, Price captured the city's grit and spirit through his dialogue. He had a gift for writing police procedurals. Previously, he'd collaborated with Spike Lee on the director's 1995 film adaptation of Price's novel *Clockers*. Singleton objected to the hire from the start and went out of his way to minimize Price.

Before filming one of the scenes in Peoples Hernandez's lair, Singleton took Coqui aside and whispered in his ear. "Don't say anything that stupid guy wrote. Say it like you'd say it. Just come with some street shit. Be you."

Coqui says he improvised most of the scene where he asks Peoples to hold on to some jewelry.

"Price didn't have a clue about the attitude of Shaft," Singleton said.

Rudin dismissed Singleton's concerns about the dialogue. But he couldn't ignore it when Jackson protested.

At the first read-through, Jackson tossed the script in disgust. "There is no fucking way I'm saying any of this shit," he said. "I don't talk like that." He urged Rudin to hire Quentin Tarantino as a script doctor.

Jackson called Price's rewrites "offensive." During production, he successfully pushed to cut material he felt uncomfortable with. In one unfilmed scene, Shaft tossed a candy bar at a girlfriend after she complained that he didn't take her to dinner. He also axed a line from the opening scene when a Black character walked into a posh lounge: "Brother comes in here like a lump of coal in a snowbank."

Before filming in Harlem's famed Lenox Lounge, Singleton urged Rudin to change the dialogue. Price had written a scene where Shaft, tired from a long day at work, turns down sex from a cocktail waitress.

"We'd look crazy doing that," Singleton said.

"You don't get to touch it," Rudin screamed at Singleton.

Jackson got in the producer's face. "Scott, I refuse to say that white man's lines."

Jackson didn't care for Singleton's rewrites, which featured the line he'd overheard and gleefully lifted.

*"You just want to be held or you want the LD?"*

*". . . I want the LD, baby. And then I want to be held. . . ." she said.*

*"You know me. It's my duty to please that booty."*

"John, that's the dumbest shit I've ever heard," Jackson said when presented with it.

Jackson remained ornery throughout production. The crew worked around his knee injury, a mysterious allergic reaction that required hospitalization (said to be an insect bite), and his tee times at local golf courses. A source told the *New York Post*, "three different times [Jackson] wouldn't work because he was playing golf."

The *Post* also suggested that Jackson's relationship with Singleton never recovered following a disagreement early on when Jackson refused to discuss a scene. "Why would I talk to him?" Jackson said about Singleton. "It's like talking to a blank wall."

But Jackson's antipathy toward his director was justified. There were times on the set of *Shaft* when Singleton would be in video village, working multiple cell phones and pagers, all hooked up to chargers. Sometimes, he wouldn't look at the take after calling "Go" to the cast and crew. Instead, he'd be texting on a tiny late-'90s cell phone he held inches from his face.

Jackson shook his head in disgust at the sight of Singleton burying his head in his devices. He thought Singleton was sloppy. Jackson was the first person to point out that an action sequence Singleton filmed lacked continuity, resulting in a Saturday reshoot.

From the start, Singleton didn't grasp the power dynamics at hand. Rudin was top dog. Then came the star: Sam Jackson. *Shaft* had languished in development until he got involved. He got to be difficult and demanding. Singleton, a director coming off a flop, didn't.

Jackson had more life experience than Singleton; when Singleton was three months old, Jackson, then an undergrad at Morehouse, was performing usher duties at Martin Luther King Jr.'s funeral. Unlike Singleton, he took a long, winding route toward stardom. After years lost to addiction, Jackson worked his way up Hollywood's ranks. Steady work. Critical acclaim. An Academy Award nomination. Leading man roles. And now with *Shaft*, his first turn as an action hero. Jackson was considered the hardest-working actor in Hollywood.

"A director has to earn my respect," Jackson said while promoting the film. "John failed to do that, so there were some tense moments. I resented that we had to pull him out of his trailer some days to get him to direct."

Singleton's conduct didn't help matters. One morning after arriving late, Singleton popped out of his car with a woman on each arm and a bag of McDonald's.

"It was a late night," Singleton said. "Had to get something to eat before work."

Singleton's social life—"the Grand Pussy Chase," as one of his close friends termed it—alarmed Rudin from early on. In June 1998, Rudin flew Singleton and Salerno to New York for a Sunday morning story meeting. Salerno arrived in Rudin's West Forty-Fifth Street offices on time at around ten a.m.

"Where the fuck is he?" Rudin said. "Call him!"

Salerno got no answer. Finally, about two hours later, Singleton sauntered in, smiling, holding a bag of food.

"What the hell is going on?" Rudin yelled.

"It's the Puerto Rican Day Parade. Finest girls from all over the city are in the streets dancing and looking fine as hell. What was I doing? I was getting numbers."

Rudin scowled. He stared him down for what felt like an hour.

"This is Shaft—the sex machine to all the chicks. I'm doing research for the script!"

Rudin shook his head. He opened the script and gave his page notes.

Singleton fell in love with the city's nightlife. Cheetah. Centro-Fly. Club New York. Chaos. Moomba. And his favorite spot, Jimmy's Bronx Café.

Following its opening in 1993, the banquet hall/restaurant/nightclub on West Fordham Road became a hot spot for celebrities, athletes (Derek Jeter celebrated two birthdays there), and politicians both local (Bronx borough president Fernando Ferrer) and international (Fidel Castro). On any given night, the clientele included local hustlers, rap royalty, and the most beautiful Latina women outside of San Juan.

"If you ever wanted to meet a J.Lo, you'd go there," says Fat Joe, the Bronx rapper who lorded over Jimmy's in the 1990s. "John liked the Latinas. He was like, 'Yo, I got to find me a fucking J.Lo.'"

Through late nights on the scene, Singleton befriended Fat Joe and his protégé Big Pun. One night, after the waiter informed Singleton that his meal had been comped, Joe rose from his seat and signaled Singleton from across the room. He made his way over to him. Joe then introduced him to Jimmy Rodriguez, the restaurant's owner and namesake.

From that point on, Singleton, and whoever was with him, never waited in line or paid for a drink at Jimmy's.

Sometimes when John met Joe at Jimmy's the night didn't end at last call. "We'd go to after-hours parties in Washington Heights tenement buildings," Joe says. "If some girls were throwing a party in Apartment 5C, me and John Singleton were up in that motherfucker pissy drunk until six in the morning, seven in the morning. We'd walk out when the sun was coming up, smiling, like, 'I'll see you tomorrow.' He was in the hood hard."

Singleton's liaisons later hit the gossip columns. "Shaft Director's Sex Time-Outs" read the headline. In January 2000, the *New York Post*'s Page Six reported he'd been spending an inordinate amount of time in his trailer auditioning female extras.

"They go in there two at a time," said an on-set source. "Next thing you know, they're sitting in the director's chair or they'll show up two weeks later as his guest, or on a second callback."

Members of the crew nicknamed the women "the domino girls" because "when you tap them on the shoulder they drop to their knees."

The report prompted a response from Singleton's agent. "If at one point or another John dated a female extra, I can't say," Jeremy Zimmer said. "But his behavior toward women on the set has never been the focus of any attention or discussion."

Singleton denied the *Post*'s account. "It was true I looked over sexy extras," he said in 2000. "But I wasn't screwing two of them in the trailer and running the crew at the same time. I mean, goddamn, you know? Give me some professional fucking consideration."

Singleton and his allies believed Rudin fed the story to the *New York Post*. But while the producer could use the press to settle scores, it didn't make sense for him to contribute to the bad buzz surrounding the film. Bad press was bad for business—and that mattered more to Rudin than humiliating a director he'd never work with again.

In the moment, Singleton brushed it aside. One night, soon after the story was published, he grabbed a late-night drink with the actress Catherine Kellner. It was around three a.m. Singleton had his usual: a Sprite with maraschino cherries.

He'd met Kellner on the set of *Rosewood*, where she played Fannie Taylor, the woman whose lie galvanized the racist mob. They became lifelong friends. Some nights he avoided the clubs for an evening at Kellner's grandparents' house, watching old movies with the sweet old Hungarian immigrant couple.

"He was comfy with us," Kellner says. "He'd put his head on my grandmother's lap. He liked people who had nothing to prove."

Sitting in a Chelsea bar, nursing his pink, sugary drink, Singleton mocked the rumors.

"This is so flattering," he said. "This is really the best kind of gossip."

"Do you think it's wonderful because it makes you look studly?"

"Yes!"

"John, they're writing in the paper that women are blowing you in your trailer."

"Yeah, I know! It's hilarious! Can you imagine that I would have women willing to do that?"

"Aren't you afraid of repercussions?"

"Why? No one who knows me would ever believe that."

Some people close to him refute the Page Six report—that Singleton held up production to have sex in his trailer with extras. Some play coy about it. Some confirm the *Post*'s reporting. But the rumors and the denials dinged his reputation. Singleton's personal life had been messy for a long time. But that was between him and the women involved in the mess. Once the New York tabloids got involved, the whole world knew about it.

The cast and crew picked up hints throughout production. Every day, he seemed to eat lunch with a different woman. He flirted with girls in the van driving to location. He constantly fielded calls from women, including his children's mothers on the West Coast.

More than the women, his relationship with Rudin stressed him out. At times, he got the good Scott Rudin, the eight-hundred-pound gorilla known to spare no expense. One night, while shooting at a bar in the Flatiron District, Rudin took a look around the location and frowned.

"This is supposed to be a bar on the Upper East Side," he groused. "These extras don't look WASPish. They look like they're from the Weehawken mall.

We're not shooting tonight." The scene was postponed at a cost and shot weeks later. Singleton appreciated the attention to detail.

But Rudin bludgeoned Singleton for the duration of the shoot. In his eyes, Singleton didn't work hard enough. He lacked focus. The women were a distraction. On set, he leaned on him. Rudin was both the irresistible force and the immovable object. "John had never encountered anyone like Scott," says Bruce Franklin, the first AD on the film. "It really took the wind out of him from the outset. It was brutal. It was painful."

"I made a deal with the devil," Singleton repeatedly told friends about working with Rudin.

Singleton was prideful though. He pushed back when cornered. One morning while shooting in Washington Heights, Singleton cranked the original "Theme From Shaft" on his car stereo after arriving late to the set.

"Shut that shit off," Rudin thundered.

"Why?" Singleton said. "Does it make you uncomfortable? If it does, you shouldn't be on the set. This is a Black movie. It's not a Paramount thing."

"Do me a favor and dance your ass behind the camera," Rudin said.

"How could you say that to me?" Singleton said.

"Because you're acting like a fucking asshole," Jackson shot back.

The movie went over budget. Filming careened into late January. At this point, Singleton accepted that his dream project had turned into a nightmare. On the heels of *Rosewood*, it shook him to his core.

"For five years, people told him he walked on water," Salerno says. "People would tell him, *'Okay, John. Whatever you think, John. This is so great. Sounds great, John.'* Do you understand how weird it is when people think you can do anything? Then, suddenly, he was hearing, *'We're just not going to be able to do that, John. We're going to need you to do it this way, John.'* When that bubble popped, everything got harder for him."

Rudin thought *Shaft* would bomb.

"You watch," he said prior to the first test screening. "We're going to have three weeks of reshoots on this thing."

But audiences loved the film. Released on June 16, 2000, *Shaft* debuted at number one with $21.7 million on opening weekend.

Singleton thought *Shaft* was "er, well . . . all right," as he told *The Guardian* a few years later. He envisioned a much different film, one more ambitious in scale, yet truer to the original. In the end, he had the wrong star and the wrong producer. Rudin didn't share Singleton's reverence for the source material. He failed to grasp what made it special. Nearly every review of the film mentioned its absence of sex. It bothered Singleton immensely that he made a prudish *Shaft* film.

"For me, *Shaft* was all about . . . that Black male hero that's not defeated," he said. "I have this thing on my chest that America, through all its media, tries to take the balls of Black men and just crushes them and dehumanizes them, desexualizes them, emasculates them."

Throughout his time on *Shaft*, Singleton felt tremendous pressure to make a film that lived up to the original. New York City cabdrivers heckled him in the street. "Listen, John, don't fuck up *Shaft*," they'd holler. A month before the film opened, the *Boondocks* comic strip addressed him directly. "If John Singleton is watching, you better not mess up *Shaft* or you got a foot comin' your way," Huey Freeman warned.

Despite *Shaft*'s success at the box office, Singleton's first foray into blockbuster filmmaking nearly broke him. "If they're not listening to me on *Shaft*, what am I even doing?" he lamented to friends in late-night phone calls.

But while filming in New York, he had another epiphany. He vowed not to compromise his vision again. It was time to return to Los Angeles. It was time to return to his roots.

# CHAPTER SEVENTEEN

Once back in Los Angeles, Singleton moved into office space on Forty-Third Street off Crenshaw Boulevard in Leimert Park, the city's Black arts hub. There was something about coming home to South LA, sleeping in his Baldwin Hills home every night, walking around the neighborhood, being back in that zone after spending so much time in New York City the last few years.

He knew his future resided in big-budget filmmaking. But after working on *Rosewood* and *Shaft*, he needed a palate cleanser. He wanted to recapture the magic and freedom he felt on *Boyz N the Hood*. He needed to regain control.

How would he do that? By making another small, intimate film set in South Central, one just as autobiographical as *Boyz N the Hood*.

While in preproduction on *Shaft*, he pulled *Fighting and Fucking* off the shelf and began revising the script he had imagined as a star vehicle for Tupac Shakur.

Now titled *Baby Boy*, the film would complete the "hood trilogy" he started with *Boyz* and *Poetic Justice* and allow him to make an artistic statement after having his voice thwarted on *Shaft*. For many years, Singleton avoided a return to South Central. But now he wanted to make, "the most ghetto movie I ever made," as he said in the spring of 2000. "Soulful. The kind of ghetto I'm talking about is the feeling you get when you were six or seven years old and your mother would sing along with Marvin Gaye records while you were eating hot links. Only someone from the ghetto could know that feeling."

*Baby Boy* also touched on provocative themes that fascinated Singleton: dysfunctional relationships between Black men and women; "nontraditional" Black family units; Oedipus; the idea of the man-child, a subject propagated by the psychiatrist Dr. Frances Cress Welsing, whose work had gained popularity in Black artistic communities in the late 1980s and early 1990s.

During this time, Singleton studied political literature—the conservative Black nationalism of Dr. Welsing and Minister Louis Farrakhan. He traded tapes of Farrakhan speeches and debated Welsing's 1991 essay collection, *The Isis Papers:*

*The Keys to the Colors*, with friends. Later in life, he refused to discuss Farrakhan in interviews. But in the 1990s, Farrakhan and Welsing were part of the culture: Chuck D credited Welsing with inspiring Public Enemy's 1990 album *Fear of a Black Planet*; her books were fixtures at African street festivals from Harlem to Leimert Park; rappers name-checked Farrakhan in their songs.

Welsing developed a controversial theory: White supremacy stemmed from the deep feeling of inferiority white people held due to their inability to produce melanin. In turn, she argued, white supremacy hindered the development of Black males in America, placing them in a permanent state of infancy. (She also theorized that homosexuality among African Americans was a ploy by white people to decrease the Black population.)

Singleton was more interested in Welsing's concept on the infantilization of the Black man.

*Baby Boy* begins with a voiceover. "There's this psychiatrist, a lady named Dr. Frances Cress Welsing. She has a theory about the Black man in America. She says that because of the system of racism, the Black man in this country has been made to think of himself as a baby. A not yet fully formed being, who has not realized his full potential. To support her claim, she offers the following: First off, what does a Black man call his woman? Mama. Secondly, what does a Black man call his closest acquaintances? His boys. And finally, what does a Black man call his place of residence? The crib."

Singleton had seen their kind around Los Angeles, usually at the mall, rocking a white tank top undershirt, flirting with teenage girls. He modeled his main character, Jody, after these young men. He also gazed internally. The story for *Baby Boy*, he said, came out of his "own dysfunctions, me purging my own demons."

By this point, Singleton's dysfunctions and demons were well known. He had five children from four women. The women didn't get along and they all competed for his attention, affection, and money. He did his best to keep them and the other women in his life siloed from one another. Singleton liked to disappear. Only a select few had full-time access to him: his publicist, his agent, his lawyer, and his mom.

The amount of bandwidth he devoted to women began to affect his work and standing in the industry. In a relaxed setting with a friend, a journalist he respected, he could open up.

"Let me say seriously that pussy has taken precedence over my business," he acknowledged to *Vibe* magazine consigliere Bonz Malone.

He couldn't change, though—not while he lived out his fantasies. As a young man, he jotted down in a notebook that his goals were to direct "epic movies and have children with a lot of beautiful women."

Young John hadn't accounted for the stress that plan would inflict on thirty-something John. The custody battles. The fights over money. The jealousy. The pettiness.

Singleton poured his life into the *Baby Boy* script. Some scenes between Jody and his girlfriend, Yvette, were actual reenactments of his time with Barlow; she insists Singleton based 'Vette, in part, on Ves'. He started writing the script following one of their numerous breakups.

The knock-down, drag-out fight at the Mark Hotel in New York? That went into the script.

The strawberry shakes? That went into the script.

The picnics in Kenneth Hahn park? That went into the script.

Singleton filled the picnic basket on set with the same contents Barlow would pack before their outings with Maasai: Fried chicken in ziplock bags. Capri-Sun. Potato salad. Bourgeois Cheetos. Hand wipes.

"I gasped on set when I saw it," Barlow says. "The chicken was actually warm in the basket. I got upset. I was like, 'If you were paying attention like that, why didn't you step up to the plate?'"

Barlow and the children now lived in Apple Valley, a city on the southwestern edge of the Mojave Desert about two hours northeast of Los Angeles. Maasai visited every other weekend or so. They'd schedule pickups at a Dave & Buster's east of Los Angeles. When he dropped off Maasai a few days later, he'd ask his son to pass a message to Barlow.

"Tell your mom she's beautiful and I love her."

"My dad didn't speak negatively about my mom," Maasai says. "It definitely wasn't proportional to the way she talked about him. He never talked about her like that, like vitriolically, except in the context of the custody battle."

Jody turned into an amalgamation of different people but shared certain traits with his creator. He was a loving father (when around) but a dishonest boy-friend and partner. When confronted with evidence of his philandering he'd get philosophical and funny about it. Jody sounded like Singleton at his worst: selfish, manipulative, and narcissistic.

"You my woman and them other hos is tricks. I make love to you. I wanna be with you. But I fuck other females from time to time. I don't know why. I just do it.

"One thing I know how to do is make some pretty babies."

It was a consensus: *Baby Boy* was the most dynamic thing he'd written since *Boyz N the Hood*. "I just wanted to make a piece of no-holds-barred ghetto poetry," Singleton said. But some friends felt he revealed a little too much of his dysfunctions and demons. One of his close collaborators confronted him after reading an early draft.

"Motherfucker, are you writing your personal diary or making a movie?"

"Motherfucker, I'm doing both," he fired back. "Do you know how many motherfucking Jody's are out here? Do you know how many men are out there and are still on the titty with their mom? Still trying to figure out their way through life?"

His mother, Sheila, was his business manager and one of his best friends; more often than not, he called her Sheila, not Mom. She did payroll at New Deal. When someone felt their check was short, they dealt with her. She wielded great influence in all facets of his adult life. They talked stories together. They talked scripts together. Sheila was first to read each one he wrote. Singleton badly wanted to please her. Some friends referred to her as the true love of his life. "In almost every conversation we had, he spoke of his mother in some way, shape, or form," says a woman he dated toward the end of his life.

Like all mothers, she had opinions on who her son dated; in her eyes, Tyra Banks was a good match for him—Barlow, not so much. But she also acted as gatekeeper and bodyguard when compelled.

On June 12, 2000, Sheila attended the *Shaft* premiere at the Ziegfeld Theatre in New York. Earlier in the day, Singleton had told Julie Brown, a producer he once dated (not Downtown Julie Brown or the comedian Julie Brown of MTV and *Clueless* fame), that he'd decided to escort another woman to the premiere. (Brown wasn't the only former fling with their sights on Singleton at the premiere. "A lot of the extras John fucked around with were there trying to get in," Coqui says.) Brown approached Singleton afterward demanding a private conversation with him. He darted down the theater stairs to avoid her. Brown claimed that Ward and another woman then surrounded her.

"Sheila wrapped her arms around me in a big bear hug and said, 'If you say anything bad about my son, I will kill you,'" Brown told the *New York Post*. She later filed a harassment complaint against Ward.

Brown told friends that she dated Singleton for three years. However, in a statement to the press, Singleton said, "I am surprised that Ms. Brown is under the impression that we have a current relationship when, in fact, our casual involvement ended three years ago. . . . Her actions appear to be [those] of a disturbed person and I am aware of a history of this type of conduct, which led to the termination of our relationship years ago."

During this time, Singleton had a strained relationship with his father. He told friends that Danny had asked him for money to cover child support payments. Following the success of *Boyz N the Hood*, he said, his father demanded a million dollars from him. "It broke John's heart," says one of his former girlfriends.

They'd reconcile—John attended the Super Bowl in Miami with Danny in 2007. But they maintained a strange dynamic. Singleton felt like his dad challenged him and competed with him, even flirting with the same women as him. Later on, Danny, who worked in real estate and insurance for most of his life, tried rivaling John as a writer and filmmaker. In 2011, Danny directed *Haterology 101*, a documentary short "teaching the world about Haters." He also wrote about a dozen books and screenplays, including *The Cultivator*, which Danny touted as "the next *Star Wars* or *Avatar*."

Yet his father held tremendous influence over him. Singleton wrote Black male characters who resembled Danny—strong, opinionated, tough. He idolized him, whether it was justified or not. He told close friends, associates, and girlfriends that he didn't want to turn into his father.

★★★★★

The script for *Baby Boy* didn't receive the reception Singleton hoped for when he shopped it around town.

Too violent. Too disturbing. Too real. Too hood. Too Black.

For a moment, he considered seeking independent financing to avoid the development process.

"There are some things in the script that I don't want to sit around a table and talk about," he said. "I want to make sure all the soul gets up there on the screen."

Eventually, he sold the project to Sony in a deal worth over seven figures. The budget was set at $14 million. He was said to receive final cut on the film.

Returning to the studio signified another homecoming for him. It had been nearly five years since he exited Columbia for what he thought were greener pastures. His experiences with Warner Bros. and Paramount left him nostalgic for

Culver City, though; he often referred to his time at Columbia in the early 1990s as his graduate school. Amy Pascal, an advocate dating back to *Boyz N the Hood*, had just been hired as studio chair. But a lot had changed since Singleton roamed the lot as the studio's golden boy. In the aftermath of *Higher Learning*, *Rosewood*, and *Shaft*, he acquired a reputation for being difficult to work with. Whether he deserved it was up for debate.

"*Difficult* is something people used to say about female directors. It's code for anyone who isn't straight, white, and male," Pascal says.

Preliminary casting began while in preproduction on *Shaft*. Though he had discussions with Mekhi Phifer, Singleton pursued the model/singer Tyrese Gibson for the role of Jody after *Baby Boy* casting director Kimberly Hardin recommended him. A few years earlier, Hardin and Jaki Brown (*Boyz N the Hood*'s casting director) had booked Gibson in the Coca-Cola commercial that changed his life. The thirty-second spot in which Gibson flashed his million-dollar voice and billion-dollar smile led to modeling campaigns with Guess and Tommy Hilfiger and a stint as an MTV VJ.

When Hardin suggested the Watts native, Singleton stopped in his tracks. Gibson, like Tupac, had sex appeal and charisma. There was a rawness to him—a ribald energy that left unconstrained could hijack a film.

"Bring him in for a reading," Singleton said.

"He was all over the place," Hardin says of Gibson's first audition. "He wasn't really in the scene. He wasn't an actor." But there were a few encouraging moments she could point to like, "Mmmm . . . that right there." Singleton saw it as well.

Singleton proposed starting him out slow. He offered him a small part in *Shaft*—ironically, the role that Mekhi Phifer went on to fill. Gibson had different plans for his career. At the time, he wanted to be *Don't Be Cruel*–era Bobby Brown: the bad-boy R&B singer who dabbled in rap and got all the girls. He signed to RCA Records. In September 1998, he released his self-titled debut. When the album went platinum, Gibson decided once and for all he didn't want to be an actor. So he ghosted Singleton.

"I was on some goofy shit chasing my music career. I wasn't ready," Gibson said. "I'm over here in the club popping bottles with models and running through every video vixen I can. I'm living my best life. I can't even attempt to wrap my head around [a movie]."

A few months later, Gibson realized his mistake. He left a rambling voicemail for Singleton apologizing for ignoring his phone calls.

One night, Singleton showed up at Gibson's condo in Gardena with the *Baby Boy* script.

"You've been avoiding me, nigga," Singleton said, brushing past Gibson. "This is your movie."

For the next two hours, Gibson devoured the script. Singleton sat across from him texting on his two-way the entire time. He left as soon as Gibson finished reading. Later that night, they spoke on the phone for hours.

"It's crazy," said Tyrese, the youngest of his mother's four children. "I feel like I'm reading my life right now."

"That's what I'm telling you, nigga. I keep telling you this is your movie."

Four months later Gibson read once more for the role.

"Do you think he can handle it?" Singleton asked Hardin afterward.

"If we get him a coach and team him up with somebody, he can pull it off," Hardin said.

For the role of Yvette, one actress stood out from the start: Taraji P. Henson, a single mother from Washington, DC, in her late twenties. Henson possessed a BFA in acting from Howard University to go along with her wealth of talent and ambition. She moved to Los Angeles and worked as a substitute teacher while taking classes at Bill Duke's acting school. Soon, she booked walk-ons and bit parts on television shows like *The Parent 'Hood*, *ER*, and *Felicity*. Hardin recommended her to Singleton after Henson auditioned. Singleton went back to New York to work on *Shaft*. About a year later, she read for him.

"She had the best reading I ever had for any person for any role," Singleton said. "It was like, boom, you knew right then and there that she needed to have the role."

The actors became Singleton's lifelong friends and collaborators. He often referred to Gibson as his little brother. After working together on three films, their relationship became something closer. "When I put him in a movie, he's speaking my voice," Singleton said. "He's my avatar." Conveniently, his avatar had a chiseled jaw, rock-hard pecs, and six-pack abs.

In Henson, he found his muse—the actress who'd inspire him for the rest of his career. "As long as I'm making films, you've got a job," he once told her. Whenever he was writing a screenplay or casting a film, Henson remained at the forefront of his mind. Soulful and sexy. Equally adept at comedy and drama. Fiercely prepared yet game for improvisation. Henson had everything he looked for in an actor. They forged a bond on set that transcended work.

He hired Snoop Dogg, Ving Rhames, and Omar Gooding, the younger brother of Cuba Gooding Jr., for vital supporting roles. As production neared, though, he'd yet to cast Jody's mother, Juanita. Some actresses were too street. Others weren't street enough. He found some to be too maternal. Some were too sexy. He prepared another round of camera tests, when his mother, Sheila, made a suggestion.

"Where is A.J.? She'd be perfect for this."

"Holy shit," he said.

Singleton first met A.J. Johnson when Brian Bellamy smuggled him onto the set of *House Party*. "*House Party* was a very intimate set. It was easy to spot a stranger," says Johnson, who played the bombshell Sharane opposite Kid 'n Play in the 1990 comedy. "I noticed him sitting around, obviously studying the filmmakers. I could tell from his posture and who he was talking to."

They ended up talking that day. About acting. About movies. About their ambitions. About Greek life—Johnson is a Delta.

Before parting, Singleton said to her in all seriousness, "Hey, Chocolate Sundae, I'm gonna work with you one day."

About a year later, Johnson auditioned for *Boyz N the Hood*. She didn't get that part. It didn't look like they'd work together on *Baby Boy* either. When Singleton reached out, Johnson was in a wheelchair after breaking both her feet in a freak jogging accident. She stopped auditioning. Her father, an electrical engineer, had come to LA to help care for her.

One afternoon, Singleton showed up to Johnson's condo to describe Juanita to her.

"She's strong. She's sexy. She's loving. She's—"

"She's a mom," said the then thirty-six-year-old actress. "I'm not playing no one's momma. I am damn sure not playing Tyrese's momma."

"John, this will kill my career," she huffed. "I don't look old enough to be his mom."

Singleton leaned forward, arched close toward Johnson. "That's the whole point."

"When you said that we'd work together, this isn't what I had in mind. I don't want this to be it. It just doesn't make sense," she said.

"I don't want it to make sense. Just read the script. Let's talk tomorrow."

That night, both Johnson and her father took turns reading *Baby Boy*.

Singleton called the next day. "What did you think?"

Soon, Johnson hobbled into the office for a screen test with Rhames, whom Singleton had cast as Juanita's boyfriend. Rhames had built a solid career since *Rosewood*, mixing blockbusters (*Con Air*; the Mission: Impossible franchise) with character work for auteurs that showed his range (Scorsese in *Bringing Out the Dead*; Soderbergh in *Out of Sight*). Rhames had hulked up to portray Melvin, the ex-con from 101st and Vermont with two strikes and a landscaping business.

"Is there anything you're uncomfortable with?" he asked Johnson, shortly after meeting her.

"No," she said.

Singleton took her aside after their first reading. "I feel like you're scared of him. I don't want to see that shit. Juanita would be like, 'This is my nigga. This is my flava. I like them big, strong, thug nigga types. I get off on that.'"

Johnson nodded along. She knew the importance of Juanita and Melvin's love story to the film.

"By the time we get to the fight where Juanita is putting out Jody, the audience has to be rooting for Juanita and Melvin—not Jody," she says. "To get there I wanted to create an image of Black love that's never been seen before on the screen. Physically. Intimately. Passionately. Everything."

She came to play on the first day of rehearsals. At one point, she stripped down to her bra and underwear and mounted Rhames. He pantomimed oral sex on her, then put her down and smacked her ass.

Singleton put down the handheld camcorder he used to record his rehearsals. He kicked his feet and punched the air. "That's the shit I'm talking about," he howled. "That's what it's all about. This shit is gonna be soulful like a Marvin Gaye record."

He carved out two weeks of rehearsals prior to filming. On most days, the cast left the script at home and focused on building their characters' backstories. Omar Gooding struggled in this environment.

"Good job, you guys. I'll see you tomorrow," Singleton announced at the end of day two. "But I have to tell you: Some of us need to step it up."

Singleton turned toward Gooding and flashed a look.

When he first contacted him about the role, he spoke to the actor's mother, Shirley, whom he had known since *Boyz N the Hood*. "I made one of your sons a movie star. Now I want to make your other son a movie star," he said. *Baby Boy* would be a departure for the actor best known for his sitcom work (*Smart Guy* and *Hangin' with Mr. Cooper*). In the months prior to rehearsals, Gooding shaved his head and hit the gym to transform into Jody's best friend, Sweetpea. "Twenty-four, thick arms, body by California State Penal System," as described in the script. But he couldn't find nuance within the character. Gooding went home and contemplated what *Boyz* had done for his older brother. He had to step it up. That night, he barely slept.

Singleton started the next day with one of his favorite improvisation drills. He had the cast form a circle around one actor who'd then answer a series of questions while remaining in character.

"Who wants to go first?"

Gooding rose from his chair and sat in the middle without raising his hand.

Henson started in. "When are you gonna—"

"Shut the fuck up."

Gooding walked over to Gibson. "Fuck you too." He went around the room.

"Little nigga," Rhames thundered. "Where you from?"

"I'm 6-0 Crip," Gooding said.

"Bitch, you from the Valley."

Gooding flared his nostrils; his chest heaved up and down rapidly.

"What the fuck are you gonna do about it?" Rhames said.

"Yeah, what are you gonna do about it?" Johnson taunted.

Gooding pointed his finger at Rhames. "Bang, you're dead."

Rhames slapped his hand away, wrestled him down, and pinned him to the floor, using every ounce of his two-hundred-plus frame to mash him. Gooding wriggled an arm free, grabbed Rhames around the neck, and planted a kiss on his forehead.

"Cut," Gooding said. "Scene over."

"Did you take an acting class overnight?" Rhames asked afterward.

"John called me out. I had to bring it."

He still had work to do. Singleton tasked a Rollin' 60s Crip named Kevin "Big Cat" Doucette with molding Gooding into a gangster. For weeks, Gooding shadowed him around Los Angeles learning how to walk and talk like a certified OG. Doucette immediately pointed out the flaws in his performance.

"You're doing too much yelling," he said. "Real G's, that's not how we do it."

Singleton stepped in. He put his arm on Gooding's shoulder and walked with him. "You have to internalize all of that," he said. "All of that anger—all of that shit that's just bubbling and jumping and screaming to get out of you—you got to find a way to internalize it."

Gooding began uttering his lines through tense jaws and clenched teeth. Soon, he found Sweetpea. "Once John sculpted me into this character, there wasn't a lot of acting," he said. "It was just something I did."

★★★★★

As much as he admired certain members of Scott Rudin's handpicked players (production designer Patrizia von Brandenstein and stunt coordinator Nick Gillard stood out), Singleton relished having total control over his crew. More so than other directors, for Singleton his team doubled as a security blanket—one less thing he worried about. They all became closer than work friends.

"I learned from *Pee-wee's Playhouse* that when you have to work as hard as you do on any production, it's nice to have a great rapport with the crew and really take care of them," Singleton said. "Film crews are like families, they're like a circus troupe, you bond for an extended period of time and then everybody goes off to the next show."

Singleton's longtime storyboard artist Warren Drummond dubbed the troupe "the Singleton Family." Drummond first met him at *The Source* magazine's Christmas party in December 1994. He joined the Family a few years later when he stepped in for Peter Ramsey and drew storyboards for *Shaft*. Singleton got the band back together for *Baby Boy*. Production designer Keith Brian Burns. Kimberly Hardin. Director of photography Charles Mills returned nearly ten years after *Boyz N the Hood*. Bruce Cannon. Cassandra Butcher and Paul Hall. Costume designer Ruth Carter. Bobbi Banks and Greg Hedgepath in the sound department. Composer David Arnold entered the fold on *Shaft* and did three more movies with him.

"There was a lot of respect and a lot of love for John in the crew," Arnold says. "John's a great filmmaker and an important voice. But, more importantly for me, I just really liked him. He wasn't shouty. Sometimes he was sort of quiet. He was funny. He seemed like a really nice person. That goes such a long way to getting people to go along with you."

His crew was always going to get his love and respect no matter what else he had going on.

"I always felt like I was coming back to family when I worked with John," Cannon says. "I'd be on another film and it would be kind of impersonal. But John made us all feel important. We always stayed in touch. He'd ask about my daughter. He asked about my wife. John was a pallbearer at my mom's funeral."

Singleton's Leimert Park office doubled as a clubhouse, with the cast and crew often gathering after hours to watch dailies and offer feedback on one another's work. On Friday nights, he screened movies in his projection room—either the latest blockbuster or a film that related to *Baby Boy* in some way, like the Italian neorealist classic *Miracle in Milan* or *Star Wars*.

"Hey, man, give me that *Star Wars* shot," he called out to Drummond. They were plotting the scene where Jody and Sweetpea hunt down Snoop Dogg's Rodney. "You know that shot on the Death Star where Han Solo and Chewbacca are being chased by the stormtroopers in the hallway and there's a low-angle shot? That's it. I want a low angle of Snoop running, cut to a low-angle shot of them chasing him."

"It's basically identical," Drummond says.

Singleton projected a different sense of energy than he had on recent pictures. He'd missed shooting in Los Angeles, going home every night, sleeping in his own bed, being in the same time zone as his children. There were no sets to construct. He shot in practical locations that didn't require altering. The neighborhood car wash. The liquor store down the street from his office.

He ran a loosey-goosey set. Everyone had an entourage. Empty forty-ounce bottles of Olde English littered the area. Snoop Dogg smoked weed out in the open.

One afternoon, Gooding played a game of dominoes outside his trailer with some of Big Cat's friends. He then went off to film his scenes. When he returned, his chain and gold cross were missing. Gooding slammed his trailer door and screwed his face. "Yo, my chain is gone," he puffed.

Cat shrugged his shoulders.

Sweat beaded down Gooding's forehead. His heart pounded.

"Should've locked your shit up," someone cracked.

One night, Sony's head of physical production, Gary Martin, visited the set with senior VP of production Andrea Giannetti.

"You're going to tell John to clear this set of all hangers-on or you're going to shut him down," he ordered her.

Giannetti arrived on set around ten p.m. She maneuvered through rows of trailers and throngs of people before arriving at Singleton's trailer. She took a deep breath and knocked.

"Gary Martin is out there and telling me I gotta do this," she said. "We have to thin this out. I know you have this under control, but I need you to do this for me."

Singleton had been here before with Martin. He knew studio executives felt compelled to flex their muscle every once in a while.

"It's not a problem," he said.

He sent all the hangers-on home, thinned out the set. The next night? Business as usual.

Singleton was in his element, working hands-on with young, inexperienced actors and nonactors like the rappers he so often cast. He had a knack for giving the right note at the right time. When doubt crept in, he urged his actors to believe in him and his vision. By the end of the shoot, they'd also believe in their own talent.

Singleton's two leads benefited the most. With Henson, he had her dig deep into her emotional reservoir. He'd take her aside and provoke her with an analogy. Before shooting the opening scene of the film, where Jody and Yvette exit an abortion clinic, he slinked toward Henson and whispered in her ear.

"Imagine if the love of your life, the person you thought would be there forever, knows you're carrying his seed, and then he tells you, 'This isn't what I want.'"

Henson nodded her head.

Early on, it became evident to Singleton, and everyone else on set, that Henson would emerge from the film a star. On the night of one of her big scenes, Singleton played Marvin Gaye's "Just to Keep You Satisfied." The following scene is the kind of clip played at awards shows. Henson's eyes convey heartbreak the moment Jody slams the door in her face. She walks slowly to her car in the rain, an umbrella in one hand, her son in the other. She collapses into the passenger seat. "He don't love me no more," she cries, over and over again.

Singleton called, "Cut."

Tracey Cherelle Jones, the actress playing Yvette's friend Sharika, then turned to Henson in the passenger seat. "Well, sister girl, it's about to happen for you," she said. "You're about to blow the fuck up."

Singleton took a less tactful approach motivating Gibson.

"John had to get in Tyrese's ass," says Kareem Grimes, an actor in the film who pulled double duty as one of Singleton's assistants and also ran lines with Gibson.

On his first day on set, they were filming the movie's opening shot of Gibson naked, suspended in his mother's womb. Gibson dipped his toe into a water tank and shrieked. "Yo, man, it's too cold."

Singleton sighed. "Shut up and get in the goddamn water," he said. "Stop being a baby. Do you want to be a movie star? We'll make you a movie star."

Throughout filming, Singleton barked variations of the line to Gibson: *Listen to me, kid, I'll make you a star.* He'd speak, then Gibson would hem and haw and break out into song and crack three jokes and go on multiple tangents. But in the end, he'd listen to Singleton.

★★★★★

During postproduction, Singleton learned that having final cut didn't actually mean he had final cut.

Sony presented him with the notes and studio interference he dreaded. One executive even called the film "misogynistic." Singleton was already furious over losing key needle drops he'd written into the film: Earth, Wind & Fire's "Fantasy" and Frankie Beverly and Maze's "Golden Time of Day." The studio deemed both songs too expensive.

Sony also asked him to rewrite the film's ending.

At first, Jody and Sweetpea kill Yvette's ex-boyfriend Rodney after he bullies his way back into her life and attempts to rape her.

"But that makes Jody a murderer," an executive cried.

His stomach churned. "Jody is protecting his family," he said. "It's like a Western. He has to take this motherfucker out."

The violence carried deeper meaning. "I'm just trying to show the dysfunctional rite of passage," Singleton said. "This guy Jody isn't a killer. But to get to where he's got to go, he's got to kill another Black man. There's a tragedy in that. It wasn't a triumphant ending."

Sony stressed that Jody needed another reason to kill Rodney. "What if he tries to kill Jody and fails? Then Jody is justified in killing him."

Another drive-by, Singleton thought. He knew audiences would compare the scene to *Boyz N the Hood.*

The disputes carried over into the film's publicity and marketing campaign. One day, while heading into a marketing meeting on the Sony lot, he ran into

A.J. Johnson, who was recording ADR (automated dialogue replacement) for the film.

"You should come with me," he told her. "I want you to see this side of the business."

In the meeting, he brought up the film's poster. *Baby Boy*'s one-sheet depicted Gibson on his bike with Snoop looming ominously over his shoulder and rows of palm trees marking the background.

"Where is the rest of the cast?"

"We're making a big push on MTV and BET. We think highlighting Tyrese and Snoop is the best way to reach the audience."

Singleton lost that battle. He no longer had the juice to pick and choose which of the studio's notes he'd ignore and where he'd acquiesce. He couldn't dictate marketing campaigns. It was one thing to get second-guessed on a historical epic like *Rosewood* or bulldozed on a big-budget piece of IP like *Shaft*. But on *Baby Boy*? They knew his story better than him?

"John was very, very upset, very, very pissed off about it," Johnson says. "John took it as they didn't have faith in his storytelling. At that point in his career, it was really devastating for him to hear."

He got his way on one aspect of the film's rollout. When it came time to unveil *Baby Boy*, he pushed to premiere the film at the Acapulco Black Film Festival.

Founded by Jeff Friday, Byron Lewis, and Warrington Hudlin, the ABFF (rebranded the American Black Film Festival after moving to Miami) showcased Black filmmakers during a weeklong networking event that doubled as a party on the beach. Singleton was one of the first celebrities Friday contacted in 1997 when he had the idea to stage a "Black version of Sundance." Through the years, Singleton taught master classes and lectured at the ABFF. In June 2001, he premiered *Baby Boy* in Acapulco.

"We didn't have many world premieres back then," Friday says. "It had to be driven by the filmmaker to get their project to play here. Nobody was more supportive of the festival than John."

He arrived in Mexico full of good cheer. He made all his movies with Black audiences in mind—none more so than *Baby Boy*. "This is very much an ethnographic film," he said. "There are no cops, no white people. It's all insular."

He figured that some segments of the Black population, the ones who championed recent films like *Soul Food* and *The Best Man*—films about upper-middle-class Black people—would recoil from it. But he looked forward to the heated debates it would spur between the Black bourgeoise and the Black working class and also between Black men and Black women.

When he introduced the film in Acapulco, he strutted to the dais, devil-may-care grin on his face. Then he leaned into the microphone, smirked, and said, "I made the ultimate nigga movie."

The lights went down. *Baby Boy* got the reception he hoped for.

"It was very controversial. Some people hated it. Some people loved it. I loved it," Reginald Hudlin says. "We argued with people about it. In *Boyz N the Hood*, he represented a full range of characters and class backgrounds and educational backgrounds. You want to show how diverse we are as a community. In *Baby Boy*, John was like, 'Nah, I'm just gonna deal with the dysfunction.' At the time, it was a very bold thing to do."

*Baby Boy* received mixed reviews from critics. Kenneth Turan of the *LA Times* called it "too messy," noting "the plot points and dramatic ideas tend to be contrived and conventional, and there's a didacticism, a lack of subtlety and sophistication, in the presentation." *Variety* praised the film for its "vibrant" characters, but also bemoaned the reshoot scenes "some late-on dramatic contrivances seemingly dragged in to provide a little violence."

Roger Ebert, however, awarded the film three-point-five stars out of four. "There has never been a movie with this angle of the African American experience," he wrote. A. O. Scott of the *New York Times* called the film "a powerful, compassionate, tough-minded critique of contemporary black manhood." He praised Gibson ("a winning combination of playfulness, vulnerability, and sexual dynamism") and Snoop Dogg ("sly, menacing, and disarmingly funny") for their performances, and Singleton for creating the most fully formed female character of his career. ("The characters of Juanita and Yvette are as richly written and solidly acted as Jody's.")

*Baby Boy* opened strong, posting $11.7 million in its first five days. But it lacked box-office legs and stalled at $29 million, surprising Singleton and disappointing Sony. The film ended up finding its audience in the rental and DVD market. Later on, it became a stalwart on BET. When Reginald Hudlin ran the network from 2005 to 2008, he'd air fan favorites to pop a rating on a weeknight or Saturday afternoon. "*Baby Boy* hit every time," he says.

What was its appeal?

"*Baby Boy* is about a dysfunctional relationship. Who doesn't understand that?" Henson said. "If you know young love, you know *Baby Boy*."

And no one knew the subject more so than Singleton. For the past decade, he'd lived in this world of young love turned complicated, of negotiated baby pick-ups and drop-offs, of man's hunger for stability while in the grasp of a selfish and toxic wanderlust that leads him astray. *Baby Boy* is Singleton distilled to his essence.

The film features no-holds-barred ghetto poetry like "I'm out in these streets telling these hos the truth. I lie to you 'cause I care about your feelings"; amusing Easter eggs like the poster of Tyra Banks on Jody's bedroom wall; memeable moments before memes existed, such as Ving Rhames cooking breakfast naked in Jody's kitchen. *Baby Boy* also contains the two quintessential sex scenes in the Singleton canon. "I took all the sexual repression from *Shaft* and put it into this film," he cracked.

In one, Jody and Yvette live up to the film's original title. They engage in some of the most passionate makeup sex ever presented in a studio film. Singleton frantically cuts between multiple positions and multiple orgasms. "I love daddy dick," Yvette cries. The scene then takes a tender turn: "Jody, when I say, 'I hate you,' what I really mean to say is 'I love you,'" Yvette says as Jody spoons with her. "But you scare me, boo, like we ain't gonna be together or something."

"Shh. I'm trying to sleep," he says. "We're gonna always be together unless I get killed or something."

The other scene is more played for laughs. "African squat fuck," Melvin grunts as he hops across the screen with Juanita straddling him while a Mike Tyson interview plays on the television. The camera cuts to Jody, tossing and turning in his bed, covering his ears with a pillow to muffle the sounds from the other room, his mother moaning in pleasure.

In a time before intimacy coordinators, Singleton got his stars to commit and they rewarded him with the best work of their careers; Henson, Rhames, and Johnson all deliver performances worthy of a nomination. Through it all, a mural of Tupac Shakur in Jody's bedroom presides over the film, acting as Singleton's take on the eyes of Doctor T. J. Eckleburg from *The Great Gatsby*, as the slain rapper watches over the characters, silently judging them.

Shakur looms large in the film's most memorable scene, a wordless two-minute encounter between Jody and Melvin following Rodney's murder. With Tupac looking down, Melvin approaches Jody, takes the gun from his palm, wipes it down, wraps it in a towel, and exits the room. When he first saw the film, executive producer Dwight Williams suggested that Jody explain the situation to Melvin.

"No," Singleton said. "The audience knows what that boy has done."

"John trusted the actors," Williams said. "He trusted his writing. He trusted what he set up."

"It's one of the best scenes in any film I shot," Singleton said proudly.

When asked to name his favorite film, he often demurred. "That's like asking me to name my favorite child," he said. But when questioned in 2018, he hinted at where *Baby Boy* stood in his own rankings.

"I love *Boyz* because it's the first," he said. "I really, really love *Baby Boy.*"

# CHAPTER EIGHTEEN

**J**ohn Singleton entered a new phase of his career following the box-office disappointment of *Baby Boy*: He became a director-for-hire.

He felt he should be in the mix for the hot new spec script. The next Bond film. The next potential franchise. If Brett Ratner could genre-hop from *Family Man* to *Rush Hour 2* to a Hannibal Lecter movie, he could as well.

The auteur in him sought to make nothing but gritty, personal films set in South Central. But the cinephile in him didn't want to be saddled to one genre. He grew up on popcorn flicks—*Star Wars* and Spielberg inspired him to get into the business. He wanted to do a Western and a comic-book movie and a courtroom drama. Then, when inspiration struck, he'd add to his South Central oeuvre. He wanted to do it all.

He chased tentpole features in the aftermath of *Baby Boy*, such as a sequel to the Vin Diesel sci-fi film *Pitch Black* and a live-action adaptation of *Sinbad* that was described as an "eighth-century *Raiders of the Lost Ark* on steroids." Then, in the spring of 2002, Diesel passed on a sequel to *The Fast and the Furious*—the *Point Break* knockoff that grossed over $140 million at the box office the previous summer, stunning the industry. The original film's director, Rob Cohen, soon followed him off the project.

Universal now needed a director on short notice.

Singleton seemed like an unconventional hire for the studio. *Shaft*, his most recent foray into blockbuster filmmaking, made headlines for the wrong reasons. But he checked certain boxes despite his lacking action-film credentials. Storytelling. Dialogue. Character development. His personal and professional relationship with Tyrese Gibson, whom the studio tagged to star opposite Paul Walker. That he was a favorite of Universal executive VP of production Holly Bario also worked in his favor. The name John Singleton still carried weight with audiences. His presence signaled that Universal wasn't phoning in the sequel.

The town was taken aback when Universal announced the hiring. Why was

John Singleton, the youngest person ever nominated for Best Director, piloting a sequel to a movie about cars that go *vroom-vroom*?

"I was sad a little bit almost. It just seemed like a waste to me," *Rosewood* writer Gregory Poirier says. "I don't have anything against those kind of movies. I just felt like John was a different kind of director."

Singleton's career detour disheartened the people who'd met him through his films—studio executives, colleagues, critics, fans. They envisioned a different path for him. Perhaps a career like Spike Lee: smart indie films with a big studio project mixed in every so often. But the people close to him knew he'd inevitably opt for a job like *The Fast and the Furious 2*.

Singleton wasn't a fan of the original film. "For me, the first Fast and the Furious was kind of a joke," he said. "I referenced the real shit in *Boyz N the Hood* with the street racing on Florence." Instead, he focused on the commercial upside. He thought a $100 million–grossing film on his résumé would lead to bigger budgets and more artistic freedom. He also wanted a break after six issue-minded films. For as much as it was a popcorn movie, he had a personal connection to *Shaft*, whereas a Fast and the Furious sequel was just a Fast and the Furious sequel.

He contemplated how best to put his imprint on every frame of the film. Early on, he met the film's cowriters, Michael Brandt and Derek Haas, for a late lunch at the Beverly Hills industry hangout, Kate Mantilini.

He leaned back in his chair and regaled Brandt and Haas, who were both around the same age as he was, with accounts of his origin story: the *Colors* screening at USC; pitching *Boyz N the Hood* to Columbia. Then he returned to the matter at hand. He spitballed ideas on how to make over Paul Walker's character ("dirty him up—make him more of a Steve McQueen type") and bring humor and levity to the film.

"John was the ultimate collaborator," Haas says. "There wasn't a meeting he didn't invite us to or not feel comfortable with us being there. I'm talking about the big major production head meetings in preproduction"—the meetings writers typically aren't invited to.

He turned his attention to casting. With Walker and Gibson in place, there wasn't work left to do above the title. He then had to replace one of the key members of the cast. Originally, Ja Rule was set to return as the street racer Edwin in an expanded role and with a bump in pay—a half million dollars, up from the $15,000 he'd received for the original. But that was pocket change compared to what the Murder Inc. star banked writing hit records for everyone from Fat Joe to Mary J. Blige; he bailed once Diesel told him that the sequel would be a bust.

Ja didn't inform Singleton of his decision—that he'd opted out of the movie to focus on a tour. After his calls went unreturned, Singleton crashed Rule's recording studio. Rule ignored him. Singleton stormed out with a plan B.

Later that night, he called Kimberly Hardin. "Get me a list of rappers," he commanded. From the names she presented, Singleton selected Ludacris. Hardin then drove down to the Chula Vista stop of the Anger Management tour and put Ludacris on tape before he hit the stage to open for Eminem. Ludacris went on to play Tej, as the character was renamed, in seven Fast and Furious movies and counting.

"Ja Rule not doing *2 Fast 2 Furious* changed Ludacris's life," Singleton said in 2015.

Preproduction hurtled forward to make Universal's planned June 2003 release date. He had around four months of prep for a film with a $76 million budget, an evolving script, and complex stunts. Singleton got to experience big-budget tentpole filmmaking in its essence—a mad dash to get product into theaters to appease shareholders and brand partners.

One morning, before a marketing meeting, Singleton approached Craig Lieberman, a technical advisor on the film.

"You're the guy helping us with the cars, right?" Singleton asked. "I expect you to speak your mind in there. Don't bullshit me."

Early in the meeting Lieberman was asked which car he wanted to spotlight in the film. "Easy," Craig said. "The Nissan R34 Skyline is the top car on the—"

"That's not going to work," a marketing executive interjected. "We already have a relationship with Dodge. We're making the Dodge Neon SRT-4 the main car."

He inhaled and exhaled through gritted teeth—loud enough for Singleton, sitting two seats down, to hear. He turned toward him. "Lieberman, what's up?"

Lieberman closed his eyes and told the truth. "You can put lipstick on a pig, but it's still a pig," he said. "The Dodge Neon is a rental car. We can put it in the film, but it can't be the main car. If we do, the people who know better will walk out."

"That ends that," Singleton said.

The 2003 Dodge Viper SRT-10 and 1970 Dodge Challenger R/T replaced the Neon in the film, while Paul Walker drove the R34 Skyline. After the meeting, Singleton sought out Lieberman. "Good stuff, man," he said, patting him on the back. "I'll see you on set."

Singleton realized early on that the success of the film hinged on the cars and the car chases. For inspiration, he rewatched *Bullitt*, *The French Connection*, and *The Road Warrior*, which he believed was the best car movie ever made. But he also drew insight from Japanese anime, old *Speed Racer* cartoons, and video games like *Gran Turismo*. When he laid out his vision for his storyboard artists, he referenced movies like *Ghost in the Shell* and *Akira*.

Singleton planned the action sequences with his second-unit director Terry Leonard, a legend in the industry, and a veteran of films with Francis Ford Coppola (*Apocalypse Now*), Steven Spielberg (*Raiders of the Lost Ark*), and John Milius (*Conan the Barbarian*). Leonard, a legit cowboy in his sixties, entered John's orbit through Warren Drummond, who'd worked with him on *Die Hard with a Vengeance*.

When they first met, Singleton said to him, "Terry, I want you to be my Mickey Moore."

Moore was a child star during the silent film era who transitioned to behind the camera as an adult. He'd recently retired at the age of eighty-five following a fifty-plus-year career as an assistant director and second unit director on films such as *The Ten Commandments*, *Butch Cassidy and the Sundance Kid*, *Patton*, and *Raiders of the Lost Ark*, on which Leonard worked as a stuntman. They became great, close friends.

"I'll do the best I can," Leonard told Singleton.

For around six weeks, they worked on the opening scene of the film—a four-car race in downtown Miami that immediately brings the audience into the new world of The Fast and the Furious. Singleton broke the scene down shot by shot for Drummond.

"I want an opening shot in the street from a low angle, kids come in from left to right and put down street markers, a pickup truck comes in and kids hop out the back, push in to the kids in the street who drive away, wide shot, exterior, boom down, Brian (Paul Walker's character) comes in."

Sometimes he'd sit in the production office with the illustrators and play with his Hot Wheels, brainstorming ideas for stunts.

"What cool things can we do with cars that haven't been done before?" he mused.

The opening scene culminated with a jump over an open drawbridge. But he couldn't shake a certain image: *What if we jump a car over another car during the bridge jump?* He collaborated with the writers and presented the idea to a visual effects designer. The second-place car would hit the nitrous oxide in midair and land in first place.

"John, that can't happen," the technician said. "Gravity doesn't work like that."

"I know—and fuck that."

★★★★★

After a week of filming, they were said to be already two days behind schedule. Locations weren't available for shooting. A permit for high-speed driving hadn't been procured. Settings didn't match the descriptions in the script. One morning, production arrived on a street corner only to discover the intersection lacked traffic lights, forcing them to reschedule the scene. With each day of principal photography costing about $300,000, the film was in danger of blowing past its already massive budget.

Rightfully so or not, the studio immediately blamed the first assistant director, Frank Davis, for the errors.

A member of the Directors Guild of America since 1988, Davis first met Singleton in the summer of 1993 coming out of a movie theater in Baldwin Hills. At the time, Davis was transitioning from the role of second AD (*Rising Sun*, *Sugar Hill*, and *Terminator 2: Judgment Day*) to first AD—one of the most important jobs in a film crew. The first AD essentially runs the set as the director's right hand. They coordinate and wrangle the cast and crew, enforce the daily shooting schedule and production timeline, and serve as the middleman between the director and the department heads and the director and the studio. On an action film like *The Fast and Furious*, the first AD also clearly delineates responsibilities between the first and second unit.

Davis's first job in the role was on Prince's *Graffiti Bridge*. He then worked on films starring Denzel Washington (*Fallen*), Sandra Bullock (*Hope Floats*), and Ice Cube (*Next Friday*). Singleton considered him for a spot on the *Golddiggaz* crew. When that film fell through, he hired him as his first AD on *Baby Boy*, and Davis steered the production without incident for the most part.

Singleton hadn't heard complaints about Davis until producer Neal H. Moritz and several executives suggested he make a change. When he told Davis about it, he reiterated that he had his back.

"I said implicitly I did not want to fire him," Singleton later said. "I didn't want to be put in that position."

He spoke with Rodney Mitchell, the assistant director of the DGA, and said he believed Davis had been targeted for his race. Privately, he told friends that Davis was "fucked over." But in the end, Singleton folded. He fired Davis, turning his back on a member of the Singleton Family.

The Equal Employment Opportunity Commission (EEOC) eventually filed a lawsuit on Davis's behalf, alleging that Universal racially discriminated against him, and accused the studio of violating Title VII of the Civil Rights Act of 1964. The government maintained there were no written records of safety violations and that production reports didn't reveal that the film was behind schedule as Universal claimed.

Singleton testified on the trial's opening day in June 2007. At times, his words conflicted with the deposition he gave three years earlier, prompting an accusation that the production deal he signed with Universal in 2006 had compromised his testimony.

On the stand he revealed that he felt his job was in jeopardy if he didn't fire his friend. "I had to make my movie, man," he said. "It was my biggest movie. . . . The movie is the most important thing."

Universal settled with Davis for an undisclosed sum during the trial. The EEOC pressed on with its case, but a federal judge ruled that the studio didn't act out of racial bias when it fired Davis. He hasn't worked in the industry since. When reached for comment, Davis declined to participate in an interview for this book.

★★★★★

Universal got the best and worst of John Singleton on *2 Fast 2 Furious*, as the film was retitled.

He went out to Barcode. Shore Club. Nobu. Satine. Nikki Beach. Pearl. Dream. A gossip columnist spotted him dining with a woman at the Delano at three a.m. But he wasn't alone in indulging in the warm weather and fine women Miami had to offer.

"Those guys were having a party," says a crew member. "Paul and Tyrese would walk into Nikki Beach and the girls would just—it was like shooting fish in a barrel for them. John too."

There are conflicting accounts of Singleton's performance on *2 Fast 2 Furious*. He either "half-assed it" or elevated the material, depending on who's talking. Before production started, he told his director of photography Matthew F.

Leonetti (*Poltergeist*, *Rush Hour 2*, the sci-fi masterpiece *Strange Days*) that he didn't have time to sit down and go over different looks. Once he got to the set, he never expressed what he wanted to do or why.

"We would kind of wing it, which, with my experience along the line, I can do," Leonetti says. "I just did what I thought was best. I never heard, 'Matt, cut that out. Let's do this different,' so I guess we got along well."

Singleton also blew off David Arnold after the composer flew in from London for a meeting about the film score. Arnold arrived at the Universal office at around one p.m. Three hours later, Singleton showed up. He hugged Arnold tightly.

"How are you, man?"

"Great, how are you doing?"

"Listen, I'm busy."

"Okay, we don't have to talk long. I just wanted—"

"No, no, I'm really busy. I can't stay. Gotta go." Singleton started to walk out of the room.

"So, what do you think about the music?"

He turned at the door. "I'm not sure, just do what you like," he said.

Arnold boarded a plane back to England. A few days later, he called Singleton.

"John, I don't think 'Just do what you like' is going to cut it. I know the sort of things you like and the sort of things you want to do. But I just need some direction."

"Think hip-hop meets *Buena Vista Social Club*," Singleton said.

Singleton's longtime collaborators noted the change. "On *Higher Learning*, he'd do shot lists at night and then again after rehearsal," Franklin says. "On *Shaft*, he also came very prepared. With Fast and Furious, he didn't show up with anything in his hand. He had no idea what he was going to do on that day." It continued into postproduction; Cannon remembers Singleton showing up later and later to the cutting room.

With his actors, he was a little less engaged than usual at times. He found the second unit's work more interesting than his own duties and could often be found standing next to Leonard, watching the veteran direct the speeding cars and the stunts. One day on set, Cole Hauser approached Singleton about fleshing out a scene.

"I'm thinking that my character should—"

"Lemme stop you," Singleton said. "Yo, it ain't that kind of movie. It ain't that kind of movie. We are just going fast. We are going hard. Be you. I just need you to be you. Don't overthink it."

Roberto Sanchez, who made his acting debut in *2 Fast 2 Furious* as Carter Verone's muscle, received the full John Singleton experience during his time on the film. After eleven years in the military, Sanchez was working as a model and handled security on the Miami Metrorail when his agent sent him to audition for the film. He read for Singleton—the scene where Verone's goons threaten the heroes on Brian O'Connor's houseboat.

Singleton just shook his head. "I'm not feeling it. Do you speak Spanish?"

"Yes."

"Okay, do it in Spanish."

Sanchez tried again.

Singleton exhaled loudly. He removed his glasses. "Where are your people from?"

"I'm Cuban."

"I know a lot of Cubans and when they get mad, they get mad."

*Oh, he wants some Tony Montana over-the-top shit*, Sanchez thought. When Singleton called action again, Sanchez grabbed his scene partner and shook him, spit flying out of his mouth. He screamed so loud that he didn't hear the casting director call, "Cut."

Singleton clapped his hands and pumped his fist. "Yes! That's what I'm talking about. Yes!"

Sanchez looked around, waiting for instruction. "What do you want me to do now?"

"Now get the fuck out," Singleton said. "We'll get back to you."

Sanchez got the call while at work about three weeks later. He'd just asked some six-foot-four dude to put out a cigar when his agent called with the news. "Smoke the whole pack for all I care—fuck you," he told the commuter. He exited the train at the next stop, returned to his office, and gave his two-week notice.

According to Sanchez and other members of the cast and crew, Singleton did a poor job handling Gibson. They claim the star goofed on set, that his focus wavered, and during one fight scene, he nearly kicked a costar in the face. Sanchez says that Gibson almost gave him a concussion during the "Ejecto seato, cuz!" scene. On five straight takes, Gibson bashed Sanchez's head on the dashboard and then blew his line. Singleton laughed it off until his frustration bubbled to the surface. "Just focus!" he shouted. Tyrese declined to comment.

"Tyrese played too much," says a member of the crew. "He knew he had a special place in John's heart as his protégé and the costar of the film. I felt like he took advantage of that a little bit."

But the cast and crew still rallied around Singleton. His enthusiasm uplifted the set. One night, at around one a.m., while shooting the lead-up to the opening race, he sensed the energy on set flagging. He cranked the stereo and started a one-man dance circle, inviting the extras to join him.

Singleton shaped the film in his image. More humor. More diversity. More eye candy. Southern hip-hop replaced techno as the sound of the franchise. He worked with Walker and Gibson throughout the picture to solidify the bond between their characters. He got Walker comfortable with improvisation. He turned *2 Fast 2 Furious* into a John Singleton film.

★★★★★

In the spring of 2003, a few weeks before *2 Fast 2 Furious* opened, Singleton, along with Universal studio executives, boarded the company jet and flew to Dallas for a test screening.

He loved watching his movies with audiences, trying to pinpoint their favorite scenes and favorite lines. When he left the theater, he felt more confident than ever about the sequel.

"We had them from the first frame," he said to Bruce Cannon during the return trip from Dallas. Cannon had been booked on a commercial flight until Singleton convinced him to hitch a ride with him.

They sat at a horseshoe-shaped table eating hors d'oeuvres and sipping champagne from a flute glass. He slapped Cannon's leg and smiled.

The future looked bright from forty thousand feet.

What would he do next? A $100 million film? A $200 million film? *Fast and the Furious 3*?

A few feet away from him, a handful of Universal executives sorted through piles of cards tabulating the score from the test screening.

Suddenly, the celebratory mood that filled the cabin moments earlier dissipated. The film scored in the mid-eighties out of one hundred. A good score—just not what Universal hoped for.

Singleton overheard the result and the murmurs that followed. But he either blocked it out or remained in denial. When the plane landed at Van Nuys Airport, he turned to Cannon. "Get used to this, Brucie," he said. He still had high hopes for what lay ahead.

Critics were not impressed with the film when it opened on June 6, 2003. Todd McCarthy of *Variety* called it "an OK follow-up" while the *New York Times'* A. O. Scott lamented Singleton's "limitations as an action director" and harped on the film's depiction of women. "[Eva] Mendes and Devon Aoki have some lines to say, and Ms. Aoki is even permitted to drive. But mostly the women, like the cars, are around to fuel adolescent male fantasies and are similarly ogled, at leeringly low angles, by the camera."

Roger Ebert, unsurprisingly, was one of the film's admirers. "*2 Fast 2 Furious* is a video game crossed with a buddy movie, a bad cop–good cop movie, a Miami drug lord movie, a chase movie and a comedy. It doesn't have a brain in its head, but it's made with skill and style and, boy, is it fast and furious," he wrote in his three-star review.

Once the franchise transitioned into globe-trotting quasi-superhero films where the stakes were nothing less than the fate of the world, *2 Fast 2 Furious* received a reassessment from critics. In 2019, Bilge Ebiri wrote in *New York* magazine, "For all its sun-drenched, candy-colored aesthetic, the film's world is steeped in mistrust: Every character has an ax to grind. Singleton takes the aggressive, one-note conflicts of the action genre and builds whole networks of resentment out of them. This lends the picture a weird authenticity, despite the general dopiness of the plot. None of the actors feel like they're posturing. You really are waiting for every scene to break out in violence. This is a testament both to Singleton's vision and to his incredible facility with actors; he gets them all to commit."

Singleton was pleased with the film. "When you watch this movie, if you know my personality, you feel the funkiness. It's not your average Hollywood blockbuster," he said. "*Shaft* was all right. But *2 Fast 2 Furious* is much closer to my vision of the kind of mainstream film I wanted to make."

The film was critic-proof. It debuted in first place with a $50.4 million opening weekend, Singleton's personal best, and, at the time, the largest opening weekend for a Black director. *2 Fast* hit with young males and diverse audiences, with Latinos accounting for 40 percent of moviegoers, African Americans making up 16 percent, and Asian Americans 8 percent. The film ended its domestic run at $127 million, slightly less than original's $144 million haul.

*2 Fast 2 Furious* performed in line with most sequels: It had a bigger opening weekend than the original ($50.4 million compared to $40 million) and a slight dip in its overall box office. Of the six films released in 2003 that were sequels to films released in 2001 (*Jeepers Creepers 2, Lara Croft: Tomb Raider—The Cradle of Life, Legally Blonde 2: Red, White & Blonde, 2 Fast 2 Furious, American Wedding, Scary Movie 3*) only *Scary Movie 3* scored a bigger box office take than the previous film in the franchise.

Singleton felt he deserved credit for the success of the film. But for Universal, *2 Fast 2 Furious* performed just well enough to green-light another sequel but underperformed to the point where the studio felt the franchise needed an overhaul. The third film in the series moved to Japan and introduced all new characters. Universal didn't invite Singleton back for the 2006 sequel *The Fast and the Furious: Tokyo Drift*, nor did they offer him another film in the pipeline.

"John did a serviceable job and the film itself was a serviceable film. I don't think he hit it out of the park," says Marc Shmuger, the former Columbia executive who ran marketing at Universal at the time. "He was now more akin to a journeyman director. I always felt like John was selling himself out or selling himself short. But that's what he wanted to do. He loved genre pictures. Of course, in doing them, he became a director among many rather than a singular voice telling stories that only he could tell. The perception of John and his talents suffered with the industry as a result of that."

Singleton thought *2 Fast 2 Furious*'s big box office would catapult him back onto the A-list. But he learned an important lesson: Directors for hire are cogs in the machine. The job is to deliver the film on time and on budget with as little drama as possible. In the eyes of the studio, Singleton didn't do his job.

He had his next move in mind, and it would be the furthest thing from what he had just experienced. He ended up violating the first rule of moviemaking: He wrote a check.

# CHAPTER NINETEEN

**W**hile prepping *2 Fast 2 Furious* in the spring and summer of 2002, Singleton fell in love with Miami.

He prized the city's multiculturalism and diversity. Its beaches. Its nightlife. Its women. The vibe.

"I remember hanging out with him a bunch of times," says Miami Beach native Brett Ratner. "Look, Miami was different. John was as real as they come. In LA, a lot of people are full of shit. A lot of people are kissing your ass. It's a lot of fake shit. Miami is more real. People don't really give a shit if you're a filmmaker."

During preproduction, Singleton stressed that he didn't want the film to resemble a postcard to South Beach. He shot in Calle Ocho, Little Haiti, and Overtown, the neighborhood often called "the Harlem of the South." South Beach got some love too. He filmed a pivotal scene inside his favorite South Beach nightclub: Nikki Beach. He captured the city's spirit. The neon. The sunshine. The grit and the glamour.

"The depiction of Miami in *2 Fast 2 Furious* may not be entirely realistic— OK, it's pure fantasy—but it's also utterly seductive," wrote the *Miami Herald*. "John Singleton, who directed the movie, portrays the city as the ultimate paradisiacal playground for grown-ups—a glittering, be-bop fantasyland that throbs and hums to a hip-hop/R&B beat, bakes under perpetually bright skies, and where only bad guys ever seem to be in a foul mood."

*2 Fast 2 Furious* was Singleton's love letter to the city that would become his home away from home.

In early September, days before filming started, Singleton paid $1.1 million for a three-bedroom, 2,340-square-foot condo steps from the Atlantic in the highly coveted SoFi (South of Fifth Street) neighborhood. Once he moved in, the cast often gathered in his luxury high-rise pad to pregame before hitting the clubs.

Postproduction took him back to Los Angeles, but he returned to Miami whenever time allowed. He was a different person as soon as he touched down from the coast. Miami John appeared more relaxed than LA John, who wore the stresses of the industry and coparenting on his face, and was beginning to feel its effects.

"One time during postproduction we were at the Universal Studios commissary and I saw him drinking red wine," Bruce Cannon says. "John told me, 'The doctor said it was good for me to keep my blood pressure down.' That is when I first learned that John was dealing with high blood pressure."

Miami John smiled more. He wore pastels. White linens. Rocked aviators. His footwear alternated between expensive leather sandals and *chancletas*.

He'd go on long walks. Swim in the ocean. Rent a boat and go sailing. Eventually, he got a cell with a 786 area code. He went out to dinner all the time. Prime 112. Smith & Wollensky. Joe's Stone Crab. Big Pink. He found a spot that sold these fancy deviled eggs he couldn't get enough of. He did the Miami scene. He hung out with the right people. Nightclub owners. Restaurateurs. Models. Celebrities. Miami celebrities. *Let's stop by Uncle Luke's table and say hello*, he'd say. He'd do Fat Joe's Terror Squad Pool Party. Later on, he cohosted industry events with Mr. 305, Pitbull. He befriended the actual mayor of Miami after meeting him at the Grand Prix in 2002.

He had this joie de vivre about him. He was down for whatever.

When Nievecita Dubuque, a music video model turned actress with a bit part in *2 Fast 2 Furious*, invited him to her birthday party, he accepted immediately.

He met her during casting. They chitchatted on the set. Singleton made sure she got a line in the movie and, with that, her SAG card. Dubuque became part of the clique of actors hanging out at Singleton's condo.

"I think John was trying to date me," she says. "I told him straight out: I didn't have an attraction to him."

Dubuque had big plans for her birthday party. She invited twenty-five people and had a party bus at her disposal. In the end, only Singleton and two of her friends showed up. "Models—beautiful women," Dubuque says. "John was happy to be a part of it. I remember the three of us girls surrounding John and dancing."

"We would go to the bar, get some drinks, talk, laugh, and then get on the dance floor. John was a dancer. Then, when we got bored of that nightclub we went to another nightclub. We partied very late into the morning. Then the party bus dropped him off at his place and drove us girls home."

Singleton hired one of Dubuque's friends he met that night to work on his new movie that was about to start filming in Memphis.

Stephanie Allain's career fell on hard times after leaving Columbia to run Jim Henson Pictures in 1996. During her four years as president of production at the studio, she made three films (*Buddy*, *Muppets from Space*, and *The Adventures of Elmo in Grouchland*), all of which bombed.

In April 2000, she landed at 3 Arts Entertainment. But she didn't want to be in the management business. Toward the end of her contract, Allain, a forty-one-year-old divorcée with two kids, faced an existential crisis: *Is this it? What else is out there for me? What am I going to do with the rest of my life?*

Around this time, she came across a script titled *Hustle & Flow*.

She opened it and started reading. A familiar feeling washed over her. With each turn of the page, her heart beat a little bit faster. The scene construction. The voice. The characters. The dialogue. Everything felt so rich.

"Pure gold," she said.

She hadn't felt this way since *Boyz N the Hood* fell into her hands over a decade earlier. About halfway through the script, she put it down and called the writer's manager.

"Where are you on *Hustle & Flow*?" she asked.

They had interest at Universal and Fox Searchlight before both studios passed, mostly due to the subject matter. *Hustle & Flow* was a tough sell: a movie set in Memphis about a Black pimp's midlife crisis. Further complicating matters, a white guy from California had written it.

Born on an army base in Newport News, Virginia, Craig Brewer had an itinerant childhood, his family ultimately settling in Vallejo. He focused on play-writing as a teenager, taking classes at the American Conservatory Theater in San Francisco. Later, he put on plays that his father helped produce, and he worked as a production manager at a Bay Area theater company.

At twenty-two, Brewer decided he needed a change of scenery. The South felt like a magical place to him. As a kid, he spent summers with his grandparents in Collierville and Fisherville, Tennessee, towns about thirty miles east of Memphis. Memories of running around barefoot holding a BB gun during sun-drenched vacations filled his heart. He soon moved to Memphis to become a filmmaker.

Brewer worked a minimum-wage job at a bookstore. After clocking out, he'd write in the P&H Cafe until late at night, before picking up his wife from her job at a nearby strip club. "It started robbing our souls a little," Brewer said of their struggle. In the fall of 1998, his father, the man he called his best friend and who was his biggest supporter, died of a heart attack at the age of forty-nine.

Brewer used $20,000 from his inheritance to help fund his first feature, *The Poor & Hungry*, which he shot on digital, as his father had suggested to him shortly before passing away. The movie ran in local theaters for a few weeks, earning Brewer back his investment. But he was still broke and closing in on thirty without much to show for it.

Inspiration for *Hustle & Flow* struck while location scouting for *The Poor & Hungry*.

One afternoon in 1999, Brewer was sitting in his beat-up Subaru outside a seedy hourly rental motel when a Chevy Caprice Classic pulled up next to him.

"Ayyy, man," said the driver, a Black man, startling Brewer. He dipped his head toward the white woman sitting in the passenger seat. "Like what you see?"

Brewer looked her up and down. She wore hot pants and styled her hair in blond microbraids.

"No, I'm good," Brewer said.

"We can get a room right here," he said, pointing back at the motel.

Brewer took another look at the woman. She massaged her sweaty brow. Her mascara-smudged eyes slowly drooped. "I'm meeting someone," he said.

The man in the Caprice pivoted. "Ayyy, man, you like rap?" He held up a cassette tape. "Ten dollars."

"Nah, I'm good."

Brewer couldn't shake the brief encounter.

"He had a dream, like me," Brewer says. "Everybody has [the equivalent of] a job at Barnes and Noble and would rather be doing something else, whether it's making a film or a rap album. Everybody's got the thing they want to be doing and the thing they're doing that they're not really thrilled about."

He sketched out a story of a Memphis pimp named DJay, harboring aspirations of rap stardom. In the fall of 2000, he started writing the script. He quickly realized how much he had in common with his lead. The stress. The frustration. The money problems. The sudden terror of mortality salient. The make-or-break moment staring them in the face.

"I had talked the talk," Brewer says. "Now it was time to walk the walk."

When he finished the script later that fall, he instructed his manager to find a home for it.

Allain ran into similar headwinds when she pitched the project to studios, though. They all had a caveat attached—even the ones that nibbled, like Focus Features and Paramount Classics. The story was too bleak. The director was too inexperienced and too white. Did DJay have to be a pimp? Could he work as a mailman or plumber instead? In the span of months, Allain went from seeking $5 million to begging for $750,000. She still couldn't find a buyer.

Sometime in late 2002, she decided to stop pitching. With the advent of digital and the changing distribution models, she calculated she could self-finance the film for around $500,000. After selling her house and downgrading to a two-bedroom in La Brea, she now had a quarter million to allocate. She needed investors. That's when she called an old friend.

★★★★★

"I have the hottest script in town!" Allain said when she sent *Hustle & Flow* to Singleton. He ignored her bluster. For months, the script sat on his office shelf as he handled postproduction on *2 Fast 2 Furious*. On Cinco de Mayo 2003, he called Allain.

"This shit is great!" he bayed.

He invited Allain to the Universal soundstage, where they celebrated over margaritas.

From the start, Singleton and Allain differed on a course for the film. Allain intended to make *Hustle & Flow* independently. When she contacted Singleton, she hoped he'd pledge a few hundred thousand bucks. They'd make the film on the cheap, share ownership, and find distribution for it.

"Nah, nah, nah, you just need me in the room," Allain recalls Singleton saying. "Fast and the Furious is about to make all this money. I got this. I can get eight million—easy."

In the early 2000s, nearly every major studio had its boutique imprint specializing in low-budget films like *Hustle & Flow*. Paramount Classics. Fox Searchlight. Fine Line at Warner Bros. Universal had Focus Features. With the DVD market still going strong, a return on investment felt guaranteed. Singleton thought he could tap into that stream. He expected to quickly close a deal thanks to his connections at each studio. Instead, he got a brutal reality check.

Singleton returned to the same executive suites and conference rooms where Allain and Brewer had been rejected. Once again they all passed on *Hustle & Flow*. Each studio had a different reason. They had uneasiness about a pimp as the film's protagonist. They believed Black movies didn't do well internationally. On more than one occasion, they told him to recast the lead. Singleton and Brewer insisted on hiring Terrence Howard, best known for his supporting turn in *The Best Man*. Singleton came close to working with the eccentric actor on *Shaft*. Howard initially had been cast as Peoples Hernandez's henchman, Tattoo. But he complained about his lack of screen time and lines. Shortly before production started, he booked the lead in a TV movie about Muhammad Ali. Singleton and *Shaft*'s producers were more than willing to let him go. Though Howard lacked an established name, Singleton deemed him poised for a breakthrough. The studios proposed other actors in pitch meetings. Don Cheadle. Snoop Dogg, Nick Cannon, and even Sisqó of "Thong Song" infamy were floated as potential stars.

Singleton and Brewer also contended with the cultural blind spots of predominantly white, older suits based in New York and Los Angeles, who were disconnected from the Southern hip-hop movement that had taken hold—and that *Hustle & Flow* felt poised to capitalize on.

The September 2003 issue of *The Source* magazine signaled the changing of the guard: A split cover featuring a collection of the South's favorite sons. On one side, OutKast, the Atlanta duo whose new album *Speakerboxxx/The Love Below* would go on to sell over eleven million copies. The B cover featured Lil Jon, David Banner, and Bone Crusher burning a Confederate flag. *The New South*, read the cover line.

"We're right," Brewer said. "Hollywood is wrong."

"We're right. Hollywood is wrong," Singleton repeated.

When he got involved with *Hustle & Flow*, he envisioned using his post–*2 Fast 2 Furious* clout to get the film financed. The sequel earned over $235 million worldwide. But he received zero credit for its success.

"He was kind of heartbroken about it," Allain says. "He felt disrespected. I think that's why he wrote the check."

After months of shopping the film, Singleton came around to Allain's thinking. He realized he didn't need $30 million or a studio to get *Hustle & Flow* off the ground. He could finance the film for about the price of his Baldwin Hills home. He put up the house for collateral and invested around $1.8 million into the film; the final, overall amount was closer to $3 million. He believed in Brewer and his script enough to mortgage his future on it.

One night in the fall of 2003, he called him to break the news.

"Listen, we've been all over town," Singleton said. "We've knocked on all the doors. Everyone is saying no to us."

Brewer paced the living room in the Memphis house he could no longer afford. He had sold his furniture and his beloved movie collection—over a thousand VHS tapes carefully curated through the years—to make rent the previous month.

"There's nothing else we can do," Singleton said.

Brewer felt a sharp pain in his throat. His eyes welled up.

"So, I'm just going to green-light this motherfucker myself. I'm getting the money together. We're going to shoot this summer. Let's get you out here. Let's start casting. Let's go make this movie."

★★★★★

*Hustle & Flow* was the passion project of three people with something to prove: Brewer, the starving artist; Allain, the former executive searching for a professional purpose; and Singleton, the auteur turned producer lugging a massive chip on his shoulder. He wasn't above holding a grudge. Singleton kept a framed copy in his office of the negative coverage Orion Pictures had given *Boyz N the Hood*. "An amateurish attempt at storytelling and does not indicate any strong talent behind it," it read. More than ever, he was driven to silence all skeptics.

With Terrence Howard cemented as the lead, Singleton turned to friends and cashed in favors to fill out the remainder of the ensemble. He cast Taraji P. Henson as Suge, the pregnant sex worker with a golden heart, and the Memphis native Elise Neal as an aggrieved spouse. He convinced Ludacris to play Skinny Black even though he had no interest in portraying a rapper. DJ Qualls (*Road Trip*), Anthony Anderson (*Barbershop*), and Taryn Manning (*8 Mile*) filled out the cast. Ike Turner read for Arnel, a club owner; in the end, they thought better of it. Isaac Hayes stepped in for the role. For the part of DJay's top moneymaker Lexus, they cast Paula Jai Parker, an actress Singleton had dated on and off for years.

*Hustle & Flow* started filming on July 9. For the next four weeks, the crew worked six twelve-hour days a week, a grueling schedule in the Memphis heat.

Before production started, the film's executive producer, Dwight Williams, took Singleton aside. "I'm going to pimp you out on this movie," he said. "You're going to need to shake hands, kiss babies, and politick."

Singleton bartered around town, putting his people skills and dealmaking prowess to work. When he needed free transportation, he took a car dealer to lunch and traded premiere tickets for a fleet of rentals. They couldn't afford to hire extras or security. Location fees weren't in the budget. But the production created goodwill with both the Memphis Film and Television Commission and the locals whose lives they'd disrupt for the next month.

Williams set up a free screening of *2 Fast 2 Furious* (free popcorn and lemonade included) for around 140 kids and teenagers. A meet and greet and Polaroid session with Singleton and the cast followed, where he busted out his best commencement speech. He spoke of the importance of hard work and education, of pursuing one's dreams. Terrence Howard also shared his unique brand of wisdom.

"You're all stars," Howard told the kids. "The hydrogen in your bodies means you share a kinship and majesty with the biggest star in the universe: the sun."

Working on a tight budget required that Brewer make his days even if it meant cutting corners. One day, while Brewer prepped a scene where Howard, Anderson, and Qualls create "Whoop That Trick," Singleton realized that shooting the scene as planned would put them behind schedule. (During preproduction, Al Kapone, the rapper who wrote and produced the song, re-created how he constructed the beat with his sampler and keyboard for Brewer and the actors.)

Singleton approached Brewer. "Hey, I'm just wondering, if you had to shoot this scene and only do it in three setups, how would you do it?"

Brewer had storyboarded the entire movie. He had more than three setups planned for the scene. "I wouldn't," he said.

"I'm curious," Singleton said, trying to draw it out of him. "What would you do?"

Brewer scratched his chin and pursed his lips. "I guess I'd start with a master shot and then do coverage shots of Terrence and Anthony."

"That's good," Singleton said. "That's what I would do. Shoot the meat."

He conferred with Allain and Williams.

"Dude," he said, walking back toward Brewer, "you only have time for three setups."

The filmmakers adjusted on the fly. Singleton had been around long enough to know that things inevitably go awry during production. But he couldn't prepare for the accusations that shook the set of *Hustle & Flow*.

About three weeks into filming, Shelby County sheriffs took Anthony Anderson and second assistant director Wayne Witherspoon into custody, charging them with aggravated rape after a female extra claimed they assaulted her in a production trailer. Both men denied the accusations and were released on $20,000 bond. They were exonerated in October when a judge dismissed the charges against them, calling it "the most suspicious rape case he'd heard in twenty years." The accuser's former boyfriend testified that she had told him the sex was consensual. According to his testimony, she said she fabricated the charges "to get us some money."

★★★★★

Singleton had learned a thing or two about producing from Scott Rudin. At times on the set of *Hustle & Flow*, he steamrolled Brewer.

"Do it again, Craig," he said, following the scene near the end of the film when DJay assaults Skinny Black. Singleton thought Skinny should say something—anything—to DJay. "If it doesn't work, you can always cut it in post. Call action."

Brewer hesitated.

"Call action, Craig!"

Allain stepped in. "John, you're not directing this scene."

Singleton and Allain fell into their old roles, with him acting like both her boss and her little brother. He liked to push boundaries on the screen. More grit. More violence. He believed there was a certain bravery in showing the brutality of life. She'd reel him in when he went too far. One night, it almost led to her shutting down the set.

They were filming one of the most uncomfortable scenes in the film—an argument between DJay and Lexus that ends with him kicking her, and her infant son, out of his house. In the script, DJay throws her down the porch's front steps. Singleton loved it as written on the page. He flew in Halle Berry's stunt double to take the fall. But Allain felt the scene didn't work in rehearsals.

"It's coming across as really violent," she told Brewer in a hushed tone. "I worry we're going to lose the audience here. They're going to hate him."

Singleton walked toward her. "No, it's going to be good," he said. "We literally saw an argument like this last week when we were location scouting. Come on, this is real."

"We're not doing that, John," she said. "He's already a pimp. It's a tough enough sell. We can't have him also be physically abusive to women."

He thought of *Taxi Driver*. "We gotta do it like Marty," he said. "We have to do it hard."

He stomped toward Howard. "Throw her down the steps—and kick her one time too," he said.

Brewer's mother visited the set that night and ended up arbitrating the dispute. "Craig, you cannot have him throw this woman down the stairs," she told him. "He can take her out onto the porch. But that's it."

Once filming wrapped on August 9, Brewer took a week off before flying to Los Angeles to work on the film. Postproduction featured one crisis after another for him. After watching the assembly edit of the film (the editor's first cut), he pulled over to the side of the road and sobbed.

A few weeks later, Allain screened Brewer's first cut for her friends.

"They weren't pleased with it," she reported back.

Brewer spent the next day in bed until Singleton called in the evening.

"It's just a first cut," Singleton said. "This is part of the process, and I'm going to help you get through it. This is an onion that you're peeling. This is a statue that you're chiseling away at. You have to get back in the edit room. Shake off that negative energy and get to work."

Singleton seemed to say the right thing at the right time throughout postproduction on *Hustle & Flow*.

One time, while working on *Hustle & Flow*, Singleton and Brewer boarded a flight in Memphis. Brewer's heart rate quickened and his breaths shortened with each step through the terminal. His hand trembled slightly as he handed his boarding pass to the gate agent. Once seated, he immediately located the emergency exit and the bathroom. Singleton sat down next to him. He closed his eyes before the plane had taxied down the runway.

About an hour into the flight, the plane dipped and wobbled. Then it plunged some more. Brewer's arms clutched both armrests. His face drained of color. The bird struggled to ascend, convulsing from side to side. He looked over at Singleton, eyes still shut, head bobbing in rhythm with the turbulence.

"You good?" Singleton asked.

"No, man, I'm not good," Brewer said.

Singleton sucked his teeth. "Oh, man, it's not our time. We're all good. Go to sleep."

The film came together slowly but steadily following Brewer's meltdown on the shoulder of a freeway. He had one good day after another in the editing room. Then he hit a wall. He realized the film lost momentum during the recording of the third song, "Hustle and Flow (It Ain't Over)."

"It was like, 'Are we really going to watch another musical number all the way through?' The movie was in trouble at the moment," Brewer says.

While driving home from the cutting room he could barely concentrate on the road. He didn't know how to fix the scene. His phone rang.

"Hey, man, swing by the Virgin Megastore on your way home," Singleton said.

"Why? What's—"

"*Purple Rain*! The Twentieth Anniversary Special Edition DVD of *Purple Rain* is out," Singleton hollered. "Oh my God, there's commentary on this bitch. You've got to hear it. It's amazing."

"I don't know, man. It was a long day and—"

"I don't want to hear that shit. Forget everything about your movie and watch this one."

*Purple Rain* was the comfort food that Brewer, a fanatic of the film, needed. He sat transfixed on his couch until the "When Doves Cry" montage started. "Oh my God, wait a minute," he said. He jolted upright. "What's the purpose of the scene?" he asked.

"It's there to remind me of the stakes of the story," he answered himself.

"Oh, that's what I have to do with 'Hustle and Flow (It Ain't Over).'"

He called his editor, even though it was after eleven.

"I'm sorry I called so late but it's important. When you wake up tomorrow, watch *Purple Rain*. Then I'm coming over. I know how to end the movie."

Soon, Brewer locked the film. Now Singleton had to sell it.

# CHAPTER TWENTY

From the moment he signed his first check on *Hustle & Flow*, Singleton planned to recoup his investment with a bidding war at Sundance. As the brainchild of Robert Redford, the Sundance Film Festival had launched the careers of Steven Soderbergh, Quentin Tarantino, and Darren Aronofsky. Sundance slowly—and then quickly—evolved into Cannes on the ski slopes. Celebrities. Wild parties. Swag bags. "A fun, amazing lovefest of filmmaking, art, and free things," says Elise Neal.

Huge acquisition deals also went down in the mountains of Park City, Utah.

In 1996, *The Spitfire Grill* sold for $10 million. Three years later, Miramax acquired *Happy, Texas* for a little north of $10 million. But there's a saying at Sundance: It's dangerous to be at high altitude with an open checkbook. Both films bombed at the box office, proving once again that picking hits at Sundance is an inexact science akin to fantasy football and day-trading. Singleton wasn't worried about the box office. He'd focus on marketing and promotion once he had a deal. In the moment, he wanted the studios to pay up.

Anticipation for the film spiked following a series of screenings around Los Angeles at the homes of Spike Lee, Will Smith, and producer Lorenzo di Bonaventura. Singleton filled the audience with friends and family and an assortment of tastemakers and cool kids. No one who could actually buy the film made it past the door.

"If you want to see the movie, buy a parka," Singleton would tell studio executives.

But he made sure to invite their assistants so they could hype the film to their bosses.

Sometime in early January, a few weeks before the film's planned premiere at Sundance, a studio head called with a blind offer of $3 million for the film. Singleton turned that down too. He remained committed to fielding a feeding frenzy of competing offers at the festival.

*Hustle & Flow* was the hottest ticket in town when it premiered on Saturday, January 22. Before the screening, Brewer climbed onstage and thanked Singleton and Allain for their trust and faith. They stood to the side beaming at each other—the picture's proud parents. Soon, Taraji P. Henson and Taryn Manning joined Brewer onstage in a rendition of Ike and Tina Turner's "Proud Mary."

Sundance hadn't seen this kind of energy before—the anticipation of a Star Wars movie on opening weekend crossed with an underground rap show.

"That was the most excited crowd I've ever seen for a movie," says former Universal executive Kevin Misher.

Immediately afterward, clusters of studio executives, including Viacom copresident and co-CEO Tom Freston and New Line chairman Bob Shaye, huddled in different corners of the Racquet Club's lobby to share their notes on the film.

*What did you think? How will it play at the multiplex? What's its potential internationally and on home video? Is it an Oscar film? Is it 8 Mile?*

They conferred with their bosses back in Los Angeles and prepared their offers; Sony's Amy Pascal, Universal's Stacey Snider, Warner Bros.' Alan Horn, and Paramount's Brad Grey attended private screenings in Los Angeles simultaneous to the Sundance premiere.

Potential buyers followed Singleton around town.

He stopped at the festival lodge on Main Street for the UTA party. Amid the ice sculptures and free booze, he fielded offers on his phone. He turned to his college friend, the producer Bill Straus.

"Harvey wants the movie," he shouted in his ear over the crunk music blaring from the speakers.

He returned to his phone.

"Focus just made an offer."

Negotiations continued at the Riverhorse on Main and the downtown Marriot Summit Watch, where Singleton and his team of agents and attorneys set up a war room. Singleton was standing in the lobby eating an ice-cream cone from a vending machine when Brewer walked in.

"Come in, we're in play," Singleton said.

Eighteen months earlier, the four bidders still involved—New Line, Columbia, Paramount, and Focus—could have bought the film for $1.5 million. They'd soon learn that yesterday's price was not today's price. At around four a.m., New Line appeared to win the auction with a $10 million offer. Singleton turned it down. He had an ace in the hole. Before arriving at Sundance, he'd promised Brad Grey, the new chairman and CEO of Paramount Pictures, that he'd give him the final offer at the end of the night.

Grey had remained fixated on winning the bidding ever since di Bonaventura called him and said, "If I've ever seen an MTV film, this is it."

Grey, a forty-seven-year-old former manager best known for producing *The Sopranos*, had been hired to take big swings. His predecessors, outgoing studio chief Sherry Lansing and her boss, Viacom chairman Jon Dolgen, had overseen huge box-office successes (*Titanic, Forrest Gump,* the Mission: Impossible series) and back-to-back Best Picture winners in 1995 and 1996 (*Forrest Gump* and *Braveheart*) during their reign. But the studio acquired a reputation for their hard negotiating tactics—they were cheap and cautious. In 2004, their sister division, Paramount Classics, lost out on acquiring *Napoleon Dynamite* at Sundance, and it went on to become the sleeper hit of the summer.

At around four thirty a.m., Singleton called Grey to tell him New Line had the highest bid. Grey deliberated with his lieutenants and countered. Soon they had a deal.

In the third largest acquisition in Sundance history, Paramount Pictures and MTV Films purchased *Hustle & Flow* for $9 million. Paramount also included a sweetener: a two-picture, $7 million "put deal" (an arrangement where the studio is required to release two additional films with Singleton producing), bringing the total package to $16 million.

Singleton celebrated with a drink. "I feel vindicated," he said to longtime *Variety* editor Peter Bart. "I also feel rich."

He boarded the Paramount jet and returned to the Toronto set of his new movie.

★★★★★

*Four Brothers* had come together quickly at Paramount. Sometime in 2004, Lorenzo di Bonaventura cooked up an elevator pitch: an R-rated revenge movie featuring foster brothers as the main characters. He commissioned a script from writers Paul Lovett and David Elliott. The writing team fleshed out the plot. They centered the film on four brothers reuniting in their childhood home in Detroit to solve their foster mother's murder; the title *Four Brothers* came from an interlude in

N.W.A.'s "100 Miles and Runnin'." ("This one goes out to the four brothers from Compton. . . .")

When they submitted their first draft, an unexpected development occurred: di Bonaventura loved it.

"I can't tell you how atypical that is," Lovett says. "We had such minimal notes that it was crazy."

Di Bonaventura, a former Warner Bros. executive who'd recently transitioned to producing, had a reputation for moving fast. He had a script. Now he needed a director. His first choice, the Hong Kong action maestro John Woo (*The Killer*, *A Better Tomorrow*, *Face/Off*), passed. He turned to Singleton, whom he had worked with on *Rosewood*. Though it bombed at the box office, Singleton's work on the picture impressed him.

"He got the right kind of performances and he didn't shy away from the intensity," di Bonaventura says. "For me, one of the hallmarks of a good action picture is that you don't shy away from the intensity. When it's violent, it should be violent. When it's emotional, it needs to be emotional. John was not afraid of the visceral."

Still, he harbored doubts about working with Singleton.

"John's reputation was that he had a hard time staying on budget," di Bonaventura says. "Everyone I talked to said, 'Great guy. Can't stay on budget.' I didn't hear *difficult*. I heard *difficult around budget*."

Singleton eased his concerns during their initial meeting. He viewed *Four Brothers* as a direct descendant of the action movies he watched late at night as a kid, urban Westerns like *Death Wish*, *Dirty Harry*, and *Point Blank*. But he also felt the film had heart—universal themes like family and brotherhood and vengeance.

At the end of the meeting, di Bonaventura made a pact with Singleton.

"This is my first production and I'm not going over budget."

"Don't worry about—"

"John, I've heard all the stories," he said. "I can't afford to go over budget. So, here's our deal. I'm going to get you everything you ask for. But I'm asking you to then use it and use it on the budget."

Singleton kept his end of the bargain. "It may just be he was never given the proper budget," di Bonaventura says.

Singleton recognized early on that the film's success hinged on casting the four Mercer brothers. For the lead role of Bobby, he had a specific actor in mind.

Singleton first met Mark Wahlberg on the Sony lot in 1993 when the former rapper and model worked on his debut film *Renaissance Man* for Penny Marshall.

They shared a passion for the movies and nightlife, partying together at Centro-Fly and Cheetah when Singleton lived in New York while working on *Shaft*.

"We always talked about working together," Wahlberg says. "John was the kind of guy you wanted to spend time with. He was very endearing and very genuine. He was charismatic, charming. He was funny. He was gangster—a guy's guy, for sure. But he knew how to conduct himself in any kind of room, any kind of environment."

Both Singleton and di Bonaventura envisioned a multiracial family unit when casting Wahlberg's three brothers. Singleton hired Tyrese Gibson, marking their third consecutive collaboration, while di Bonaventura enlisted Garrett Hedlund, a twenty-year-old farm boy from Minnesota, who'd booked roles in *Troy* and *Friday Night Lights* shortly after moving to Los Angeles. When a scheduling conflict removed Ice Cube from consideration for the role of Jeremiah Mercer, the most complex character out of the four Mercer brothers, Singleton pivoted to another rapper, André 3000, from OutKast.

André 3000 (born André Benjamin) had recently undergone a massive career shift. Now in his late twenties, he'd grown restless within the act he formed in 1992 with his high school friend Big Boi. He thirsted for something different. On OutKast's subsequent album, André fused hip-hop with psychedelic pop, funk, and electronic music. He also pursued creative outlets such as fashion and acting. *Speakerboxxx/The Love Below* won three Grammy Awards, including Album of the Year. André's solo record "Hey Ya!" topped the Billboard Hot 100 while drawing comparisons to Little Richard, the Beatles, and the Ramones. But he struggled transitioning to Hollywood.

André says he "bombed" his audition for the role of Tej in *2 Fast 2 Furious*. "My nerves overtook any chance to get in that film," he says. "I'm horrible in auditions. Coming from rapping, the audition process was so weird for me because I'd step in the room and all these people would see me as that rapper and I felt that pressure."

Eventually, he started booking jobs: *Hollywood Homicide* and *Be Cool*, where he was typecast as a rapper in both films. Then he branched out in the Guy Ritchie caper *Revolver* and *Idlewild*, the Prohibition-era musical starring OutKast that had just wrapped prior to *Four Brothers* going into production.

Paramount announced Singleton's involvement in *Four Brothers* in October 2004. Less than three months later, principal photography started in Toronto and Hamilton, Ontario, which stood in for Detroit. Singleton had two editors cutting the film during production (Bruce Cannon and *Hustle & Flow* editor Billy Fox) to make Paramount's scheduled late summer release date.

For the first time since *Boyz N the Hood*, it was a straightforward shoot.

"It was a very relaxed set," says the veteran actor Barry Shabaka Henley, who played a crooked politician in the film. "There was little tension or drama going on. Everybody was working in concert. That always starts from the top down. I remember John as a quiet, powerful presence."

He'd finally found the right collaborator in di Bonaventura. Singleton didn't go over budget or over schedule. There were no blowups on set that made the gossip columns. No one of note got fired. Singleton and di Bonaventura were friends prior to filming and remained so afterward. Despite the truncated shooting schedule and complicated stunts and set pieces, the greatest challenges on the $40 million film proved to be the weather ("It was fucking brick," Wahlberg says) and keeping Singleton upright on the ice during his cameo as a hockey goaltender.

"John had never been on ice skates before but was like, 'I can skate,'" says production designer Keith Brian Burns. "He was holding on to everyone to not fall. It was like, 'John, you're going to kill yourself.'"

From the moment he arrived in Toronto, he tried building chemistry among the four brothers. The film's rehearsal time consisted of the stars bro-ing out together. Watching playoff football at Singleton's condo. Boys' nights at restaurants and clubs. They'd play the dozens over drinks and then insert the jokes into the script the next morning. Singleton compared the improvisation in certain scenes to members of a jazz band riffing off one another.

"I don't think I had that much fun on a movie in my entire career," Wahlberg says. "We all really bonded with each other. We knew the movie was only going to be as a good as the guy next to you, so it was about putting everybody in position to be the best. Normally, you get on a movie and it can be pretty competitive— everybody is trying to get their moments. But John did a good job of empowering everybody."

And then *Four Brothers* opened on August 12, 2005, to some of the worst reviews of Singleton's career. The *Miami Herald* proclaimed it "Singleton's sloppiest, laziest movie to date." *Entertainment Weekly* called *Four Brothers* "oafish." The *Detroit News* deemed it "ridiculously violent, crude, homophobic, brash, and plain absurd."

"Loud, stupid, unrealistic, overdone, without a thought in its ugly little head and kind of enjoyable," wrote the *Washington Post*.

*Variety* praised the "engaging interplay" between the four brothers and hailed the directing. "Singleton is unafraid to slow the tempo for scenes like a character-revealing Thanksgiving dinner (brightened with a touch of magical realism). But when Singleton kicks out the jams during the hard-core rough stuff—especially during a slipping-and-sliding car chase during a snowstorm, and a full-out assault on the Mercer home—he delivers the goods with edgy kinetic flair."

Audiences loved the film. *Four Brothers* debuted atop the box office with $21.1 million. It was a throwback of sorts—a brawny, hypermasculine '70s-style action flick with no connection to existing IP. *Four Brothers* had more going for it, such as an A-list movie star playing to his blue-collar strengths; fun chemistry amongst the ensemble; a scenery-chewing villain (Chiwetel Ejiofor channeling Yaphet Kotto as per Singleton's suggestion); and a director who could elevate a good script.

"John used to talk about flavor. 'How do you create flavor?' he'd ask. In *Four Brothers*, a lot of the success is because there is a ton of flavor in it," di Bonaventura says. "Flavor makes for more colorful characters. Flavor makes for less generic decision-making."

*Four Brothers* would be a much different, and much less effective, film in the hands of another filmmaker. Singleton nailed the casting. He seemed to make the correct choice at each turn, such as reinserting the Thanksgiving dinner scene and pushing back on Paramount's request for a hip-hop score and soundtrack. From the opening credits, Marvin Gaye's "Trouble Man" established a mood and tone for the film.

"These four brothers are from Detroit and are dealing with the death of their foster mother," he said. "We had to play music that she would've listened to and that's late '60s/early '70s Motown B-sides."

*Four Brothers* ended its domestic run at $74.4 million. But di Bonaventura believes the studio left money on the table.

Sometime in July 2005, Brad Grey asked di Bonaventura to send a copy of the film to his boss, Tom Freston. Di Bonaventura declined. When word got back to Grey, he immediately called the producer.

"What the fuck are you doing, man?" Grey howled. "You can't deny a copy for the chairman."

"Yes, I can!"

"Why?"

"Because piracy, Brad. Every time you make a DVD you risk piracy."

"I don't care. Do it!"

He messengered over a watermarked DVD. About a month later, a few days before the film opened, di Bonaventura and Singleton strolled through a flea market in Santa Monica. They came upon a vendor selling bootleg DVDs.

"Oh man, we love movies," Singleton gushed. "How do we keep in touch? We want to stay on top of things."

The bootlegger gave Singleton his name and number.

"I'll take every copy of this one," Singleton said, holding up *Four Brothers*.

Shortly thereafter, the FBI arrested the vendor.

Later that afternoon, di Bonaventura and Singleton watched the *Four Brothers* bootleg. The watermark encryption on the DVD read *Property of Tom Freston*.

★★★★★

Singleton was the hottest he'd been in over a decade leading up to *Hustle & Flow*'s July 22, 2005, release. He'd become the king-making producer he envisioned when he first launched New Deal. He enjoyed being back in the spotlight. His press run that summer turned into an extended victory lap.

"My last film made $240 million," he said in an interview with the *New York Times*, referring to *2 Fast 2 Furious*. "Hello, I've been here."

*Hustle & Flow* pierced the conversation through a storm of publicity and good reviews. The *New York Times* profiled Singleton. Terrence Howard profiles ran in both the *Los Angeles Times* and *Vibe*. Taryn Manning appeared on the cover of *Nylon*. The ensemble made the cover of *Jet*. Singleton and Brewer appeared on *Charlie Rose*. Its stars blanketed Viacom properties like BET and MTV. The film earned raves in the New York *Daily News*, the *Los Angeles Times*, *Entertainment Weekly*, *Ebert & Roeper*, *Newsweek*, and *USA Today*.

Then it opened in seventh place before dropping out of the top ten the following weekend. What went wrong?

Singleton and Brewer were prescient about the rise of Southern hip-hop. By the summer of 2005, Lil Wayne, T.I., and Young Jeezy were the three hottest rappers in the game.

But Allain believed the film's marketing, and its poster, crucially, leaned a bit too much into crunk music and hip-hop. She preferred a campaign focusing on both its indie cred and its story about a guy wanting to elevate himself through art.

Singleton remained fixated on piracy. A few days after *Hustle & Flow* opened, law enforcement officials in eight major cities confiscated 2,500 DVDs of the film.

Paramount positioned *Hustle & Flow* as counterprogramming to the big, dumb blockbusters populating multiplexes in late summer (*The Island, Fantastic Four, Stealth,* and *The Dukes of Hazzard*). At first, it appeared they stuck the landing. *Hustle & Flow* earned a little over $8 million on opening weekend, with the second highest per-screen average in the top ten. But it fell 49.7 percent in its second frame and dropped precipitously through August until ending its theatrical run at $22.2 million domestic.

From the start, the studio misjudged *Hustle & Flow*'s box-office potential. Following the Sundance screening, Paramount Classics executives told Brad Grey that they believed *Hustle & Flow* had a $30 million ceiling at the box office. Tom Freston, Grey's boss, was said to disagree with that assessment. Viacom thought the film could be another *8 Mile*—Eminem's semiautobiographical crowd-pleaser that opened at $51 million and banked $126 million domestically in the fall of 2002.

*Hustle & Flow* wasn't *8 Mile*. It didn't star the highest-selling rapper in the world. It was an art house film and should've been treated as such. Paramount went too wide, too soon, opening the film on 1,013 screens.

"It was just a shit show," says Ruth Vitale, then copresident of Paramount Classics. "It should've opened on four screens. Then we build it up from there. If we did a hundred thousand dollars on opening weekend on four screens, that would've been the headline."

Paramount could've purchased the film for around $1.5 million two years earlier. Then it doubled down on its error after catching a whiff of the Sundance vapors. In the end, the studio spent around $25 million on *Hustle & Flow* once P&A (prints and advertising) factored into overhead.

"We all drank the Kool-Aid," Vitale says. "Every acquisitions expert has sat in a screening room and watched the ceiling blow off it. Then it doesn't play anywhere else."

*Hustle & Flow* found redemption during the winter of 2006. The studio's Oscar campaign built momentum through awards season before capitalizing on a well-timed DVD release in January, three weeks before Oscar nominations were revealed. *Hustle & Flow* earned Academy Award nominations for Best Actor (Terrence Howard) and Best Original Song (Three 6 Mafia's "It's Hard Out Here for a Pimp"). Singleton viewed the honors as validations. He'd overpaid Three 6 Mafia despite cost concerns and cast Howard despite his lack of star power and his reputation.

"Terrence played Ralph Abernathy in an HBO movie about the Montgomery bus boycott. He was a mess on that movie, just a total pain," says Preston Holmes, a producer on *Boycott*, and an associate producer on *Hustle & Flow*. "He created all kind of problems on the set. He ran up a big bill at the hotel. He was just being a bad boy. When I arrived in Memphis for *Hustle & Flow*, my very first day I went to the set, got out of the car, and saw Terrence. He walked up to me and he apologized for how he acted on *Boycott*. Terrence was definitely on his best behavior on *Hustle & Flow*."

Singleton relished his role as the film's biggest booster during the endless cocktail parties and schmoozefests that define awards season. Over and over again, he recounted the film's Cinderella story. How he financed the film. His Sundance triumph. The challenges they faced along the way.

"So, I told Craig, 'If you fuck up, my kids will have to go to public school!'"

"The same fools who turned us down were now begging for the movie!"

On Oscar night, Three 6 Mafia were surprise winners for Best Original Song; Howard, as expected, lost Best Actor to Philip Seymour Hoffman (*Capote*). Singleton and the Memphis rappers piled into a limousine afterward and headed to the *Vanity Fair* gala, where they partied alongside Madonna, Jamie Foxx, and Russell and Kimora Lee Simmons. From there, Singleton planned to meet Craig Brewer and Ludacris at Prince's party. A slight problem occurred when he arrived at the Hollywood Hills mansion: He wasn't on the guest list.

Singleton turned to Juicy J. "I know Prince. Let me handle this."

He exited the limo and approached a security guard. "I got Three 6," he said. "They just won an Oscar. Let Prince know we're out here."

A few minutes later, the security guard returned. "He said no."

★★★★★

Singleton didn't waste time to collaborate once more with Brewer. By the time the Oscars rolled around, they were already in postproduction on their follow-up movie.

In the fall of 2005, they returned to Memphis to shoot *Black Snake Moan*.

Though the film was not part of the two-picture deal he signed at Sundance, Singleton, along with Allain, produced it at Paramount. *Black Snake Moan* didn't have the long, torturous road to production that *Hustle & Flow* did. Studio executives read the script on the flight back from Sundance. Paramount quickly pounced to strike a deal despite the film's controversial subject matter. The plot involved a Black bluesman named Lazarus chaining a white sex addict to his radiator in an attempt to heal her.

Singleton bore little resemblance to the micromanaging producer from *Hustle & Flow*.

"John's paycheck was on the line on *Hustle & Flow*, so he was far more participatory in a producorial role," Allain says. "We were spending somebody else's money on *Black Snake Moan*. I think he was just having a good time."

He fancied himself the set photographer and spent much of his time in Memphis shooting stills and footage of the production. His greatest contribution to the film came during casting when he recruited Samuel L. Jackson to star as the lead; they had become friends following their ambivalent relationship on *Shaft*.

Singleton's relationship with Brewer had taken a turn since *Hustle & Flow*'s release. "This was probably the only time there was some weirdness between him and I," Brewer says.

Singleton received his first multi-million-dollar installment from the Sundance deal in the spring of 2005. By the time *Hustle & Flow* was released in July, Paramount had paid him 99 percent of the $9 million owed. Allain, Brewer, and the main cast were primed for a share. They negotiated a slice of the potential back-end profits in return for working for close to scale. But even as *Hustle & Flow* receded from theaters and summer turned to fall, no one had been paid.

Singleton deflected attempts to discuss the situation. Eventually, Brewer and members of the cast took their complaints to UTA. "His agents were not pleased," Brewer says. "But they were like, 'This isn't our problem. We're staying out of it.'"

In November 2005, as filming on *Black Snake Moan* came to an end, the dispute went public. "For All the Sacrifice and Luck, the Cash Isn't Flowing," read the headline in the *Los Angeles Times*. Singleton went on the defensive in the article, arguing that the money from Paramount paid for additional costs.

"I took all the financial risk on the film," he said. "We made a collective agreement to do a professional mix for the film, and that cost was not covered by Paramount. That was covered by me. They're dealing with me as an individual and not as a studio—I had to act like a studio. I was making sure that no one would get paid until after all the bills would get paid. I always planned to pay everybody by the holidays."

At times during the interview, he could barely hide his contempt for the situation. "I don't like somebody saying I'm a shyster. I resent people making comments when everybody's life has been changed from *Hustle & Flow*. Everyone has a career now."

Nearly two decades after the film's release, the profit dispute was still tied up in litigation. In November 2021, Taryn Manning sued Singleton's Crunk Pictures LLC, claiming she is "entitled to one percent of 100 percent of the net profits derived from exploitation of the picture," which, the suit alleges, totals at least $812,245. They settled in June 2023.

Brewer remembers approaching Singleton about their agreement.

"The contract isn't right," Singleton said, pacing his office.

"What are you talking about? We both signed it."

"I never agreed to ten percent. It should be seven percent. That's a typo."

"A typo?"

He stared through him. "Yeah, a typo."

Brewer shook his head. "John, it's in the contract. It's ten. Oh, and by the way, it's not ten. It's five and five—five for writing and five for directing."

"Well, that's not what I agreed to," he said. Singleton then turned back to Brewer. "I don't know why you're so pissed, anyway. We're only talking about thirty thousand dollars."

"John, that's a lot of money for me. I got a kid."

Brewer eventually received his share, though it was slightly less than he had negotiated.

"It was such a lame excuse: a typo," Brewer says. "If that's the case, it was a typo from your office. It's something that I learned quickly not to hold against him. But it's something that baffled me through the years. John was very much about his business. He really was. If it wasn't for his contribution and if it wasn't for his risk, I wouldn't have a career."

Brewer had witnessed a side of Singleton that he had shielded from the public. But it was one that the women closest to him knew far too well.

# CHAPTER TWENTY-ONE

One night while filming *Four Brothers*, Singleton walked onto the set, a bowling alley in Toronto, cell phone glued to his ear, and started flirting with one of the extras.

"Why do you look like that?" he asked.

"What do you mean?" said Mitzi Dee Andrews, a thirty-year-old Toronto native.

He ended the call and looked her up and down. "You're in full makeup and wearing a dress."

"Oh, I just came from an audition."

Singleton laughed. "Don't you know the rule?"

"What's the rule?"

"If you're working on my show, you can't work on any other show in town."

"I have a rule too. If you don't live in Toronto, you can't tell me what to do in Toronto."

"Well, I'm leaving Toronto in a few hours. A private jet is waiting to take me to Sundance."

Andrews rolled her eyes. "Cool." She walked away, shaking her head.

Years later, they'd laugh about the lame flex. "Remember when I tried to impress you with the plane?" he'd say.

When they met, Andrews had decided that 2005 would be her last year working as a background actor. She had a day job as a teacher and a ten-year-old daughter, Oriah, at home. She craved a normal schedule with normal hours. Then she met Singleton. Soon she'd be traveling across the world by his side.

One night after he returned from Sundance, he leaned over in bed. Told her he loved her. Andrews, head on the pillow, eyes closed, ignored him. The next morning, he said it again.

She grabbed his face with both hands. "John, you don't love me. You love fucking me. You don't know me well enough to say that, and I don't know you."

He tried once again on his last day in Toronto. Andrews had come to terms that he'd soon be back in Los Angeles and their whirlwind romance had concluded.

He chased her down the street outside his condo. "I love you," he said.

This time she didn't push back.

Two weeks later she was in Miami. Then Las Vegas. Then Los Angeles. Then the Memphis set of *Black Snake Moan*. Then LA again.

She tried jumping off the carousel after five or six months. She missed her daughter during long weekends with Singleton. There was also a full-time job and bills to pay.

"Well, how much do you get paid for teaching?" he asked her.

"Twenty-two hundred a month," she said.

"Okay, that's taken care of. I want you with me. How else am I going to see you?"

Andrews quickly got an idea of how Singleton rolled—and also of the tangled personal life he kept.

He had five children from four women and had issues with all of their mothers—each relationship volatile in its own unique way. Coparenting had turned into a series of arguments and negotiations about visitation rights, money, and past and present transgressions. Around this time, he started a process that resulted in all of his children moving in with him with the exception of Hadar, his daughter with Akosua Busia.

Justice, now a teenager, had already been shuttling between parents but lived with Singleton around this time. In late 2005, Selenesol moved in following an incident with their mother. (Selenesol is nonbinary and uses they/them pronouns.)

Singleton became embroiled in a long, painful custody battle with Maasai and Cleopatra's mother, Vestria Barlow, shortly after she moved to Houston with them without telling him.

Singleton had been seeing the kids less often with all the long stretches on film sets in Memphis and Toronto and then back in Memphis. He started spending more time in his South Beach condo. Once he started dating Andrews, he'd occasionally fly to Toronto for the weekend. Due to all the travel, Barlow claims she couldn't serve Singleton with a move-away order before she decamped for Texas. Singleton became apoplectic upon finding out. Barlow says he demanded custody of both Maasai, eleven, and Cleo, six, initiating a child custody evaluation.

Barlow believes Singleton took these steps out of spite. She had remarried. Soon she'd be pregnant with her third child.

Maasai and Cleopatra moved into the Baldwin Hills home.

This was what Singleton knew. It's how he was raised. He'd live here, there, then split time between the two. Mom's place. Dad's. Grandma's. Kids adjust. Furious took in Tre when it was time for him to become a man and look how that turned out. Now, with the idea of domesticity suddenly appealing to him, he collected his children under one roof. In the process, some of them became collateral damage.

"To be raised by your mother for eleven years and then be pulled away was traumatizing," Maasai says. "I got into fights with my dad about it all the time. I held anger about it for a decade."

Cleopatra desperately missed her mom as well, so much so that everyone from Maasai to Andrews, Singleton's new girlfriend, begged him to send the six-year-old home to her mother. She moved back to Houston once the evaluation was complete about six months later, Barlow says. Maasai stayed with his dad.

Singleton struggled with the new arrangement and the full house. "When I got my kids full-time, they drove me so crazy I could've made a movie about that shit," he said. "I wanted to throw them out the window." He excelled at creating moments with his children. The day-to-day intricacies and routines of parenting (school, meals, appointments, activities) proved more challenging. He loved his kids. He also loved his work and his alone time and his social life. He struggled to remain present, both mentally and physically, on occasion.

He'd wake up early, load the kids into the car, drive to IHOP for breakfast, and then unload Justice and Maasai at their school before dropping off Selenesol at Page Academy. His mother helped out. His assistants doubled as nannies. Then, after school, once homework was done, they'd play video games. He'd cook spaghetti with turkey meat, tacos loaded with sour cream, cheese, and tomatoes. When it was time for dinner, they'd usually sit on the couch and watch television.

"We would eat together and enjoy each other's presence," Selenesol says. "It wasn't like a nuclear family where we were eating together at the kitchen table. As I got older I realized we did do that. It was just different."

He always kept a camcorder around in the hopes of capturing organic moments.

As a parent, he wrestled with how best to deploy his money and privilege. He paid for the best private schools and tutors. But he worried about spoiling his kids. He talked about it endlessly, even to journalists and friends he normally didn't talk personal matters with. He grew up hard and wanted his children to emulate the toughness and independence he'd exhibited as a child.

One afternoon, he took Maasai and Cleo to a movie at the El Capitan Theatre. Afterward they went next door to the recently opened Disney Soda Fountain and Studio Store. They sat near a window, eating ice cream, watching the people come and go on Hollywood Boulevard.

"I remember being a young boy and looking into an ice-cream shop similar to this, not having enough money for anything," he said in a shaky voice. He looked at his kids. "Do you know how happy I am, being a man, being able to take you guys here?"

Singleton's father brought him to the Toho La Brea Theatre to watch Godzilla movies as a child. Now he indulged Maasai's fascination with Japanese culture. He bought him Miyazaki movies on DVD. Sometimes he'd take him out to sushi in Sawtelle Japantown followed by a visit to the video game import store. He took him to Comic-Con.

"Maasai, you don't realize how much we have in common," he said to his teenage son.

He said this having realized how his own father had shaped his parenting style. How he also parented through axioms like *Trust, but verify*. How he'd look at his own son and ask, "Are you a leader or a follower?"

One time, after Maasai tossed his pencils in disgust, he asked, "What's the matter?"

"I'm having trouble drawing Cyborg from *Teen Titans*. I can't—"

"Don't say you can't. You're not going to be handed anything in life. You have to do the work. I don't want to hear *can't*."

He put his own spin on parenting. When it came time to warn his son about drugs and alcohol, he turned to his Blu-ray collection. One night, Maasai sat on the floor of John's bedroom watching Kurosawa's *Seven Samurai*.

"Do you know why they're making fun of Kikuchiyo?" John asked.

"He's drunk."

"He can't defend himself because he's drunk. I want you to remember that."

"My dad loved the role of father and he thought of it as being a teacher," Maasai says. "My dad was really like a friend to me. Some parents, there is a saying, some Black parents say, 'I ain't one of your little friends or whatever.' My dad was my friend. As a teenager my dad trusted me to come in and out of the house when I wanted. . . . I can't imagine my dad was strict about anything."

For high school, he enrolled Maasai at Cate, a prestigious boarding school in Santa Barbara, where tuition ran close to $50,000. Every other weekend, he'd pick him up in his brown Mercedes convertible for the two-hour drive back to Baldwin Hills. He used these long drives on the Pacific Coast Highway to introduce his son to the classics.

"You have to listen to this," he'd say.

"It was on one of these drives I first heard *The Chronic*," Maasai says. "I just remember riding with my dad in his convertible, looking out at the ocean with 'Let Me Ride' playing."

★★★★★

Singleton remained an in-demand director-for-hire following the success of *Four Brothers*. But he struggled getting projects out of development.

Throughout 2005, he worked on *John Singleton's Fear & Respect*, a video game that Paramount planned to later adapt into a feature film. Pitched as *Grand Theft Auto* meets *Boyz N the Hood*, it told the story of Goldie, an ex-con from South Central trying to go straight. Though Midway shot footage for it, the video game developer canceled it in 2006.

For the most part, the movies offered to him bore little resemblance to the ones on which he made his name: *Executive Order: Six*, a supernatural thriller similar to *The Thing* for Relativity Media; *Convoy*, an action-adventure film about truck drivers in the Afghanistan war zone that would've reunited him with producer Lorenzo di Bonaventura, and a live-action adaptation of *The Wheelman*, another di Bonaventura production, and another video game adaptation, but with the added draw of The Fast and the Furious's Vin Diesel as the titular character.

He pursued potential franchise films even after *Shaft* flamed out and Universal didn't invite him back for the next Fast and Furious installment. Singleton was considered by 20th Century Fox for *Live Free or Die Hard* (aka *Die Hard IV*) before they opted for Underworld creator Len Wiseman. He resurrected *Luke Cage* for Sony with Tyrese Gibson as the Hero for Hire, yet the project languished in development hell. His best bet at a series was an adaptation of Tom Clancy's espionage thriller *Without Remorse* for Paramount.

Set in Clancy's lucrative Jack Ryan universe (the first four films, *The Hunt for Red October, Patriot Games, Clear and Present Danger,* and *The Sum of All Fears,* banked close to $800 million worldwide combined), *Without Remorse* told the origin story of John Clark, a Navy SEAL turned CIA officer. In January 2006, Singleton signed on to write and direct the film. He immediately targeted Joaquin Phoenix for the lead. Paramount put the film in turnaround in June.

Shortly thereafter, Singleton left UTA and returned to CAA.

He came close to making *Tulia,* an adaptation of the Nate Blakeslee book about the national scandal that unfolded in the small Texas city of the same name. The subject matter fit snugly into Singleton's wheelhouse. In July 1999, the Panhandle Regional Narcotics Trafficking Task Force arrested forty-six people in a drug sting—thirty-nine of whom were Black, representing approximately 10 percent of Tulia's Black population. Authorities found no drugs, paraphernalia, weapons, or significant bundles of cash on the defendants, yet they received sentences of up to 361 years in prison. The convictions were soon overturned.

Halle Berry had been attached to produce and star alongside her *Monster's Ball* costar Billy Bob Thornton. When Singleton signed on to the Lionsgate Films production in the summer of 2007, he pursued Jennifer Hudson, fresh from her Oscar win for *Dreamgirls. Tulia* was a go picture. An October start date was announced. But before they could begin filming, Berry announced her pregnancy and dropped out of the film.

Singleton also considered optioning *Confessions of a Video Vixen,* the "tell-some" memoir by Karrine Steffans that spent over twenty weeks on the *New York Times* Best Seller list.

Published in June 2005, the book became an immediate sensation for its graphic depiction of the author's sexual escapades with some of the biggest stars in hip-hop and sports, such as DMX, Jay-Z, Puff Daddy, Shaquille O'Neal, Ja Rule, and others.

Singleton viewed Steffans's story as made for the big screen. At its heart, it's a #MeToo precursor. *Confessions* tells of a young woman's journey from an abusive childhood in St. Thomas to the rampant misogyny of the entertainment industry. For years, he urged her to share it with the world.

They met sometime in early 2001, a little over a year after Steffans (aka Elisabeth Ovesen) arrived in Los Angeles. She'd just a left an abusive relationship with the legendary rapper Kool G Rap, whom she met at seventeen and had a son with. She started over at twenty-two, working as a model in music videos for

Jay-Z, R. Kelly, and M.O.P. From there, she descended into a blizzard of sex, drugs, and rock 'n' roll.

On one of their first dates, Singleton took her to the inaugural BET Awards in Las Vegas. He paid for her styling, got her hair done professionally. They walked the red carpet together. During the show, they sat behind Bobby Brown (who she later dated) and Whitney Houston. Steffans woke up early the next morning to find Singleton packing his suitcase.

"Where are you going?" she asked.

"LA. I have shit to do."

*This is kind of a letdown*, she thought.

"I have to get back," he said. Singleton attended the *Baby Boy* premiere the next night.

She sighed and rolled over in the king-size bed, pulling the covers over her head.

"Look, enjoy the suite," he said.

"What do you mean?"

"Enjoy the suite. Charge whatever you want to the room."

"I did. I ordered everything on the menu," Steffans says. She was surprised that Singleton was leaving so soon, especially after her experiences with other rich, powerful men. "We hadn't gotten to the intimate part yet. He wasn't even trying to."

Eventually, they started sleeping together. For the next year or so, they saw each other sporadically, mostly at Singleton's office in Leimert Park or his house in Baldwin Hills. Their relationship soon evolved into something more platonic.

"I never really enjoyed that other part of our friendship," she says. "I don't think John is a great lover. I don't mean that in a physical sense. I mean that in an emotional sense.

"Being his lover was so unfulfilling because you're not getting *him*. John didn't give a fuck about pussy like that. It was an exercise. For him, the first thing was always film and the words. He will always leave you for it and you'll feel left. You might have had an amazing week or two together. But then it's writing time or shooting time and you're going to fall back in the line. How wonderful was it to be the person he called and was like, 'Listen to what I just wrote'? That was way more intimate than having sex with John."

They'd go out and indulge in steaks, drinks, desserts. In time, Steffans shared her poetry with him as well. Later on, she read him excerpts from *Confessions of a*

*Video Vixen.* Singleton, an eager gossip, loved to hear her stories about the rappers she knew intimately. When the book became a phenomenon in the summer of 2005, he suggested turning it into a movie.

Singleton had started thinking casting. Before she knew it, Steffans was being shadowed by both Jill Marie Jones from *Girlfriends* and Elise Neal for the role. Suddenly, she had a change of heart. Steffans felt the industry, Singleton included, viewed her as a fad.

"You've got to strike while the iron is hot," he'd tell her.

Steffans looked at the long game. "John, I don't think you know what I'm doing. I'm a writer for real, for real. *Confessions* was a money grab."

"But think about how much attention a movie will get."

"You want to make this story. I get it. But tell me: How does it end?"

"It ends with you writing a book and becoming a millionaire."

"There's no arc. I'm twenty-seven years old. If we do the movie now, there's no growth. Let's revisit it when I'm in my forties. Let me get to where I'm going and then we'll make a movie."

"Well, lemme know when you feel it's time," he said. "I'd love to turn your story into a movie."

Steffans's press run continued with profiles in the *Washington Post* and the *New York Times,* and television interviews with Bill O'Reilly and Geraldo Rivera. In September 2005, she appeared on Tyra Banks's new nationally syndicated talk show, *The Tyra Banks Show.*

Did Banks know about Steffans's relationship with Singleton? Steffans isn't sure.

"Some women cannot get enough of men who have money and power and influence" is how Banks introduced "Kiss-and-Tell Karrine," as she nicknamed her guest. The sit-down interview in front of a studio audience quickly went off the rails. Banks was seemingly unable to hide her contempt for Steffans, frequently interrupting her guest in a condescending tone.

"It doesn't bother me that you're not ashamed," Banks said. "I admire the fact that you're not ashamed. I think what bothers me is that . . . you knew that naming names would be the thing that made the press—because you were attracted to that. You are attracted to names. You are attracted to celebrity."

She wrapped up the segment asking Steffans, "You're dying inside, aren't you?"

"I wanted to say so bad to her, 'So, you didn't fuck John Singleton for the role in *Higher Learning*?'" Steffans says.

In June 2006, Singleton agreed to a deal with Universal that inched him closer to his long-standing goal of movie moguldom. As part of the pact, he'd finance and produce five low-budget films (no more than $15 million) that the studio would then market and distribute. He had full creative control on the projects.

Universal hoped for Singleton to produce economical genre pictures from Black and Latino filmmakers that appealed to Black and Latino audiences—a formula that had recently made the studio millions. In 2002, Universal purchased *Empire*, a gritty thriller starring John Leguizamo as a South Bronx heroin dealer, for $650,000 at Sundance. The film went on to gross $17.6 million domestic.

As a fan of *Empire*, Singleton wanted to get into business with its creator, the writer and director Franc. Reyes. Sometime in early 2006, he ran into the Bronx native at a Coffee Bean on Fairfax and Sunset. A couple days later they met in Singleton's office on the Paramount lot.

"What do you got for me?" he asked Reyes.

Reyes pitched him the idea for *Illegal Tender*, an action drama about a Puerto Rican family from the South Bronx escaping their violent past.

"I love it," Singleton said. "Write that in a month and we'll get it done."

Reyes submitted his first draft three weeks later. "I considered him a legend at that point," Reyes says. "The fact that he wanted to work together was a pretty big deal for me."

Though the script needed work, Singleton rushed into preproduction, eager to move forward with his first film under his Universal deal. They'd shoot through the summer of 2006 in New York and Puerto Rico. He envisioned *Illegal Tender* as a chance to re-create the magic of the mentor-protégé relationship he enjoyed with Craig Brewer on the set of *Hustle & Flow*.

But Singleton shared a different dynamic with Reyes. They were strikingly similar, for better and for worse: Both Singleton and Reyes were stubborn type-A personalities with healthy egos.

"Craig had a certain respect and reverence for John and certainly would listen," says Preston Holmes, an executive producer on *Illegal Tender*. "Franc. thought he knew best."

Immediately, they clashed on matters ranging from casting to the crew. The friction continued into principal photography with Singleton second-guessing Reyes's choices on set. At one point, he started directing the second unit and tried overruling Reyes's shot list.

"Push in on Millie!" he hollered during a shootout involving the film's heroine, Millie DeLeon (played by Wanda De Jesus). "Push in! Push in! She's having a moment here!"

Reyes gritted his teeth and moved on.

*Illegal Tender*'s problems continued in postproduction. For weeks, Singleton and Reyes butted heads over cuts, transitions, and needle drops until the Puerto Rican director departed for New York to shoot his next film. Singleton took over editing duties, cutting the film with Reyes's editor Tony Ciccone.

"I have a substantial personal stake in this picture," Singleton told him early on. "I don't want this shit to be bootlegged on the internet. No DVDs of the film can leave here. None."

Before leaving for New York, Reyes demanded a copy of the first cut. Normally, Ciccone wouldn't hesitate to burn a DVD; he'd never worked on a film where the producer denied a director a copy of their film. But he remembered Singleton's edict and explained it to Reyes. "Franc. kept persisting and then I relented," Ciccone says. "Ultimately, I learned that was a mistake."

A few days later, they were in the cutting room when Singleton received a text from a colleague in New York. Reyes had shown them the film.

"Great movie, John! Can't wait to see it on the big screen!"

Singleton glowered at him until Ciccone wanted to crawl under a rock.

"How many more ways can I explain this to you?" he said, in a condescending tone. "I have a lot of money invested in this film. If it gets bootlegged, I will lose money. No DVDs."

Ciccone couldn't bring himself to make eye contact. He grimaced and gazed toward the floor.

Singleton fired him a few days later. He told him it was for budgetary reasons.

★★★★★

Universal had low expectations for *Illegal Tender*. The studio released the film on just 512 screens in the dumping ground of late August.

"Not exactly the film we were hoping we might get," says then Universal chairman Marc Shmuger.

Critics hated it (15 percent fresh on Rotten Tomatoes) and audiences ignored it. *Illegal Tender* debuted in sixteenth place with $1.4 million before topping out at $3.1 million. Singleton had now produced two flops within six months; *Black Snake Moan* earned just $9.3 million after its March 2007 release.

Singleton still loved *Illegal Tender*. One night, a few years later, the film's co-lead Rick Gonzalez was up at three a.m. watching television with his wife when the phone rang.

"What's up, J?" Gonzalez asked.

Singleton had come across *Illegal Tender* on the tube and wanted to reminisce. "Hey, man, I just want you to know: We made a classic. We made a fucking classic."

The Brooklyn-born actor had caught Singleton's attention with his performance in 2005's *Coach Carter*. "I can tell you've been putting in the work," Singleton told him during preproduction on *Illegal Tender*. "I also know that Hollywood doesn't understand how to work with you."

*Oh snap*, he thought, *John gets it.*

Singleton worked closely with Gonzalez during their time together. He'd sidle up next to him on set and explain the thinking that went into certain shots. Once production wrapped, he pulled Gonzalez aside and extended some career advice. "Hey, you're gonna have to keep fighting for your roles," he said. "They're not gonna write for you. They're not gonna create any roles for you. You have to hang in there and keep going."

On August 23, 2007, Singleton drove to the USC campus in his Lexus SUV to give a commencement speech for the 2007 Inner-City Filmmakers summer program, an eight-week course for underprivileged incoming freshmen. Lee Davis, a director Singleton had worked with in the 1990s, taught the class; Davis had finally made his film *Running Meters* (retitled *3 A.M.*) in 2001 with Spike Lee producing for Showtime.

Earlier in the summer, Singleton had promised him he'd speak at the kids' graduation. But they lost contact during the preceding weeks. Davis wasn't sure Singleton would show, until he walked onto campus that evening. Singleton delivered a short address to the graduates. Afterward, he sat and chatted for about twenty minutes with Davis and his students.

Later that night, at around eight thirty p.m., Singleton was driving west on Jefferson Boulevard when he struck and killed a pedestrian later identified as a fifty-seven-year-old woman named Constance Russell. "A tragic accident," police called it; Russell was not in the crosswalk when Singleton's Lexus SUV hit her.

Police questioned and released Singleton at the scene. A preliminary investigation found he wasn't speeding or under the influence of drugs or alcohol. He had no legal exposure and wasn't hurt in the accident. But he did not escape unscathed.

# CHAPTER TWENTY-TWO

"**A**re you all right?"

There was no answer on the other side of the line.

"John, are you all right?"

Singleton took a deep breath and exhaled loudly. For the next two minutes, he didn't say a word.

"No," he said finally. "No, I'm not."

"Do you want me to come over?"

"Yeah, come over."

Dion Fearon hung up the phone and scurried to his home in Baldwin Hills. When she arrived, she found Singleton, still dejected from the accident a few days earlier. He sat shoulders slumped, eyes heavy, almost sinking into his couch. She went to his side. Grabbed his hand. Together, they sat in silence.

Singleton first met Fearon in 1993 at Magic City, the fabled Atlanta strip club where she worked. He requested a table dance from her. She declined.

They'd call and hang out sporadically over the years until reconnecting for good around 2005 at Robi Reed's annual barbecue. For years, Reed, who was Spike Lee's go-to casting director on his early films, and who cast *Poetic Justice* for Singleton, hosted a cookout that attracted a who's who of Black Hollywood. Fearon had just returned from a short stint as a television producer in her native Jamaica and needed a job; previously, she executive-produced DMX's 2004 movie adaptation of Donald Goines's *Never Die Alone*.

"Red Ants!" Singleton cried, calling her by his nickname for her.

"Oh, God, what do you want?"

"Where have you been? I've been calling and texting."

She explained what she'd been up to.

"Bad idea," he said. "Those Jamaicans don't know what to do with someone like you. Are you looking for a job?"

"Yeah, I am. But what kind of job? I'm not gonna work as no fluffer," she joked.

He laughed. "No, a real job," he said. "You can come in and be my assistant and we can rock this Hollywood thing together."

In a short time, she became one of his most trusted lieutenants. "He introduced me as his producing partner," Fearon says. "But I did everything for him. When he needed to send a wolf or a barracuda, I'm who showed up."

About three days after the car accident, she appeared at his home. They hadn't spoken since a brief exchange on the night it happened, when Singleton called her to confirm he hadn't been injured.

"I can't believe I took a life," he repeated over and over again in a quiet voice. They talked about the accident, then sat on the couch and watched *The Outlaw Josey Wales.*

After the accident, Singleton cut back on driving. He became more dependent on Fearon and others to chauffeur him around. But he still had to address the lingering trauma.

A friend recommended a collection of essays: *The Extraordinary Nature of Ordinary Things.*

"My simplest book," says Rabbi Steve Leder, "and my most Jewish book."

Singleton reached out to Leder, a Hollywood rabbi out of central casting, through his public email address. They scheduled a meeting in his office on Olympic and Barrington. Leder remembers Singleton as subdued through their initial encounter.

"He didn't blame himself," Leder says. "But he felt understandably awful. I'm not a trained psychologist or psychiatrist, but certainly, in my opinion, John was living with some low- to medium-grade depression as a result of the car accident."

They shared a long conversation. At one point, Singleton asked, "How did this happen?"

"That's not how it works, John," Leder explained. "Expecting that being a good person can protect you from evil is like expecting the bull not to charge because you're a vegetarian. Can I tell you about this guy named Job whose life fell apart due to no fault of his own?"

Singleton visited Leder two or three times a month. Then he'd go six months or so without seeing him. "He worried and thought a lot about being a good dad and a good son," Leder says. They talked about storytelling and parenting, friends and family, slavery and the Holocaust, Baldwin and Hughes, their shared love of the film *Pixote*. They also discussed Abraham and Sarah, Isaac and Rebekah, Jacob, Rachel, and Leah.

Leder spoke the language of God in simple Joel Osteen–like terms using metaphors and similes that an everyman could follow. This new form of religious dialogue intrigued Singleton.

"I think John wanted religion in his life," Leder says. "But he felt that the religion he was raised with and surrounded with lacked answers and perspective. He was a nondogmatic person. The religion he was exposed to was mostly rigidly dogmatic, and it didn't square with his reality and he knew it. He knew particularly after that accident that he wanted and needed faith and perspective in his life and he knew he wasn't finding it within his own religious tradition."

Was Singleton religious? Some girlfriends say they prayed together regularly. Others can't recall seeing him do it at all. In the late 2010s, he told a reporter: "I thank God every day. God guides me and leads me. [Faith] led me through a lot of different journeys where there could have been another path for myself."

"I always thought of my dad as an agnostic person, maybe spiritual but not religious," Maasai says. "He definitely seemed to believe there was an order to the universe—that there was a god, karma, whatever. But to give it a name? I don't know. He didn't talk about prayer. When I converted to Islam in college, he respected my spiritual journey. He also talked about the influence the Nation of Islam had on him growing up."

"I think sailing was John's form of prayer," Leder says. "He felt like much of the rest of his life was out of touch and that when he was sailing, he was in touch with something he very much longed for and needed."

Singleton found peace in sailing. Eventually, he received certification in long-haul sailing from the American Sailing Association. In 2011, he purchased a new fifty-one-foot cruiser—a large vessel for a novice sailor. He named the yacht *J's Dream*.

By the fall of 2008, Singleton still hadn't landed a follow-up to *Four Brothers*. He'd spent the last year or so developing a remake of the Reagan-era television series *The A-Team* for 20th Century Fox. Upon landing the gig, he hired his *2 Fast 2 Furious* collaborators Michael Brandt and Derek Haas, and they rushed to get in a draft before the November 2007 writers' strike.

Singleton had a dream cast in mind that included Bruce Willis as Colonel Hannibal Smith and Woody Harrelson as Murdock. For the role of B. A. Baracus, both Ice Cube and MMA star Quinton "Rampage" Jackson were considered. Singleton envisioned the film as a gritty international thriller, and dispatched his production designer, Keith Brian Burns, to scout locations in London, Jordan, Berlin, Dubai, and Marrakesh. Then the strike halted momentum and creative differences between Singleton and the studio arose. He exited the film in late 2008.

"I left because they were going to make a corny movie," he said. "I wanted to do an '80s-style action picture, a man's movie like *The Dirty Dozen*. They made a mess." Fox reworked *The A-Team* with new writers and Joe Carnahan (*Narc, Smokin' Aces*) directing. Shot primarily in British Columbia, the film was a critical and commercial disappointment upon its release in June 2010.

Shortly after departing the film, Singleton left CAA to sign with Endeavor, his third agency in four years.

He felt like he was losing jobs to inferior directors. When Frank Darabont exited the Jamie Foxx and Gerard Butler revenge thriller *Law Abiding Citizen*, Singleton angled to replace him. He ended up losing the sweepstakes to F. Gary Gray. Singleton had a tough time stomaching the result. Gray had started as a cameraman on *Pump It Up!* with Dee Barnes before graduating to directing music videos for Ice Cube, Coolio, and OutKast, and, eventually, *Friday* for Ice Cube.

Gray reached out to Singleton before directing his next film, *Set It Off*. "He wanted to talk about how John worked with actors," remembers Howard Hobson, who had been a producer on *Pump It Up!* "When I asked John, he gave me a look like, *Do I really have to do this?* But he spent ten to fifteen minutes walking Gary through his process and all the exercises he does with actors. That was generous of him."

The success of *Set It Off* propelled Gray to bigger budgets and pushed him toward genre films such as *The Negotiator*, *The Italian Job*, and the *Get Shorty* sequel, *Be Cool*. Gray had a nice visual eye, but story and character weren't his strengths; the industry, Singleton included, considered him more of a shooter. Singleton vented to friends after the producers hired Gray for *Law Abiding Citizen*, rationalizing that his rate cost him the gig.

Lorenzo di Bonaventura was willing to meet his price for a *Four Brothers* sequel. But the producer would first have to convince Paramount chairman Brad Grey to green-light the film.

"Movies like *Four Brothers* aren't chic to the chairman of a company," di Bonaventura says. "When I was at Warner Bros., Steven Seagal movies made more than everyone else's pictures, but they're not something you talk about at cocktail parties."

Di Bonaventura and Grey ran into each other on the Paramount lot the next January after the release of *Four Brothers*. "Congratulations!" Grey said.

"For what?"

"You made Paramount's most profitable movie last year."

"On a dollar-for-dollar basis?" di Bonaventura asked.

Grey nodded.

"More than *War of the Worlds* and *The Longest Yard*?"

Grey nodded.

"Great, let's make *Three Brothers*!"

Grey looked at di Bonaventura. "Eh, it's not really my type of movie."

"Brad, you just told me that it was your most profitable movie of 2005. You run a studio."

"Yeah, but it's not really what I want to do."

"People love that movie," Mark Wahlberg says. "But I don't think the studio understood how it resonated within the culture and with audiences. I can't go anywhere without people saying, 'Oh! Bobby Mercer back in town!'"

By early 2010, Paramount came around. Singleton and the three surviving brothers (Wahlberg, Tyrese Gibson, and André 3000) seemed poised to return. Titled *Five Brothers*, the sequel would be set on Devil's Night in Detroit and introduce two new brothers: a young foster brother and Bobby Mercer's biological brother. For the latter, the studio discussed Mickey Rourke, who was hot following *The Wrestler*, to play the film's villain. But it never made it past the development stage.

His frustration started to build each time a film fell through. A pattern emerged. "It was a little like back when he was at USC," Bill Straus says. "He'd be like, 'This is going to be great! This is going to be the best! Blah, blah, blah.' Then, once it fell apart, he wouldn't mention the film again."

Singleton tried writing his way out of the slump. In the late 2000s, he worked on scripts that would've added to his "hood trilogy": small films, close to his heart, set in South Central.

"I have to do this for me," he'd tell friends about these personal projects. "I have to get this out of my system."

Friends remember Singleton at his happiest when working on these scripts. Sometimes, he'd email fifteen pages over with the subject line reading *Enjoy*.

He wrote *Brick* with Rampage Jackson in mind for the title role: Charles "Brick" Whitehouse, a gruff ex-con making his way through life juggling two women: an old flame named Shamekka, who changed her name to Shelia after becoming an attorney, and Paige, "a SEXY WHITE GIRL . . . about twenty-five, thick in a way Black men like," who works at Walmart and lives in a trailer with Brick.

Singleton enjoyed writing Paige. She made grilled cheese sandwiches for Brick like one of his girlfriends did for him. For the role, he wanted the former child star Amanda Bynes.

*Brick* made *Baby Boy* and *Hustle & Flow* look commercially appealing by comparison. The language. (The n-word appears forty-three times in the script.) The subject matter. The third act problems. The dialogue ("You want this big Black dick, you white bitch?! That what you want?! Come here! You shaking that big muthafuckin' marshmallow ass up in my face?!"). The full-frontal male nudity, which Rampage Jackson also had a problem with.

"There was one scene where I'm smashing this big white girl from the back and smacking her ass," Jackson says. "But somebody knocks on the door and Brick goes to the door butt naked with his dick hanging. I was like, 'Man, I'm going to need a cock double.' I'm a fighter. Most of my fans are male. I didn't want to be nude in the movie and I didn't want any sex scenes."

*Brick* went out to producers, where it received some interest. "I remember Jason Blum called me because he wanted to make it," Reginald Hudlin says. "But all the other executives in his office hated it. I guess he was asking other Black folk for their opinions. I don't know if he had Black people in his office. So he sent me the script. I read it. Told him I loved it. But the film didn't get made."

*Fight for Love* was an even more personal film—and a greater disappointment. He pitched the project as an unofficial sequel to *Baby Boy* with Tyrese Gibson and Taraji P. Henson starring as Sir and Cookie, ex-lovers with two kids. When he told Vestria Barlow about the idea, she said, "What's it going to be about? There's no more material."

Set at the start of the Great Recession, the film explores how everyday people resort to extreme measures to pay the bills. *Fight for Love* opens with Sir losing his pit bull Rocky in a lengthy dogfighting scene. Afterward, he challenges the dog's owner to a fight and walks away holding his winnings. When Sir and Cookie lose their jobs, they team up in unsanctioned street fights for big bucks (and fall back in love all over again).

Singleton depicted characters and wrote scenes straight from his own life. Sir's seven-year-old daughter is named Cleo. His grandmother Irena closely echoes Singleton's maternal grandmother, Audrey. She lectures Sir: "What did I always tell you, boy? A bitch will dig a nigga a ditch. I say that from experience, 'cause I dug a few holes for many a man that crossed me the wrong way. Take my advice next time and wrap your worm up 'fore you make more babies and have another angry bitch gunning for you."

At times, the women characters seem to be addressing Singleton. "You learned your bad habits from ya momma or grandmomma who always catered to anything you ever wanted but never asked you to do nothing. . . . By the time you got grown, in the back of your mind you resented when women did anything for you because it made you seem less of a man and more like a little boy! Furthermore, you didn't even know how to be a real man because all your sorry life you had nothing but women telling you what to wear, when to eat, when to go out and play!"

At one point in the film, Sir's grandmother tells Cookie, "He strong on the outside but hurting deep on the inside so deep he ain't even seeing it. Sir been walking around with a broken heart way before he even met you, Cookie."

*Fight for Love* ends with Cookie and Sir dancing at their wedding with their children. "I want everybody in the same place. Let's just try to be together as a family for real. You and I can be grown and sexy with no drama, can't we?" he tells her prior to them getting back together.

Singleton announced the project in August 2008. But he couldn't get a studio to green-light the film or his two stars to commit.

"The dogfighting turned everybody off. Everyone who read it told him that," Bruce Cannon says. "But John loved it and wasn't going to change it."

"I told him I couldn't get it made," Sony executive Andrea Giannetti says. "It felt like an indie movie where he would be the star of the Spirit Awards. I think he had Taraji. I was like, 'You're never going to get a big star to play the male lead, because it's her movie.'"

Singleton needed a male lead after Gibson unexpectedly dropped out; Gibson had recently shot the *Transformers* sequel and would soon return to the Fast & Furious franchise in *Fast Five*. Singleton told friends that Gibson's then wife advised him against making "hood films" like *Baby Boy* or *Fight for Love*.

He had drawn up a budget for the film, talked to Preston Holmes and Paul Hall about producing it. There was a lot of excitement there. Once Gibson dropped out, it felt like the rug was pulled out from under him.

"That hurt him," says a friend. "I saw a turn. All of a sudden, he just didn't believe in himself. He started having doubts."

The movie industry had shifted beneath his feet. Studios were no longer content to hit singles and doubles, resulting in the slow death of Singleton's bread and butter, the mid-budget feature. He could've gone the independent route. But he wanted to make mainstream Black movies for major studios.

Everyone was scared to take a risk, and anything that didn't have an A-list actor attached, a superhero, or a numeral in the title was deemed a risk. Singleton became a victim of Hollywood's changing economics. IP had taken over multiplexes; 2007's top ten grossing films were all based on existing material. Foreign markets were more vital than ever. Before green-lighting a film, studio executives would ask, *How does this play in Germany? In Indonesia? Does this work in Mexico? Will this appeal to Chinese audiences? Will we have to edit the film to gain entry into the Chinese market?*

The DVD market also cratered, wiping out a huge ancillary source of income for the studios. DVD sales, which peaked in 2005 at $16.3 billion, had slumped to $11.6 billion in 2008. The Great Recession and the rise of on-demand and streaming would put a stake into the heart of that revenue stream.

Suddenly, it became difficult for Black directors not named Tyler Perry to get funded for character-driven films that didn't include multiple action set pieces.

"As much as Tyler Perry was a success story, we were all impacted by his success," says *Idlewild* director Bryan Barber. "We were told that audiences didn't desire the movies we tried to make. It was like, 'Hey, these are the kind of movies Black people are responding to. You should make these three-million-dollar movies. You should give your actors one take. You should have someone run through in a wig.'"

Nearly two decades into his career, Singleton remained competitive with the next crop of Black directors like Perry. (Singleton soon became embittered toward the multi-hyphenate. He believed Perry's *Madea's Big Happy Family* [2011] lifted a scene from *Fight for Love*.) One afternoon in 2010, he ran into his former assistant Joe Doughrity at Legends Barbershop on Fairfax.

"I'm about to do this film that's going to show everyone," he crowed.

"Show everyone what? Man, you're a living legend," Doughrity said. "These niggas wouldn't be here if not for you. You ain't competing with them."

"I have to remind people sometimes."

Doughrity put his arm on Singleton's shoulder. "Do you ever not want to be the number one guy?" he asked.

Singleton chuckled and made his way over to his barber's chair.

★★★★★

Singleton landed his comeback project in March 2010. On the surface, the film sounded promising: a million-dollar spec script starring the most in-demand young action star in town. But that wasn't what attracted him to the film. Singleton needed a go picture, and *Abduction* was a go picture.

*Abduction* started as a one-line idea inside producer Lee Stollman's office. What if a teenager sees his picture on a milk carton and starts digging for answers? Shawn Christensen, the lead singer of the rock band Stellastarr, then banged out a draft on spec while on tour. Once Christensen filed the script in early 2010, Stollman set his sights on finding a movie star.

He quickly recruited Taylor Lautner. The eighteen-year-old actor had rocketed to stardom after portraying werewolf Jacob Black in *Twilight* and its sequel *New Moon*. Adapted from Stephenie Meyer's best-selling novels, the first two entries in the supernatural romance franchise grossed over a billion dollars combined. With his washboard abs, Lautner became an object of desire for both teenage girls and studio executives. His attachment turned *Abduction* into one of the hottest projects in town. Lionsgate bought the script for a million dollars and handed Lautner $5 million to star.

"It was a really fast sale to production," says Stollman, a former talent agent, who repped Tupac Shakur when Singleton made *Poetic Justice*. "I've only seen one faster, and that was when we represented Kevin James and sold *Paul Blart: Mall Cop* to Sony."

Lionsgate had a window to make the film in the summer of 2010 before Lautner departed for the next *Twilight* sequel in the fall. They needed the best available director. Fortunately, Lionsgate's president of production, Allison Shearmur, a friend for almost twenty years, knew Singleton was available and sent him the script.

"John came in and talked about the story and how he saw it and wanted to shoot it," Stollman says. "It was more of a conversation than him auditioning for us because we all knew him and had a good relationship with him."

Singleton was cognizant that he was a director-for-hire on the project. But he viewed the film as a potential Bourne Identity–like franchise.

Lautner's fame complicated the Pittsburgh-based production. Every morning, hundreds of teenage girls and their parents clustered nearby for a glimpse of the heartthrob. As a result, a cloak-and-dagger mentality permeated the set. Paparazzi were deemed the enemy. Grips erected massive twenty-by-twenty black cartons whenever Lautner went shirtless. One morning, Singleton arrived on set, only to be stopped by security for not displaying his security badge properly.

Singleton rolled his eyes. "Really?" he said. "This is how it goes now? That's what's happening? Interesting."

From the start, Singleton struggled to connect with Lautner. He tried relating to him through film. "I want you to think about this like *Chinatown*," he instructed Lautner before a scene. "I want it to feel like when Jack is uncovering the case." Lautner stared back at him. Eventually, Singleton got him an acting coach.

Lautner was well-liked on set. "A really hardworking, dedicated kid," Stollman says. He handled the bulk of his stunts and addressed everyone, including Singleton, as *sir*. But he carried a tremendous amount of pressure—Lionsgate had bet a $35 million production on him—and it may have been too much for the young actor.

Singleton struggled physically during the shoot. The mandatory physical for insurance purposes typically administered prior to production didn't raise any red flags. But his terrible vision became a point of concern amongst the crew in Pittsburgh. "His peripheral vision was gone," says Doug Torres, the first AD on the picture. "His head had dinks and dents in it from walking into lights and crane arms. I remember oftentimes being like, 'John, are you okay? He'd just say, 'I'm fine. I'm fine.'"

But he wasn't fine. Later on, after he got back to Los Angeles, he had lunch with *New Jack City* producer Doug McHenry at Matsuhisa. He told McHenry that his eyesight had eroded.

"You can't tell anybody," Singleton said. "I don't want to be known as the blind director."

Singleton said this knowing his idol Kurosawa was practically blind when he directed his late-career masterpiece *Ran*.

"You're a storyteller, John," McHenry said, "and some of the greatest storytellers in history had impaired vision. Your gift as a storyteller will not be diminished, because writing is your real gift. Don't let this stop you from telling stories."

His sagging health didn't affect his work on *Abduction*. The dailies looked good. The film didn't need extensive reshoots, only a handful of pickup shots over two days. Singleton was optimistic leading up to *Abduction*'s release. Test screenings were decent. He believed Team Jacob would support the film. When he spoke of sequels during his press run, he genuinely believed it.

In September 2011, *Abduction* opened in fourth place with $10.9 million before ending its domestic run at $28 million. The reviews were more brutal than the box office. Though Singleton had received negative write-ups in the past, critics challenged his basic skills as a director.

"Coming six years after his decent last feature *Four Brothers*, Singleton's directorial hand betrays a bit of rust," said *Variety*. The *New York Times* called Singleton's efforts "cynical hackwork." "The film contains neither the passion nor the competence of his previous genre efforts—*2 Fast 2 Furious* and *Four Brothers*," wrote the *Los Angeles Times*.

Singleton texted with Stollman throughout opening weekend. "It was a crushing moment," Stollman says. "It was devastating for all of us and for John in particular."

Singleton barely left a trace on the film. Aside from Lautner rocking a Roberto Clemente jersey in one scene, *Abduction* didn't include any of Singleton's trademark flourishes that made him, up until now, a distinctive filmmaker.

"A lot of John's special sauce got lost," Stollman says. "This was a job, frankly. We were thrilled to have him. He did great work. It's not a John Singleton movie, per se."

*Abduction* ended Lautner's bid to be a leading man. But it also handed Singleton a one-way ticket to movie jail. He'd spend the next few years clawing his way out.

# CHAPTER TWENTY-THREE

In the summer of 2008, Singleton took Mitzi Andrews island-hopping in the Caribbean. He was a father of five from four women and hadn't directed a movie in years. When they reached Trinidad, the island where her family is from, he proposed. Singleton had asked and secured her father's blessing before the trip.

Andrews and her now-teenage daughter Oriah moved into Singleton's home around 2006 or 2007. For a moment there, he considered relocating. "He wanted to start over with me," she says. Singleton looked at homes in Calabasas before deciding to stay put. He'd never leave the neighborhood. Around this time, he realized how moving had impacted him during his formative years. He and his children had put roots down on Don Carlos Drive in Baldwin Hills. He wasn't about to displace them. Andrews didn't have an issue with being the latest girl-friend to cohabitate with him. She lounged on the same couch as the last woman. Watched the same television set. Used the same toaster.

"The only issue I had was the bed—that bed had just seen too much," she says. Singleton refused to replace it. "But he bought really, really expensive sheets, like five-thousand-dollar sheets. I didn't see the point. Then I lay down on them and was like, *Wow, they were worth it.*"

She made some slight changes, rearranged the furniture, hung some more family photos, "changed the flow of the house, the energy of the house," Andrews says. Then she moved on to planning the wedding. But one thing or another happened, causing a delay.

By the next summer, she was pregnant. The hope was to get married before the baby arrived, but Andrews had a complicated pregnancy. She felt constant pain starting around five months in and spent the remainder of it in and out of doctor's offices and hospitals.

On January 6, 2010, Singleton's forty-second birthday, she gave birth to their child Isis Adonia Syxx Singleton.

Around five weeks later, they planned to celebrate their first Valentine's Day together as new parents. The florist delivered a huge bouquet for Andrews shortly after breakfast. A few hours later, she heard a knock at the door. When she peered outside, she saw a white woman holding the same bouquet she had received that morning. She opened the door.

"Are you Mitzi?" the woman asked.

Andrews recalls looking her up and down.

"My name is Angelina. I've been seeing John for the last thirteen years."

"Come inside," Andrews said. "Would you like some tea?"

Angelina (not her real name) entered and placed her bouquet next to Andrews's flowers. She took out her phone. For the next few minutes, she flipped through pictures of her and Singleton together through the years.

Angelina looked at Isis resting on a blanket. "How did you get pregnant?" she asked. "I've been trying to get pregnant this whole time."

"You can look at me and I'll get pregnant," Andrews said in her bold, Trini accent.

Shortly after Angelina departed, the phone rang. It was Singleton. He'd heard about the encounter.

"Didn't I tell you not to let anyone in the—"

"Nigga, that bitch looked like a fucking delivery girl. Why the fuck would I ever think you were fucking that?"

Later that night when he came home, they argued while the kids ate dinner in the other room. Afterward, Selenesol, now ten, approached Andrews and asked, "Mitzi, you're not going to leave us, are you?"

"These poor babies were caught in this cycle of bullshit," Andrews says.

She tried to make it work. But after a while, she felt embarrassed to be in the relationship. His infidelities revealed themselves at the most arbitrary moments, smacking her in the face when she least expected it. She found a stack of nude pictures when reorganizing his office. Random women posted on her Facebook page to tell her that they'd just been with him or were having his baby.

In September 2011, one of Singleton's girlfriends approached Andrews at the *Abduction* premiere.

"We need to talk as women," she said.

"No, we don't," Andrews responded. She knew the woman's face from her profile picture on social media.

Singleton avoided eye contact when confronted with his indiscretions. He'd make promises—try to talk his way out of the doghouse. They'd have a few good weeks or months. "Then it was right back to the nonsense," Andrews says. She ended up leaving in 2012.

"I had to maintain my sanity," she says. "I couldn't be the happy person that he fell in love with when I'm angry due to all these things. I was never an angry person before."

Andrews's breaking point coincided with her breast cancer diagnosis. She moved back to Toronto with their child—"a better place for her to be living." She could also afford her surgery thanks to Canada's public health care system.

Singleton turned combative toward Andrews in the months following her departure even as she dealt with cancer. "You were with me for the money," he said. Eventually, he apologized, although he did so in broad strokes without specifics. "I'm just really sorry I hurt you," he told her. He came to all her surgeries connected to her cancer—her mastectomy and her breast reconstruction. Soon after, he got her a job as an extra on *The Best Man Holiday*, which was shooting in Toronto.

By that point, she'd forgiven him. "I understood who he was and who he needed to be," Andrews says. "I accepted him for that, and we became good friends afterward."

Who was he? A guy who grew up admiring men like Danny Singleton and John Shaft. A guy who was still defending R. Kelly as late as 2017. "He has a bunch of girlfriends—a lot of people have a bunch of girlfriends," he said to a TMZ reporter. "The women he is with are adult women and they made the decision to be with him. They know what they're getting into, so I don't see what the controversy is really about."

Singleton approached relationships with a cynical mindset. They were using each other. Everything became transactional. He wanted something from them: sex and some level of companionship. They must want something from him, whether it was a role, a fancy vacation, red-bottom heels, a car payment, or next month's rent. When he obliged, he gained a sense of control in the relationship. He'd grown accustomed to people taking from him, extracting, leveraging him, trying to monetize and manipulate him. He became guarded and questioned who loved him for him.

Most of these women did love him. Some knew what they were getting into when they entered his toxic vortex. Yet they'd soon learn about his tendency to hurt the people closest to him.

The loyal ones had a high tolerance for it and, in time, grew accustomed to the pain. They stuck around waiting for their time as The One. The one he'd move into his home. The one he'd take to premieres and the Oscars. The one who'd eventually make him change his ways.

Singleton had women all over the world. New York. Miami. Rio de Janeiro. Paris. Hollywood. The Valley. Down the street from him in Baldwin Hills. He didn't slow down even after turning forty. During this time, he dated famous actresses, unknown actresses, authors, producers, models, and postal workers.

"On Valentine's Day, I would send nine, ten, twelve different floral arrangements to women," Dion Fearon says. "It might go up to fifteen depending on who was in his good graces."

How did he have the time and energy for it? Did he have a sex addiction?

"Oh yeah, we were having a lot of sex and this man still had time to cheat," Andrews says. "We all have vices. John wasn't a smoker. He wasn't into drugs. His vice was women. When he was on a high, he wanted to celebrate with a woman he loved in that moment. When he was low, he needed to fuck something."

He wanted love and stability. But he didn't consider monogamy—settling down felt too much like settling. He told friends he had a fear of being stuck in one place with one woman. He preferred to be always moving. Always writing. Always thinking. Always texting. Next thing. Next thing. Next thing. Nothing is finite. You finish a script; you write another one. You don't hear from one woman; you text the next one in your phone. With time, the behavior became compulsive.

Que Jacobs had recently dropped out of dental school when she met Singleton on the set of *Black Snake Moan*. They crossed paths one morning. On set later that afternoon, he saw Jacobs—an assistant on the film but an aspiring actress—and walked over to her.

"Didn't I just see you?" he asked.

They talked on their lunch break and exchanged numbers. Back in Los Angeles, they ended up meeting for lunch. Some part of him knew that a woman who looked like her wouldn't be interested in him were he not director John Singleton. But in the moment he didn't mind. This was part of the deal.

Jacobs brought up a recent homework assignment in her theater class: a monologue written from the perspective of your complete opposite. Jacobs, a "super-girly" beauty with stunning curves, performed as a "butch lesbian." Singleton asked to read it.

"This shit is so good," he said afterward. "Oh my God, Que. You are a writer."

She took writing courses at UCLA and expanded her monologue into an entire stage play. Over the next eighteen months, she'd send him drafts, which he'd critique. His notes could be brutal. Eventually, she finished the play, titled *It Affects 1, It Affects All*. Singleton financed an April 2011 production of it at the Edgemar Center of the Arts in Santa Monica.

Singleton nicknamed her "the Come-Up Girl," which seemed to double as both a compliment and an insult. One year, he gifted Jacobs a director's chair for her birthday with the sobriquet inscribed on the back. She later wrote a play based on the moniker. It's about "a young woman robbed of her childhood by her mentally ill mother who leverages her assets to seduce wealthy men in order to provide for her family."

They went on like this for years. Hollywood dating. Singleton took her out on the boat. Paid for her certification. She was aboard with him and his instructor, Captain Chuck, on his first overnighter, a three-day trip to Catalina. Shortly after Andrews departed for Toronto, Jacobs moved into his Baldwin Hills home.

He took her to the Oscars three years in a row. *Vanity Fair* parties. He introduced her to Spielberg and Coppola. She talked shop with Halle Berry, who encouraged her to produce her own projects. Flicked it up with Oprah Winfrey and Paul McCartney.

This made her a target of his other girlfriends—the ones who weren't The One. The cycle repeated. She engaged with them just as she did before she had been anointed. Singleton moved on as he always did. Some of his close friends had a rule about not attempting to learn the women's names until after the third introduction. Someone new would always come along.

The women in his life couldn't fill the void he felt inside. There was a certain loneliness to him hinted at in his late-night phone calls and texts to friends. They would be about any random thing. The new Spider-Man movie. An idea. A memory. A story. Tomorrow's shot list. Things that could've waited for the morning. Things that could've been an email.

He didn't sleep much. He had trouble shutting off his brain. But in those late-night hours when he reached out to friends, he was searching for a connection.

The pressure started to get to him. He told friends that he felt like he had "the weight of the world on his shoulders." The lack of work. The women. The kids. The drama. Being stretched so thin that sometimes he just wanted to disappear. Occasionally, he'd show up at Andrews's house in Toronto unannounced.

"I knew he was running away from something," Andrews says. "He just needed to rest his head. I would make some island food for him, maybe some stewed chicken, and he would just sleep and play with Isis."

The simplest things made him happy. He liked to get up in the morning, have a plate of eggs and slices of heirloom tomatoes sprinkled with salt and pepper, sit on the carpet in his bedroom, and watch the news in his boxers.

He'd take an Uber to the marina, jump in his kayak, paddle past the breakwater, turn back toward the shore, clear out his mind, and let the tide bring him in. Then he'd haul back to his boat.

*J's Dream* doubled as a bachelor pad, a man cave, an office, a pied-à-terre. The yacht had the finest slip in Marina del Rey, right on the main channel with views of the other boats coming and going. He took business meetings aboard. In later years, he lived there intermittently. He hosted parties—Fourth of July barbecues with the family; big gatherings with celebrities; one-on-ones with friends where he grilled sea bass and asparagus and poured wine.

More than anything, the boat offered solitude. He'd vanish for days to write or to simply get away from it all. When that didn't provide the distance he craved, he'd itemize his checklist, pack supplies, study the tide, check the weather, chart a course, and set sail for Mexico.

Nine or ten days later, he'd return and hit the grind again.

★★★★★

In October 2011, a few weeks after *Abduction* opened and bombed, Singleton took a meeting with Trevor Engelson at the Soho House in West Hollywood. A thirty-four-year-old talent manager, Engelson had set it up through his friend, Ari Greenburg, Singleton's agent at William Morris Endeavor.

Engelson was swimming in deep waters. At the time, his biggest clients were the writers of *Hotel Transylvania* and some unknown actors he found on YouTube. Growing up in Great Neck, Long Island, he dreamed of working in the entertainment industry and working alongside John Singleton.

As a sixteen-year-old, Engelson made $6.50 an hour cleaning tennis courts for the parks department in the summer of '93. He spent most of his time in a little shack making plans for the future. For inspiration, he hung a one-page advertisement for *Poetic Justice* that he'd ripped out of *People* magazine.

Soon, he headed west, attending USC, majoring in communications after the film school rejected him again and again. He interned. Worked for free. Unloaded equipment on the sets of music videos and commercials, going wherever he could to make contacts. He got a job at *The Tonight Show*. A PA gig on the LL Cool J shark movie *Deep Blue Sea* followed that. He landed in Endeavor's mail room, where he worked his way up to creative assistant before getting fired for stealing a script off his boss's desk.

Engelson started Underground Films, a small management firm/production company. For the next decade he built the business while earning producer credits on forgettable films like *Zoom*, *All about Steve*, and *Remember Me*. When he met with Singleton in the fall of 2011, he'd just bought out his partner and married his future ex-wife Meghan Markle.

"What do you got for me?" Singleton asked.

"I'm gonna help you become the Black Jason Blum," Engelson puffed in his thick Long Island accent. "This is how we're gonna do it. We're gonna raise twenty million. No, no, no, make that forty million. Forty million—no problem. Then, get this, we'll make a bunch of five-million-dollar movies, the way Blum is doing it with horror."

Singleton bit his lip and looked away, stifling a smile.

"But we're not gonna make horror movies—unless you want to make a horror movie. We're gonna make, you know, the kind of movies you make, the ones in your wheelhouse, movies like *Hustle & Flow*. We do that, and then ten years down the line we sell the company for a billion dollars."

"Yeah, I don't need you," Singleton said. "You know I put up my own money for *Hustle & Flow*, made fifteen million bucks, and won an Academy Award. But I like you. What else you got?"

Engelson tapped his foot and rubbed his hands on his knees. "What are you doing in television?" he asked. "Let me tell you what we're gonna do."

"I came up with some bullshit that I pulled out of my ass," Engelson says. "I think he knew I was bullshitting. He liked that mentality." Singleton hired him the next day.

After the meeting, they walked down a grand staircase leading to an elevator. About halfway down, Engelson put out his hand and stopped Singleton mid-stride.

"Um, John, you might not want to take this one."

"Why? What's up?" He couldn't see that far.

Paramount executives Rob Moore and Adam Goodman were waiting for the elevator. Earlier in the week, Singleton had filed a $20 million lawsuit against Paramount Pictures.

"Let's wait for the next one," Engelson said.

"Nah, man, fuck that," Singleton said. "Let's go." He picked up the pace and followed them, squeezing in before the doors closed.

"What's up, Adam? What's up, Rob?" he said, smiling. "How are you guys doing? What's going on?" The elevator ticked down slowly, what seemed like forever. Singleton hopped out and shouted, "See you guys around!"

Singleton accused the studio of breaking the agreement they'd signed at Sundance in 2005. His story went like this: He turned down more money from other studios because Paramount added a two-picture $7 million "put deal" on top of the $9 million to distribute *Hustle & Flow*. Over the next five years, Singleton brought them a number of projects. Some ideas in pitch form. Some package deals, like a Tracy Morgan concert film directed by Spike Lee. Paramount rejected them all. He became convinced that the studio had no intention of honoring the agreement.

What tipped him off? Sometime in 2009, Paramount informed Singleton's reps that the contract voided after five years. Singleton had until January 22, 2010, to deliver the completed pictures.

Singleton's lawsuit argued that Paramount "actively concealed and failed to disclose these conditions" during the negotiations.

People close to him urged him not to pursue litigation. But he insisted it was justified, consequences be damned. That he was standing up for the little guy. Standing up for Black filmmakers. That might've been true. But he also wanted to prove a point: Don't mess with John Singleton.

Singleton settled with Paramount in November 2012, days before the trial's start date. He told friends he received about $5 million. But the damage had been done. Suing a studio was still taboo at the time Singleton took his beef to court. Nowadays, Neal Moritz can sue Universal, settle, and then return to producing Fast & Furious films for the studio.

The combination of box-office failure and litigation made him toxic to potential employers.

Before Singleton got hired for *Abduction*, Lionsgate head Allison Shearmur called Lorenzo di Bonaventura and asked, "Just how difficult is John?" He had a reputation for being difficult about budgets—arguing about budgets and coming in over budget. But everyone liked him. He was part of this big club. The lawsuit changed this perception of him. The upper echelons of Hollywood now looked at him and muttered, *Oh, this guy's a problem.*

Singleton believed his track record would help him avoid movie jail—the term for when a director temporarily can't land work due to personal or professional failures. *Abduction* was the first critical and commercial bomb of his career. Prior to that he had a sparkling résumé: *Boyz N the Hood*, one of the most important movies of the 1990s; two-time Academy Award nominee; four number-one movies; discovered countless movie stars.

Why couldn't he get a job?

He noticed that his white colleagues seemed to get second, third, even fourth chances before facing repercussions. Bryan Singer had a reputation for problematic behavior on set and a dubious box-office record outside the X-Men franchise. But studios handed him big-budget features, until sexual assault accusations during the height of the #MeToo movement derailed his career. For John McTiernan to land in movie jail, he had to make three consecutive bombs (*The 13th Warrior*, *Rollerball*, and *Basic*) and get convicted of making false statements to the FBI after hiring a private investigator to dig up dirt on a producer.

Singleton told marketing people their ideas weren't shit. He talked trash in the press. Pushed back on notes from studio executives. He'd tell them, in so many words, "Shut the fuck up and let me do what I do." So did James Cameron, Michael Bay, David Fincher, Oliver Stone, and countless other directors. Somehow they had managed to avoid the consequences of the label *difficult*.

"I think part of my reputation is that I'm some Black militant guy, really serious, and I don't like white people," Singleton said in an interview. "And it's like, dude, I'm kind of a goofball. I'm funny. I'm self-effacing and everything. But I am very serious about storytelling."

Out in the wilderness, he became disillusioned with the industry. He tried to remain optimistic. But cracks started to form. People close to him are split as to whether his confidence wobbled during this time. But how could it not?

Singleton was a product of the studio system. From the age of nine years old, he wanted to be in their club. To be down. Then it happened, and it was amazing. The money. The women. The respect from his peers, which meant more to him than he let on. The opportunities it opened up. Chats with Spielberg. Visits to the Skywalker Ranch. Parties with Eddie Murphy. Dinners with Spike Lee. Sometimes, he'd visit Carrie Fisher in her house in the Hollywood Hills, and they'd drink wine and watch movies together. The industry that made all that possible had now rejected him.

While he privately grumbled that he'd been ostracized due to the color of his skin, in public, he both attacked and defended the industry for how it handled race. In 2013, he wrote an op-ed for the *Hollywood Reporter* where he tackled the trend of white directors telling Black stories, such as the James Brown biopic *Get On Up*. In the piece, he called out the "latent racism" in the studio system. "Even when there are Black directors or writers involved, some of the films made seem like they're sifted of soul," he wrote. "It's as if studios are saying, 'We want it Black, just not that Black.'"

But then, a few months later, he came to the defense of former collaborators Amy Pascal and Scott Rudin after leaked emails revealed them making racially insensitive jokes about President Barack Obama.

"Pascal and Rudin's comments in the hacked emails are troubling, but from my perspective they don't read as 'racist,'" he wrote in another *Hollywood Reporter* op-ed. "These two people have consistently hired people of color. They stand differently from industry figures who would never hire a Black person, no matter how qualified for any position."

No matter how much he pitched. No matter how hard he pushed. He couldn't get another directing job. Despite his long relationship with Ice Cube and the lobbying efforts of MC Ren, he lost the N.W.A. biopic *Straight Outta Compton* to F. Gary Gray.

"It wasn't like I'd pitch him and people would go, 'Yes, let's go!' It was like, 'Oh, that's an old name. What's he done lately? Oh, he did that Lionsgate movie with that kid from *Twilight*. I don't know. What's he up to now?'" Engelson says.

He didn't have much to fall back on. The five-picture deal that he signed with Universal in 2006 had fizzled away and the studios weren't interested in his original screenplays. He never stopped writing. But during this time the quality of his work diminished. *Blame Rio!*, a script he finished in 2013, was a disastrous attempt to expand into out-and-out comedy.

In the script, an unfunny facsimile of *The Hangover* crossed with a horndog version of *The Bucket List*, Joe, a middle-aged guy, tags along with his dying father to Brazil for one "last wild ride." Joe's dad is described in the script as a "cool-ass player" who "always gotta be the center of attention."

About halfway through the script, Joe's dad pops a little blue pill and suffers a heart attack or stroke in a Rio de Janeiro "whorehouse." Joe rides with him in the back of the ambulance, tightly grasping his hand. There, on the way to the hospital, Joe shares his dying wish for his son.

"I want you to promise me you'll find someone you love with all your heart and soul and who loves you back, that you can take care of and who will take care of you. Have kids and a family."

"What happened to never get married and conquer as much as you can in a lifetime?"

"Macho bullshit. I said that to make sure you weren't gay. There's only so much ass you can conquer in one life, believe me, I've tried. Put my all into it but it leads to nothing, son. Don't end up like me."

Then the blanket covering the dad's naked body flies off, revealing a fourteen-inch erection.

★★★★★

In February 2014, he agreed to write and direct a Tupac Shakur biopic for Morgan Creek. He felt emotionally ready to tackle the project after turning it down several times in the past; Antoine Fuqua had the job prior to him but couldn't find the right star or script.

Singleton decided early on he had to tell the truth about Tupac, or at least his version of it. "There's a lot of stuff I may do that may piss a lot of people off," he said of his planned warts-and-all biopic.

Shortly after signing the deal, he visited the scene of the rapper's murder at the intersection of East Flamingo and Koval in Las Vegas. He reflected on what Shakur meant to him. What he meant to Black people. What was lost with his murder. The void he left.

Before writing, Singleton sat on his boat and contemplated their time together. The *Poetic Justice* set. Freaknik. *Yo! MTV Raps.* He thought about the complexities of Tupac. His brilliance. His madness. His rapid descent into violence, incarceration, and death. What was he like in the days prior to his murder? He reached out for conversations with people who knew him. His early manager Atron Gregory. Suge Knight. Afeni Shakur, who gave John her blessing on the project.

Shakur started to visit Singleton in his dreams.

"Tupac was very much alive to him," says Cheo Hodari Coker, who'd written a draft for Fuqua. "It was almost like writing a movie was an opportunity to have a conversation with his friend."

As part of his preparation, Singleton studied classic films featuring singular performances from strong male leads. *Taxi Driver. All That Jazz. Scarface. American Gangster. The Wolf of Wall Street.* For visual inspiration he pored over his

F. W. Murnau box set, hoping to pick something up from the German silent film master. His chief concern with the script was the dialogue. "I have to get the words right," he'd tell his friends.

Singleton banged out a script in the spring of 2014. When he finished, he asked Engelson to read it.

"I'll send a messenger," Engelson said.

"Come to my boat."

"Why can't I just send a messenger?"

"This thing is not leaving my sight. Come to the boat. Read it here."

On a Saturday afternoon, Engelson and Singleton's feature agent, Rich Cook, arrived at *J's Dream* for a curated reading of *Tupac Amaru Shakur*. Singleton handed each a cocktail and a hard copy of the script.

"All right, enjoy," he said. He skipped across the deck and set up a Bluetooth. Marvin Gaye's "Don't Mess with Mister 'T,'" which Singleton planned to open the movie with, then pierced through his speakers.

A few minutes later, he returned.

"Hey, what page are you guys on? Sixteen?" He cued up Curtis Mayfield's "Little Child Runnin' Wild." It went on like this for the next few hours. More drinks. More records. "Play at Your Own Risk" by Planet Patrol. Eric B. and Rakim's "My Melody." Marlena Shaw's "Women of the Ghetto." When Shakur bobbed his head along to the "So Many Tears" instrumental on page one hundred, Singleton played the Shock G–produced track for his audience.

At a colossal 156 pages, Singleton aimed for something epic with *Tupac Amaru Shakur*. The film had to hit all the expected beats for a movie on Tupac's life: the "Same Song" video; the Quad Studios shooting; Afeni spiraling into drug addiction; the *Juice* audition; the violence and excess that marked his time at Death Row Records. But Singleton also aimed to avoid the standard music biopic format.

Scenes of Shakur's birth are interspersed with Inca chief Túpac Amaru leading troops into battle in sixteenth-century Peru. Singleton wanted to emphasize the revolutionary elements of Shakur. At one point in the film, Tupac's face is superimposed onto that of George Jackson, the Black Panther activist and cofounder of the Black Guerrilla Family, as he's shot in the San Quentin yard.

In the script's most bizarre scene, Tupac travels back to eighteenth-century Peru and morphs into Tupac Amaru II. An *Apocalypto*-like battle follows, with him slaughtering the invading Spaniards. He's then captured, drawn and quartered, and beheaded. Then things get weird. Modern-day Tupac picks up his decapitated head, shares a blunt with it, and they have a conversation ending with the head christening him Makaveli.

Singleton's script also had a whimsical quality to it. After Tupac attacks the Black Hollywood establishment during a BET interview, the film cuts to John Singleton in his home ("black, thin, horn-rimmed glasses . . . eating a BOWL OF SUPER SUGAR SMACKS"). "That's who I need to fucking work with! Tell them, Tupac!" he says before the film returns to Shakur conferring with his publicist.

The script isn't perfect. It's at least ten to twenty pages too long. The Madonna cameo is cringeworthy. "People who busy themselves with caring what others think about them aren't free. They are slaves," she tells Tupac as they share a bed. "You define who you are and let the world accept it or not."

As he expected, the script pissed a lot of people off. It implied that Afeni Shakur had a threesome while nine-year-old Tupac sat in the next room watching television. An early version of the script also included a scene where six "PREDATORY and DEGENERATE" inmates attack Shakur. Prior to that, one of the prisoners licks his lips, eyeing him.

"As [the guards] walk away we see the six men rush toward TUPAC and him fighting them off from the glass in the doorway. The camera pulls away and down the hallway as we hear the HORROR sounds of the prison. The cacophony of the men in their cells."

"I thought the script was excellent," says Preston Holmes, a longtime friend of the Shakur family. "I thought that should be the movie."

But the studio and the film's producer L. T. Hutton, a Dogg Pound associate who knew Shakur during his time at Death Row, hated it. The numerous sex scenes. The severed head. Singleton's self-referential cameo. ("It's not about you," Hutton said. "This isn't *My Long Walk with Tupac*. It's not *Tupac and Me*.") More than anything, he hated the prison rape scene. Called it defamatory.

Singleton felt the studio leaned on Hutton to play it safe. "Hutton was cool until the white folks tried to take over. He had to toe the line but what he did wasn't necessary," he told a friend.

Morgan Creek wanted a concert film. Hutton preferred a hagiography of the rapper. Singleton submitted rewrites, but the studio wouldn't approve the script. In the end, he wasn't going to make anything but the Tupac movie he wanted to make. He'd learned his lesson from *Shaft*. In early 2015, about a year after signing on to it, he left the project.

"He was devastated," says Kimberly Hardin, who set up casting calls and auditions for the film.

Singleton didn't exit quietly. Upon the announcement that Carl Franklin would replace him, he posted a lengthy screed on Instagram. "Real talk! The reason I am not making this picture is because the people involved aren't really respectful of the legacy of Tupac Amaru Shakur. . . . If Tupac knew what was going on he'd ride on all these fools and take it to the streets. But I won't do that."

For years, he blasted the project during interviews, taking swipes at Hutton, Morgan Creek, and Benny Boom, who ultimately replaced Franklin as the film's director.

Singleton's predictions came true when *All Eyez on Me* opened in June 2017. "The movie churns out Tupac's story like sausage meat," wrote the *Financial Times*. *New York* magazine called it a "faithful adaptation of the rapper's Wikipedia entry." RogerEbert.com dubbed the film "one of the most useless biopics ever made."

*All Eyez on Me* received an 18 percent score at Rotten Tomatoes and disappointed at the box office, earning $44.9 million domestic against a $40 million production budget. Singleton claimed to have never watched the film.

"That was supposed to be our generation's Malcolm X," he said. "Now we have a rapper movie that was in theaters for two weeks."

# CHAPTER TWENTY-FOUR

**B**orn into a military family in 1976, Eric Amadio grew up loving his country. His dad flew in the air force. Mom worked for J. Edgar Hoover's FBI. His uncle fought in Vietnam. As a kid living on the border of Downey and Pico Rivera, Amadio had a front-row seat to the explosion of crack and the war between the Bloods and Crips. He lost his first friend to gang violence at the age of eleven. It wouldn't be the last.

After graduating high school, Amadio, the grandson of an undocumented Italian immigrant, attended San Francisco State, a public university with a very activist and anti-government bent. And that's where he learned that everything he had believed in was, in fact, a lie.

At the age of nineteen, Amadio read Dark Alliance, an investigative series published in the *San Jose Mercury News*. Over the course of three articles, reporter Gary Webb spun a tangled, shocking tale. Webb alleged that CIA agents smuggled cocaine into the United States, then used the profits to arm the Contras, a Nicaraguan anticommunist rebel group.

And what happened to the tons of nearly pure cocaine? It hit the streets, igniting the crack epidemic of the 1980s with South Central LA serving as its epicenter.

"I was furious," Amadio says. "This was personal for me. I was raised to be a full-blown patriot and this notion that our government was involved in this really threw me for a loop."

For the next fifteen years, he went down the rabbit hole researching the story. He hadn't decided yet whether it would be a novel or a movie. But one thing remained certain: At some point, he'd write it. He came up with a plot. A good kid with family obligations meets a CIA agent with his back up against the wall. Together, they unleash a plague on the community. Amadio tabled the idea, though, as he worked his way into the film industry, writing and directing two small indie films in the late 2000s.

Like many young filmmakers of this era, Amadio transitioned to television. "It felt like getting sent to the minors," he said. But he held an advantage over his peers. His experience in film allowed him to skip past the writers' room grind and straight to pitching shows. He quickly sold a series to Starz about the business of professional football called *Offseason*.

"What's next?" asked his agent, Evan Silverberg of Underground Films.

And that's when Amadio mentioned his dream project: *Red, White, and Blue*. The red stood for the Bloods, the blue for the Crips, and the white was for the cocaine.

"That's cool as shit," Silverberg said. "Let's bring it to Trevor."

A few weeks later, Trevor Engelson invited Silverberg and Amadio to City Spa, a shvitz on Pico, to celebrate. They ordered some beers. Got a good sweat going.

Silverberg turned to Amadio. "Tell Trevor about your idea," he said.

Amadio laid out his plans for *Red, White, and Blue*.

"I want to do something about where I grew up," Amadio said. "The neighborhood changed in the 1980s and it had everything to do with the CIA bringing in coke."

Engelson scoffed and shook his head. "That's an urban legend," he said. "Folklore."

Amadio recited a CliffsNotes version of Dark Alliance. "Look it up if you don't believe me," he said.

Engelson's eyes shone with excitement. "I just signed John Singleton," he said. "He has something similar he's really passionate about. Let's put you guys together. See what happens."

★★★★★

Singleton also considered television to be the minor leagues.

Back when he started out in the early 1990s, being referred to as a "TV director" was a slur. Singleton once compared the work to selling drugs: Once you get in, there's no getting out. But he dabbled a bit, even though it felt like slumming.

In November 1997, he signed a seven-figure development and production deal with Warner Bros. TV to create programs for the studio. He immediately procured a six-episode commitment for *CRASH*, a one-hour drama about the LAPD SWAT team. ABC planned for it to debut in their fall 1998 lineup. But Singleton couldn't be pried away from *Shaft* to work on a network show.

Every so often, he'd flirt with television. In the early 2000s, he developed a show with *Menace II Society* writer Tyger Williams at FX. He sold an hour-long drama about high-class sex workers to Showtime in 2007 called *Trade*. Epix showed some interest in a miniseries he pitched about the first government agents. But none of the shows made it out of development. His heart was never really in it. He had a blind spot toward television, missing out on opportunities to direct episodes of *The Wire* and *The Shield*. In 2008 Warner Bros. terminated his deal.

Singleton altered his stance once *Abduction* flopped and he landed in movie jail. The perception around television had also changed.

The prestige TV era was in full effect. *The Sopranos. The Wire. Sex and the City.* Suddenly, the writing improved, the storytelling became more ambitious, the production values increased. HBO changed the game. Then everyone got in on it. Showtime had *Dexter, Weeds*, and *Homeland*. American Movie Classics shifted from airing reruns of *The Basketball Diaries* and *Volcano* to original programing such as *Mad Men* and *Breaking Bad*. FX's *The Shield* and *Rescue Me* scored millions of viewers and dozens of Emmy nominations.

With the movie industry focused more than ever on sequels and superheroes, feature film writers and directors flocked to television for the storytelling opportunities—and for the paychecks.

"When I realized they were going to give me twelve million bucks to make a one-hour pilot, I figured I'd take a shot at it," Brett Ratner says about his decision to direct the pilot episode of *Prison Break* and executive-produce the series.

More than anything, television had overtaken film as a driver of pop culture. The internet acted as an accelerant—social media turned both big hits and niche shows into can't-miss communal experiences. Facebook and Tumblr posts. Twitter watch-alongs. Reddit threads. The comments section on blogs.

Singleton slowly came around to recognizing the moment. Now in exile, he had no choice.

The movie offers weren't coming in. Meanwhile, Engelson haggled him to adapt his films into television. "Low-hanging fruit," he called it.

About three months into working for him, Engelson approached Singleton with a compelling idea.

"I know it's sacred, but what about doing *Boyz N the Hood* as a TV show?" he suggested.

"Nah, I'm not doing that."

"Just call it: *Boyz N the Hood: The Series*."

Singleton pursed his lips. He moved on.

"He never used the word sacrilege, but that's the vibe I got," Engelson says.

Singleton wasn't against mining his filmography for potential television. In August 2009, he tweeted, "Writing like a beast. *Baby Boy* the TV show coming in 2010." But he didn't have a clear vision of it yet.

Around this time, he could be found slouching in the beanbag in his office binge-watching *The Sopranos* on repeat. The more he learned about television, the more he realized he had to learn. Singleton studied how to write for episode cliffhangers and commercial breaks. He noticed the pacing in television moved faster. Close-ups were utilized more often than he preferred.

He had the benefit of several cicerones, friends and colleagues who worked in television, willing to walk him through the ins and outs of the business. The radically different shooting schedule. The limited prep time. They gave him feedback on his scripts. Put him on to the politics of the industry. Schooled him on how the showrunner is king in television, while directors are interchangeable. How the network hovers over every part of the process. They're looking at dailies, giving notes on actors, commenting on the script.

"It's ten times worse than film," Ratner says. "You have these television executives who've never made a film second-guessing every casting decision, every page. Who wants to be a part of that? The whole reason to be a feature film director was to have freedom."

Singleton started taking some swings. In 2013, he sold *Club Life: Miami*, a drama about a reformed criminal falling into South Beach's nightlife, to HBO, and was set to co-executive-produce the series with Russell Simmons. But he struggled with the script, cramming three episodes worth of plot into the pilot. The series didn't move forward at the network.

But he soon met the right collaborator, a writer almost as obsessed with 1980s Los Angeles as he was, and who also wanted to make a television show about it.

★★★★★

Amadio committed the instant he heard the name John Singleton.

"I'm a kid from the neighborhood," he says. "John is one of the reasons why I became a filmmaker. He showed an entire generation of kids, where there wasn't hope. All my friends are tradesmen. We weren't encouraged to dream. John was one of those dudes that made you go, 'Fuck, it's possible.'"

He showed up late for a meeting on Singleton's boat after Engelson handed him a slip number and wished him good luck. When Amadio arrived in Marina del Rey, he parked his car and meandered through the port, searching for the right dock. Finally, he found it. Singleton stood on his boat wearing board shorts and flip-flops. Big, warm smile on his face. He welcomed him aboard. They settled on the deck.

"Tell me about this idea," Singleton said.

For the next hour or so, they talked about growing up in Los Angeles.

Singleton remembered an era before crack—when the Spanish art deco homes didn't have bars on their windows. Neighbors raised each other's kids. People took pride in their lawns. Children played in the streets past dusk with streetlamps illuminating touch football games.

Then everything changed.

*Red, White, and Blue* offered Singleton an opportunity to tell these very Black, very California, very human stories he held dear. He jumped at the idea of partnering with Amadio.

They met frequently throughout early 2014, brainstorming storylines, hatching ideas, coming up with characters like a luchador turned cartel courier. Amadio would trigger Singleton's memory and off he'd go for five, ten, fifteen minutes. He loved to tell stories about things that happened to him and events he had witnessed. He'd act out scenes. Maintain eye contact. Raise his voice. Sprinkle in little details he remembered (and some he embellished). Then he'd let out that cackle. The Laugh. If he was really feeling it, he'd just go crazy, clapping his hands and smacking his knee. Singleton, unassumingly, straddled the line between socially awkward and charismatic.

Both he and Amadio realized early on there were parallels between the dramatic series they were creating and the life of Freeway Rick Ross, the Los Angeles crack kingpin who, according to prosecutors, amassed nearly $300 million in profits between 1982 and 1989. Ross was sentenced to life in prison in 1996—the same year the Dark Alliance series reported on the link between his operation and the Iran-Contra affair.

Singleton had breakfast with him in the early 1990s and encountered Ross again after he got out on appeal in 2009. There was talk of a collaboration, maybe a movie. "He was helping me put my script together," Ross said. From there, Ross claims, Singleton ghosted him.

"John and I always made a point not to do the Freeway Ricky story," Amadio says. "It was more a correlation of these different neighborhood legends. Certainly,

Freeway Ricky was the guy and the biggest. But there was a bigger story about America that we were more interested in telling."

One afternoon, Amadio showed up at the marina to review the final pitch document with Singleton—one last appraisal before meeting with the networks. When he got there, he noticed him smiling from ear to ear.

"Come on, come on," Singleton said, sliding across the deck. "So, I was thinking about the title. I don't know, man."

"I'm not in love with it either," Amadio admitted.

"So, I think I have something. It's good."

"What is it?"

"Guess."

"I can't. Just tell me."

"Are you sure? You don't want to guess? It's good."

"John, what's the new title?"

"*Snowfall*."

Engelson partnered with the veteran film and television producer Michael London to shop the project around town. They quickly found a buyer. In April 2014, Showtime acquired the series with an aggressive offer. But the network couldn't figure out what to do with it. After a short development cycle, they put it in turnaround. The *Snowfall* team regrouped. They remained confident they'd find a new home in no time.

"We were disappointed, obviously," Amadio says. "But the truth was we now had a good script and we still had John directing."

★★★★★

One afternoon around this time, Singleton was watching a movie on his boat when Lee Daniels, the Academy Award–nominated director of *Precious*, called.

"I need you to come to Chicago," Daniels said.

Singleton immediately knew what was in Chicago. A few weeks earlier, Taraji P. Henson had told him all about Daniels's new series *Empire*.

"I need you to come in and show these white people what this show can be," Daniels said.

Singleton snickered. "Man, you wouldn't have this show if I didn't pay for *Hustle & Flow*."

He felt he'd birthed *Empire*, a one-hour Fox drama starring *Hustle & Flow* duo Terrence Howard and Henson as Lucious and Cookie Lyon, a divorced couple battling over Empire Entertainment, a record label/management firm in the mold of Jay-Z's Roc Nation.

Reuniting DJay and Shug proved to be a casting coup. *Empire*'s pilot received rapturous reviews and blockbuster ratings when it aired on January 7, 2015. With over 9.9 million viewers, it was Fox's highest-rated debut in three years. *Empire* arrived at the right moment: a fun, opulent series at a time when television had gotten too dark and depressing. Daniels aimed to make a Black version of the 1980s prime-time soap *Dynasty* set in the gilded world of the hip-hop industry and had stuck the landing.

"You've got to do an episode," Malcolm Spellman, the show's writer and coproducer, urged Singleton. "This is, by far, the Blackest shit on TV."

Daniels booked him to direct the fifth episode of the series, "Dangerous Bonds." But he encountered pushback from Fox network executives after advocating for Singleton.

*He can't. He's never directed TV before. He doesn't know how to do it.*

Singleton met with *Empire* showrunner Ilene Chaiken. "The things that he said to me indicated that he understood the rigors of television directing," she said. Chaiken sent him to meet with the network. Through a series of interviews, he won them over as well. Then he stepped onto the set and validated each and every one of the concerns the network had about him.

Over twenty years into his career, Singleton had his way of working. He broke down the script and mapped out each shot and each scene and went about directing as if it were a film. Television doesn't work that way though. Showrunners and producers prefer having a lot of options in the editing room. They want directors to shoot extraneous coverage. When Singleton failed to provide it for them, it irked certain higher-ups on the show.

He put his stamp on "Dangerous Bonds." One of the episode's main storylines centered on the Lyons' youngest son, Hakeem, shooting a music video for his new single "Drip Drop." Singleton imagined it as the kind of ornate, big-budget clip from the industry's halcyon pre-Napster days. He requested video vixens, a giant bed, and a wall of water.

"We can't do that," production said. "It costs too much and we don't have the stage space for it."

"Well, I'm going to do it," Singleton said.

Production didn't expect him to go through with it. But he figured out how to get it done within the budget.

*Empire*'s viewership had climbed each week since its premiere. By the time Singleton's episode aired on February 4, the show was the ninth-highest-rated series on television and approaching pop culture phenomenon status. Critics called "Dangerous Bonds" one of the standouts of the first season. "The rollicking episode cemented the force-of-nature status of Cookie Lyon's character, played by Taraji P. Henson," *Variety* exclaimed.

Singleton walked away from the experience surging with confidence. Afterward, he told Dion Fearon, "We are going to take over TV."

★★★★★

Once Showtime put *Snowfall* in turnaround, Michael London started talking to FX EVP of Series Development Nicole Clemens, while Engelson simultaneously reached out to his college pal Eric Schrier, the network's president of original programming.

If HBO and Showtime were the New York Yankees and Los Angeles Dodgers of cable television—the glamour franchises with deep pockets and championship banners—FX operated like the *Moneyball*-era Oakland Athletics, an outsider brand looking for an edge while maintaining a sensible budget.

Led by chairman John Landgraf, long considered one of the sharpest minds in the business, FX had guided a diverse array of hit shows onto the air, such as *Rescue Me, Louie,* and *It's Always Sunny in Philadelphia.* But the network had entered a transition phase when *Snowfall* appeared on its radar in early 2015. Longtime hits *Sons of Anarchy* and *Justified* had just ended their run; *The Strain,* a goofy vampire thriller from Guillermo del Toro, debuted with strong ratings before viewership fizzled; one of the best shows on television, the Cold War spy drama *The Americans* struggled to find a sizable audience; and *The Bridge,* a whodunit set on the El Paso/Juarez border, floundered after its promising start. More than ever, the network needed a hit. Clemens scheduled a meeting with Singleton.

Amadio handled the bulk of the presentation with Singleton enthusiastically punching in like John Madden on color commentary. Together, they explained the narrative at the heart of *Snowfall*: the saga of Franklin Saint, the young striver from South Central who develops into a crack kingpin over the course of the series. They framed the show as a sweeping history of America and evoked Henry Ford when describing Saint. But their pitch also honed in on extremely specific and personal details—the show's flavor.

"South Central Los Angeles, 1983," Singleton said, standing at the head of a long conference room table. "Franklin and his friends walk up to a house party. Outside, two lowriders are parked on the lawn. Smoke from a barbecue grill billows into the air. We follow Franklin into the party. Everyone is dancing to funk-based early hip-hop. 'Clear' by Cybotron. We follow him through the party. People are doing the freak, grinding on each other. It's like sex with clothes on. You're gonna see the sweat on people. The music is gonna be bumping. . . ."

"It was one of the best director pitch-tone meetings we ever had," Schrier says.

Before they left the conference room, a development executive offered some advice.

"Make it a little less Showtime and a little more FX," he said. "Be weird."

Amadio went home and started rewriting the pilot. He fixated on the note.

Be weird.

Be weird.

Be weird.

He remembered something that happened at a party long ago. He filed it away, knowing he'd eventually put it in a script. Be weird? He'd seen some weird shit in his day.

Amadio started spiraling after hitting send on the email. "He's going to think I'm fucked up. John's going to think I'm some weirdo. Shit, this is bad."

About an hour or so later, Singleton called.

"You crazy motherfucker!" he screamed. "Oh my God. Oh my God! You crazy motherfucker. I can't believe it. I can't—"

Amadio added a scene during which a woman fills a straw with cocaine and blows it up a character's ass while he's receiving oral sex from another woman.

"They said be weird. I've never seen that on television before."

"You sick fuck," Singleton said. "This is either gonna make us or break us. They're either gonna say, 'Never come back again' or they're going to order the show."

They ordered the show to pilot.

From the start, FX planned to hire an experienced writer/producer to act as showrunner on the series. Singleton approached Charles Murray about the job. Over the last fifteen years, Murray had worked in all areas of television, ascending from writer to story editor to supervising production on a host of shows: *Third Watch*, *Criminal Minds*, *V*, and *Castle*. Having recently wrapped a stint as a co–executive producer on *Sons of Anarchy*, he knew the inner workings of the network.

They'd formally met a few years earlier after appearing on a panel together about breaking into the television business. After it concluded, Singleton approached Murray.

"Hey, man, I'd love to stay in touch, maybe grab some coffee or something, because I'm getting into television, and would love to talk about TV and—"

"John, I know you already."

"Huh?"

Murray looked at him. Turned his head. Looked back at him. Staring.

"Your dad is married to my wife's aunt. I sat across from you at the wedding. We've spent Thanksgiving together."

Singleton laughed.

"Yeah, we can get together," Murray said.

Murray had been one of the voices Singleton leaned on when he started out in television. Now he hoped he could marshal *Snowfall* to the screen. But Murray had just agreed to executive-produce *Luke Cage* for Cheo Hodari Coker over at Netflix.

FX turned to Dave Andron, a writer and producer on *Justified*, the neo-Western crime drama based on Elmore Leonard's stories. Over six seasons, Andron, a writer and producer raised in Philly, learned how to master Leonard's voice and perspective. He did his homework on Harlan County, Kentucky, the show's setting. The network believed he could replicate the feat vis-à-vis John Singleton and South Central.

"Dave had come up through a really good farm system and just had a lot of good technical facilities," Landgraf says. "He was ready to take on a leadership role."

Andron assembled a mini writers' room consisting of Singleton and Amadio, the two creators of the show, the *Justified* writer Leonard Chang, and, at Singleton's behest, Walter Mosley, the novelist best known for creating the Easy Rawlins series. For the next month or two, they prepped the pilot and broke down a ten-episode first season. Singleton now had to find his Franklin Saint.

★★★★★

During casting, Singleton reunited with the kid people had once dubbed the Next John Singleton.

"Are you going to the audition?" he asked Malcolm M. Mays, a twenty-five-year-old actor, writer, and director.

"Yeah," Mays said, looking at him.

"Good luck, man," Singleton said as he walked out of the elevator.

*This nigga didn't realize it was me,* Mays thought.

Singleton didn't catch on until after Mays auditioned. Singleton removed his glasses and squinted. Then put them back on. "Malcolm? Is that you?"

"You know him?" someone asked.

"Nigga, that's my son!"

Singleton and Mays hadn't spoken to each other in two or three years prior to the audition. They first met in early 2008, a few months after the *New York Times* profiled Mays in the Arts section.

He had a familiar story. A smart, precocious kid from Los Angeles, Mays bounced around schools hoping to avoid the street violence that claimed his friends. All the while he dreamed of making movies. He told his junior high school friends he'd become a rich and famous filmmaker. Then, through a mix of talent, ingenuity, hard work, and a little luck, he made it happen.

Mays scored an interview with Peter Guber when the former Sony chairman spoke at his church; he procured an internship with director Martin Campbell (*GoldenEye, The Mask of Zorro, Casino Royale*) through the athletic trainer at his high school. At the age of fifteen, his short film *Open Door* gained acceptance into a film festival. Soon after, he wrote a screenplay about racial tension between Black and Latino high school students that led to recognition from Panavision's New Filmmakers Program. UTA selected him for a mentorship program. When one of the agents applauded him for taking an interest in filmmaking, Mays shot back, "It's not what I want to do. It's what I'm going to do."

Mays climbed the industry ladder accumulating mentors and admirers along the way. A junior executive at Sony introduced him to Denzel Washington's long-time collaborator, the producer Todd Black, who put him in touch with Sony's president of studio operations, Gary Martin—the same Gary Martin who had an office next door to John Singleton during the summer of 1990. Martin had little success putting Mays in touch with him until Singleton read about Mays in the *New York Times.*

One afternoon in February 2008, Singleton called Mays, then an eighteen-year-old high school student, as he sat in math class.

"It's John Singleton."

Mays thought his cousin had pranked called him. "Right, bro, please. Stop playing. I'm gonna fight you."

"This is John Singleton, and I'll fight you too!"

Suddenly, the bass exited Mays's voice. "Hey, how are you doing? Sorry about that."

"What are you doing tonight?"

"Nothing, I think."

"Can you come to the Skirball Cultural Center? Bring your momma."

Later that evening, Singleton hosted a screening of the 1970 Hal Ashby film *The Landlord*. Afterward he met the kid he'd heard so much about.

"How are you here?" Singleton told Mays. "I thought there was just one of me."

Their relationship quickly progressed past that of mentor and protégé.

"He was really a father figure for me," Mays said. "I have daddy issues. He has son issues. And we connected. He looked at me like a son figure."

Singleton's "son issues" were deep-rooted, emanating from when Maasai moved in with him. Maasai resented him for how he handled the custody battle with his and Cleo's mother. Singleton, with time, came to think of his son as spoiled; he had immense respect for people like Mays who paved their own path.

After graduating high school, Maasai followed in his father's footsteps, enrolling in USC film school.

Singleton's presence loomed large on campus.

As an underclassman, Maasai registered for a two-semester writing course taught by Tyger Williams, the *Menace II Society* screenwriter and a friend of his father. A vintage *Boyz N the Hood* poster from Cannes hung in the classroom.

"I know it was hard for him. It's hard enough he had to sit there and stare at his dad's poster every time he walked into the classroom," Williams says. "We had a couple of conversations about establishing his own identity and what it's like to live in the shadow of someone like his dad."

Over the next three years, Maasai converted to Islam, studied abroad in Japan, and met his future wife, Jasmine Joy. Maasai remained on pace to graduate from the Writing for Screen and Television program in the spring of 2016. Then, in December 2015, his father took him aside. "You need to apply for a loan," he said.

People close to Singleton believe he pulled his son's tuition due to financial concerns. A few months earlier, Akosua Busia sued him for over $200,000 in back child support payments. In court filings, Singleton claimed to have negative cash flow—earning approximately $14,500 a month against $24,000 in expenses.

(Despite their fraught history, Singleton still carried a torch for Busia. "Don't let her come near me," he told an associate one morning prior to a hearing. "If I smell her. It's all over. I'll give her everything.")

He wanted to teach his son a lesson. Earlier in the year, Singleton asked Maasai to sublet his apartment while he studied abroad in Japan. He dawdled prior to his departure. "I'm in the middle of college. I've never really handled something like this before," Maasai says. "I didn't get any guidance. It was like, *You need to do this and I'm not going to give you any advice on how it's done. But I'm going to get mad at you for not accomplishing it.*"

In the end, Singleton's mother found a tenant to take over the lease. When Maasai returned from Japan, he lost the apartment and moved into his childhood bedroom in Singleton's Baldwin Hills house. He complained to his father throughout the fall semester about his commute.

"I had to walk down the hill to get to the bus or train to go to school and then I would have to walk up the hill after taking the bus or train to get back home," Maasai says. "It's a fifteen- to twenty-minute walk down or up the hill, and that wore down on me over and over again. It was like, *Why am I in this situation and not the one I was in before I left for study abroad?*"

Maasai blamed his grandmother for Singleton pulling his tuition. "She always tried to come between me and my dad's relationship," he says. "I think it comes down to the fact that she never liked my mother." Around this time, he also wrote a public blog post accusing her of manipulative and controlling behavior.

Singleton denied Maasai's accusations. When his son pressed him on it, Singleton shot back, "You were rude to your grandmother at Thanksgiving."

"I barely said anything to her at Thanksgiving," Maasai says. "My dad wanted the love of his mother, so he was never going to confront her."

Maasai then launched a GoFundMe page for the $30,000 needed to cover his tuition. The gossip sites pounced.

"Huh? John Singleton's Son Needs You to Pay His College Tuition," proclaimed the headline on BET's home page.

Singleton hadn't anticipated the story going public or the inevitable blowback. "He went ballistic," Fearon says. Eventually, he helped his son obtain a loan. Maasai kicked in the $5,340 he raised on his GoFundMe. He graduated in May 2016.

Singleton fell out, in part, with Malcolm Mays just as he did with his biological son.

Singleton wanted Mays to enroll in USC film school, so much so that he set up a meeting between him and the dean. Mays had different plans for his future. Though he intended to continue making movies, and even act, Mays petitioned to apply to the Marshall School of Business at USC.

"John was like, 'Nigga, I didn't raise all this money for you to go to business school,'" Mays said. "He was really a hood nigga, so we got physical about it. We moved some furniture around."

They didn't speak again until Kimberly Hardin brought Mays in to audition for the part of Franklin Saint.

"You were so fucking good," Singleton exclaimed at Mays following his read. But it wasn't enough to win the role.

★★★★★

Born in Peckham, Southeast London, to Nigerian parents, Damson Idris studied drama at Brunel University and performed at the Royal National Theatre. His audition tape wowed FX executives. When he met with them in person, he quoted *Boyz N the Hood* and *Menace II Society* in a flawless American accent. The executives in the room fell in love with him. "It was pretty evident to everyone that Damson was a star," Landgraf says.

Everyone but John Singleton.

One night, when it appeared that Idris had won the role, he called Hardin. "Kim, you've got to find me someone else," Singleton said, his voice rushed and frantic. "They're trying to make me take this guy."

He hoped to cast someone from the neighborhood. Singleton tossed out alternatives: Kofi Siriboe (*Queen Sugar*), Mays, anyone Black and from Los Angeles—just not the British kid.

Idris's eighth audition made Singleton a believer. Afterward, he bought him lunch at a Jamaican restaurant. Sitting there, picking at his food, Idris sensed he'd landed the role. He thought Singleton might need some reassurance from him.

"Hey, if I get this part," Idris said, "I promise you, I won't let you down."

Singleton leaned back and smiled. "Okay, all right. We'll see."

He took Idris under his wing as he had previously done with Shane Salerno, Tyrese Gibson, and Craig Brewer. He hosted Idris on his boat; invited him to white linen parties at Gibson's house; took him to the Oscars. Singleton opened up about his own life, telling Idris about his love for his mom and the genius of Spielberg. He recounted tales from his early days in the industry. What he experienced. What he learned. Where he envisioned Idris taking his career.

"He called me Dam-zel," Idris says. "He would constantly tell me stories of people like Fishburne and Denzel and how I reminded him of them so much. How I was going to go so far. How he was so proud of me. He told me that from the very beginning. It's like he knew exactly where I was going from day one."

Singleton wanted Idris to connect with the neighborhood. He often spoke of the victims of crack, the people who made Franklin Saint rich. One afternoon, after a long talk in Singleton's office, they walked to a nearby park and sat on a bench.

"Hey, man, you see that guy over there?" Singleton said, pointing to a homeless man. "Maybe at some time he was a lawyer, and this is how he turned out."

Idris soaked it all in.

"A lot of people are relying on you," Singleton told him. "It's the auntie who lived through it. It's the guys in the jailhouse, the kids in the foster system, the people in recovery. You need to prove yourself to all these people. That's the responsibility you have. This isn't going to be a walk in the park."

"That was a huge responsibility to place on a twenty-three-year-old kid," Idris says. "But I think pressure is what this industry needs more of. We've gotten to a place where it's okay to fail. That's cool. But sometimes you should really strive to win too."

Singleton filled out the cast around Idris. For the other two leads, he hired the Madrid-born Sergio Peris-Mencheta (*Resident Evil: Afterlife*) to play the hulking luchador El Oso, and the Tony-nominated actor Billy Magnussen (*Vanya and Sonia and Masha and Spike*) for the role of Logan Miller, the hard-partying CIA agent. He also set Jill Scott, Lauren London, and DeRay Davis in supporting roles.

Slowly, it became apparent that the *Snowfall* pilot was heading for disaster.

Before going into production, Eric Schrier sat down with him to address some of FX's concerns. Singleton continued to pursue other projects while prepping *Snowfall*. He tried angling his way onto the *Roots* remake underway at the History Channel as an executive producer. When that failed, he asked to direct the first episode of the miniseries.

"John, it's really hard to multitask on these jobs," Schrier told him. "If we're going to do this, I'm going to need your full attention on this. We can't have you off doing four other projects."

Singleton told Schrier what he wanted to hear. But he didn't stop chasing work.

Singleton also became unwilling to compromise his vision of the show. During preproduction, he refused to listen to suggestions about the script or setups.

"He would go into production meetings and really blow up against the producers," says a member of the crew. "Then he'd turn to me and say, 'That's what it takes to play the angry Black man in Hollywood.'"

Once on set, he worked as if he were on a film set. He got bogged down in minutiae. At one point, he did six takes of a shot of a record spinning on a record player.

"John, you've got to move on," Andron pleaded. "We have these other huge scenes to shoot."

"I don't want to hear it."

Singleton hadn't learned from mistakes he made on *Club Life: Miami* and *Empire*. He went too long on the script and didn't shoot enough extraneous coverage.

"I've done twenty-nine pilots," says Stewart Lyons, the line producer on the *Snowfall* pilot. "Going in somewhat long is not uncommon. Going in that long is not common."

Some collaborators begged him not to go down that route. Singleton responded with a shrug. "Trust me, they're going to love what I do," he said. "They'll let it go as long as it needs to be." His pilot ran seventy minutes.

He assumed that if he could deliver the best possible version of the pilot that it would be embraced. But he ignored the strict parameters he worked under—the pilot had to come in at around forty-four minutes. Because he used mostly master shots and mini masters, he couldn't whittle scenes down in the edit room. Even if he had more options, it would be nearly impossible to cut twenty-six minutes and maintain a coherent linear story.

Why didn't the network or Andron step in beforehand? "I didn't feel like it was my job to blow it up," Andron says. "I loved its ambition, but it was too ambitious. I wish I thinned it out more. But a lot of smart people looked at it and thought this could be executed."

FX scrapped the pilot, yet still believed in the series. They'd previously been in this position, having reshot the pilots for *Rescue Me* and *Sons of Anarchy*, two of their biggest hits.

*Snowfall* still had a lot going for it. Idris and the concept both tested off the charts.

Landgraf and his team decided to double down. They were willing to rework the pilot, albeit with a revised script and a new director.

Singleton now had a choice before him: Take his ball and go home, or make it work.

With *Snowfall* in flux, he went back to school.

In late 2015, Singleton reached out to USC's film school dean Elizabeth Daley about teaching at his alma mater.

"I'm taking a pause," Singleton said when Akira Mizuta Lippit, the vice dean of faculty at the film school, asked about his motivation for teaching. He needed a break from the grind, the relentless pressure of getting his projects off the ground.

"College is a place to reflect and think and engage in a dialogue about film," he told Lippit. "I want to reconnect with that creative space, just breathe, and regain that energy."

Over the next few weeks, he put together a syllabus with the help of a teaching assistant. He had no interest in standing in front of a small group of students and recounting war stories from his twenty-five-year career. Singleton proposed a course modeled after Drew Casper's Cinema 190, where, each week, he'd introduce a film, host a screening, and then steer a vibrant discussion—an open forum where students contributed and explored.

USC offered Emergence of Multicultural Cinema with John Singleton in the spring semester of 2016 with classes held every Friday in Ray Stark Theater from 10:00 a.m. to 1:50 p.m. Enrollment spiked once word leaked that Professor Singleton had returned. The class topped out at around a hundred students.

"This course is based on my theory that film culture had to evolve with cultural trends to include various cultures in different genres of filmmaking and away from what I term a 'Manifest Destiny' viewpoint of other ethnic groups," Singleton said. "This fundamentally changed film culture and pop culture and, ultimately, the world."

From the first class of the semester, Singleton demonstrated he wouldn't play it safe. He screened D. W. Griffith's *The Birth of a Nation*.

"Most of my colleagues will not go near it these days," Lippit says.

Once a staple in film schools, Griffith's groundbreaking silent film from 1915 had been swept into the dustbin of history. Film scholars like Singleton considered it a technical masterpiece—Griffith pioneered the use of close-ups and fade-outs and staged the grandest battle scenes committed to film at that point. But *The Birth of a Nation* depicted Black Americans in such a racist manner that it was considered racist back in 1915. The *Washington Post* later dubbed it "the most reprehensibly racist film in Hollywood history."

Singleton didn't avoid the ugliness. He had a unique take on the film.

"*The Birth of a Nation* is a science-fiction film," he told the class. "Science-fiction films speak to the fears of a society. In the 1950s, it was nuclear war. In the post-Vietnam era, it was US imperialism. This shows Black people rising in the South, running the political structure, taking all the white women, and subjugating white people to poverty. This was the fear back then. So, it's *Star Wars*, but different."

Later that semester, he screened *Blazing Saddles*, *Duck Soup*, and *Enter the Dragon*.

One Friday morning, while Singleton lectured on Gordon Parks, someone in the back of the classroom began heckling him.

"What do you know about *The Mack*?"

Singleton squinted toward the person interrupting him.

"What do you know about *Sweet Sweetback's Baadasssss Song*?"

He slowly made his way toward the back row of Ray Stark Theater. The heckler then removed his hat.

"Brett Ratner, ladies and gentlemen," Singleton announced to the class. "We've been friends twenty-five years, way back before *Boyz N the Hood* and before *Rush Hour*. We weren't even directors when we met at Russell Simmons's apartment in New York City."

Ratner sat in on the rest of the class. Afterward, they spent the afternoon together on campus. "That's when he told me about *Snowfall*," Ratner says. "He was very proud of the work he'd done. He thought it was great."

★★★★★

When John Landgraf decided to reshoot the *Snowfall* pilot, he told Dave Andron, "Don't be afraid to make changes." Andron took the advice to heart.

Idris and Peris-Mencheta were the sole holdovers from the original pilot's cast, while Singleton Family members were excised from the crew. The Logan Miller character, who overdoses in the new pilot, and his father, a wealthy oil man with political connections, played by Tim Matheson, were also jettisoned.

Miller's death opened the door for Franklin Saint's new CIA contact, Teddy

MacDonald, a dour agent with daddy issues of his own; the introduction of a major new character also enabled Andron to earn a cocreator credit on the series.

Singleton vented to friends.

*They made this guy cocreator of the show two years after I created it!!!* he texted. *And I hired this guy! My dumb ass. I was being inclusive not knowing or seeing how jealous this dude was.*

Singleton never had a full heart-to-heart with Andron about him taking over the pilot. Shortly after the announcement, they had a short conversation over the phone, where Singleton offered a lukewarm endorsement of the plan.

"Okay, whatever, "he said. "If this is what gets the thing going, then fine, figure it out."

"It was hard to get a read," Andron says. "I'm sure it was a blow. But he understood. He wanted it to go forward. He wanted the story to have a chance to live. He also had a lot to gain financially."

In the spring of 2016, the new *Snowfall* pilot filmed with the young Belgian directing team of Adil El Arbi and Bilall Fallah at the helm.

Singleton remained in the writers' room. The show still had his DNA running through it. But tension lingered between him and both Andron and the network.

While awaiting notice of *Snowfall*'s ultimate fate, Singleton moved forward in hopes of landing more television work. He sold *Straight Outta Heaven*, a drama about a dead rapper returning to Earth as a guardian angel, to The WB, and he executive-produced the A&E documentary *L.A. Burning*, a twenty-fifth anniversary retrospective on the 1992 Los Angeles uprising.

In the fall of 2015, he directed an episode of *The People v. O. J. Simpson: American Crime Story*, an anthology series about the O. J. Simpson trial, from showrunner Ryan Murphy (FX's *Nip/Tuck* and *American Horror Story*) and writers Scott Alexander and Larry Karaszewski (*Ed Wood* and *Man on the Moon*).

"I remember being a little stupefied that Singleton wanted to interview with us," Alexander says. "Interview with us? He's John Fucking Singleton. It was these weird formalities. We were like, 'Of course Singleton should be on the show.'"

Singleton's work on "The Race Card," episode five of the ten-part series, netted him an NAACP Image Award for Outstanding Directing in a Drama Series, and Emmy and Directors Guild nominations.

He also directed an episode of the hit Showtime series *Billions*. In April 2016, shortly after the season one finale, Singleton texted Brian Koppelman, the show's cocreator and co-showrunner, along with David Levien, that he'd watched it three times in a row.

Koppelman showed Levien the text.

"That is so cool," Levien said. "You should ask him to direct an episode."

Koppelman texted him.

*I'm down*, Singleton wrote back immediately.

Despite his stellar work on *The People v. O. J. Simpson*, Singleton's reputation had followed him over to television.

"There were all these voices from the network with vague warnings like 'Be careful when an auteur director comes to your show. They will ride off with their vision,'" Levien says. But Singleton put them at ease following a preproduction meeting at a diner in Long Island. "He sits down and starts talking about the thematic of the episode in the deepest way of anybody we'd worked with on the show. It was unbelievable."

While on the set of *Billions*, Singleton received the call that would set up his final act. He was on Billionaire Lane in Southampton preparing to film a scene when the phone rang. Eric Schrier and other FX executives were on the line with news. The network loved the new pilot of *Snowfall*. They were picking up the series.

"All right, guys," Singleton said. "That's great. I'm so excited. Let's go make a classic."

He hung up and returned to work.

"And . . . action."

# CHAPTER TWENTY-FIVE

n early 2014, Dallas Jackson, a thirtysomething screenwriter from Denver, made the rounds at Lee Daniels's Oscar party in Beverly Hills. He took in the scene. The A-listers in Tom Ford and Prada. The spread. The free-flowing booze. For one day at least, he could pretend not to be a broke writer living in the projects.

Jackson had sold about a dozen scripts since entering the business. But work had dried up. His most recent project, a remake of *The Last Dragon*, fell through at Sony about a year earlier. When the checks stopped coming in, he moved his pregnant wife and toddler son from a rental house in Baldwin Hills to a one-bedroom in the Jungles, home of the Black P. Stones Bloods.

He didn't know what to do next.

Jackson placed his bets on a reboot of the 1979 film *Penitentiary*—the script he'd written tackled the prison industrial complex through a modern lens. When he set out to acquire the rights to the franchise, he met Leon Isaac Kennedy, star of the first three *Penitentiary* films and a partial rights holder. They soon became friends. Then, one night, Kennedy invited Jackson to the bash that would change his fortunes.

"I never got a check or anything from going to a party," Jackson says, "except for that party where I met John Singleton."

They made their way through the party. Kennedy introduced Jackson to Sharon Stone and to Daniels. He spotted Singleton sipping champagne near the bar.

"John, you should meet this young brother, Dallas," Kennedy said. "He's super talented and already doing big things with the studios."

Kennedy turned to Jackson, leaned in, and whispered in his ear. "You should do something with John."

He left them alone once he made the introduction.

"Hey, man, where'd you go to college?" Singleton asked.

"Howard."

Singleton beamed. "Man, I wanted to go to Howard."

"Really?" Jackson said, stepping back. "You're Mr. USC."

"Yeah, but I got so much love for that school."

For the next few minutes, they talked shop: about the nominated films, the state of the industry, the studio executives they each detested.

Jackson heard a familiar voice speaking in a British accent. He looked over his shoulder. "Oh shit," he said. "That's Dr. Quinn, Medicine Woman."

Singleton turned and bolted toward Jane Seymour. "Jane!"

"John!"

"Take a picture of us, Dallas," Singleton said.

Jackson obliged. "Um, can I get a picture too?" he asked.

Singleton grabbed his phone and twisted his body into a professional photographer's stance—knees bent, elbows out—to snap the pictures.

He looked at his phone. "Hey, do you want to go to another party?"

"Sure."

"Ride with me."

They climbed into Singleton's Mercedes and drove off to the Weinstein party at the Montage Beverly Hills. When they arrived, Singleton immediately started talking to a group of women.

"Don't leave me," Jackson said. "I don't have my car."

"I won't. Now go have fun."

Jackson mingled. He looked for familiar faces, someone to chitchat with, a possible networking opportunity. Less than an hour later, Singleton returned.

"Let's go."

Later on, he dropped Jackson off at his car. "Let's exchange numbers," Singleton said. "We should hang out."

Jackson barged in through the front door. He couldn't believe his luck. For a while now, he'd wanted to get in touch with Singleton. Back when he lived in Baldwin Hills, he'd see him working out at the 24 Hour Fitness on Slauson. On a few occasions, he came close to walking over and saying, "Hey, I'm a writer, too." He decided against it each time.

*Dude is here to work out just like me,* he thought.

But now he had a number and an open invitation.

"I met John Singleton at the party," he told his wife. "I'm going to pitch him *Rebel.*"

For the past few months, Jackson's wife, Amani Walker, had been fleshing out a concept for a show set in contemporary Oakland about a John Shaft–like PI nicknamed Rebel. The twist? Rebel was a woman. *Scandal* had just popped at ABC, and they figured network executives would be more open to Black female leads in the mold of Olivia Pope: sexy, tough, morally ambiguous. Jackson needed someone to walk them into the room. About a week later, he texted Singleton about it.

They met inside a sporting goods store near the marina. "Come on, walk with me," Singleton said. Singleton, Jackson, and his potential producer, Kate Lanier, the writer of *What's Love Got to Do with It* and *Set It Off*, then settled onto a bench near the camping equipment section. Jackson broke down the show for him.

Singleton smiled. Suddenly, he was a kid, staring out his window toward the Century Drive-In. "You know, one of my favorite movies was *Coffy* with Pam Grier," he said. "This could be a modern-day *Coffy*."

He cut to the chase. "What do you want me to do?"

Jackson flinched. "Um, well, it would be great if you could executive-produce it, and then we can shop it."

"Sounds cool."

Jackson exhaled.

"I'm developing a show called *Snowfall*. I could develop this too—but I'm not setting up no meetings! You set the meetings and I'll show up. You tell me where to be and I'll be there. But I'm not gonna pick up the phone. I'm not gonna—"

"Fair!"

The name John Singleton opened up some doors. Jackson secured cofinancing largely through his involvement. But it didn't carry much weight with the networks.

"Life is too short to work with difficult people," said a Black female television executive once Jackson mentioned Singleton's involvement with the project.

BET had some interest in *Rebel*, with one slight caveat: Singleton had to direct the pilot. At first, he balked at the request. At this point, he was still in preproduction on the original *Snowfall* pilot. He expressed concern that his work on *Rebel* violated his FX contract. So the series remained in limbo while Singleton shot his doomed pilot.

Singleton called Jackson soon after learning he'd been replaced on *Snowfall*. "Fuck it, tell BET I'm directing it." He fumed.

Six weeks later, they were in preproduction on the pilot. Soon after, the network green-lit a first season.

When they learned the news, Singleton turned to Jackson and said, "Tell your wife to get a house."

★★★★★

Singleton felt energized working on a Black show created by a Black woman airing on a Black network. With *Snowfall* slipping through his grasp, he became determined to flex his power on *Rebel*. He pledged to hire Black producers. Black directors. Black writers.

He brought in the veteran writer and producer Randy Huggins (*The Unit, Criminal Minds, Power*) to interview for the job of showrunner.

"You want to run this show for me?" Jackson asked at the outset of the meeting.

Huggins looked around. "I can get hired just like that?"

"Randy, do you see who I'm sitting here with?" Jackson asked, pointing to Singleton.

"Yeah, but you don't have to run it up the flagpole or anything?"

"I don't," Jackson said. "So, do you want to run this show for me?"

"Hell yeah."

Singleton thought of the many, many young Black writers and directors he'd met through the years. He'd read their scripts, watched their reels and short films. They just needed a shot. Now he was now in a position to offer one.

"John opened the door for them," says Bruce Cannon, who edited the *Rebel* pilot. "There's a whole generation that just worshipped him. They treated him like royalty on that show."

One day, Natasha Tash Gray snuck up behind Singleton in the production office and whispered in his ear, "Hey, wanna see a dead body?"

When they started working together, Gray, a writer and director from South Central, incessantly quoted *Boyz N the Hood* to Singleton—even though it was *Poetic Justice* that inspired her to become a writer. They met through a mutual friend, Cheo Hodari Coker, who passed one of Gray's scripts to Singleton. In June 2015, she approached Singleton following a DGA event honoring Tim Story.

"I'm Tash," she said.

He stared at her.

"Cheo gave you my script."

"Right, right. He said you're from LA."

"I am."

"Which LA?"

"South LA."

"LA, LA?"

"You want me to Crip Walk?"

They exchanged numbers. She didn't hear back from him until months later when he asked her to read the *Snowfall* pilot. "There's something wrong with it, but I don't know what," he said.

She got back to him immediately. "You've written yourself into a corner," she said. "This is not a terminal show. This is television. It's too closed-ended."

"Why didn't anyone tell me that?"

"I don't know. You're John Singleton. People don't want to offend you."

Gray soon joined *Rebel* as a staff writer. Singleton didn't come to the writers' room often. But he remained heavily invested in the show—he attended the big production meetings and handpicked the directors.

Singleton first encountered Sheldon Candis over fifteen years earlier when the Baltimore native attended USC. Candis would seek him out at USC events, both as an undergrad and as an alum, after graduating in 2003. Candis landed on Singleton's radar in 2012 with his debut feature, *LUV*. A semiautobiographical coming-of-age story set in Baltimore, *LUV* was nominated for the Grand Jury Prize at Sundance. Singleton caught it a few months later at an AMC in Miami. He called Candis immediately afterward.

"Sheldon, it's John."

"John who?"

"John Singleton, negro. Hey, I just wanted to tell you that your movie is beautiful. I'm taking you with me."

"Thanks, John. Where are we going?"

"Don't worry, just be ready."

A few years passed before Singleton invited Candis to shadow him on the set of the *Snowfall* pilot and on "The Race Card," the episode he directed on *The People v. O. J. Simpson: American Crime Story.*

"There was no shadow program," Candis says. "I wasn't supposed to be there. But John made sure I was."

Soon after, he hired Candis to direct two episodes during *Rebel*'s first season. On the night before Candis's first day on set, Singleton called him into his office.

"Sheldon, remember you're here because you're a filmmaker," he said. "I don't want that basic, standard TV stuff. I want us to be telling this as a cinematic story."

He arrived on the set the next day about an hour before the crew broke for lunch and found Candis.

"How many setups you got done?"

Candis hadn't kept track all morning.

"When I met Spielberg, he always loved to talk setups. He asked about mine on *Boyz N the Hood*. That's why I'm asking. Let's go talk to the script supervisor."

They walked over to her. She flipped through the book and announced, "Twenty-one."

Singleton raised his eyebrows and turned to Candis. "You got twenty-one setups before lunch?" He extended his arm, shook Candis's hand, and walked back to the production office.

The *New York Times* accurately assessed the show following its March 2017 premiere. "Not exactly good . . . but definitely not boring." The nine-episode first season averaged a little over five hundred thousand viewers—enough to warrant a look for a second season. But shortly before the first season aired, BET fired the executive who'd been the show's biggest supporter. In November 2017, the network canceled *Rebel*.

By that point, Singleton and his band of acolytes had moved on. Gray settled on the USA miniseries *Unsolved: The Murders of Tupac and the Notorious B.I.G.* She'd soon work alongside Singleton on *Snowfall*. Candis codirected *Baltimore Boys*, the ESPN 30 for 30 documentary on one of the greatest high school basketball teams of all time. Jackson made the leap into feature films. In March 2017, a week after Jordan Peele's *Get Out* topped the box office with $33 million on its way to $176 million domestic, Blumhouse Productions green-lit *Thriller*, a slasher film that Jackson would write and direct for Netflix.

Jackson had never directed. The first thing he did was ask Singleton for advice.

"Of course you can direct," Singleton said. "What have you been following me around for? What have you been taking notes for?"

Before filming the *Rebel* pilot, Singleton told Jackson to get a notebook, tail him on set, and write down everything he did and said during the shoot. "This is going to be your directing class," he said.

Jackson reviewed his notes prior to *Thriller* shooting in the summer of 2017.

Singleton stopped by the set twice a week during production. Early on, he pulled Jackson to the side and shared the lesson he first learned from Paul Reubens.

"Treat the PA the same way you treat your actors," he advised. "Treat the caterer the same way you treat the director of photography. Treat the extras the same way you treat the grips. Because they are all here for you. If you treat everybody with respect and with love, they will show your movie love—and they will bust their ass for you."

"A lot of people don't share knowledge because they're afraid that you might surpass them one day," Jackson says. "John didn't have that insecurity. He had already fulfilled his dreams of making movies."

# CHAPTER TWENTY-SIX

After four years in development at two networks, *Snowfall* debuted in July 2017 to mediocre reviews and so-so ratings. Its strengths and weaknesses were evident to both audiences and critics.

"It's hard to understand why the show isn't just about Idris's phenomenal Franklin," wrote *Variety*'s Sonia Saraiya.

Nowadays, Dave Andron can admit he should have just focused on Franklin. But during *Snowfall*'s early days he consistently advocated for the Teddy MacDonald/CIA storyline over the more dynamic thread involving Saint.

There was a sense he felt insecure regarding ownership of the series—that he pushed Teddy because Singleton couldn't stake claim to the character. Andron may have been the showrunner and cocreator. But Singleton was its soul. He shaped the feel and tone of the show, particularly whenever it turned its eye to South Central. That was his world—the world he introduced in *Boyz N the Hood*. The space where *Snowfall* resided in pop culture could not be if not for John Singleton.

A series of incidents on the original pilot between Andron and close Singleton collaborators Dion Fearon and Kimberly Hardin permanently stained their relationship and heightened any tension that already existed between them.

"[Andron] disrespected so many people," Hardin says. "It was very infuriating, nauseating. . . . Because of all that happened, I never watched the show."

Hardin and production designer Keith Brian Burns didn't return for the second pilot, while Fearon transitioned to an associate producer role on *Rebel*. Not surprisingly, with Singleton no longer in the director's chair, the racial composition of the crew changed dramatically from the original pilot to the one shot in 2016.

The friction between them spilled over into the first season. There would be moments in the writers' room when Andron, or another writer, might propose an idea, only for Singleton to shoot it down in a curt manner.

*That's not how things were done. That would never happen. No one talked like that.*

They acted like they weren't on the same team, often disparaging each other to coworkers. Andron trashed Singleton's efforts on the original pilot to anyone who'd listen. He never missed an opportunity to remind people that Singleton "fucked it up." He had to step in to fix it—even though he was technically in charge of the original pilot as well.

Singleton couldn't look past Andron's supposed lack of deference. He expected to be the authority on all things pertaining to Franklin Saint and South Central. Instead, he felt challenged over and over again. Would someone question Scorsese about the Little Italy of his formative years? Singleton wanted similar respect. He'd earned it.

He grumbled about it to whoever would listen. *These people have empowered a person who knows nothing about the world, specifically Black people, to tell an important story,* he texted a friend. *Meanwhile, I, and several other professionals, are being disrespected, sometimes harassed off the jobs.*

Singleton had previously clashed with collaborators. *Higher Learning. Rosewood. Shaft. Baby Boy.* He didn't respond well to criticism and turned anyone blocking his creative vision into a mortal enemy. But his contempt for them—the Scott Rudins; gutless studio executives—paled in comparison to how he felt about Dave Andron.

Singleton told friends he once relinquished his first-class seat and squeezed into coach to avoid sitting next to him on a flight.

They argued out in the open, creating an environment that led to a high turnover rate in the writers' room. Amadio exited about midway through the first season. "I didn't see how the show benefited and I didn't see how I benefited from staying day-to-day," he says.

Singleton made fewer appearances in the office around the time of Amadio's departure, as he felt more comfortable on the set. Yet he still managed to contribute to the scripts in ways that played to his strengths. He touched up dialogue—polishes that focused more on texture—and marked sections he felt could be more authentic to the South Central of his era.

Naturally, he gravitated toward the characters based in South Central. He began his career filtering his stories through Ricky, Tre, and Doughboy. Now he had Franklin, Kevin, and Leon.

Singleton worked closely with the actors portraying the three friends: Idris, Malcolm Mays, whom he cast as Kevin, the most reckless member of the crew, and Isaiah John, who portrayed Leon. A twenty-year-old from Atlanta, John was working as a janitor when he landed the role of Franklin's best friend. His biggest job to date had been "Gang Member #1" in *Barbershop: The Next Cut*.

Before the pilot filmed, Singleton invited John and his mother onto his boat. For the next five hours, he answered any question John had about his character and the show. Over Italian sausages and peppers, he regaled them with stories about *Boyz N the Hood*, and shared the lessons he learned from his time in the business.

"I can tell you grew up in a tight-knit family," Singleton said to John. "Here's what I can say: Keep your family close. Keep Atlanta home. It's working for you."

When John struggled on the set, Singleton sought him out, called him over, whispered in his ear. "You got this." Then he'd give a fist bump and move on.

He also worked closely with Amin Joseph and Angela Lewis to sharpen their characters, Uncle Jerome and Aunt Louie. Their presence. Their mannerisms. Their look. How to suck their teeth. How to be "nice/nasty." Early on, he'd yell at Lewis. "Be more Detroit!"

"I would get so mad. I knew what that meant," says Lewis, a Detroit native. "Every Black person from Detroit ain't gangster. Then, one day, I realized what he meant. I can't play Louie from a place of fear. I can't be afraid to be gully. I can't be afraid to let that part out of me. I can't be afraid. I have to be in my power. That's what he meant. You got to let go of the fear. You got to be more Detroit."

He was not at his best on *Snowfall*. The health problems that plagued him in recent years had grown more serious. His vision had eroded to the point where his cousin Smokey, now a consultant on the series, guided him on routine strolls. Singleton walked with his hand on Smokey's shoulder and listened for instructions.

"Curb, step down," Smokey would say. "Curb, step up."

Singleton had multiple surgeries on his eyes, the nature of which couldn't be confirmed.

"About five or six years before he passed away, I think a blood vessel burst in his eyes when he went snorkeling," Selenesol says.

They say Singleton had retinitis pigmentosa, a rare genetic condition that he passed on to Selenesol and Isis. Symptoms include a loss of peripheral vision, sensitivity to bright light, and decreased vision at night. Though he claimed it didn't affect his job, frank conversations were had behind the scenes about whether he could still handle directing. In video village, he'd press his face within an inch of the monitor to watch playback. He worked slow. He began to feel self-conscious.

His chronic high blood pressure as an adult exacerbated the condition.

The condition was said to be genetic. But Singleton's neglectful diet, poor sleeping habits, and the overwhelming stress he created both in his personal life and career potentially made things worse. He was prescribed a regimen of pills—a chart on his refrigerator door reminded him of which ones to take and when. The medication generated unsettling side effects. He felt drowsy and sluggish, and sometimes he slurred his words. He nodded off in the occasional meeting. "I can't let people see me like this," he'd tell friends. When he felt he had to be sharp at work, he'd skip doses, which then prompted his readings to spike to hypertensive crisis levels of above 180.

Singleton's aversion to his medication frustrated and alarmed those who loved him. Girlfriends routinely took his blood pressure readings for him. He'd snap a picture and send the numbers to his mom. Sometimes, he'd FaceTime to provide video evidence of him taking his pills. Throughout the day, his assistants passed him apple slices and sweets for little bursts of sugar.

Singleton's appearance changed during this time. He aged rapidly and his midsection ballooned. He took a stab at going vegetarian but it didn't hold. He did manage to give up some of his favorite foods though.

One time Maasai suggested they go to Roscoe's Chicken and Waffles for dinner.

Singleton winced. "You know I can't eat that stuff."

His face appeared to have discolorations. Bags formed under his eyes. His laugh lines and wrinkles became more pronounced. He often brushed off questions about his health. *No, I'm good. I'm fine. I'm just tired.* He didn't admit to pain or discomfort. He worried about people worrying about him.

Mortality had been on his mind since his health problems had mounted. Prince's death from a fentanyl overdose in April 2016 also shook him tremendously. For the first time, he projected some vulnerability. He came across as fragile. When he saw old friends, he mended old wounds.

"John just showed up at my house. It was weird," says Stanley Clarke. Singleton had lost touch with the bassist and composer since *Higher Learning.* He'd recently seen Clarke at a *Boyz N the Hood* retrospective. A few days later, he made an unannounced house visit.

"It's not like he was apologizing, but the way he was talking I almost blurted out to him, *Are you in a twelve-step program or what, man?*" Clarke says. "It was just strange."

He took stock of his relationships with his children and their mothers.

"I used to have conversations with him when he got upset with Justice or Selenesol and he'd threaten to kick them out of the house," Mitzi Andrews says. "I would have to tell him, 'Your [children] aren't like these women you're having relationships with. You can't just get rid of them when they don't do what you ask them to do. That's not how you treat your children. That's not how you treat anybody.'"

Selenesol says the house became "a little more toxic" after Andrews departed. They didn't get along with Que Jacobs when she moved in.

"I would get trauma-dumped by her in middle school," Selenesol says. "She'd be like, 'Your dad is cheating on me' and would tell me about their drama and vent to me about him. Having to listen to stories about my dad changed my view of him. It was tough for me to process. As I grew up I was like, 'Yeah, I really shouldn't have been in those situations.'"

He hadn't been around as much since starting the process of launching *Rebel* and *Snowfall*. Selenesol would visit him on set. Sometimes, they'd go out to dinner together. Singleton would be on his phone throughout—emailing, texting, making calls. Once they returned home he'd be more present. "We'd talk about school and things happening in my life. I'd confide in him and tell him I'm struggling in school," Selenesol says. "I remember being in his bed, crying in his lap, and him telling me things were going to be okay."

At the heart of it, they just wanted to spend more time with their dad. "It's like that song 'Cat's in the Cradle,'" Selenesol says. "When I first heard it, I burst out crying like, 'This is my life.'"

With Singleton keeping long hours on *Snowfall*, Selenesol had a lot more freedom than their siblings did. "Freedom to do dumb shit," they say. "Then we'd argue and I would always talk back. He would get frustrated with that."

"John was great when the kids were cute and cuddly and he could dress them and smooch them. He just wanted to be loved and hugged," Andrews says. "The minute they got mouthy he wasn't up for it."

Sometime during Selenesol's senior year of high school, they left the house. After couch surfing for a few days, they ended up staying with one of Singleton's ex-girlfriends, a television writer and producer, who lived down the street from him. She provided the structure they were searching for. A drama-free household with church on Sunday. Selenesol made overtures toward a reunion, texting their dad after running into him at a movie theater.

*I just think it's important that you know I love you and I really want to start over.*

Singleton accepted them back into his house. But another argument occurred around the time of Selenesol's prom. Singleton ended up not attending their high school graduation (and neither did their mom following a disagreement about where to attend college).

"I guess my dad was working. He came after to the Cheesecake Factory. It was just Justice and Maasai," they say. "I had to forgive a lot. I had to forgive them for a lot of things. There's definitely some cases where I could have been supported more or treated better. I know our parents are human, but that really hurt me."

Soon after graduation, Selenesol moved to New York.

The health problems. The blowups at work. The disputes with his kids. They had been building for some time. He felt a seventh child—a son—could be the remedy for it all. He wanted a second shot at turning a baby boy into a man. He talked about passing down his knowledge. Having a protégé. Mentoring on a daily basis, not just every other weekend like the first time around. He thought it would be easier to start from scratch rather than mend relationships filled with decades' worth of baggage. He felt a sense of urgency.

In early 2017, he propositioned Rayvon Jones, a forty-year-old ex-girlfriend from a small town in Louisiana, whom he first dated in the early 2000s. One afternoon, while together on his boat, he asked if she'd bear him a son. Jones said she would on the condition they "settle down and get married" at some point. Once Singleton acquiesced, they started visiting IVF clinics to ensure the gender. By the summer, she was pregnant.

Jones says she remembers meeting Singleton one day in his office. For the previous few weeks, he'd been fielding angry calls from his other girlfriends. He flashed a devilish grin, knowing what was about to come out of his mouth was vile.

"Bitches are mad," he said. "They're all asking, 'Why her? Why her?'"

"That's a good question," Jones said. "Why me?"

Singleton's close friends and family were as curious as Jones: Why her?

Some of them knew her by another name: Raquel Lee. (Jones says she assumed the alias—a combination of her middle name and both of her parents' middle names—following a bout of self-consciousness. She thought Rayvon sounded like a stripper's name.) In the early 2010s, Jones, a former music video model and *Jet* magazine Beauty of the Week, worked on the fringes of the fashion industry. She owned an online boutique named Raquel's Closet and founded Fifi LeRoux, a kids' clothing brand. On social media, she showcased her work as a "red carpet designer" for the actress Meagan Good, Destiny's Child's Michelle Williams, and Tila Tequila, the MySpace-era reality TV queen.

One of Lee's good friends happened to be V. Stiviano, who, according to media outlets at the time, was also the mistress of Los Angeles Clippers owner Donald Sterling.

In the spring of 2014, TMZ released recorded conversations between Stiviano and Sterling during which the eighty-year-old billionaire scolds her for associating with Black people. "Why are you taking pictures with minorities? Why?" Sterling asked.

Within a week, NBA commissioner Adam Silver banned Sterling from the league for life, forcing him to sell the team. Stiviano, a thirty-one-year-old walking meme in a full-face reflective visor, became an immediate media star. She attracted swarms of paparazzi and sat for an exclusive interview with Barbara Walters. By that point, Sterling had broken up with his "right-hand arm—man, [his] everything, his confidant, his best friend, his silly rabbit," as Stiviano described her role in his life.

Sterling appeared to move on. In June 2014, he was spotted on vacation in Palm Springs with Raquel Lee, aka Rayvon Jones, and three other women.

Singleton was said to distance himself from Jones after learning of her association with the disgraced billionaire. But James claims that Singleton recognized her links with Sterling and even hosted him on his boat. "It was V. Stiviano, me, Donald Sterling, and my friends," she says. "We all hung out."

In 2017, he selected her to be the mother of a baby he planned to name John Singleton Jr.

Why her? Singleton told Jones that he trusted her and admired how close her family was to one another—their kinship.

The people closest to him weren't pleased.

"Nobody in his family liked Rayvon," says his cousin Smokey. "Everybody looked at her as a gold digger."

To her detriment, she didn't connect with Sheila. "We didn't have a relationship," Jones says. "I would ask John, 'Why doesn't she speak when she comes over? Why isn't she friendly?' He giggled and said, 'Oh, she's cool. She's kinda like your mom.' I was like, 'Absolutely not.'"

Jones spent the early months of her pregnancy living in his downtown apartment but soon moved into Singleton's house in Baldwin Hills. Around this time, he started spending more and more nights in the marina.

Singleton expected to die. He didn't believe death was imminent. He thought he had a little more time. But it felt like he was putting things in order as if the end was near.

One day, while out on the boat, he recorded a message for his children:

"I love you first and foremost. Never ever be afraid to live and seek adventure, to go to exotic places and see exotic things, and meet different people, and taste different food . . . Learn a little a bit of a different language all the time. Never be afraid of that because that's what life is about—exploring different things and meeting new people . . . Also, to everybody I love, and the kids and everybody, understand that I'm doing this for you because I want to show you guys how great life can be and I want to be able to take you guys to different places around the world. That's what living large is about . . . It's about enjoying the gifts that God has really given us. It's not about all the other stuff . . . It's about the true gifts that God has given us. That's what it's about. I love you all. Alright, bye."

He still had a lot of life to live. So, as he approached his fiftieth birthday in January 2018, he decided he wanted a big party, one glorious night with the crew he'd assembled over the last half century. On Saturday, January 6, 2018, around five hundred of his closest friends, family, and colleagues packed into Paloma Hollywood, a taqueria on Hollywood Boulevard, to celebrate him.

Singleton wanted things to be perfect—free of drama. "He was very stressed about Rayvon," Maasai says. "There were all of these women in the room trying to get my dad's attention. Some of them were very comfortable not being the only one. Rayvon wasn't playing that. She was trying to get married."

The party went off without a hitch aside from an appearance by a disgraced but not yet convicted and canceled R. Kelly; Rayvon's cousin invited the singer after meeting him backstage at a November 2017 concert in Houston that Singleton and Jones also attended.

Singleton made the rounds. He tried to greet every guest, though it proved impossible. Wherever he walked, a small circle would form around him. His mother commandeered a slideshow featuring photographs of him from childhood to USC to his film sets. He delivered a short speech. Then, one by one, some attendees told stories about how John Daniel Singleton had changed their lives.

"He was taken aback," says Natasha Tash Gray. "I told him, 'What's wrong with you? You know you did all of this.'"

"He was always creating, so I don't know if he ever had time to reflect," Dallas Jackson says. "But there was a lot of love in the room for his fiftieth birthday. After that night, I think he probably had a good idea of who he had helped and how much he had done."

On January 29, Singleton attended the *Black Panther* premiere at the Dolby Theatre in Los Angeles. Over two decades earlier, he'd tried and failed to get the film off the ground at Columbia. Now superhero movies had conquered Hollywood. He always knew comic books were fertile ground for storytelling, with unlimited box-office potential. Disney had entrusted director Ryan Coogler (*Fruitvale Station, Creed*) with steering the $200 million film to the screen.

Coogler had moved to Los Angeles in early 2008 after enrolling in the three-year master's program at USC film school. A former college football player from Oakland, he had recently graduated from Sacramento State with a bachelor's degree in finance. Coogler couch surfed with friends and family during his first few weeks in LA. Eventually, he moved in with a friend who was born and raised in South Central. Early one morning, they went to work out at the 24 Hour Fitness on Slauson.

Before hitting the gym, Coogler's friend warned him, "I work out with my headphones on because people will come up to you and ask questions—especially the older guys. They're always trying to work in."

A few minutes into their workout, Coogler and his friend were super-setting pull-ups when an older man approached them to chitchat. Coogler's workout partner ignored him. But Coogler recognized the face.

"Holy shit," he said to himself. "Man, what's the chances of this?"

*Boyz N the Hood* was the first film Coogler had seen in theaters. He was just five years old when Singleton announced his arrival in the summer of '91. But Ira Coogler, a juvenile hall probation officer in his mid-twenties, deemed Ryan old enough to watch the rated-R film. He'd read about *Boyz* in the newspaper and considered it his duty to bring Ryan to see this movie about Black fathers and sons. On the film's opening day, Ryan sat on his father's lap at the Grand Lake Theater in Oakland staring in awe at the big screen.

*Boyz N the Hood* felt like a documentary to him. Doughboy, Tre, and Furious reminded him of his cousins, uncles, and father. He sat in the dark mesmerized. "I understood all of it, bro," Coogler says. He cried when Tre got pulled over and when Ricky got shot. He cried so much that another theatergoer turned to his father and said, "Shut that baby up."

"It wasn't a good idea for that person to do that," Coogler said. "My dad might've threatened him. He was quiet the rest of the movie."

Back at the 24 Hour Fitness, Coogler collected his thoughts and walked toward Singleton.

"Are you guys athletes?" Singleton asked.

Coogler laughed nervously. He briefly went over his college football career. Four seasons at Colorado State. Wide receiver. Number 17. One hundred and twelve receptions. Six touchdowns. "Then I started explaining to him why I was in LA," Coogler says. "That I was there for film school and that he was a big influence on why I went to USC."

They exchanged numbers.

Coogler stayed in touch while remaining careful not to sweat him too hard. But the further he got into the program, the more he reached out. They'd link up whenever Singleton visited campus. He also put a word in for Coogler with Dean Daley. Eventually, Coogler was selected for a 546 project, a group workshop in narrative filmmaking considered to be the program's crown jewel. Coogler wrote a short film titled *Fig* (short for Figueroa Street), about a sex worker and her young daughter. When he finished the script, he sent it to Singleton.

Singleton shared his notes with Coogler. "He didn't like the ending," Coogler says. "But I kept it in. I was being a knucklehead."

*Fig* went on to claim the HBO Short Film Award at the American Black Film Festival in 2011. Coogler was on his way. *Fruitvale Station*, his feature debut as a writer/director, was the Sundance darling in 2013, winning the Grand Jury Prize. Released that July, the film grossed $17 million worldwide against a $900,000 budget. Coogler entered the big leagues with *Creed*, the $40 million *Rocky* spin-off starring Michael B. Jordan and Sylvester Stallone that grossed $173 million worldwide.

Singleton texted him following the *Black Panther* premiere. Told him he sat in the balcony with director Ava DuVernay screaming his head off.

*This is a serious game changer,* Singleton said. *You've done it.*

*It's like I told Spike, I'll be forever chasing y'all,* Coogler responded.

*So proud. Just enjoy this.*

*I'm just glad y'all show me love. It helps so I can peep game from you guys when I can. I feel like I have a privilege that you guys didn't, being able to tap into all of your experience and wisdom*, Coogler said.

*All love.*

*Black Panther* took in $202 million on its opening weekend, at the time the fifth largest debut in history, and over $700 million during its domestic run, good for the sixth highest of all time. Now, in his late thirties, Coogler looks at Singleton's run in the mid-1990s through a different lens.

"I realized, *Holy shit, this dude made a movie every two years for a big chunk of time.* It fucked me up a little bit. He was as prolific as you can be and he started when he was twenty-two," Coogler says. "What I put my finger on was how that must have taxed him. *Creed* and *Fruitvale* were two years apart. *Panther* was three years after *Creed* and that shit almost killed me, bro. The constant stress, man. When you got movies that come out two years apart, you basically never stop working. He was doing his movies with musicians and shit. It had to be a fucking circus to work with Cube and then Pac and Janet Jackson."

Coogler still looks at his texts with Singleton from time to time. Did Singleton know how much he influenced the younger generation?

"He knew how much he meant to me. I would tell him," Coogler says. "I think it was clear. He knew, man. I like to believe he did."

★★★★★

On March 4, 2018, Singleton returned to the Dolby Theatre for the 90th Academy Awards. For the second consecutive year, he attended with Damson Idris. He cheered wildly when Nicole Kidman announced Jordan Peele had won Best Original Screenplay for *Get Out*, and when Kobe Bryant won Best Animated Short Film for *Dear Basketball*.

Through the course of the night, Singleton alternated between pinot and vodka. Later on, he polished off several In-N-Out burgers. "Bad idea," he said afterward.

Along with Idris, he attended the *Vanity Fair* party before heading to Jay-Z and Beyoncé's bash at the Chateau Marmont, a secret casino-themed party that reminded Singleton of the clubs he frequented in New York during the late '90s, such as Nell's, Cheetah, and Centro-Fly.

"Singleton was a people's person but also a star," says Idris. "At parties, most superstars sit on a couch and have people come up to them. John would be both.

He'd float around the room. He didn't care about the hierarchy of the business. He'd walk up to a young actor and be like, 'Hey! I saw that movie you did!' Equally, someone like Quincy Jones or Sam Jackson would walk up to him."

Singleton's health had taken a profound turn for the worse. One day in early 2018, he was on his boat with Smokey when he suddenly felt a sharp pain in his head. Smokey found him laid out on a couch, looking pale and gray. When Smokey suggested calling him an ambulance or driving him to the hospital, Singleton shot it down.

"I let him kick back and relax," Smokey says. "I took him to the doctor a couple of days later."

A few weeks later, he had another incident. He felt a similar, somewhat sharper, pain as he drove around with a friend. This time, it was debilitating enough that he had to be admitted to a hospital. There, he learned he had suffered a TIA, a transient ischemic attack, also known as a ministroke. A TIA is a temporary blockage of blood flow to the brain that typically lasts less than five minutes. Symptoms include numbness or weakness in the face, arm, or leg, particularly on one side of the body, impaired vision and speech, dizziness, confusion, and a loss of balance. Though the blood clot usually dissolves on its own, a TIA is still considered an emergency requiring immediate medical attention. According to the National Institute of Neurological Disorders and Stroke, "a prompt evaluation (within sixty minutes) is necessary to identify the cause of the TIA and determine the appropriate therapy."

"TIAs are often warning signs that a person is at risk for a more serious and deliberating stroke. About one-third of those who have a TIA will have an acute stroke sometime in the future."

He kept quiet in the industry about his health and went dark on Twitter and Instagram between March 7, 2018, and April 4. Few friends knew the specifics and the extent of the ailments. Those who did pleaded with him to slow down and to prioritize his health.

Singleton was still rehabilitating when his son was born on April 2, 2018. Jones had gone into labor suddenly and Singleton missed the birth; she says he arrived moments after her sister cut the baby's umbilical cord. He named the boy Seven John Singleton. He decided against making his son a junior, fearing the name could place too much of a burden on him.

Fatbacc died soon after Seven's birth. He had been sick for some time. Singleton cried in front of friends after receiving the news. He posted two separate

Instagram tributes. But he had already arranged for a more fitting way to honor him. Season three of *Snowfall* featured a heavyset character named Fatback, a loyal enforcer in Franklin's crew.

Singleton tried to resume what he considered a normal schedule. But Fatbacc's death—occurring so soon after his own brush with mortality—left him shaken.

"John had survivor's guilt," Kevin Powell says. "*Why am I still here?* That's a question virtually every Black male in America will ask himself as he sees those around him, including the gifted ones, fall one by one. John became a young elder. There's a sadness to it. You think of the people you came up with and then you look around and it's like that Tupac song, 'I'm trying to find my friends but they're just blowing in the wind.' That's what John felt."

The journalist sat down with Singleton for a long interview in 2018 for a book he planned to write on Tupac Shakur. "He had gained a lot of weight. He didn't look well."

Singleton soon returned to work on *Snowfall* on a somewhat reduced schedule. The series found its footing once crack was introduced late in its first season, and when Franklin and Teddy finally collided, early in season two.

Unlike in the first season, Singleton maintained a steady presence in the writers' room. Once, while discussing the scene where Franklin and Jerome confront their friend's father for stealing their cocaine, Singleton blurted out, "Jerome's got to say, 'Tell Rob to slap his daddy.' *Slap yo' daddy! Slap yo' muthafuckin' daddy!*"

The cast and crew erupted in laughter. Later on, once the show aired, social media turned the phrase into a meme.

"It was just one line," Andron says, "but it became this hugely iconic moment."

The second season finale, "Education," marked a crossroads both for the series and for the partnership between Singleton and Andron. *Snowfall* collapsed from being a three-legged stool into Franklin Saint's show on the Singleton-directed episode, which took part mostly in prison after Franklin shot, and inadvertently killed, Kevin. Throughout the episode, Saint surfed a wave of emotions, and Idris delivered an intense, Emmy-worthy performance.

"It was just a very emotional day. I remember my girlfriend at the time, I just sent her home," Idris says. "Singleton was really intelligent. We had conversations about my personal trauma, if you will, my relationship with my father, and he brought that into the scene."

"I'm proud of you," Singleton told Idris at the end of the day.

He said that to Idris all the time. This time he believed him.

But the day dragged on. Singleton's poor vision and unsteadiness contributed to the shoot running behind schedule. At one point, Andron inferred he had to pick up the pace.

"Why the fuck are you telling how to do my job?" Singleton shouted back at him. "You need to back the fuck up."

"Dave and John got into it," Smokey says, "and it almost turned physical on set."

As he promoted season two, Singleton contemplated burning the series to the ground. Behind the scenes, he felt his power had been diminished. Yet, once again, the network put him front and center as the anchor of *Snowfall*'s publicity and marketing campaign.

"From executive producer John Singleton, the creator of *Boyz N the Hood*," blared the promo spots. Posters and billboards prominently featured Singleton's name.

The previous summer he'd gone on a eleven-city promo tour. Once again, he sat on panels. Conducted countless interviews with overcaffeinated local anchors. Fielded questions from rap morning show radio hosts fishing for clickbait.

Singleton lent *Snowfall* his heft and authenticity—twenty-five years of goodwill he'd accumulated on the subject of South Central. Meanwhile, the three leadership positions in the writers' room were held by Andron, a Korean American man, and a white woman.

Shortly after filming concluded on the season, Singleton texted a friend, *Thinking of how to blow this white boy off my show. I gotta do it. He's thinking the same thing. How to get me out. I gotta be smart.*

*This shit is giving me a heart attack. Mixture of emotions. Anger. Hurt. Disappointment. More anger. This situation is a microcosm of everything that's wrong with this country. If I don't fight it, it'll eat me alive.*

But in the midst of plotting his coup, he received a call from FX's human resources department.

In November 2017, at the height of the #MeToo movement, a journalist publicly accused Singleton of sexually harassing her during a press junket at the American Black Film Festival in Miami several months earlier.

"I conducted the interview, and afterward I went over to Singleton to grab my mic and he grabbed my wrist and pulled me toward him, saying, 'Bring that juiciness over here,'" Danielle Young wrote in an essay for *The Root*. "He was sitting in a director's chair, so when he pulled me, I fell forward and stopped myself by placing my hands on his legs. He then leaned forward and kissed me on my cheek."

Singleton panicked following the essay's publication. He called his allies in the press. His girlfriends. His female friends. "Did I do something wrong?" he'd ask after frantically recounting his version of what happened.

"He did hug her," says one of Singleton's girlfriends, who'd witnessed the encounter. "I don't want to assume because of someone's reaction they're comfortable with the situation, but she was trying to paint the picture that she was antsy and trying to get away and just completely obviously uncomfortable and she was not. It was the exact opposite. She was kind of making comments toward the fact that she was a thick girl. It wasn't what she painted it as. If she was uncomfortable, that was not evident at all. I also didn't see him grab her breast."

The story quickly dissipated.

Singleton's quest to get Andron fired failed. But he refused to walk away from the show. "I'm not going to give that motherfucker the satisfaction," Singleton told a friend. He had a lot to gain financially. He couldn't afford another dent in his professional reputation either. In the end, FX renewed *Snowfall* for a third season in September 2018. Andron remained showrunner. The writers' room and the crew became more diverse.

But the battles had taken a toll on Singleton.

"In retrospect, I think I can see that he was taking on a lot of stress," John Landgraf says. "He cared so deeply about the show. Every bump in the road was painful for him."

# CHAPTER TWENTY-SEVEN

From the start of their romantic relationship, Whisper Williams noticed Singleton's shady cell phone habits. Williams, a visual merchandiser living in Miami, began to recognize the names of callers he'd send to voicemail and the ones he'd scurry out of earshot to answer. He purposefully left his phone in unoccupied rooms of his Miami condo. Then he'd sneak off and make calls or answer texts furiously.

In the fall of 2017, Williams figured out his password.

"I saw a lot of things in his phone," she says.

She knew there were other women. They already had the monogamy conversation. He liked to keep the door open for them, he said. She just hadn't imagined the scope of it. But one thing in this enormous digital trove troubled her more than any thirst trap she found—a picture of him kissing a pregnant woman in a fancy restaurant.

"Who is this pregnant lady and why are you so close to her?" she asked him.

"Oh, she's just a friend," he said.

"Who is she?"

He chuckled. "She's just a friend."

"I just couldn't fathom the idea of him having somebody else pregnant," Williams says. "I just prayed on it. 'Whatever the truth is, just let it come out because I'm not interested in being involved in something so chaotic and messy.'"

The relationship became a little more chaotic and messy a few weeks later when Williams began to think she was pregnant. She called Singleton in Los Angeles.

"Have you ever been pregnant before?" he asked.

"No."

"Take a test."

She called him back later that day to tell him the news.

"Yeah, that's what I thought," he said. "We'll figure it out. Let's take it day by day. We'll make it work."

"He was very matter-of-fact about the situation," Williams says. "I didn't feel like he was as supportive as I thought he'd be."

She didn't understand his iciness toward her. Earlier, he'd told her he wanted a baby. Williams wasn't ready for motherhood. Now he didn't seem too excited. She figured it had to do with the recent #MeToo accusations against him. He had a lot on his mind. She couldn't imagine he had a pregnant woman living in his Baldwin Hills home. (Williams miscarried weeks into her pregnancy.)

Over two decades his junior, Williams had been one of Singleton's closest companions since they met at the South Beach nightclub Dream in September 2016. Singleton dispatched a mutual friend to introduce him after he spotted Williams, five foot nine with big hair and high heels, sauntering through VIP. They convened near the DJ booth for a quick conversation that ended with Singleton asking for her phone number. The next day they had lunch at Smith & Wollensky. Later that afternoon, he let her know he wanted to be more than just friends. He invited her up to his condo to show her his artwork.

"Our creative minds balanced each other out. I felt like I understood him and he understood me," she says. "I just loved his free spirit. He just wanted to be a kid. He found so much joy in beautiful things."

Throughout their relationship, Singleton praised her—her intellect, her beauty. He photographed her constantly. He asked questions about her background and aspirations. He told Williams she had unlimited potential. "How can I help you reach your goal?" he asked. He had connections in so many industries. He could provide funding. Though she worked in merchandising, she wanted to coach fashion models on how to build a portfolio and transition from Instagram to the runway. He spoke of getting her a job on the set of *Snowfall* in costume design.

His friends dubbed her the Teenager. Singleton nicknamed her Eyebrows.

Williams became one of his favorite travel partners. They took trips to the Caribbean. Once, while in Turks and Caicos, he woke her up to watch the sunrise. Later that day, they hung around a small plaza, ate at a cute restaurant, and grabbed drinks at a cozy bar. His signature laugh reverberated through the joint. When his song came on, he danced, an awkward two-step. He didn't care who watched. He could get used to this—island life.

In August 2018, they took a trip to Italy.

From the moment they landed in Rome, Williams remembers something feeling different. His phone rang, buzzed, and vibrated. The name *Rayvon* continuously popped up. Missed calls. Voicemails. Unread text messages. Later that night, when she searched his phone again, she went straight to his text thread with Rayvon Jones.

The first text she opened confirmed her fears. Jones had sent him a photo of an insurance card for a four-month-old named Seven John Singleton. Williams kept scrolling. Jones had inquired about the obscene room charge from the hotel in Rome. There were pictures of the baby. Videos of the baby. Updates on the baby. She scrolled some more. "Oh wow, she thinks he's on a business trip," Williams murmured to herself.

They had another night in Rome before traveling to the Amalfi Coast for a few days. She contemplated her next move. *How do I even approach this? Should I bring it up? What would I say? Do I ruin the trip? Do I try and enjoy it?* She decided to confront him once they returned to Miami.

They went directly to his condo from the airport, Williams says. There, she pulled up the screenshots she'd taken of his texts.

"When exactly were you going to tell me about your baby?"

She remembers Singleton looking straight ahead, not making a sound when she confronted him.

She brandished her phone. "When exactly were you going to tell me about your baby?"

"I don't—I didn't—" He struggled to find his words. "I don't know." He rubbed his head. "The reason why I wanted a baby—it's going to sound really weird to you. You're not—"

"You can try me."

"I feel like I'm going to die. That's why I wanted another child."

She knew about his ministrokes. She asked about Jones.

"I'm taking care of her," he said. "She's the mother of my child." Williams says he spoke about his relationship with Jones as if it were a business transaction. Jones, meanwhile, asserts that they were talking marriage and looking at engagement rings.

Williams sent Jones a long message over WhatsApp, recounting her relationship with Singleton. How long they'd been together. How he told that he wanted to have a baby with her.

"All the women say John said he wanted to have a baby with them," Jones says.

She knew about his cheating long before Williams contacted her. One day, she confronted him over it. "Why are you being so selfish," she asked. "Why are you still doing these things?"

"I'm still not fulfilled," was his response.

Singleton dismissed Jones's distress over Williams. "Oh, whatever," he said when Jones showed him the WhatsApp text. "That's just a stalker. She won't leave me alone."

But Jones knew he wasn't telling the truth. He was the one initiating contact, leading them along.

The two women spoke on the phone shortly thereafter. The conversation wasn't hostile. Jones made her position clear—she lived in his house and was the mother of his youngest child.

"She told me that John was sick, spiritually," Williams says. "She took a very strong stance that the things John did, and how he deals with women, were based on trauma."

Slowly, Williams pulled back—but not all the way and not for long. He texted and called zealously. Sometimes she answered. She felt she had to be there for him. But things changed. Soon, she started seeing other people.

"John was looking for love. He was lonely," she says. "He wanted people to like him. He wanted people to love him genuinely. He loved to be loved. He loved to show love. He was very affectionate. He loved women. I don't think he was truly happy. I think he was a very joyful person. But I always got the sense that he felt he was missing a little something."

★★★★★

The advent of social media made it more difficult for him to conceal his deceptions. The actress from a long-running network television drama he'd been dating stopped responding to him around this time; Williams scrolled through their text thread when she penetrated Singleton's phone. He became forgetful when it came to covering his tracks. He got sloppy.

"He wanted to be a good person," Mitzi Andrews says. "He wanted to be a certain kind of man. It's hard to do it if you've never seen it, though. He tried. But it's something he wasn't really built for."

In the past, Singleton had shared sparks with the entertainment journalist Tanisha Laverne Grant during their red carpet interviews. They finally acted on their mutual attraction in January 2018 after she dipped into his DMs. She met him for drinks at the Loews Hotel on Hollywood and Highland after covering the red carpet at the NAACP Image Awards.

"I saw the heaviness on him," Grant says. "I remember looking at him and even questioning how much more time he had here."

Singleton suggested a change of scenery. "I want to take you out to my boat. I want to take you out to the marina."

"I would love that," she said.

They jumped into a cab, headed to a nearby Mexican restaurant for an hours-long dinner, then climbed aboard *J's Dream*. He moved slowly across the deck. When he tried picking up the pace, he lost his balance. Earlier, at the restaurant, he'd asked for her help signing the check. He couldn't find the glasses dangling from his shirt collar.

She looked around the boat. The piles of clothes. The stacks of books. The electronics. Computers. Televisions. Speakers.

"Do you live here?" she asked.

"The house is for my children," he said. "This is my peace. My sanctuary. I'm on my boat."

She thought back to their first encounter. The African American Film Critics Association Awards in February 2015. "There is no way I can be attracted to John Daniel Singleton," she said to herself. "This is not a path forward." Then she looked at him in the cabin of his boat and thought, *This person is just really shattered.*

And yet she stayed the night.

"Just out of my ego, I wanted to be a part of his cypher," Grant says. "As a Gen Xer coming out of an HBCU, coming out of consecutive Republican presidential administrations, and coming into the Clinton era, there was this great bubbling of enthusiasm and hope for young Black creatives coming into Hollywood. You had shows like *In Living Color* and *Living Single* and then John Singleton, who was so serious and so cerebral—it felt like it was our time. John was a marker saying *It's our turn now.*"

They got up early the next morning and shared a taxi. As soon as he entered the car, he reviewed his notes for *Snowfall*.

Grant was hooked despite the red flags. She loved his mind. She loved how he affirmed her. When she discussed her career, he made her feel like she could move the world. As a journalist, she wanted to know more. *What else is there to his story?* she thought. They lived on opposite coasts, and so she didn't see him for a few months. Singleton often reached out with last-minute plans.

*Hey T, finally landed, let's meet for a late dinner. . . . Hey T, do you want to grab breakfast? . . . Let's go to Miami this weekend. I'd love for you to see the condo, T.*

They finally got together again that summer, around the time of Grant's birthday. He had returned to the East Coast to promote *Snowfall*. They spent four days together at the Edition in New York and the Park Hyatt Bellevue in Philadelphia.

On July 23, Grant worked the red carpet at the *Snowfall* season two screening at the Landmark Theater in midtown Manhattan. Later that night, following a Q&A with the cast, Singleton wanted to take her out on the town for an early birthday celebration. A big dinner. Cake. The whole shebang. But she felt worn down from the heat and suggested they stay in.

When she opened his hotel room door, she found Singleton lying in bed with trays of room service scattered about. He'd wolfed down most of a cheeseburger and an entire ice-cream sundae. "I could tell that he was fighting to look like he was a thousand percent," Grant says. "But I could see clear through it."

She pointed to the room service.

"John Daniel, what are you doing?" she recalls saying to him.

"What do you mean?"

She walked into the bathroom, gathered the bottles of pills on the bathroom sink, and marched back out. "This doesn't bode well for you," she said, her eyes watery.

He grimaced. "T, don't do that," he said. "The medication isn't working."

"You have to sit this press tour out."

"I can't."

"Please go home, rest, go see—"

"If I sit it out, they're going to take my show, T. Those white boys are going to take my show."

"They can't. You're John Daniel Singleton. *Snowfall* is your baby."

"They can and they will. If they know I'm sick, they're going to hijack it."

He knew how vulnerable he was at this moment. This wasn't the same John Singleton who kicked in the door as a twenty-three-year-old wunderkind. This wasn't the same firebrand who might bring a gun into the cutting room to protect his vision. This wasn't the same John Singleton who put up his house to fund a passion project. He was a fifty-year-old man in failing health slumped in a hotel-room bed contemplating his mortality. He knew he'd die soon. All he wanted to do was finish his show the way he wanted. And then make a few more movies.

# CHAPTER TWENTY-EIGHT

Sometime in early 2018, Scott Alexander and Larry Karaszewski floated Singleton's name as a potential director for their next film, *Dolemite Is My Name*, a biopic on the making of *Dolemite*, starring Eddie Murphy as Rudy Ray Moore.

"It had come back to us that he was not in good shape," Alexander says.

Craig Brewer got the job. Throughout the summer of 2018, he urged his assistant to get in touch with Singleton regarding a set visit. They never heard back. Toward the end of the shoot, he tried one last time.

"John is nervous about being around Wesley," Brewer's assistant told him.

Snipes's comments to the *Hollywood Reporter* earlier in 2018 about his proposed *Black Panther* film had hurt him. "I love John, but I am so glad we didn't go down that road, because that would have been the wrong thing to do with such a rich project," Snipes said about Singleton's vision for the film.

They set up a date for when Snipes—who was costarring in the film as D'Urville Martin, the director of the original *Dolemite*—wouldn't be on the set.

Upon his arrival, Singleton greeted Eddie Murphy and the rest of the cast. They all sat around laughing while Brewer played scenes from the film. "He didn't look good," Brewer says. "There was a tiredness to him." Then, without warning, Wesley Snipes walked onto the set.

Brewer looked at his assistant. *Oh fuck*, he mouthed.

Singleton got out of his seat as soon as he noticed Snipes. They embraced for a long time.

"How are you, my brother?" Snipes asked, both arms clutching Singleton's shoulders. "It's good to see you."

Singleton plotted his return to film. True to form, he secured an array of options. He signed on to direct a documentary on comedian Andrew Dice Clay. Cheo Hodari Coker had written a *Four Brothers* sequel; Malcolm Mays adapted

*Intercepted: The Rise and Fall of NFL Cornerback Darryl Henley* into a screenplay for him. He also looked at *Middle Passage*, Charles R. Johnson's 1990 National Book Award winner, and had been in contact with Atron Gregory, Tupac Shakur's former manager, about a lost Tupac script, a semi-autobiographical account of his sexual assault trial—the script differed from *Live to Tell*, which Preston Holmes's production company had acquired years earlier.

Singleton had written a two-hour pilot called *Black Power*, a series in develop-ment at Amazon that he described as "the civil rights movement mixed with *Game of Thrones*." He was also developing a show with the creators of *Billions* about Willy Ribbs, one of the first Black NASCAR drivers.

His main focus throughout 2018 was getting an Emmett Till movie into production.

The producer Laray Mayfield first approached Singleton about directing *Till* years earlier. She had all the pieces in place: Jerry Mitchell, a journalist at the *Clarion-Ledger* in Jackson, Mississippi, whose investigative reporting helped bring Medgar Evers's killer to justice, had cowritten a script, and Taraji P. Henson, whom Mayfield cast in her Oscar-nominated role in *The Curious Case of Benjamin Button*, showed interest in playing the lead, Till's mother, Mamie Till Mobley.

Mayfield reached out to Singleton to direct. Initially, he didn't want to travel down that road again. *Rosewood* had been the most taxing shoot of his career.

"No, I'm not doing it—and no, I don't want to talk about it" is how he replied to her overtures.

A few years later, he attended a performance of August Wilson's *Joe Turner's Come and Gone*, starring Henson. Backstage, he ran into Mayfield. He told her that he felt he could now tackle the project.

Singleton recognized the importance of telling Emmett Till's story in a post–Trayvon Martin, post-Charlottesville world. "It's a microcosm of what a lot of women are still going through when they're raising men on their own," he said. "How can any Black woman prepare their son for any of this stuff?"

They brought the project to Holly Bario at Amblin and hired Gregory Allen Howard (*Remember the Titans*) to write a new draft. Henson would produce and star. Singleton reached out to Samuel L. Jackson about a role. Despite his health problems, Singleton regularly stayed up until three a.m. working, doing research, thinking about the story.

Singleton had a dark vision for *Till*. He wanted to remind the world of what had happened to the fourteen-year-old boy. He watched film noir and old horror films to prep, and in the fall of 2018, he attended screenings of Ida Lupino's *The Hitch-Hiker* and Edgar Ulmer's *Detour*.

"John pitched it like a horror movie," Bario says. "There were moments where you are in Till's point of view in the back of the truck, hearing all these sounds. It was so visceral."

*Till* fell apart before making it into production. People close to him claim Singleton and Amblin haggled about the budget and were about $2 million apart. Bario says "a script thing" made them put the film on hold in early 2019. "That's a hard movie to get made," she says. "It's a brutal subject. The visuals are very intense."

Mayfield believes those issues were mere speed bumps and that *Till* would move forward later in the year. "There was still some work to do on the script," she says. "But we were starting to talk line producers and budget. We were very, very close."

MGM ended up making an Emmett Till movie from a different script. Released in October 2022, the film received positive reviews (96 percent on Rotten Tomatoes) but grossed just $9 million domestically against a $33 million budget. The Nigerian-born writer-director Chinonye Chukwu took a much different approach to *Till* than Singleton's planned version. In her film, Till's murder occurred off camera.

★★★★★

One night in February 2019, Singleton called Mitzi Andrews to discuss his upcoming slate. After wrapping season three of *Snowfall*, he intended to shoot *Till* and another feature back-to-back. Then he'd move to Toronto to research a different project.

Recently, he'd been speaking with the rap star Drake about collaborating on a film—a *Baby Boy*–type story set in late '80s/early '90s Toronto about an immigrant from the Caribbean having babies with white women. Singleton planned to live in Toronto for at least a year. He told Andrews he had to experience all four seasons there before writing about the city.

Normally, when discussing the potential Drake project, Singleton prattled on, full of energy. But on this night he spoke in clipped sentences. His heavy breathing muffled the phone.

"Are you okay?" Andrews asked.

"I just came from the hospital."

"What's going on?"

"Nothing. I just had another episode. It's okay. I'm—"

"Dude, what's really going on?"

"I don't know," he said. For a few seconds the line went silent. "I just want you to know that if anything happens, I love you. Thank you for giving me the happiest child I ever had. Everything will be taken care of."

"He had hero syndrome," Andrews says. "He liked to be the knight on the horse. He always wanted to save the day for the people he loved: *Don't worry about me. Everything is okay.*"

Singleton was a bit more forthcoming about his health with Yon Styles.

He'd reconnected with his college friend following his fiftieth birthday party. Singleton hosted Styles on the *Snowfall* set shortly afterward. Then, in June, they traveled to Miami for T. David Binns's fiftieth birthday party.

"Bottles," Singleton said as soon as he sat down in a nightclub.

"We partied all night," Styles remembers.

Singleton showed no sign of the ministroke from a few months earlier. They did USC homecoming together in the fall and then caught up at Singleton's Christmas party. Styles stuck around until well past midnight. As the guests filtered out, Singleton took him aside.

"Hey, man, do you remember that night in the limo when *Boyz* came out?"

"How could I forget?"

"Do you remember what you said to me?"

"We all have opinions. But you have a voice now."

"You were a hundred percent right," Singleton said.

In early 2019, Styles returned to New York City, where he worked as a consultant for the MTA. For the last few years, he'd been embroiled in bitter litigation with a real estate developer over his grandmother's Harlem brownstone. Then, just as the court battle came to its conclusion, Styles suffered a hemorrhagic stroke. At first, he could only move his left arm. He was confined to a wheelchair for some time and spent months in a hospital.

Singleton texted him upon finding out and offered his advice.

*You have to move your limbs,* he wrote.

*How do you know?* Styles texted back.

*I had four of them.*

*Huh?*

*I went to rehab and worked it out. I did what they told me to do and I got better.*

*How come we've never talked about this before?*

*Oh, they were minor, mini strokes, so I didn't tell you guys.*

Singleton remained active during the last few months of his life. He sailed with friends out to Palos Verde to see the whales. He told Andrews that his mother gifted him a trip to Napa Valley. In late January, he spoke at Taraji P. Henson's Walk of Fame ceremony.

"She's a trooper. She's my soldier. She's my favorite person to work with," he said.

He visited Selenesol in New York, surprising them at their job at a downtown Manhattan restaurant. Since moving to New York, they'd worked a series of service industry jobs and bounced around the city: a few months with their tía in Corona, then with an NYU friend, before staying in East New York for a spell.

"He told me that he was dreaming about me and wanted to check on me," Selenesol says. He bought them some new clothes and took them to see *Chicago* on Broadway, starring Cuba Gooding Jr. "I remember my dad telling me, 'You're the only kid that went to work out of high school.' I threw myself into the cold, hard world. I definitely think he was proud of me."

On February 21, Singleton attended the ICON MANN Power 150 Dinner at the Waldorf Astoria celebrating Samuel L. Jackson, Ruth E. Carter, and Spike Lee. Later that night, he hit up a MACRO party at Casita Hollywood. He wore a midnight-blue velvet tuxedo blazer and a skinny black tie.

"He was the best-dressed person there," Geoffrey Fletcher says.

The former NYU film student had almost exited the business after his brush with Singleton in the mid-1990s. He worked odd jobs to pay the bills. Through it all, he kept writing. He never stopped believing in himself. "Because John had taken an interest in me, I felt like I could one day get back," he says.

Fletcher scored his long-awaited breakthrough in 2009 with *Precious*, for which he later became the first Black person to win the Academy Award for Best Adapted Screenplay. When he ran into Singleton at the *Vanity Fair* Oscar party, it felt like "a warm pause in a whirlwind night," Fletcher says. "I thanked him for inspiring and believing in me."

Fletcher had crossed paths with Singleton a few times since then. But he'd never seen him like this.

"He wasn't moving much and had a look on his face that was between absent and preoccupied," Fletcher says. "For someone who was always so present, he felt a little faraway. I said hi to him briefly and he nodded. But there was something unmistakably different. It looked like he was fighting to hang in there."

Some friends walked away from their encounters thinking it might be the last time they saw him. Others didn't notice a change. "Come on the boat!" he'd say.

He learned that parenting adults came a little easier for him. Now, with Justice and Maasai in their mid-twenties, their relationship had evolved.

"I remember Justice telling me, 'Dad and I are talking about girls. How weird is that?'" Andrews says. Justice has since come out as a trans man. "The responsibilities with the kids were different. The conversations were different. He could be raw and real and share with them."

Toward the end of March, he spent a weekend in Miami for Trevor Engelson's bachelor party. Singleton had to miss Brett Ratner's fiftieth birthday party in Paris. But he sent his director friend a video message from the pier.

"We want to wish you a happy fiftieth birthday. We hope you have many more. You stay out of harm's way. Troublemaker number one. You don't need any lawyers—any extra lawyers—in your life right now," Singleton said. In the fall of 2017, six women had accused Ratner of sexual misconduct and harassment. "You know we love you. Miami loves you. Ladies. Ladies. Everybody come in, come in."

Five young women ran toward Singleton. "Happy birthday, Brett!" they shouted. Then, one woman, holding a cocktail, toppled to the floor.

On Saturday, they partied on a yacht—"a fucking ship you could throw a bar mitzvah on," Engelson says. The next day they went to Prime 112 for lunch: Engelson. His friends. Singleton. Damson Idris. The rapper turned podcaster N.O.R.E.

"We were there for hours," Idris says. "Everyone had to get a flight."

"I'm not leaving," Singleton said quietly, quoting Leonardo DiCaprio from *The Wolf of Wall Street.*

"I'm not leaving," Engelson repeated.

"I'm not leaving," Idris said.

"I'm not fucking leaving," Singleton shouted. The table erupted in cheers.

"We ended up staying in Miami for another few days," Idris says.

Singleton and Idris went on long walks together in Miami during which they discussed plans for the series. Filming on season three of *Snowfall* had gotten underway in February.

Singleton and Andron were in a better place following the chaotic end of season two. At the time, FX feared Singleton would exit the show. That didn't happen. He stuck around. Whether he knew it or not isn't clear, but Singleton controlled *Snowfall*'s fate. In a way, he held all the power. "If John had pulled the plug or given up in any way, shape, or form, then we would have too," Landgraf says. "Despite all the assets, we would have not continued with the show if John had chosen to walk away from it."

"It was very mature of John just on his part that the show must go on," Malcolm Spellman says. "I was tight with both John and Dave and got to hear both sides. I was really proud of those dudes. They both seemed to understand that the mission was bigger than the emotions. They made it work when things got tense. That doesn't happen a lot. In TV, someone can get pushed out very easily. Motherfuckers get pushed out all the time in Hollywood. They didn't do that."

In the end, the fractious partnership between Singleton and Andron worked. *Snowfall* would not exist if not for Singleton's vision. Andron shaped that vision into something the network felt comfortable with.

"Dave had been working with FX since *Justified*," Eric Amadio says. "He knew how they worked. He knew what they wanted. He knew how to get shit done within that infrastructure. The show doesn't succeed without Dave. He did a fantastic job in delivering to the network exactly what they wanted."

Singleton secured some victories. The network appointed more Black crew members and more Black directors, including Singleton favorite Carl Seaton from *Rebel*. Natasha Tash Gray was now in the writers' room every day. For the first two or three weeks, Singleton showed up as well. Then, one day, Gray and Andron got into a little spat—a heated, but healthy, disagreement about character or story that happens every so often in the room.

"In John's mind, I shut Dave down," Gray says. Once it was over, Singleton clapped his hands and stood up. "Tash got it," he said. "I don't have to come here anymore. I'll see you later." From that point on, Gray says Andron referred to her as "John's girl."

Singleton started to think he needed to be everywhere and involved in everything *Snowfall*-related. A few weeks before Engelson's bachelor party, he accompanied the crew on a scouting trip to Costa Rica. Friends suggested he cut back on his travel, but he couldn't be persuaded.

He planned to return to Costa Rica in April and fly to New York later that month for a meeting with Levien and Koppelman, the *Billions* team, about the series they were kicking around. While in New York City he intended to meet with the *Rosewood* and *Shaft* actress Catherine Kellner.

"He liked going off the radar. It was going to be a secret," she says. "We spoke on a regular basis, but I hadn't seen him in a while. He was finally going to meet my children."

He celebrated Seven's first birthday with a *Sesame Street*–themed party at a kid's event space in Los Angeles. About a week later, on April 11 Singleton attended an event at the Samuel Goldwyn Theater celebrating the USC film school's ninetieth anniversary. He sat on a panel with fellow USC alums: Marvel's head honcho Kevin Feige and the producers Stacey Sher and Jennifer Todd. At one point in the evening, they each showed a clip from a film that influenced their career. Singleton chose *Seven Samurai*.

"John was on fire that night," Scott Alexander says. "It was like a dissertation. He was just going on and on, shot by shot, about Kurosawa and his use of light and sound. He was teaching a master class to this packed theater full of USC alumni and film freaks."

★★★★★

While in Miami for Engelson's bachelor party, Singleton met up with Whisper Williams. She had started dating someone that winter. Slowly, her ire toward Singleton receded. "I felt this slight obligation to be there with him even though I wasn't going to be able to be romantically involved with him," she says.

He told her about his trip to Costa Rica—how he immediately fell in love with the country and could envision buying property there at some point. Williams agreed to accompany him when he returned a few weeks later.

They checked into a boutique hotel near the water in Puerto Viejo de Talamanca, a small town on the Caribbean coast. On their second day in the country, a tour guide named Jungleman took them snorkeling in a shallow reef. After returning to shore, they hiked through a dense, hilly jungle.

John lagged behind the group. He tripped a few times, struggling to step over the thick tree roots protruding from the soil. Williams turned and scolded him. "Please pay attention to where you're going," she said. Singleton took a tumble, opening a gash on his kneecap. He limped back to base camp.

"I'm fine. I'm good," he said as blood seeped from his wound.

Jungleman then mashed a local antiseptic plant into a juicy paste and slathered it on Singleton's knee. Eventually, he had it cleaned and bandaged at the hotel.

The next day they took a shuttle to the capital. They shared a long conversation over dinner that night in San Juan—a sort of postmortem on their relationship.

"There was a lot of closure," Williams says. "I told him he was never going to find true happiness until he let go of whatever he was searching for. It's never going to live up to what you need to be happy."

They were intimate with each other once during the trip. "It felt more like an obligation—not to allude that he forced me or demanded it," Williams says. "But it was more like, 'Well, we've done it before. We're here. We're staying together in the same bed.'"

The next morning Williams returned to Miami, while Singleton ventured into the jungle where *Snowfall* filmed. The trip left him visibly fatigued. "I spoke to him on FaceTime while he was in Costa Rica," says the director Bryan Barber. "He looked sick. When I saw him I thought, 'I'm gonna tell him he looks sick.' But I didn't because I didn't want to hurt his feelings."

Once on the set, he stuck close to the episode's director, Alonso Alvarez. The Mexican-born filmmaker had made an impression on Singleton when he shadowed him a year earlier. One day, Singleton asked him to grab lunch.

"Hey, TV is great and all, but what do you really want to do?" he asked Alvarez.

"I have this movie I want to direct."

"What's it about?"

Alonso pitched his dream project. Set in the United States and Mexico, *Un Viaje al Corazon* would tell the story of a widowed dad who gets deported shortly before his daughter's heart transplant and has to journey back across the border.

"Send me the script," Singleton said.

Nine days later, Singleton called him. "I'm going to produce your movie," he said. "You're going to need a real budget. I know you were thinking three million, but this is a twenty-five-million-dollar movie. I'm going to take you around."

(Alvarez eventually got the film made for $3 million. *The Wingwalker*, as it was called in the United States, opened the Chicago Latino Film Festival in April 2024.)

Alvarez was hired to direct an episode in season three of *Snowfall* that featured locations in Panama and Nicaragua.

The producers then scheduled a logistics meeting. They already had a spot in Los Angeles that doubled for Panama but needed to review options for a Nicaragua stand-in.

They went around the table. Alvarez suggested Costa Rica.

"We can't do it at the Botanical Gardens in Pasadena," Alvarez said, as someone had previously suggested. "Did you read the script? There are waterfalls. Costa Rica is cheap. Let's go down there with a skeleton crew and shoot there."

"Fuck yeah, someone is thinking right," Singleton said. "We have to go."

They walked through the jungle together in Costa Rica. "I couldn't believe he was just fifty-one years old," Alvarez says. "He was a little frail to be walking up those hills. But he never went back to the hotel. He kept pushing through." Singleton shared his war stories from *Boyz N the Hood*—how he faked it until he made it. Then he offered advice about directing television.

"You're here for a reason," Singleton said. "Your essence is what got you here. Follow your gut, have some balls. People are going to tell you what it's supposed to look like. Fuck them. A lot of TV directors come here and just do a master shot and two close-ups and move on. Don't do that. Think outside the box. Have an artistic vision. Do that and you'll be fine."

Alvarez's shoot went as planned. On one of his last nights in Costa Rica, he dreamed about Singleton. They were hiking together when Singleton tripped and nearly tumbled off a cliff. Alvarez caught him in time. He scrambled to yank him up. For a second there, he thought they were in the clear. But he suddenly couldn't handle the weight. His arm strained. His grip slipped. "I couldn't bring him back to my side," Alvarez says.

He watched Singleton plummet to his death. In the morning, Alvarez woke up in a sweat.

They parted at the airport. Alvarez and most of the production returned to Los Angeles. Singleton caught a flight to Miami.

★★★★★

Singleton met Williams for an alfresco lunch at Smith & Wollensky. Throughout the meal, he appeared tired and disoriented.

"I think I want to order the . . ." Singleton lost his train of thought. "I think I want the . . ." He snapped his fingers. "What do you call it?" He picked up the menu. When the waiter arrived, once again he forgot what he wanted to order.

They had a full meal—steak or crab with mashed potatoes and vegetables.

He sipped water. "God, I'm so tired," he said with an exhale while signing the check.

They went back upstairs to take a nap. When he woke up three hours later, he wanted to eat again. "Hey, can you go get Joe's?" he asked.

Williams shot him a curious look. During their entire time together, they always made the short walk to Joe's Stone Crab together. He gave her money. While at the restaurant, her phone buzzed. John had texted her a series of random words—gibberish, mostly.

She thought he had butt-texted her. When she responded, he answered, "Joe's. Joe's."

She hurried back to the condo with their dinner. "Yo, are you good?" she asked. "Do you want to go to the hospital? You're acting kind of funny."

"No, no, no, I'm fine," he said. "I'm just so tired."

"John, I think you could be having a stroke—or that you might have just had one."

"No, no, no," he insisted. "I just have a headache. I'm going to eat and go to sleep. Once I'm back in LA, I'll go to the doctor."

"I didn't think that was the best idea," Williams says. "But he didn't want to go to a doctor in Miami. You couldn't really tell him anything. If he wanted to do something, he was going to do it his way."

He ate part of his dinner, then immediately threw it up in the bathroom. "I started freaking out," Williams says. She pleaded with him to go to a hospital. Singleton deflected. "I think I just ate something bad," he said.

"He would not let me call anything," she says. "He was very prideful that way."

He moved unsteadily when he woke up in the morning. "I could tell he was not expressing the true pain he was in," Williams says. Once again, he refused to check into a hospital. His car arrived to take him to the airport. "As soon as I land, I'll go to the doctor," he said.

Singleton's text messages to Jones and to others from the airport were garbled and confused. He called Williams to let her know he landed. He told her he'd see a doctor in the morning.

An argument was inevitable once Singleton walked through the front door of his house. Before he left, Jones had asked him to take her to Costa Rica.

"No, no, no, it's too dangerous," he said.

Then he made plans to bring Williams, the much younger woman whom he still called and texted all the time and who his live-in girlfriend harbored suspicions about; Williams claims Jones followed her on Instagram, or lurked on her page, at least. Later that night, she'd view Williams's Instagram post from Costa Rica. But that's not how she unearthed the truth.

What happened over the next twelve to eighteen hours remains unclear, unaccounted for, and up for intense debate.

Jones's account is as follows.

"He came home that night, around nine or ten. As soon as he opened the door, he did not look right. He looked really dark, and skinnier than when he had left. I said, 'What's wrong with you? Why do you look like that?' 'I think I got food poisoning' is what he told me. I was like, 'Have you been taking your medicine?' 'Yeah, yeah, yeah.' I immediately got his blood pressure pump to check his blood pressure. His blood pressure was like two hundred something like it always was."

The American Heart Association says a systolic blood pressure reading of two hundred requires immediate hospitalization.

"I went and got his medicine and made him take it," Jones says. "He played with the baby and asked me to run his bathwater. So I ran his bathwater. We were there while he took his bath. He wanted to hold the baby while he was bathing. He bathed the baby. I asked him about his trip. He said it was good."

At this point, Jones says, she went to unpack Singleton's bag, and that's when she made her revelation. "The bag tag had Miami on it and I knew that girl lived in Miami," Jones says. "I asked him. He goes, 'Oh, I had to stop by there to come back.'" Jones denies screaming at Singleton. "But I knew he was lying to me, so I was cold to him."

"After he got out of the bath, he lay in the bed for a little with the baby," Jones says. "Then, I guess, the medicine started kicking in. Me and Seven went to sleep. I didn't notice him going to sleep. I noticed he kept going in and out of the bedroom all night. So he didn't sleep. That next morning, he tapped me on my shoulder and said, 'I'm going to go to the hospital, but I should be back. I'm not going to go to work. I'm going to spend the day with you and the baby.'"

Around this time, Smokey says he called him.

"John was like, 'Hey, man, I got a headache. I'm finna go to the hospital.' I'm like, 'What's going on?' He told me he got a headache from arguing with Rayvon. When he got home, Rayvon confronted him about the Instagram pic and they got into a big-ass argument. That was the last time I talked to him. He's like, 'Hey,

I'm going to Cedars-Sinai Hospital in the marina. I got a headache.' Then I say, 'Well, you want me to come get you and take you?' He's like, 'Nah, I'm gonna take an Uber.' I'm like, 'All right, when you get through, call me.' He never called me."

"So, I didn't hear from him for a couple of hours," Smokey says. He went to the house looking for Singleton. "Rayvon called me over. She was crying and all this and all that.

"Come to find out, because of the argument that him and Rayvon was having—because Rayvon was talking about she was finna leave him because he lied to her about, you know, she can't go to Costa Rica because it's dangerous, but [Whisper] posted all this shit on Instagram. And she called me over and was crying about the shit [Whisper] posted—talking about 'Look what he's doing.'"

Some of Singleton's loved ones proposed a different series of events. In August 2019, Singleton's mother wrote an anguished Facebook post suggesting that Singleton vomited blood and suffered a massive stroke while in his bathtub. She lamented that Jones (who she didn't name in the post) did not call 911 or contact her immediately. Soaked in pain, her words embody a mother in mourning.

Tosha Lewis made similar claims over social media on August 9, 2019. Writing on Instagram, she accused Jones (who she also didn't name) of withholding medical attention from Singleton until it was too late. She also alleged that Jones and Smokey dropped off Singleton at the hospital before abandoning him.

Smokey denies that he drove Singleton to the hospital or that he helped Jones take him to the hospital.

"John took an Uber to Cedars-Sinai Hospital in the marina and checked himself in," Smokey says. "I went up there to talk to the nurses at Cedars-Sinai. One of the nurses said, 'I remember telling [John] "How did you get here?" [John] said, "I took an Uber and I walked." She said, "I'm surprised you ain't dead."' Because his blood pressure was so high."

Singleton's death certificate confirms he checked in to the hospital on April 17, 2019. But it doesn't state which Cedars Sinai location he was initially admitted to. Cedars Sinai wouldn't confirm or deny anything related to his stay. As for how he reached the hospital, in June 2019 "a source close to the famed filmmaker" told TMZ that "there are no Uber or Lyft receipts to confirm how he arrived."

Jones says she had booked tickets to go to Texas for her grandfather's ninety-fourth birthday, and only got on the plane after talking with Singleton's mother.

"She said he was all right," Jones says. "I thought it was the same kind of episode it's always been. Then when I get to Texas a day later his cousin Avance [Smokey] calls crying like, 'You need to get home. You need to get home. They're saying John is not going to wake up again. He's brain-dead and you got to get home.' I immediately got back on a plane and left the baby in Texas with my parents. When I get to the hospital they start mistreating me and didn't want me to be there."

On April 20, when the press first reported Singleton's condition, they said he had suffered a "mild" stroke. He was in far worse shape. TMZ later reported that Singleton had been placed in a medically induced coma. Slowly, and then all at once, his friends and loved ones rushed to Cedars-Sinai Medical Center on Beverly Boulevard.

The scene at the hospital mirrored the chaos of his personal life. Friends, family, the mothers of his children, business colleagues, celebrities, and acquaintances from all walks of life jockeyed for leverage and position. Rifts spilled out into the open.

When Danny Singleton found out that his son had been placed in a medically induced coma, he went on a long, loud rant about the medical profession and Big Pharma, and pushed to transfer him to another hospital.

Dave Andron's presence sparked an uproar among Singleton's family.

"Justice had a problem with him being there and seeing my dad in that state and told Malcolm Mays to get rid of people. Malcolm came out yelling like, 'Y'all need to get the fuck out of here,'" Maasai says. "But it wasn't just Dave Andron who was there. It was some of my dad's close friends, some he knew from before I was born. My wife tried to calm him down. She said, 'Malcolm, you're not the only person to have a relationship with him.' He said, 'Shut the fuck up, bitch.' My dad's friends pinned him down. I was standing there like, 'Dude, it's not shameful to die. It's normal.' I was on this weird philosophical thing. Other people were holding me back because I guess they thought I was going to jump on him. That's not the type of person I am." When reached for comment, Mays declined to participate in an interview for this book.

With Singleton hospitalized, Singleton's mother filed papers in court asking to be appointed his temporary conservator, or guardian.

The *New York Times* reported that, "Ms. Ward requested to be named his conservator for now because her son had not signed any health care directive or power of attorney that would let someone make medical or financial decisions for him, the papers said. As is required in a conservatorship case, the papers included a declaration from a doctor attesting to Mr. Singleton's impaired state, though the declaration did not specify whether he was in a coma."

The newspaper also reported that Singleton "had been set to sign a lucrative settlement agreement in or around April 30. The documents say that if a conservator cannot sign the papers on his behalf, it will mean a big financial loss." Singleton's daughter Cleopatra and others opposed the application, despite Sheila's role as her son's longtime business manager. (The matter wouldn't be settled until years later.) Cleopatra gave a statement to the *New York Times* that caused further confusion.

"My father is not in a coma," she said. "My father had a stroke on April 17, 2019, and at this point we are optimistic about a full recovery."

A few visitors claimed that Singleton responded to stimuli. He smiled at the sounds of certain voices. It gave some hope that he'd recover. Taraji P. Henson wrote on Instagram that she visited him with Tyrese Gibson and that Singleton jumped when he heard her voice.

Gibson backed her up in the comments, stating that he remained confident God would safeguard his recovery.

Shane Salerno visited Singleton later that day. He didn't share Gibson's optimism.

"I went into the room with this cousin of his. It was clear to me sitting in there for forty minutes that John was gone. . . . And this goofball Tyrese Gibson—I was walking in while he was walking out—goes out there and starts tweeting that John's going to make it and John's coming back. It was terrible. People were calling me and I was like, 'I'm telling you what I'm hearing from the doctors, I was literally just holding John's hand. He is not coming back—ever.' I remember my mom, who loved John and John loved my mom, saying to me, 'Hey, I heard on the news that John was going to come back.' This Tyrese thing had gotten around like it was a fact, and I'm like, 'Mom, stop. He's not coming back. He's gone.'"

On the morning of April 29, Fox4 Kansas City film critic Shawn Edwards reported that a member of Singleton's family had told him that Singleton had died. Singleton's publicist immediately denied the claims, telling *People* magazine, "John is still on life support. That reporting is inaccurate."

But later that morning, a spokesperson for the family released a statement. "It is with heavy hearts we announce that our beloved son, father, and friend, John Daniel Singleton, will be taken off of life support today. This was an agonizing decision, one that our family made over a number of days, with the careful counsel of John's doctors."

He died from an acute ischemic stroke, intracerebral hemorrhage, and hypertension. He was fifty-one.

A week later, TMZ obtained his death certificate. Singleton's time of death: April 28 at three thirty p.m., about twenty-four hours prior to the announcement that he was going to be taken off of life support.

**F**ollowing the announcement of Singleton's death, colleagues, collaborators, and fans paid tribute to him.

"Condolences to the family of John Singleton. His seminal work, *Boyz N the Hood*, remains one of the most searing, loving portrayals of the challenges facing inner-city youth. He opened doors for filmmakers of color to tell powerful stories that have been too often ignored," former president Barack Obama tweeted.

Singleton meant so much to so many. He was everybody's friend. He was everyone's champion. He mentored hundreds—maybe thousands.

"He used the clout he got from Academy Award nominations for *Boyz* and called us all to him," Veronica Chambers wrote in a *New York Times* piece published in May 2019. "So many of us who worked on *Poetic Justice* had spent so much of our lives being the only black kid, or one of a handful. We were the sprinkles on our vanilla campuses and in our vanilla workplaces, and it had its effect: It made us mute our voices, code switch so we could be understood, get in where we could fit in.

"John, with his exuberant confidence, gave us jobs and invited us to be bold in our blackness."

He was laid to rest on May 6 at Forest Lawn Memorial Park—Hollywood Hills following a service at Angelus Funeral Home in South LA.

Danny Singleton gave a weird, self-referential eulogy where he seemed to take credit for his son's success. He mentioned the books he had written and various other accomplishments. On and on he went in a belligerent tone to the point where some people in attendance felt uncomfortable. "What Danny did was so fucking corny," said one spectator.

"Kanye-like," added another observer.

Later that night, around twenty to thirty of Singleton's loved ones gathered at Il Cielo, an Italian restaurant in Beverly Hills, to celebrate the man who brought them together.

Guests were invited to share their memories of him with the room. Some declined. Some told two-minute stories. Some went long. There were heartfelt odes and humorous anecdotes.

Two weeks later, a memorial nearly as star-studded as the Oscars was held at USC. Regina King acted as master of ceremony. Speakers included Tyrese Gibson and Singleton's children but not any of the women who bore his children.

"I think this is what happened," Mitzi Andrews says. "Nobody wanted Rayvon to speak, so we're not going to have anybody speak. It's just better to have the kids speak."

At one point in the memorial, one of the speakers said, "Stand up if John Singleton gave you your start in the business." Immediately, a wave of attendees got out of their seats.

★★★★★

The business came together to celebrate Singleton. FX named a conference room after him and established the FX Storytelling Legacy Scholarship in his honor. The network also continued to pay Singleton's episodic fees on the seasons of *Snowfall* that were shot after he was gone and kept his backend points in place as well. Sony Pictures renamed their largest screening room the John Singleton Theater. At the 2020 Oscars, his directing hero, Steven Spielberg, introduced the In Memoriam montage. Stephanie Allain, who produced the show, arranged for Singleton to be the last to appear. But Kirk Douglas died four days before the ceremony. Ultimately, he replaced Singleton in the anchor slot of the segment.

USC also recognized one of its favorite sons. The USC School of Cinematic Arts and the USC Black Alumni Association created the John Singleton Scholarship for the Arts at USC, benefitting students of color pursuing arts degrees at the university. SCA paid tribute to him throughout the 2022–23 academic school year, presenting "John Singleton: A Celebration." The film series kicked off on September 9, 2022, with a screening of *Boyz N the Hood*, followed by a panel discussion moderated by Robert Townsend featuring Sheila Ward-Johnson, former Columbia chairman Frank Price, and *Boyz* location manager Kojo Lewis.

"There were lots of tears," says Adrianne Shropshire, who met Singleton as freshmen at USC. "It was a family affair—actual family and USC family. I took my kids who have certainly seen it before but only on television. Oftentimes it will come on and they'll watch the whole movie. They had never seen it on the big screen. They were completely blown away."

The year-long celebration ended with a screening of the *Snowfall* series finale and USC announcing plans for the John Singleton Lounge, a memorial outside of the dean's suite in the School of Cinematic Arts building.

A flurry of litigation followed Singleton's death. He wrote a will in 1993 leaving his estate to Justice. Since then, he'd fathered six other children. Per California law, unless Singleton specifically disinherited the other children, they had claim to equal shares from his inheritance.

In July 2023, Sheila Ward-Johnson, as conservator, submitted her final report. Singleton's $6.8 million estate would be split equally between the seven children.

A few weeks later, Vestria Barlow filed a $15 million lawsuit against Ward-Johnson and several movie studios claiming she was owed 7–10 percent of Singleton's residuals from all his films following *Boyz N the Hood*. A judge later dismissed the lawsuit.

The children split Singleton's journals and memorabilia related to his films. Maasai was awarded his father's 895 laser discs and his entire comic-book collection.

Sometimes, when he thinks of his father, Maasai's reminded of one of Singleton's favorite quotes, a saying attributed to the Malian historian Amadou Hampate: "Whenever an old man dies, it is as though a library were burning down."

"Besides all the other emotions that's how it felt when he passed away," Maasai says. "There's all this knowledge he didn't get a chance to share."

Maasai followed his father into the business. In the last few years, he has worked as a writer on the animated series *Transformers: EarthSpark* and *Transformers: Cyberverse*.

"The best times I had with my dad were in the last few years. I'm happy to have been on good terms with him before he passed away," he says. "He was excited to see me grow professionally. We never got to this point, but he said, 'I can't wait until you and I go out to eat and you're like, 'Dad, I've got the check.'"

Maasai honored his father the best way he knew how. He named his daughter Johanna.

Selenesol returned to Los Angeles on March 17, 2019. "We did get a chance to talk, but that was in the midst of him shooting, so we didn't get a chance to hang out a bit," they say. "We planned to go kayaking. He went to Costa Rica and sent me a picture of this cheetah, like, *Hey, check this out.*"

Selenesol ended up working on *Snowfall* as a second camera assistant for three years. There, everyone constantly approached them to profess their love for Singleton. The hairdresser. The security guard Singleton personally hired. Bobby Thomas from Black Pack, now thirty years into a career that started with *Boyz N the Hood.*

*Snowfall*'s series finale, which aired in April 2023, featured a tribute to its cocreator. Toward the end of the episode, Franklin Saint, now broke, destitute, and a drunk, goes for a walk with Leon through the streets of South Central. They stumble across a set.

"Heard they shooting a movie," Leon says.

The director is a thin young Black man in jeans and a black baseball cap. He's talking to child actors—one wears a USC jersey; another is in a blue-and-yellow striped shirt. It's the fall of 1990. John Singleton is directing *Boyz N the Hood.*

Franklin scoffs. "Y'all ain't gonna win no Oscar."

Damson Idris approached Selenesol that day on set. He wore a filthy tank top. Ragged beard. Rotten teeth. He put his arm around them. "I loved your dad," he said, slurring his words, not breaking character. "I know he's here with us. I really feel it." Selenesol appears in the background of the scene as a camera operator, looking through the viewfinder.

In October 2023, Mitzi Andrews and Jeremiah, her child with Singleton, visited friends in Pennsylvania. (Jeremiah is nonbinary, uses they/them pronouns, and often goes by Miah.) *2 Fast 2 Furious* was on television. It was their first time watching the film. They immediately gravitated toward Suki, the street racer driving a hot pink Honda S2000. Jeremiah, like their brother Maasai, is into Japanese anime, and creating digital art. "They were like, 'Huh, Dad's cinematography was pretty good,'" Andrews says.

Seven mimics the father he lost at one year old. Sometimes, he wakes up in the morning, asks for his glasses, and eats heirloom tomatoes for breakfast. He loves watching movie trailers. "That's the most important part of the movie," he says. His mother is trying to find the right time to introduce him to *Boyz N the Hood.*

They live in Atlanta now where Jones homeschools Seven. He takes classes in Spanish, Japanese, public speaking, financial literacy, improv, coding, chess, and

Minecraft math. Jones says Seven was reading at the age of two and is a Mensa member. He has an agent, a manager, an IMDb page, and his own YouTube channel. In November 2024, he made his acting debut in an episode of *Abbott Elementary*. He aspires to be a multi-hyphenate like his dad.

"He sits home and writes his own scripts," Jones says. "He grabs his toys, gets his camera, and record mini-movies."

For a long time, Seven struggled to understand what happened to his dad. Singleton would be comforted to know that a movie guided his son toward the answer. One day, right before his fourth birthday, he watched Disney's *Soul*. He then walked up to his mother and proclaimed, "That's where Dada is. Dada is in the great beyond."

# ACKNOWLEDGMENTS

L et me start from the beginning at the top of the list: This book wouldn't be possible without the contributions of the hundreds of people who spoke with me on the record, off the record, and on background. Thank you for trusting me with this important story. The goal was always to deliver an honest, forthright, and accurate depiction of John Singleton, an iconic filmmaker who packed a lot of life into fifty-one years.

The portrait provided here is a piece of journalism based on what I've been told, what I've researched, and what I think.

Over the last few years I've had many conversations with people who were close to Singleton at some point in his life. One of the first calls I made was to Cheo Hodari Coker. Thanks for imparting your wisdom and for the genuine support. Thank you, Trevor Engelson. Thank you, Howard Hobson. Yon Styles was kind enough to meet me in Astoria and the Bronx to talk about his fellow Black Pack alum. Thank you, Joe Doughrity. Bruce Cannon was very generous with his time. He was candid and caring when talking about his friend John. Thank you, Karrine Steffans. Dallas Jackson said the right thing to me when I was feeling incredibly low. Thank you, Shane Salerno. Warren Drummond is a living legend from the borough that reigns supreme. Thanks for making time for a three-hour breakfast to talk movies and boxing. Warren's love for Singleton was palpable. His words resonated with me throughout this long process. My first conversation with Dion Fearon lifted my head during a particularly tough time. She contributed mightily in so many ways. Thank you, Adam Schroeder. Thank you, Mitzi Dee Andrews, Vestria Barlow, and Rayvon Jones. Eternal gratitude to Maasai Singleton and Selenesol Singleton. Rest in peace, Ed Pressman, Paul Reubens, and Paula Weinstein.

The work of other journalists provided the foundation of this book. The writers and reporters who documented Singleton's three-decade-long career. The staffs at *Variety*, the *Hollywood Reporter*, *Deadline*, and the *Los Angeles Times*. The writers

Craigh Barboza, Dr. Joi Carr, Veronica Chambers, and Patrick Goldstein. The late Joe Wood wrote the definitive Singleton magazine profile: "John Singleton and the Impossible Greenback Bind of the Assimilated Black Artist," *Esquire*, August 1993. George Alexander, Garvia Bailey, Stephen Galloway, Ron Silverman, and Jacqueline Stewart all conducted revealing, wide-ranging interviews with Singleton. Thank you to all who interviewed Singleton over the years. Thank you for putting in the work and recording history.

Tim Wojcik at Levine Greenberg Rostan is an absolute ace. The book doesn't exist without him. He worked tirelessly to sell it and fought for me every step along the way. He is my greatest advocate. Thank you.

Shout-out to the team at Andscape. Thank you, Jen Levesque, for recognizing the project's potential. Olivia Zavitson is one of the hardest workers I've been around. Thank you. Many thanks to my brilliant editor, Aliya S. King. I've known Aliya for twenty years. We both wrote Ja Rule cover stories for the *Source* and are former keepers of the Biggie Belt. (You see, The Notorious B.I.G. once wore a fifty-two-inch belt to a photo shoot and . . . Google can finish the story.) She's a dogged reporter and gifted writer. Here's a secret: She's an even better editor. Thank you for holding me up to your high standards. (We're not making Big Macs here.) Thank you also to designer Amy King, copy editors Guy Cunningham, Meredith Jones, Jill Amack, and Mark Amundsen, compositor Susan Gerber, and managing editor Iris Chen. Thank you, Michele Soulli, for the digging and bonus therapy sessions. Brendan Frederick was clutch, coming through with a treasure trove of old magazines. Thank you.

Because this is my first time doing this, I must recognize the people who were present at the start. Kim Osorio put the ball in my crib at the *Source*. She hired me as her intern after a meeting on December 4, 2001—a day forever known as Ether Day, at least in Queens and on the internet. She was a great boss and protector. If not for her, I might not have all ten of my fingers. (Long story.) She is still a friend. Jermaine Hall is the only person I've ever referred to as my mentor. He helped shape me as a writer and editor and gave me every opportunity to succeed. In January 2006, he assigned me an oral history of *Boyz N the Hood*, which set me on this path. Working with him at *KING* magazine was the highlight of my career. I still look forward to our late night phone calls about the Lakers, although "late night" comes around much earlier these days.

At the *Source*, I was fortunate to have Jerry L. Barrow as an editor. Thank you, Siobhan O'Connor. Thank you, Adam Matthews. Thank you, Timmhotep Aku.

I learned so much from the late Dave Bry at *XXL*. Clover Hope is a cherished friend. Thanks for always being there for me. Thank you, Jordan Rosenfeld. Shout-out to John Castellano, Thomas Goldstein, Bobby O'Connor, and George Rontiris for the late night texts, encouragement, and support.

Athanasios and Georgia raised me in a loving, stable household and provided me with everything I ever needed. My father demonstrated what a real work ethic looked like 24/7/365. My mother encouraged my love of reading through trips to the library. She also taught me to value kindness and empathy. Antonia is like a big sister crossed with a bonus best friend. She always has my back. Love you all.

My wife, Karen Philip, is the strongest person I know. She's a great mom and all I ever wanted in a partner. Love you forever. Emery and Giannis are everything to me. They make me smile. They inspire me every day. Watching them grow has been the best. I am so proud to be their dad.

I'd like to say something about John Singleton. His story is awe-inspiring. His talent and drive, astonishing. From the start, he recognized he had a voice and that it mattered. He touched the lives of so many people, both as a mentor and an aspirational figure through his films. He was also a man of many complexities. He made missteps. He was flawed.

I never met Singleton. The first time we spoke was in spring 2006 for the *King* article. It was late in the process. I must have been outlining my first draft. Then my landline rang and a now-familiar voice shouted, "You know, I'm kind of sick of talking about *Boyz N the Hood*. I've made a lot of movies since then. I'm a veteran. But my publicist says I should talk to you. I got about twenty minutes." Nearly an hour later, he gave me his email address in case I ever needed to interview him again.

I struggled with the responsibilities that accompanied writing a book like this on a titan like Singleton. There were moments when I felt like a fraud, an imposter—and worse. Singleton was cognizant of his legacy. He'd want it to be recorded and remembered the right way. But would he want me tasked with the assignment? This led to much internal strife and some uncomfortable conversations. Singleton was critical of white filmmakers telling Black stories, even writing an op/ed for the *Hollywood Reporter* on the topic. Yet time and time again he collaborated with white filmmakers to bring Black stories to the screen: Gregory Poirier on *Rosewood*, Shane Salerno on *Shaft*, Craig Brewer on *Hustle & Flow*, almost everyone on *Snowfall*.

The response from his friends was mixed. *Yes. No. Maybe. I don't know. It's too late anyway.* "No, but he would have respected your [chutzpah]" was the answer that made me laugh the hardest and the one that, as his biographer, I find myself agreeing with.

Lastly, a few weeks before this book went to press, the world lost a beautiful person, my cousin Betty Paralikas. For the last twenty years or so, she was a junior high school teacher in Queens. Before that, she owned a video store during the pre-Blockbuster days of the 1980s. I remember talking movies with her at holidays as a kid. She loved *The Godfather* and *Coming to America*. The Val Kilmer star-vehicle *The Saint* was a personal fave. She was so supportive throughout this process. More importantly, she was the kindest person in my family. It's unfair that she's no longer here.

# AUTHOR'S NOTE

*The Life of Singleton: From* Boyz N the Hood *to* Snowfall is an unauthorized biography of filmmaker John Singleton and not endorsed by the Singleton family or estate. Consequently, a number of people close to Singleton, most notably his mother and father, declined to participate.

I conducted nearly four hundred interviews over the course of three years of reporting. During this process, I never misled anyone into thinking the book was sanctioned by the estate. When asked, I clearly communicated with sources which persons had declined to partake in the book.

This is a condensed version of the research notes. For the full version of the research notes, please visit the author's website or the book's page on the Disney Books website.

## BIBLIOGRAPHY

John Singleton interview, Jacqueline Stewart, Academy of Motion Pictures Arts and Sciences Visual History Program, July 11, 2017.

John Singleton interview, Stephen Galloway, *Hollywood Reporter*, Masters Series, March 24, 2014.

Joe Wood, "John Singleton and the Impossible Greenback Bind of the Assimilated Black Artist," *Esquire*, August 1, 1993.

Thomas Golianopoulos, "Acting Up: An Oral History of *Boyz N the Hood*," *KING*, July/August 2006.

Thomas Golianopoulos, "2Pac: A Thug's Life on Film," *Vibe*, October/November 2011.

Thomas Golianopoulos, "Twin Killing," *Vibe*, Winter 2010.

Joi Carr, *Boyz N the Hood: Shifting Hollywood Terrain*, Peter Lang Publishing, 2023.

John Singleton and Veronica Chambers, *Poetic Justice: Film-Making South Central Style*, Dell Publishing, 1993.

Craigh Barboza, *John Singleton: Interviews*, University Press of Mississippi, 2009.

## CHAPTER ONE

California, Court of Appeals (2nd Appellate District) Records and Briefs.

United States Census Lines.

John Singleton speech, Hollywood Walk of Fame Ceremony, August 20, 2003.

Sheila Ward interview, John Singleton: A Celebration, USC, *Boyz N the Hood*, September 9, 2022.

Joe Wood, "John Singleton and the Impossible Greenback Bind of the Assimilated Black Artist," *Esquire*, August 1, 1993.

John Singleton interview, Andrew J. Rausch, *Fifty Filmmakers: Conversations with Directors from Roger Avery to Steven Zaillian*, Michael Dequina McFarland, 2008.

John Singleton interview, Jacqueline Stewart, Academy of Motion Pictures Arts and Sciences Visual History Program, July 11, 2017.

Patrick Goldstein, "His New 'Hood Is Hollywood," *Los Angeles Times,* July 7, 1991.

John Singleton and Veronica Chambers, *Poetic Justice: Film-Making South Central Style,* Dell Publishing, 1993.

*Boyz N the Hood,* Director's Commentary.

John Singleton interview, Terry Gross, NPR, 1991.

John Singleton interview, Carl Seaton and Jeff Byrd, *Screenwriters Rant Room,* re-released on January 7, 2020.

Sheila Ward interview, Joi Carr, *Boyz N the Hood: Shifting Hollywood Terrain,* Peter Lang Publishing, 2023.

Sheila Ward, LinkedIn profile.

George Alexander, *Why We Make Movies: Black Filmmakers Talk About the Magic of Cinema,* Broadway, First Edition, 2003.

Janice C. Simpson, "Not Just One of the Boyz," *Time,* March 23, 1992.

John Singleton interview, Alex Haley, *Dialogue with Black Filmmakers,* 1992.

Sam Kashner, "How *Boyz N the Hood* Beat the Odds to Get Made—and Why It Matters Today," *Vanity Fair,* August 4, 2016.

John Singleton interview, Joi Carr, *Boyz N the Hood: Shifting Hollywood Terrain,* Peter Lang Publishing, 2023.

John Singleton interview, *Drink Champs,* July 6, 2017.

John Singleton interview, *On Story: 601,* Austin Film Festival, April 16, 2016.

John Singleton interview, Stephen Galloway, *Hollywood Reporter,* Masters Series, March 24, 2014.

John Singleton interview, Donald Bogle, *From Classic Hollywood and New Hollywood to South Central,* TCM, 2016.

John Singleton interview, *Friendly Fire: Making an Urban Legend,* Director: Todd Williams, Columbia TriStar Home Entertainment, 2003.

John Singleton interview, *Poetic Justice* Q&A at the Mark Taper Auditorium, July 14, 2018.

John Singleton DGA Q&A with Spike Lee, August 13, 2018.

## CHAPTER TWO

Aljean Harmetz, "U.S.C. Breaks Ground for a Film-TV School," *New York Times,* November 25, 1981.

Myrna Oliver, "Ray Stark, 88; Hollywood Legend, Insider . . ." *Los Angeles Times,* January 18, 2004.

USC Yearbook, *El Rodeo: A Closer Look,* Volume Eighty Four, Student Publications, 1989.

John Singleton, "PERSONAL PERSPECTIVE: In Hollywood, Writer Basically Gets the Blame," *LA Times,* March 22, 1992.

Patrick Goldstein, "Polonsky Never Lost His Sense of Humor or Zest for Life," *LA Times,* November 3, 1999.

Susan King, "From Douglas Fairbanks to George Lucas: USC's School of Cinematic Arts Turns 90," *LA Times*, April 6, 2019.

Alan Light, "JOHN SINGLETON: Not Just One of the Boyz," *Rolling Stone*, September 5, 1991.

John Singleton interview, Jacqueline Stewart, Academy of Motion Pictures Arts and Sciences Visual History Program, July 11, 2017.

kappaalphapsi1911.com/history.

Laurence Fishburne interview, *Game Changers* Q&A, July 8, 2019.

George Alexander, *Why We Make Movies: Black Filmmakers Talk About the Magic of Cinema*, Broadway, First Edition, 2003.

John Singleton and Veronica Chambers, *Poetic Justice: Film-Making South Central Style*, Dell Publishing, 1993.

John Singleton interview, *On Story: 601*, Austin Film Festival, April 16, 2016.

James Andrew Miller, *Powerhouse: The Untold Story of Hollywood's Creative Artists Agency*, Mariner Books, 2016.

Martha Southgate, "Boyz II Men," *Premiere*, August 1993.

Philip Thomas, "Who the Hell Does John Singleton Think He Is?" *Empire*, November 1991.

John Singleton interview, Elvis Mitchell, Los Angeles Film Festival, June 14, 2014.

William Raspberry, "The Chief and the Choke Hold," *Washington Post*, May 16, 1982.

"Race, Rap & the L.A.P.D.," *PBS Frontline*.

## CHAPTER THREE

John Singleton interview, Jacqueline Stewart, Academy of Motion Pictures Arts and Sciences Visual History Program, July 11, 2017.

John Singleton interview, *Charlie Rose*, January 6, 1995.

Greg Tate, "Sex and Negrocity: John Singleton's *Baby Boy*," *Village Voice*, June 26, 2001.

John Singleton interview, Walter Mosley, *Boyz N the Hood* 25th Anniversary Q&A, June 12, 2016.

John Singleton interview, 2011 Los Angeles Film Festival.

John Singleton interview, Stephen Galloway, *Hollywood Reporter*, Masters Series, March 24, 2014.

John Singleton interview, Garvia Bailey, *An Evening with John Singleton*, March 15, 2013.

*Boyz N the Hood* Director's Commentary.

George Alexander, *Why We Make Movies: Black Filmmakers Talk About the Magic of Cinema*, Broadway, First Edition, 2003.

Ice Cube interview, *WTF with Marc Maron*, May 11, 2023.

Ice Cube interview, *The Howard Stern Show*, August 25, 2019.

## CHAPTER FOUR

Aljean Harmetz, "Aspiring Moguls Take M.B.A.'s to Hollywood," *New York Times*, May 13, 1986.

John Singleton interview, Jacqueline Stewart, Academy of Motion Pictures Arts and Sciences Visual History Program, July 11, 2017.

Veronica Chambers, "Singleton," *Dirt*, Issue No. 5, 1993.

James Andrew Miller, *Powerhouse: The Untold Story of Hollywood's Creative Artists Agency*, Mariner Books, 2016.

John Singleton interview, AFI Harold Lloyd Master Seminar, March 8, 1995.

John Singleton interview, Alex Haley, *Dialogue with Black Filmmakers*, 1992.

George Alexander, *Why We Make Movies: Black Filmmakers Talk About the Magic of Cinema*, Broadway, First Edition, 2003.

Alan Light, "JOHN SINGLETON: Not Just One of the Boyz," *Rolling Stone*, September 5, 1991.

Nancy Griffin and Kim Masters, *Hit & Run: How Jon Peters and Peter Guber Took Sony for a Ride in Hollywood*, Simon & Schuster, 1996.

Alan Citron, "A Messy and Drawn Out Fight at Columbia," *LA Times*, September 25, 1991.

John Singleton interview, *Charlie Rose*, January 6, 1995.

*Boyz N the Hood* Director's Commentary.

John Singleton interview, *Sway in the Morning*, September 24, 2011.

Darralynn Hutson, "The Ruler Is Back," *The Source*, July 2003.

Frank Price interview, National Endowment of the Arts, February 21, 2013.

Frank Price interview, John Singleton: A Celebration, USC, *Boyz N the Hood*, September 9, 2022.

## CHAPTER FIVE

Frank Price interview, National Endowment of the Arts, February 21, 2013.

Steve Nicolaides interview, Joi Carr, *Boyz N the Hood: Shifting Hollywood Terrain*, Peter Lang Publishing, 2023.

Ice Cube interview, *WTF with Marc Maron*, May 11, 2023.

Laurence Fishburne interview, *Game Changers* Q&A, July 8, 2019.

Regina King interview, *Friendly Fire: Making an Urban Legend*, Director: Todd Williams, Columbia TriStar Home Entertainment, 2003.

*Boyz N the Hood*, Director's Commentary.

Jaki Brown interview, *Friendly Fire: Making an Urban Legend*, Director: Todd Williams, Columbia TriStar Home Entertainment, 2003.

Sam Kashner, "How *Boyz N the Hood* Beat the Odds to Get Made—and Why It Matters Today," *Vanity Fair*, August 4, 2016.

John Singleton interview, *Access Hollywood,* July 18, 2016.

John Singleton interview, AVFF Remembers *Boyz N the Hood,* June 16, 2015.

Nelson George, "CPT Time," *Village Voice,* August 7, 1990.

John Singleton interview, Donald Bogle, *From Classic Hollywood and New Hollywood to South Central,* TCM, 2016.

John Singleton interview, Stephen Galloway, *Hollywood Reporter,* Masters Series, March 24, 2014.

John Singleton interview, Phillip Williams, "An Interview with John Singleton," *MovieMaker,* June 2001.

John Singleton interview, AFI Harold Lloyd Master Seminar, March 8, 1995.

John Singleton interview, "*Boyz N the Hood* Rings Out, 20 Years Later," NPR, July 8, 2011.

## CHAPTER SIX

John Singleton interview, Donald Bogle, *From Classic Hollywood and New Hollywood to South Central,* TCM, 2016.

John Singleton interview, *Friendly Fire: Making an Urban Legend,* Director: Todd Williams, Columbia TriStar Home Entertainment, 2003.

George Alexander, *Why We Make Movies: Black Filmmakers Talk About the Magic of Cinema,* Broadway, First Edition, 2003.

John Singleton interview, Jacqueline Stewart, Academy of Motion Pictures Arts and Sciences Visual History Program, July 11, 2017.

Nancy Griffin and Kim Masters, *Hit & Run: How Jon Peters and Peter Guber Took Sony for a Ride in Hollywood,* Simon & Schuster, 1996.

*Boyz N the Hood,* Director's Commentary.

Cuba Gooding Jr. interview, Elvis Mitchell, *Boyz N the Hood* 25th Anniversary Celebration and Conversation.

Thomas Golianopoulos, "The Life and Death of Lloyd Avery II," *LEVEL,* July 22, 2021.

Morris Chestnut interview, Elvis Mitchell, *Boyz N the Hood* 25th Anniversary Celebration and Conversation.

Sam Kashner, "How *Boyz N the Hood* Beat the Odds to Get Made—and Why It Matters Today," *Vanity Fair,* August 4, 2016.

Jason Jones, "'John Always Wanted to Tell Our Story': Los Angeles, *Boyz N the Hood,* and the Enduring Legacy of John Singleton," *The Athletic,* July 12, 2001.

dream hampton, "Hip Hop Cinema . . . South Central Style," *The Source,* September 1991.

## CHAPTER SEVEN

Stereo Williams, "Revisiting the *Boyz N the Hood* Soundtrack," *Rock the Bells*,
    July 15, 2021.

Joe Wood, "John Singleton and the Impossible Greenback Bind of the Assimilated
    Black Artist," *Esquire*, August 1, 1993.

*Boyz N the Hood*, Director's Commentary.

Sam Kashner, "How *Boyz N the Hood* Beat the Odds to Get Made—and Why It
    Matters Today," *Vanity Fair*, August 4, 2016.

John Singleton interview, "Memories of Cannes," *LA Times*, May 7, 1997.

George Alexander, *Why We Make Movies: Black Filmmakers Talk About the Magic of Cinema*,
    Broadway, First Edition, 2003.

Spike Lee interview, Nasser Metcalfe, "Spike Lee on Filmmaking," Blackfilm.com,
    July 1999.

Ice Cube interview, *The Untold Story Behind the Making of* Boyz N the Hood,
    BlackTree TV, December 4, 2012.

Roger Ebert, *Siskel & Ebert*, June 1, 1991.

Duane Byrge, *The Hollywood Reporter*, May 15, 1991.

David Ansen, *Newsweek*, July 15, 1991.

Scott Poulson-Bryant, "Dreaming America," *Spin*, September 1991.

Janet Maslin, "A Chance to Confound Fate," *New York Times*, July 12, 1991.

Gene Siskel, *Siskel & Ebert*, July 13, 1991.

Roger Ebert, *Chicago Sun-Times*, July 12, 1991.

Tammerlin Drummond, "The Early Buzz on *Boyz*: It's All Too Real," *LA Times*,
    July 7, 1991.

Seth Mydans, "Film on Gangs Becomes Part of the World It Portrays," *New York Times*,
    March 13, 1991.

John Singleton interview, *Friendly Fire: Making an Urban Legend*, Director: Todd Williams,
    Columbia TriStar Home Entertainment, 2003.

John Hartl, "Violence Mars Film Premiere," *Seattle Times*, July 14, 1991.

Frank Burgos, *Chicago Sun-Times*, July 14, 1991.

Scott Harris and Jim Herron Zamora, "*Boyz* Film Opens to Violence," *LA Times*,
    July 14, 1991.

## CHAPTER EIGHT

John Singleton interview, *Access Hollywood*, July 18, 2016.

Stephanie Allain interview, *Friendly Fire: Making an Urban Legend*, Director:
    Todd Williams, Columbia TriStar Home Entertainment, 2003.

Janice C. Simpson, "Not Just One of the Boyz," *Time*, March 23, 1992.

Alan Light, "JOHN SINGLETON: Not Just One of the Boyz," *Rolling Stone*,
    September 5, 1991.

John Singleton interview, *Drink Champs*, July 6, 2017.

John Singleton interview, Jacqueline Stewart, Academy of Motion Pictures Arts and Sciences Visual History Program, July 11, 2017.

John Singleton interview, Garvia Bailey, *An Evening with John Singleton*, March 15, 2013.

Billy Frolick, "Back in the Ring," *LA Times*, October 25, 1992.

Patrick Goldstein, "His New 'Hood Is Hollywood," *LA Times*, July 7, 1991.

David Rensin, "John Singleton Talks Tough," *Playboy*, September 1993.

John Singleton interview, *Charlie Rose*, January 6, 1995.

Bruce Fretts, "John Singleton on Early Success," *New York Times*, April 30, 2019 (from 2017).

John Singleton interview, Andrew J. Rausch, *Fifty Filmmakers: Conversations with Directors from Roger Avery to Steven Zaillian*, Michael Dequina McFarland, 2008.

John Singleton, *AFI Lifetime Achievement Award: A Tribute to Sidney Poitier*, March 12, 1992.

Gary Dauphin, "Ashes and Embers," *Village Voice*, May 21, 1996.

Nina J. Easton, "The Invisible Woman," *LA Times*, September 29, 1991.

Billy Norwich, "The Scene," *Palm Beach*, February 25, 1993.

Bernard Weinraub, "Black Filmmakers Are Looking Beyond Ghetto Violence," *New York Times*, September 11, 1995.

*The Signal*, March 12, 1993.

John Singleton interview, George Rush and Joanna Molloy, "Singleton's Family Saga," *New York Daily News*, June 17, 2001.

Todd Williams, "Higher Ground," *The Source*, February 1995.

Karen Grigsby Bates, "They've Gotta Have Us," *New York Times Magazine*, July 14, 1991.

Jack Fleming, "Longtime Home of Late *Boyz N the Hood* Director John Singleton Surfaces for Sale," *LA Times*, October 21, 2020.

Ryan Naumann, "Late Director John Singleton's LA Home Sold for $1.6 Million," *Radar Online*, December 23, 2021.

"Self-Assured," *New York Times Magazine*, September 15, 1991.

John Singleton interview, *A Conversation with John Singleton at the 15th Annual ABFF*, July 23, 2011.

John Singleton interview, *The Real*, March 6, 2017.

John Singleton interview, Joi Carr, *Boyz N the Hood: Shifting Hollywood Terrain*, Peter Lang Publishing, 2023.

John Singleton interview, AVFF Remembers *Boyz N the Hood*, June 16, 2015.

John Singleton Instagram post, June 4, 2015.

John Singleton interview, *The Breakfast Club*, March 28, 2017.

*MTV Rockumentary: The Making of* Remember the Time, 1992.

Beth Kleid, "TV & Video," *LA Times*, January 14, 1992.

Jon Pareles, "Review/Video: Michael Jackson's Costly New Promotional Clip," *New York Times*, February 4, 1992.

Betsy Sharkey, "For the Oscars, It's a Familiar Tune," *New York Times*,
    February 16, 1992.

Lacey Rose, "Race, Barriers and Battling Nerves," *Hollywood Reporter*,
    February 23, 2018.

David J. Fox, "Streisand: Thrilled, Disappointed," *LA Times*, February 20, 1992.

Beth Kleid, "Movies," *LA Times*, April 15, 1992.

John Singleton interview, *Friendly Fire: Making an Urban Legend*, Director: Todd Williams,
    Columbia TriStar Home Entertainment, 2003.

Bill Higgins, "Social Climes: The Oscars," *LA Times*, April 1, 1992.

## CHAPTER NINE

John Singleton and Veronica Chambers, *Poetic Justice: Film-Making South Central Style*,
    Dell Publishing, 1993.

Craigh Barboza, "Being John Singleton," *Uptown*, September 2011.

Nancy Griffin and Kim Masters, *Hit & Run: How Jon Peters and Peter Guber Took Sony
    for a Ride in Hollywood*, Simon & Schuster, 1996.

Bob Thomas, "Singleton of *Boyz* Conquers the Welles Syndrome," *Desert News*,
    August 24, 1993.

John Singleton interview, Jacqueline Stewart, Academy of Motion Pictures Arts and
    Sciences Visual History Program, July 11, 2017.

John Singleton interview, Garvia Bailey, *An Evening with John Singleton*, March 15, 2013.

David Ritz, "Janet Jackson: The Joy of Sex," *Rolling Stone*, September 17, 1993.

Mark Savage, "Janet Jackson on Being a Child Star: 'I Don't Remember Being Asked,'"
    BBC, July 24, 2024.

Roger Ebert, "John Singleton Recites the Poetry of Cinema," *Chicago Sun-Times*,
    July 18, 1993.

John Singleton interview, Elvis Mitchell, Los Angeles Film Festival, June 14, 2014.

John Singleton interview, *The Breakfast Club*, March 28, 2017.

John Singleton interview, Stephen Galloway, *Hollywood Reporter*, Masters Series,
    March 24, 2014.

Thomas Golianopoulos, "2Pac: A Thug's Life on Film," *Vibe*, October/November 2011.

John Singleton interview, *Poetic Justice* Q&A at the Mark Taper Auditorium,
    July 14, 2018.

Martha Southgate, "Boyz II Men," *Premiere*, August 1993.

Bernard Weinraub, "From Errand Boy to Studio Chief," *New York Times*,
    October 4, 1991.

Veronica Chambers, "The Director," *Vibe*, Fall 1992.

Tosha Lewis Instagram post, January 6, 2022.

## CHAPTER TEN

John Singleton interview, *Poetic Justice* Q&A at the Mark Taper Auditorium, July 14, 2018.

Yvonne Villareal, "John Singleton Looks Back on the 1992 LA Riots in New Documentary," *LA Times*, April 18, 2017.

John Singleton and Veronica Chambers, *Poetic Justice: Film-Making South Central Style*, Dell Publishing, 1993.

Jeffrey Wells, "Mickey Rourke Slams Spike Lee," *Entertainment Weekly*, May 22, 1992.

Patrick Goldstein, "The Mission Beyond Hollywood," *LA Times*, May 31, 1992.

Jann S. Wenner, William Greider, "Bill Clinton: The *Rolling Stone* Interview," *Rolling Stone*, December 9, 1993.

J. D. Vance interview, *The Joe Rogan Experience*, October 31, 2024.

John Singleton, "Children at War: Violence and America's Youth," Senate Labor and Human Resources subcommittee hearing, August 25, 1992.

Kevin Allman, "Fashion a Matter of Poetic Justice," *LA Times*, July 23, 1993.

Jason Deparle, "For Some Blacks, Social Ills Seem to Follow White Plans," *New York Times*, August 11, 1991.

Mary Ann French, "Great Expectations," *Washington Post*, July 25, 1993.

Jill Nelson, "Single-Minded," *USA Weekend*, July 23–25, 1993.

David Rensin, "John Singleton Talks Tough," *Playboy*, September 1993.

Gideon Bachmann, "US Leads Charge at Africa Fest," *Variety*, March 7, 1993.

Gideon Bachmann, "African Film Biz Marks Era of Unity, Productivity," *Variety*, April 13, 1993.

Roger Ebert, "John Singleton Recites the Poetry of Cinema," *Chicago Sun-Times*, July 18, 1993.

John Kisewetter, "*ER* Actress Dreams About Having It All," *The Cincinnati Examiner*, April 7, 1999.

Monte Williams, "He's Up to No Hood," *New York Daily News*, July 21, 1993.

## CHAPTER ELEVEN

Henry Louis Gates Jr., "Niggaz with Latitude," *New Yorker*, March 21, 1994.

Thomas Golianopoulos, "Twin Killing," *Vibe*, Winter 2010.

John Singleton and Veronica Chambers, *Poetic Justice: Film-Making South Central Style*, Dell Publishing, 1993.

Michael Upchurch, "Black on Black—Director's Debut, *Boyz*, Does Some Right Things," *Seattle Times*, July 12, 1991.

Philip Thomas, "Who the Hell Does John Singleton Think He Is?" *Empire*, November 1991.

Roger Ebert, "*Menace II Society* Review," *Chicago Sun-Times*, May 26, 1993.

Elaine Dutka, "It's Not All Black and White," *LA Times*, February 19, 1995.

Bernard Weinraub, "Black Filmmakers Are Looking Beyond Ghetto Violence,"
    *New York Times*, September 11, 1995.

George Alexander, *Why We Make Movies: Black Filmmakers Talk About the Magic of Cinema*,
    Broadway, First Edition, 2003.

John Singleton interview, *Yo! MTV Raps*, aired July 23, 1993.

Veronica Chambers, "All Black Everything," *New York Times*, May 14, 2019.

John Singleton interview, *The Whoolywood Shuffle*, September 2011.

Beth Coleman, "Justice Is a Lady," *Village Voice*, August 3, 1993.

Mary Ann French, "Great Expectations," *Washington Post*, July 25, 1993.

Monte Williams, "He's Up to No Hood," *New York Daily News*, July 21, 1993.

Joe Wood, "John Singleton and the Impossible Greenback Bind of the Assimilated
    Black Artist," *Esquire*, August 1, 1993.

Roger Ebert, "John Singleton Recites the Poetry of Cinema," *Chicago Sun-Times*,
    July 18, 1993.

Tupac Shakur interview, "*Poetic Justice* 1993 Behind the Scenes," https://www.youtube
    .com/watch?v=Q6wGXPMmIzE.

Kenneth Turan, "*Poetic Justice*: Traveling on a Bumpy Road," *LA Times*, July 23, 1993.

Terry Pristin, "The Rise and Fall of *Poetic Justice*, *LA Times*, August 13, 1993.

Owen Gleiberman, "Best and Worst of 1993: Movies," *Entertainment Weekly*,
    December 24, 1993.

Vincent Canby, "*Poetic Justice*: On the Road to Redemption," *New York Times*,
    July 23, 1993.

*Poetic Justice*, Director's Commentary.

Richard Johnson with Florence Anthony, Timothy McDarrah and Seth Kaufman.
    Page Six, *New York Post*, July 21, 1993.

## CHAPTER TWELVE

Jim Newton, "Skinheads Get Prison for Bombings, Plot," *LA Times*, January 14, 1994.

Jim Newton, "Bail Sought for Suspect in Church Bomb Plot," *LA Times*, July 20, 1993.

Associated Press, "Skinhead Pleads Guilty to 'Race Wars' Plots," *New York Times*,
    October 21, 1993.

Associated Press, "Skinheads in Bomb Case Are Tied to Earlier Plots," *New York Times*,
    September 9, 1993.

Christopher John Farley, "Today Los Angeles, Tomorrow . . ." *Time*, July 26, 1993.

"Los Angeles Racial Tension Won City Role in White Supremacist Plot,"
    *Washington Post*, July 16, 1993.

Adam Sandler, "White Racists Busted," *Variety*, July 16, 1993.

John Singleton interview, AFI Harold Lloyd Master Seminar, March 8, 1995.

*Higher Learning*, Director's Commentary.

Terry Pristin, "The Rise and Fall of *Poetic Justice*," *LA Times*, August 13, 1993.

Andy Marx, "Col Aims for *Burnout* as Singleton Next Pic," *Variety*, June 11, 1993.

John Singleton interview, Toronto International Film Festival, Audience Q&A, February 12, 2013.

Roger Ebert, "John Singleton Recites the Poetry of Cinema," *Chicago Sun-Times*, July 18, 1993.

Leonard Klady, "Shakur Nixed at Colpix," *Variety*, November 29, 1993.

Michael Rapaport interview, *The Breakfast Club*, October 24, 2017.

John Singleton interview, *Poetic Justice* Q&A at the Mark Taper Auditorium, July 14, 2018.

Christian Moerk, "Learning Inks Epps," *Variety*, January 3, 1994.

Marilyn Beck and Stacey Jenel Smith, "The 'Prince' Takes a Fresh Look," *New York Daily News*, December 10, 1993.

Eric Ducker, "How a 1995 John Singleton Film Presaged Today's Sex, Gun and Race Issues," *LA Times*, February 1, 2020.

Cassandra Butcher interview, John Singleton: A Celebration, USC, *Higher Learning* screening, October 12, 2022.

Richard Johnson with Florence Anthony, Timothy McDarrah and Seth Kaufman. Page Six, *New York Post*, July 21, 1993.

*Jet*, January 23, 1995.

Aidore Collier, "John Singleton: *Higher Learning* in Hollywood," *Ebony*, April 1995.

Tyra Banks interview, "Tyra Banks Had to Shoot Her *Higher Learning* Sex Scene on Her First Day," *People TV*, December 12, 2018.

Paul Hall interview, John Singleton: A Celebration, USC, *Higher Learning* screening, October 12, 2022.

Michael Rapaport interview, Nick Cannon on Power 106, September 17, 2019.

Omar Epps interview, *I Am Rapaport*, June 26, 2018.

Michael Rapaport interview, *Talib Kweli's People's Party*, February 10, 2020.

Michael Rapaport interview, *All the Smoke*, January 7, 2021.

Ice Cube interview, *WTF with Marc Maron*, May 11, 2023.

Carol Schatz and Vicki Sheff-Cahan, "Higher Yearning," *People*, January 23, 1995.

Tim Appelo, "Tyra Banks Struts Her Stuff Onscreen," *Entertainment Weekly*, January 13, 1995.

James Ryan, "Tyra Banks Is the Real Thing," *GQ*, May 1995.

Roger Ebert, *Chicago Sun-Times*, January 11, 1995.

Todd McCarthy, "*Higher Learning*," *Variety*, January 8, 1995.

Peter Travers, *Rolling Stone*, January 11, 1995.

Owen Gleiberman, "*Higher Learning*," *Entertainment Weekly*, January 13, 1995.

Kenneth Turan, "Higher Learning at Singleton U," *LA Times*, January 11, 1995.

Janet Maslin, "Higher Learning: Short Course in Racism on a College Campus," *New York Times*, January 11, 1995.

## CHAPTER THIRTEEN

John Singleton interview, Jacqueline Stewart, Academy of Motion Pictures Arts and Sciences Visual History Program, July 11, 2017.

John Singleton interview, Carl Seaton and Jeff Byrd, *Screenwriters Rant Room*, re-released on January 7, 2020.

George Alexander, *Why We Make Movies: Black Filmmakers Talk About the Magic of Cinema*, Broadway, First Edition, 2003.

Jordan Levin, "Dredging in the Deep South," *LA Times*, June 30, 1996.

John Singleton interview, *Charlie Rose*, February 26, 1997.

Jay Carr, "John Singleton Searches for Justice in *Rosewood*," *Boston Globe*, February 16, 1997.

John Singleton interview, Stephen Galloway, *Hollywood Reporter*, Masters Series, March 24, 2014.

Bill Moss, "Rosewood Survivors Negotiating Movie Deal," *Tampa Bay Times*, September 16, 1994.

Judy Brennan, "Clash of the Titans," *LA Times*, August 28, 1994.

Michael Kaplan, "Heidi Fleiss Reveals How Wild H'wood Producer Jon Peters' Parties Got," *New York Post*, March 24, 2022.

Nancy Griffin and Kim Masters, *Hit & Run: How Jon Peters and Peter Guber Took Sony for a Ride in Hollywood*, Simon & Schuster, 1996.

John Singleton interview, *In Conversation with John Singleton*, Complex Con, DeRay McKesson, November 2016.

Mike Fleming, "'Band' on the Run," *New York Daily News*, November 12, 1995.

Steve Pond, "Schwarzenegger's Drill," *Washington Post*, June 19, 1992.

Ryan Parker and Aaron Couch, "Wesley Snipes Reveals Untold Story Behind His 'Black Panther' Film," *Hollywood Reporter*, January 30, 2018.

"Singleton Snags Daniels Negro League Brushback," *Variety*, May 15, 1995.

"Singleton Shift to U, Too," *Variety*, December 3, 1995.

"New Studio Shuffles Put Deals on Wheels," *Variety*, December 10, 1995.

Big Gipp interview, *The Art of Dialogue*, February 25, 2023.

Jay Boyar, "The Making of *Rosewood*," *Orlando Sentinel*, February 19, 1997.

Stephen Forbes, "A Changing Type," *LA Times*, February 19, 1997.

Gary Dauphin, "Ashes and Embers," *Village Voice*, May 21, 1996.

*Rosewood*, Director's Commentary.

Wolfgang Saxon, "Minnie Langley, 83, Sought Recompense for Racist Rampage," *New York Times*, December 19, 1995.

"Minnie Langley, Rosewood Survivor and Fighter," *Tampa Bay Times*, December 18, 1995.

Bernard Weinraub, "Stirring Up Old Terrors Unforgotten," *New York Times*, February 19, 1997.

## CHAPTER FOURTEEN

Lola Ogunnaike, "His Name, and Money, at Stake, Director Takes Producer's Risk," *New York Times*, July 21, 2005.

"*Rosewood*: About the Production," *Film Scouts*.

Gary Dauphin, "Ashes and Embers," *Village Voice*, May 21, 1996.

*Rosewood*, Director's Commentary.

Jerry Fallstrom, Mary Murphy, Don Fernandez, and Dianne Copelon, "Rains Stall *Rosewood* Shooting Schedule," *Orlando Sentinel*, January 9, 1996.

John Singleton interview, Jacqueline Stewart, Academy of Motion Pictures Arts and Sciences Visual History Program, July 11, 2017.

John Singleton interview, *In Conversation with John Singleton*, Complex Con, DeRay McKesson, November 2016.

John Singleton interview, Carl Seaton and Jeff Byrd, *Screenwriters Rant Room*, re-released on January 7, 2020.

Stephen Forbes, "Singleton Takes Pride in Quantum Leap," *LA Times*, February 19, 1997.

## CHAPTER FIFTEEN

Kim Masters, "Dark Prince of Hollywood, Producer Gavin Polone Opens Up About Unlikely Directorial Debut," *Hollywood Reporter*, January 6, 2012.

"Smith Takes on New Role," *Variety*, February 5, 1995.

"Antsy Agents Make Mutant Managers," *Variety*, March 19, 1995.

Elaine Dutka, "The New World Order," *LA Times*, June 23, 1996.

"New Studio Shuffles Put Deals on Wheels," *Variety*, December 10, 1995.

Tupac Shakur phone call with Sanyika Shakur f/k/a Monster Kody, October 18, 1995.

John Singleton interview, *Drink Champs*, July 6, 2017.

John Singleton interview, Jacqueline Stewart, Academy of Motion Pictures Arts and Sciences Visual History Program, July 11, 2017.

John Singleton interview, Stephen Galloway, *Hollywood Reporter*, Masters Series, March 24, 2014.

Glenn Whipp, "From Boyz to Boy," *Los Angeles Daily News*, June 29, 2001.

Jeff Commings, *The Baton: A John Williams Musical Journey*, May 27, 2020.

*Rosewood*, Director's Commentary.

Jay Boyar, "*Rosewood* Debut Delayed by Composer's Schedule," *Orlando Sentinel*, October 16, 1996.

Jerry Fallstrom, "Oprah Devotes Today's Show to Rosewood," *Orlando Sentinel*, February 27, 1997.

Gregory Poirier, "John Singleton and the Making of *Rosewood*: Screenwriter Gregory Poirier on Moments and Regrets," *Deadline*, July 12, 2020.

George Alexander, *Why We Make Movies: Black Filmmakers Talk About the Magic of Cinema*, Broadway, First Edition, 2003.

Bernard Weinraub, "Stirring Up Old Terrors Unforgotten," *New York Times*, February 19, 1997.

Jay Carr, "Powerfully Recalling a National Disgrace," *Boston Globe*, February 21, 1997.

Jay Boyar, "*Rosewood*: A Powerful Truth," *Orlando Sentinel*, February 21, 1997.

Stanley Crouch, "A Lost Generation and Its Exploiters," *New York Times*, August 26, 2001.

"The People Column," *Miami Herald*, November 17, 1996.

Superior Court of California, County of Los Angeles, Declaration of Akosua Busia, June 3, 1997.

George Rush and Joanna Molloy, "Going, Going, Ghana," *New York Daily News*, April 17, 1997.

*LA Times*, October 6, 1996.

## CHAPTER SIXTEEN

Bernard Weinraub, "Stirring Up Old Terrors Unforgotten," *New York Times*, February 19, 1997.

Eric Harrison, "Can You Dig It? Not Quite," *LA Times*, June 23, 2000.

Erich Leon Harris, "The Shafting of John Singleton," *MovieMaker*, July 2000.

"Singer Set to Direct Fox's *Men*," *Variety*, December 9, 1996.

John Singleton interview, *In Conversation with John Singleton*, Complex Con, DeRay McKesson, November 2016.

Jon Burlingame, "How Isaac Hayes' 'Shaft' Reinvented the Game for Film Music," *Variety*, June 25, 2021.

Desa Philadelphia, "The Importance of Being Gordon Parks," DGA.org, Summer 2006.

Douglas Perry, "He Could Dig It," *Fort Worth Telegraph*, June 16, 2000.

John Singleton interview, *Politically Incorrect*, June 22, 2000.

Anita M. Busch, "*Shaft* Shifts to Paramount," *Variety*, June 30, 1997.

Steve Daly, "Who's the Man?" *Entertainment Weekly*, June 16, 2000.

Michael Fleming, "Singleton Sweet on *Golddiggaz*," *Variety*, December 18, 1997.

Stephen Forbes, "Singleton Takes Pride in Quantum Leap," *LA Times*, February 19, 1997.

"*Golddiggaz* Scripters Ink Pic Deal with U," *Variety*, June 18, 1997.

Diedre Johnson, "Lead Writer Camille Tucker Gives the Blueprint for How *The Clark Sisters* Was Done," *Black Girl Nerds*, April 8, 2020.

John Singleton, "John Singleton on Sony Hack: Jokes by Amy Pascal and Scott Rudin Aren't 'Racist,'" *Hollywood Reporter*, December 17, 2014.

Benjamin Wallace, "Scott Rudin in the Wings," *New York* magazine, August 4, 2021.

Paul Hall interview, John Singleton: A Celebration, USC, *Shaft* screening, November 30, 2022.

Shane Salerno, "My Time Making *Shaft* with John Singleton," *Deadline*, May 15, 2019.

Kevin Brass, "Up Against His Own Deadline," *LA Times*, April 7, 2002.

Danny Leigh, "John Singleton: *Shaft*, the Melodrama," *The Guardian*, September 5, 2000.

"Wesley Snipes Damns *Shaft*," *The Guardian*, August 17, 2000.

"Jackson Gets Shaft," *Variety*, February 15, 1999.

Michael Fleming, "New Line Goes with the Flow for Singleton," *Variety*, November 11, 1998.

Melanie Rehak, *San Francisco Examiner*, December 5, 1999.

Troy Patterson and Clarissa Cruz, "Monitor," *Entertainment Weekly*, September 24, 1999, https://ew.com/article/1999/09/24/monitor-426/.

George Rush and Joanna Molloy, "Drag for Singleton," *New York Daily News*, September 10, 1999.

Mitchell Fink, "Singleton Seeks Justice in Custody Battle," *New York Daily News*, March 9, 2000.

Mitchell Fink, "Ex-galpal Rips *Shaft* Daddy," *New York Daily News*, June 26, 2000.

Kristal Brent Zook, "Rocking the Cradle," *Washington Post*, June 30, 2001.

Andrew Hindes, "Leguizamo May Get Singleton's *Shaft*," *Variety*, April 30, 1999.

Jeffrey Wright interview, "Jeffrey Wright Breaks Down His Most Iconic Characters," GQ.com, May 1, 2020.

Michael Fleming, "Par Trying to Give Collette the Shaft," *Variety*, October 6, 1999.

Mitchell Fink, "*Shaft* Bigs Lock Horns over Few Black Hires," *New York Daily News*, August 23, 1999.

Soraya Sarhaddi Nelson, "Protesters Say Hollywood Favors White Stuntmen," *LA Times*, September 28, 1999.

Glenn Whipp, "Can Ya Dig It?" *Los Angeles Daily News*, June 11, 2000.

Richard Johnson with Ian Spiegelman, Page Six, *New York Post*, December 11, 1999.

Flo Anthony with additional reporting by Michael E. Ross, "BETONHOLLYWOOD," *New York Daily News*, February 6, 2000.

Richard Johnson with Paula Froelich and Chris Wilson, Page Six, "*Shaft* Has Its Fill of Snarky Sam," *New York Post*, April 21, 2000.

*Calgary Sun*, May 5, 2000.

John Singleton interview, *Drink Champs*, July 6, 2017.

Seth Kugel and Alan Feuer, "Fidel Castro Ate Here, but Now It's a Piece of Bronx History," *New York Times*, January 3, 2004.

Richard Johnson with Paula Froelich and Ian Spiegelman, Page Six, "*Shaft* Director's Sexy Time-Outs," *New York Post*, January 21, 2000.

Ryan Gilbey, "John Singleton: A Change of Gear," *The Independent,* June 13, 2003.

John Singleton interview, *All Arts: Hollywood's Best Film Directors*, 2011.

Aaron McGruder, *The Boondocks*, May 12, 2000.

## CHAPTER SEVENTEEN

John Singleton interview, *All Arts: Hollywood's Best Film Directors*, 2011.

Alex Demyanenko, "John Singleton, the Chronicler of L.A.'s Mean Streets," *Capital and Main*, April 30, 2019.

Bill Chappell, "Activists Mourn Race Theorist Dr. Frances Cress Welsing," NPR.org, January 2, 2016.

Greg Tate, "Sex and Negrocity: John Singleton's *Baby Boy*," *Village Voice*, June 26, 2001.

Patrick Goldstein, "A Difficult Coming of Age," *LA Times*, February 27, 2001.

Bonz Malone, "Growing Pains," *Vibe*, August 2001.

*Baby Boy*, Director's Commentary.

Cassandra Butcher interview, John Singleton: A Celebration, USC, *Higher Learning* screening, October 12, 2022.

Mitchell Fink, "Did Singleton's Mom Shaft Ex?" *New York Daily News,* June 14, 2000.

Richard Johnson with Paula Froelich and Chris Wilson, Page Six, "*Shaft* Sneaks in Slander of Rudy," *New York Post,* June 14, 2000.

Danny Singleton, author bio, Amazon.com.

Andrew Hindes, "Indie Baby Boy," *Variety*, February 25, 1999.

Claude Brodesser, "Col, Singleton Near Deal to Make *Baby*," *Variety*, October 16, 2000.

*Higher Learning*, Director's Commentary.

Tyrese Gibson interview, *The Fat Joe Show*, August 5, 2020.

John Singleton speech at Taraji P. Henson's Hollywood Walk of Fame Ceremony, January 28, 2019.

Taraji P. Henson, *Around the Way Girl: A Memoir*, 37 Ink, 2017.

John Singleton interview, *Sway in the Morning*, September 24, 2011.

Jawn Murray, "John Singleton: Hollywood's Star Maker and Rule Breaker," *Savoy*, July 2005.

Omar Gooding interview, DJ Vlad, October 30, 2021.

John Singleton interview, Jacqueline Stewart, Academy of Motion Pictures Arts and Sciences Visual History Program, July 11, 2017.

John Singleton interview, Garvia Bailey, *An Evening with John Singleton*, March 15, 2013.

Kenneth Turan, "This Isn't Neverland," *LA Times,* June 27, 2001.

Todd McCarthy, *Variety,* June 26, 2001.

Roger Ebert, *Chicago Sun-Times,* June 27, 2001.

A. O. Scott, "Be a Man? But Where Are the Role Models?" *New York Times,* June 27, 2001.

Greg Braxton, "Life pre-Cookie: Taraji P. Henson Reflects on *Baby Boy* in TV One Special," *LA Times*, March 25, 2015.

Glenn Whipp, "From Boyz to Boy," *Los Angeles Daily News*, June 29, 2001.

Dwight Williams interview, Phillip Goldfarb, DGA, November 18, 2019.

John Singleton interview, *Poetic Justice* Q&A at the Mark Taper Auditorium, July 14, 2018.

## CHAPTER EIGHTEEN

Patrick Goldstein, "Cool Is the Fuel," *LA Times*, December 10, 2002.

Michael Fleming, "Sinbad Sails for Col," *Variety*, December 13, 2001.

John Singleton interview, Jacqueline Stewart, Academy of Motion Pictures Arts and Sciences Visual History Program, July 11, 2017.

Lorenza Munoz, "Co-workers Testify in Studio Case," *LA Times*, June 15, 2007.

Lorenza Munoz, "Director Says He Disagreed with Firing," *LA Times*, June 13, 2007.

Lorenza Munoz, "Judge Oks Race Suit Against Universal," *LA Times*, April 28, 2006.

Lorenza Munoz, "Universal Settles with Black Movie Worker," *LA Times*, June 14, 2007.

Gabriel Snyder and Chris Gardner, "Singleton Gets a High Five from U," *Variety*, June 20, 2006.

Leslie Simmons, "Judge Sides with Uni in *2 Fast* Suit," *AP*, July 13, 2007.

Joseph Menn, "Studio Prevails in Racial Bias Case," *LA Times*, July 13, 2007.

Liz Balmaseda, "South Floridians Exercise and Celebrate the Right to Be Different," *Miami Herald*, July 4, 2002.

*2 Fast 2 Furious*, Director's Commentary.

*Miami Herald*, August 23, 2002.

Lesley Abravanel, "Babes in Clubland Stalking Denzel," *Miami Herald*, June 28, 2002.

Todd McCarthy, "*2 Fast 2 Furious*," *Variety*, June 6, 2003.

A. O. Scott, "Classy Chassis, Unleaded Love," *New York Times*, June 6, 2003.

Roger Ebert, *Chicago Sun-Times*, June 6, 2003.

Blige Ebiri, "John Singleton's Best Movies Beyond *Boyz N the Hood*," *New York*, April 30, 2019.

Ryan Gilbey, "John Singleton: A Change of Gear," *The Independent*, June 13, 2003.

Lorenza Munoz, "*Furious* Sequel Is 2 Fast for *Nemo*," *LA Times*, June 9, 2003.

## CHAPTER NINETEEN

*2 Fast 2 Furious*, Director's Commentary.

Rene Rodriguez, "The Reel South Florida," *Miami Herald*, June 8, 2003.

condoreports.com.

Stephanie Sayfie Aagaard, "Speedy Streets," *Miami Herald*, October 9, 2002.

Stephanie Allain interview, New York Film Academy, April 19, 2016.

Stephanie Allain interview, *I Blame Dennis Hopper*, Illeana Douglas, August 28, 2018.

"Poor and Hungry, Craig Brewer Gave His Chancy Movie *Hustle* All He Had—and It Paid Off Big," *San Francisco Gate*, July 20, 2005.

Sharon Waxman, "Wee Hours Wheeling and Dealing at Sundance," *New York Times*, January 24, 2005.

John Singleton and Craig Brewer interview, *Charlie Rose*, June 29, 2005.

Rob Tannenbaum, "The *Playboy* Interview: Ludacris," *Playboy*, October 2006.

Dwight Williams interview, Phillip Goldfarb, DGA, November 18, 2019.

*The Commercial Appeal*, July 17, 2004.

*The Commercial Appeal*, October 10, 2004.

## CHAPTER TWENTY

Lola Ogunnaike, "His Name, and Money, at Stake, Director Takes Producer's Risk," *New York Times*, July 21, 2005.

Peter L'Official, "Rhyme Scheme," *Village Voice*, June 28, 2005.

Sharon Waxman, "Wee Hours Wheeling and Dealing at Sundance," *New York Times*, January 24, 2005.

Robert W. Welkos, "After Credits Roll, Deals Are Struck," *LA Times*, January 29, 2005.

Laura M. Holson and David M. Halbfinger, "At Paramount, the New Chief Spends Freely," *New York Times*, March 25, 2005.

Robert W. Welkos, "Paramount, MTV, Do the Hustle for $9 Million," *LA Times*, January 24, 2005.

Peter Bart, "John Singleton the Auteur Was Also Skilled in Hollywood Gamesmanship," *Deadline*, May 1, 2019.

John Singleton interview, *Charlie Rose*, August 18, 2005.

*Four Brothers*, Director's Commentary.

John Singleton interview, *Sway in the Morning*, March 27, 2017.

Dave McNary and Michael Fleming, "Par Rounds Out Its Band of Brothers," *Variety*, October 12, 2004.

John Singleton interview, Carl Seaton and Jeff Byrd, *Screenwriters Rant Room*, re-released on January 7, 2020.

John Singleton interview, *On Story: 601*, Austin Film Festival, April 16, 2016.

*Four Brothers*, Director's Commentary.

Rene Rodriguez, "This Family Is as Dysfunctional, Erratic, as the Film Itself," *Miami Herald*, August 12, 2005.

Tom Long, *Detroit News*, August 12, 2005.

Stephen Hunter, "*Four Brothers* in Mayhem," *Washington Post*, August 12, 2005.

Joe Leydon, *Variety*, August 10, 2005.

John Singleton interview, IMS Engage with Arthur Baker, April 21, 2016.

Lloyd Grove, "Singleton Eyes Flow of Bootleg," *New York Daily News*, July 26, 2005.

John Singleton and Craig Brewer interview, *Charlie Rose*, June 29, 2005.

DJ Paul, as told to Seth Abramovitch, "Three 6 Mafia Star Remembers His Oscar-Winning Night: 'Like That, Salma Hayek Killed My Hard-On,'" *Hollywood Reporter*, February 24, 2016.

Juicy J interview, "Juicy J Recalls Oscar Win with Three 6 Mafia," *HipHopDX*, December 18, 2020.

Rachel Abramowitz, "For All the Sacrifice and Luck, the Cash Isn't Flowing," *LA Times*, November 25, 2005.

Tom Tapp, "Taryn Manning Sues John Singleton's Crunk Pictures for Share of *Hustle & Flow* Profits," *Deadline*, November 16, 2021.

## CHAPTER TWENTY-ONE

Craigh Barboza, "Being John Singleton," *Uptown*, September 2011.

*ADAGE*, January 12, 2005.

Dave McNary, "It's Spring Time for Par," *Variety*, October 24, 2005.

Michael Fleming, "Singleton to Direct *Executive Order*," *Variety*, November 19, 2007.

Michael Fleming, "Vin Diesel to Star in *Wheelman*," *Variety*, May 7, 2009.

Dave McNary, "Scribe's Getting Roses," *Variety*, March 31, 2005.

Josef Adalian, "Showtime Lures George Clooney," *Variety*, July 11, 2007.

Tatiana Siegel, "Relativity Announces Presale Lineup," *Hollywood Reporter*, May 18, 2007.

Brian B., "John Singleton to Helm Tom Clancy's *Without Remorse*," Movieweb.com, January 16, 2008.

"Phoenix is Without Remorse," Gamesradar.com, February 24, 2006.

"Exclusive: Wilson's War, Singleton's Grenade," TMZ, June 19, 2006.

Stephanie Frederic, "John Singleton Breaking New Ground Again," *LA Sentinel*, August 23, 2007.

Dave McNary, "John Singleton to Direct *Tulia*," *Variety*, August 1, 2007.

"Halle Berry . . . Baby on Board!" TMZ, September 4, 2007.

George Rush and Joanna Molloy, "Protesting Tyra-ny," *New York Daily News*, August 10, 2005.

Patrick Goldstein, "More Color, Please," *LA Times*, June 20, 2006.

Gabriel Snyder and Chris Gardner, "Singleton Gets a High Five from U," *Variety*, June 20, 2006.

"Film Director Kills Woman in Tragic Accident, Police Say," *LA Times*, August 25, 2007.

## CHAPTER TWENTY-TWO

Tatiana Siegel, "Singleton Hunts for A-Team," *Variety*, December 16, 2007.

Geoff Boucher, "Ice Cube Talks *A-Team*," *LA Times*, August 1, 2008.

"'A-Team' Goes to Plan B," *LA Times*, January 28, 2009.

Chris Lee, "Quinton Rampage Jackson Fits *The A-Team* to a Mr. T," *LA Times*,
   May 30, 2010.

Craigh Barboza, "Being John Singleton," *Uptown*, September 2011.

TMZ, May 11, 2009.

Steven Zeitch, Borys Kit, "Gray Makes Citizen Arrest," *Hollywood Reporter*,
   October 17, 2008.

Borys Kit, "Paramount Eyeing *Four Brothers* Sequel," *Hollywood Reporter*,
   January 13, 2010.

*Brick*, an original screenplay, John Singleton, August 19, 2009.

*Fight for Love*, an original screenplay, John Singleton, June 23, 2013.

Steven Zeitchik, "John Singleton Will Be Taylor Lautner's Next Director,"
   *LA Times*, March 25, 2010.

Steven Zeitchik, "On *Abduction*, Taylor Lautner Could Be a Boy in the Hood,"
   *LA Times*, March 9, 2010.

Amy Kaufman, *"Abduction* Will Definitely Have a Sequel," *LA Times*,
   September 16, 2011.

Andrew Barker, *"Abduction,"* *Variety*, September 22, 2011.

Stephen Holden, "At Least His Abs Get a Workout," *New York Times*,
   September 22, 2011.

Glenn Whipp, *"Abduction* an Abs Fest," *LA Times*, September 23, 2011.

## CHAPTER TWENTY-THREE

Patrick Goldstein, "John Singleton on His *Hustle & Flow* Suit Against Paramount,"
   *LA Times*, October 19, 2011.

Eriq Gardner, "Paramount, John Singleton Settle *Hustle & Flow* Litigation,"
   *Hollywood Reporter*, November 5, 2012.

"Singleton Settles Suit with Studio," *LA Times*, November 7, 2012.

Alex French and Maximillian Porter, "Bryan Singer's Accusers Speak Out,"
   *The Atlantic*, January 23, 2019.

"Director John McTiernan Headed to Prison," *Deadline*, October 4, 2010.

Lacey Rose, "You're Not Gonna F***in' Tell Me What My Story Is: Sam Esmail,
   Nic Pizzolatto and *The Hollywood Reporter* Drama Showrunners Roundtable,"
   *Hollywood Reporter*, June 3, 2019.

John Singleton, "Can a White Director Make a Great Black Movie?" *Hollywood Reporter*,
   September 19, 2013.

John Singleton, "John Singleton on Sony Hack: Jokes by Amy Pascal and Scott Rudin
   Aren't 'Racist,'" *Hollywood Reporter*, December 17, 2014.

TMZ, October 1, 2011.

"John Singleton, Peter Berg in Mix to Direct NWA Biopic," *LA Times*,
   September 22, 2011.

Borys Kit, "F. Gary Gray in Talks to Direct NWA Movie *Straight Outta Compton*," *Hollywood Reporter*, April 10, 2012.

*Blame Rio!*, an original screenplay, John Singleton, October 23, 2013.

Justin Kroll, "John Singleton Back as Director for Tupac Shakur Biopic," *Variety*, February 12, 2014.

John Singleton interview, Stephen Galloway, *Hollywood Reporter*, Masters Series, March 24, 2014.

John Singleton interview, Elvis Mitchell, Los Angeles Film Festival, June 14, 2014.

*Tupac Amaru Shakur*, an original screenplay, John Singleton, May 20, 2014.

L. T. Hutton interview, *The Breakfast Club*, June 14, 2017.

Oliver Gettell, "Carl Franklin Replaces John Singleton as Tupac Director," *LA Times*, April 8, 2015.

John Singleton Instagram post, April 7, 2015.

Emily Yoshida, "*All Eyez on Me* Is a Faithful Adaptation of Tupac Shakur's Wikipedia Page," *New York*, June 16, 2017.

Nick Allen, Rogerebert.com, June 16, 2017.

John Singleton interview, *Sway in the Morning*, July 21, 2017.

## CHAPTER TWENTY-FOUR

Gary Webb, "Dark Alliance," *San Jose Mercury News*, August 1996.

Jenny Hontz, "Singleton Segues to TV," *Variety*, November 17, 1997.

Christopher Edward Jackson obituary, March 18, 2013.

Josef Adalian, "Showtime Lures George Clooney," *Variety*, July 11, 2007.

John Singleton interview, *The Breakfast Club*, March 28, 2017.

Nellie Andreeva, "Studios Terminate More Deals," *Hollywood Reporter*, January 16, 2008.

John Singleton Instagram post, August 22, 2009.

Lesley Goldberg, "John Singleton, Russell Simmons Team for Miami Set Club Drama at HBO," *Hollywood Reporter*, December 4, 2013.

Nellie Andreeva, "Showtime Drama to Chronicle Origins of Crack Cocaine Epidemic in Los Angeles," *Deadline*, April 29, 2014.

Maureen Ryan, "*Empire* Boss on Director Diversity: It's the 'Right Thing to Do,'" *Variety*, November 10, 2015.

Cynthia Littleton, "Filmmaker John Singleton Rides the Peak TV Wave to Recharge His Career," *Variety*, May 22, 2017.

Dominic Patten, "FX Picks Up John Singleton *Snowfall* Pilot," *Deadline*, May 1, 2015.

Malcolm Mays interview, *The Breakfast Club*, September 2, 2021.

David M. Halbfinger, "Based on a True Story," *New York Times*, December 27, 2007.

Malcolm Mays interview, *Build Series*, April 10, 2017.

"John Singleton and Ex-Wife in Ugly $200K Child Support Fight!" *Bossip*, July 4, 2015.

maaswaar.blogspot.com.

gofundme.com/f/uscfilm.

Evelyn Diaz, "Huh? John Singleton's Son Needs You to Pay His College Tuition,"
   BET.com, January 25, 2016.

Demetria L. Lucas, "*Snowfall* Star Damson Idris Is Hollywood's Hottest Antihero,"
   *Hollywood Reporter*, March 10, 2022.

John Singleton Instagram post, November 10, 2015.

Ed Rampell, "*The Birth of a Nation*: The Most Racist Movie Ever Made," *Washington Post*,
   March 3, 2015.

John Singleton interview, Carl Seaton and Jeff Byrd, *Screenwriters Rant Room*, re-released
   on January 7, 2020.

Cynthia Littleton, "John Singleton Sets *Straight Outta Heaven* Guardian Angel Drama at
   CW," *Variety*, November 2, 2016.

## CHAPTER TWENTY-FIVE

Mike Hale, "In BET's Police Drama *Rebel*, Blaxploitation Matters," *New York Times*,
   March 28, 2017.

tvseriesfinale.com.

## CHAPTER TWENTY-SIX

Sonia Saraiya, "John Singleton's *Snowfall* on FX," *Variety*, June 30, 2017.

Amber Ryland, "Donald Sterling's New Girlfriend Revealed: It's V. Stiviano's Former
   'BFF For Life' Raquel Lee—PLUS, Her Link to Rob Kardashian," *Radar Online*,
   June 25, 2014.

Shyam Dodge, "Donald Sterling and New 'Girlfriend' Raquel Lee Leave Beverly Hills
   Restaurant Separately . . . After Billionaire Called His Wife a 'Pig' in Court,"
   *Daily Mail*, July 14, 2014.

facebook.com/raquelleesworld.

raquelleesworld.wordpress.com.

raquellee.brandyourself.com.

V. Stiviano interview, Barbara Walters, *ABC News*, May 2, 2014.

Deborah Hastings, "Donald Sterling Spotted Cavorting with Young Woman in
   California," *New York Daily News*, June 17, 2014.

Denise Goolsby, "Donald Sterling Spotted in Palm Desert with Young Woman,"
   *Desert Sun*, June 25, 2014.

Lil Rel interview, *Club Shay Shay* podcast, March 13, 2024.

John Singleton Instagram post, March 7, 2018.

Tosha Lewis Instagram post, April 29, 2019.

John Singleton Instagram post, April 29, 2018; May 8, 2018.

Danielle Young, "Don't Let the Smile Fool You, I'm Cringing on the Inside," *The Root*,
   November 6, 2017.

## CHAPTER TWENTY-SEVEN

Datwon Thomas, "FX Network's *Snowfall* Cast and Crew Showcase the New Season on NY Tour Stop," *Vibe*, August 13, 2018.

## CHAPTER TWENTY-EIGHT

Ryan Parker and Aaron Couch, "Wesley Snipes Reveals Untold Story Behind His *Black Panther* Film," *Hollywood Reporter*, January 30, 2018.

Maggie Coughlan, "*Boyz N the Hood* Director Signs On to Andrew Dice Clay Doc," *New York Post*, November 1, 2018.

Debra Birnbaum, "Amazon Increases Production Spending for 2018, Developing Three New Sci-Fi Series," *Variety*, September 28, 2017.

Katie Kilkenny, "Taraji P. Henson to Star in and Produce Film on Emmett Till," *Hollywood Reporter*, January 11, 2018.

John Singleton interview, *The Breakfast Club*, July 25, 2018.

John Singleton speech, Taraji P. Henson Hollywood Walk of Fame Ceremony, January 28, 2019.

Sheila Ward Facebook post, August 2019.

"John Singleton's Mother: His Baby Mama Did Nothing to Prevent His Death . . . But Baby Mama Denies It," TMZ, August 9, 2019.

Tosha Lewis Instagram post, August 9, 2019.

"John Singleton Hospitalized After Stroke," *Variety*, August 20, 2019.

Bruce Haring, "John Singleton Is in Coma, Court Papers Reveal, As Mother Seeks Conservatorship," *Deadline*, April 25, 2019.

Sophie Haigney, "John Singleton's Family Fights for Control of His Affairs After Stroke," *New York Times*, April 26, 2019.

Rosemary Rossi, "Tyrese, Taraji P. Henson Visit John Singleton in Hospital, Ask Fans to 'Keep Praying,'" *The Wrap*, April 28, 2019.

"Tyrese Describes 'Heavy Heart' After Visiting John Singleton with Taraji P. Henson," *Urban Hollywood 411*, April 28, 2019.

"Following Report of Death, John Singleton's Representatives Say He's Still in a Coma," CNN Wire, April 29, 2019.

Ale Russian, "John Singleton Is 'Still on Life Support' Despite Report That He Has Died, Says Publicist," *People*, April 29, 2019.

Nellie Andreeva, Patrick Hipes, "John Singleton to Be Taken Off Life Support Today," *Deadline*, April 29, 2019.

"John Singleton Death Certificate Released . . . Died Day Before Announcement," TMZ, May 6, 2019.

## EPILOGUE

Barack Obama Twitter post, April 30, 2019.

Veronica Chambers, "All Black Everything," *New York Times*, May 14, 2019.

Bruce Haring, "John Singleton Private Funeral Set for Monday as Larger Memorial Planned," *Deadline*, May 3, 2019.

"Details on John Singleton's Private Funeral, Plus: What His Death Certificate Revealed," *Extra TV*, May 6, 2019.

"John Singleton Big Memorial Planned at USC Alma Mater," TMZ, May 13, 2019.

John Singleton Memorial Program.

Denise Petski, "Disney Television Writing Program Opens Applications for 2024; Sets FX Singleton Scholarship," *Deadline*, October 24, 2023.

Desa Philadelphia, "A Transformative Trojan," *In Motion*, Winter 2019.

Amaya Nakpodia, "Celebrating John Singleton," USC, School of Cinematic Arts News, September 2, 2022.

Desa Philadelphia, "SCA Dedicates New Lounge to Close Out Year-Long Celebrating of SCA Alum John Singleton's Career," USC, School of Cinematic Arts News, April 27, 2023.

Danielle and Andy Mayoras, "The John Singleton Estate Teaches Why No One Should Procrastinate Updating Their Will," *Forbes*, November 4, 2019.

"John Singleton Will Filed in Court . . . Daughter Justice Is Beneficiary," TMZ, May 3, 2019.

Ryan Naumann, "John Singleton's Screenwriter Son Awarded Late *Boyz N the Hood* Director's Massive Comic Book Collection, Will Split $6.8 Million Estate with 6 Siblings," *Radar Online*, January 10, 2024.

Ryan Naumann, "Family War! John Singleton's Mom Refusing to Resign as Executor of Son's Estate After Being Sued for $15 Million," *Radar Online*, July 28, 2023.

Ryan Naumann, "Judge Sides with John Singleton's Mom in Family War over Late Director's $6 Million Estate," *Radar Online*, December 7, 2023.